HEROMAN 4

Original/Stan Lee + BONES TAMON OHTA

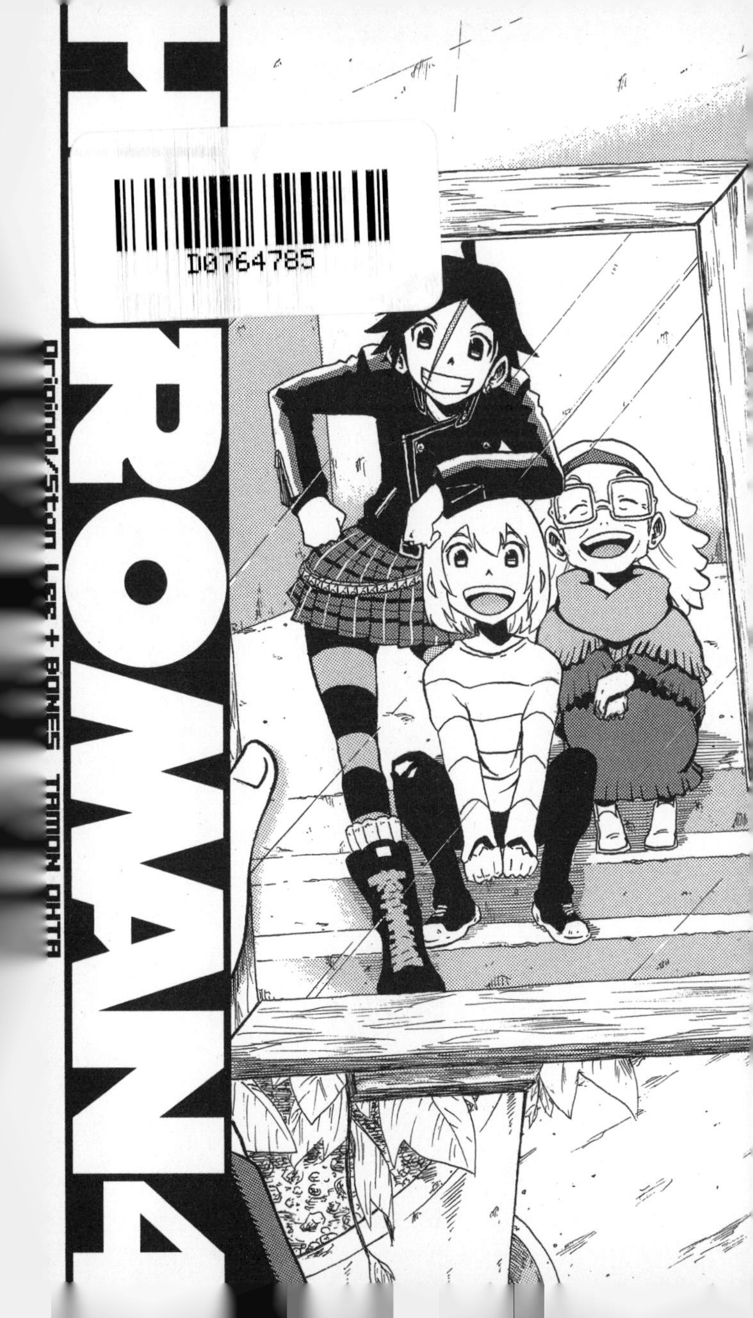

HEROMAN
04 ▸ contents

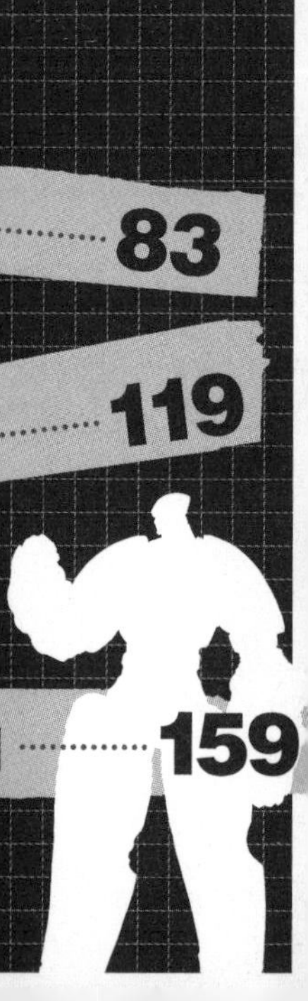

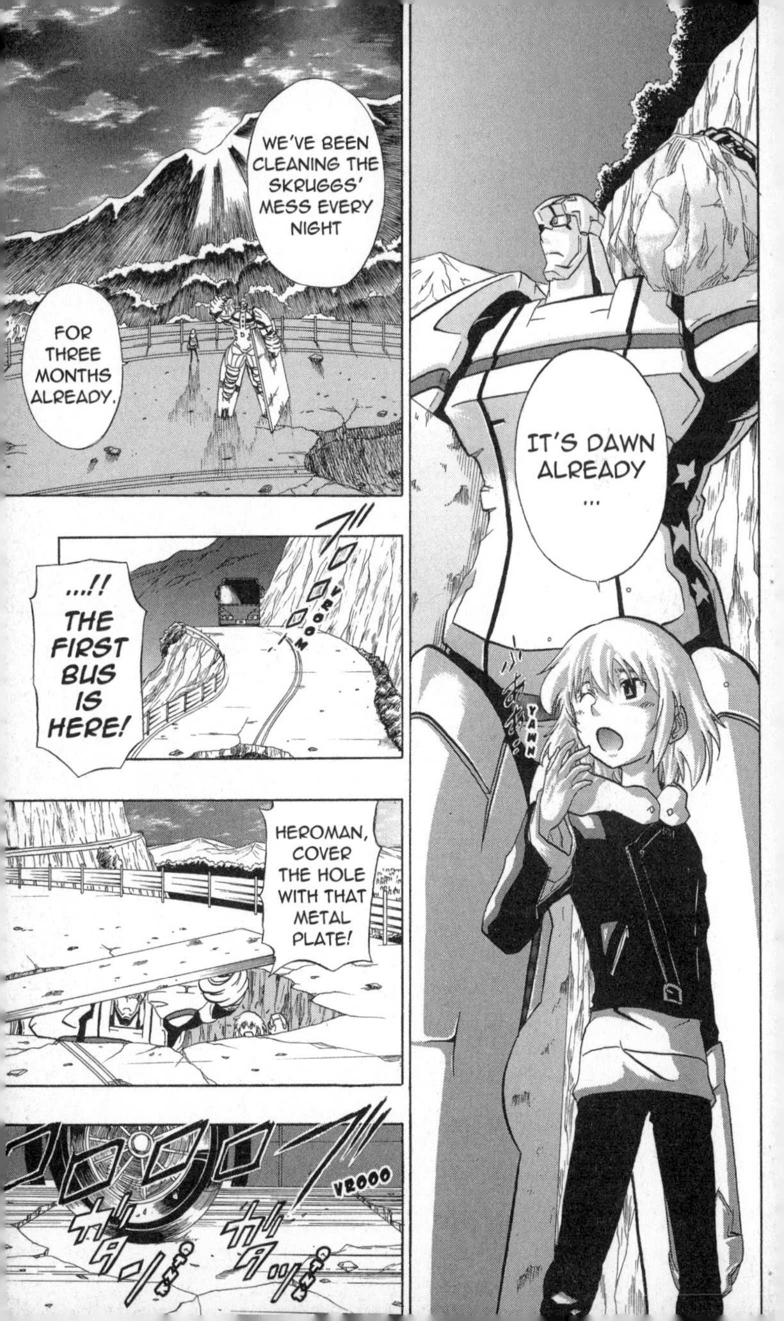
IT'S DAWN ALREADY ...
YAWN
WE'VE BEEN CLEANING THE SKRUGGS' MESS EVERY NIGHT
FOR THREE MONTHS ALREADY.
VROOM
...!! THE FIRST BUS IS HERE!
HEROMAN, COVER THE HOLE WITH THAT METAL PLATE!
VROOO

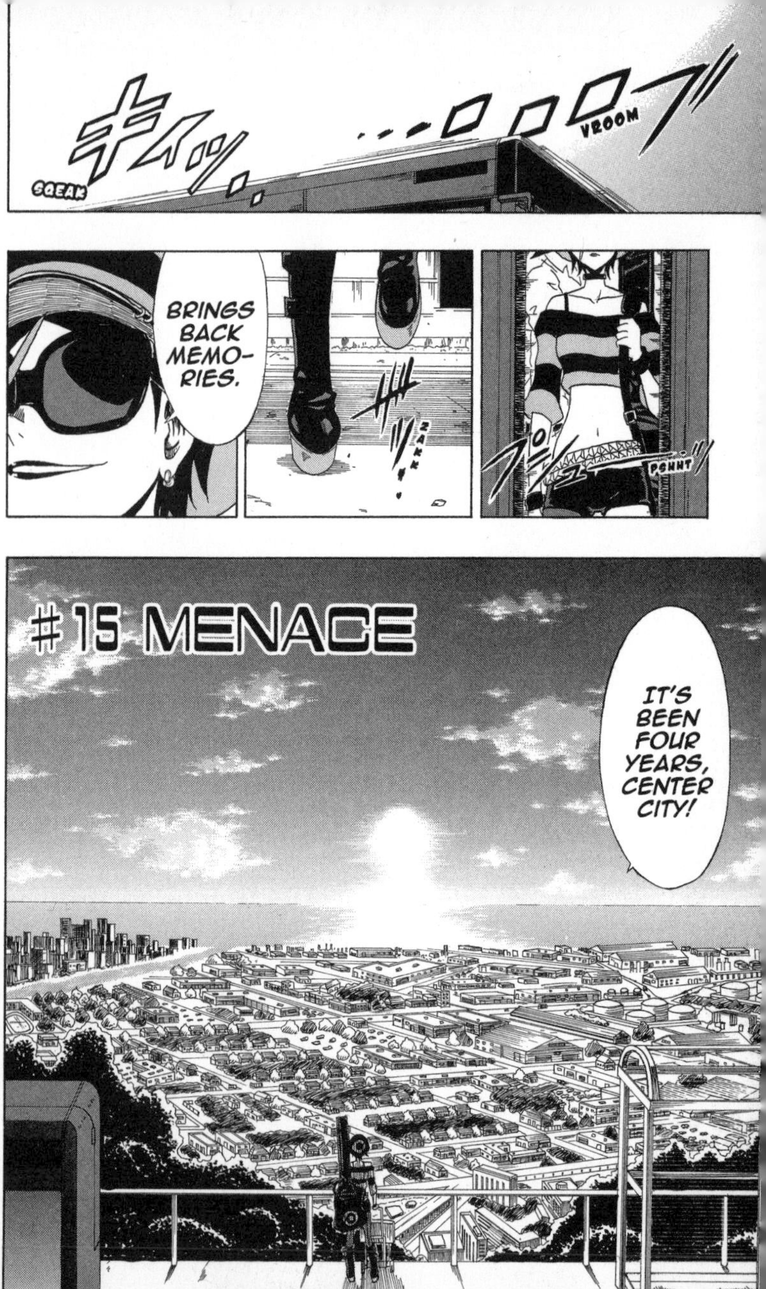
VROOM
SQEAK
PSHHT
ZAKK
BRINGS BACK MEMO-RIES.
#15 MENACE
IT'S BEEN FOUR YEARS, CENTER CITY!

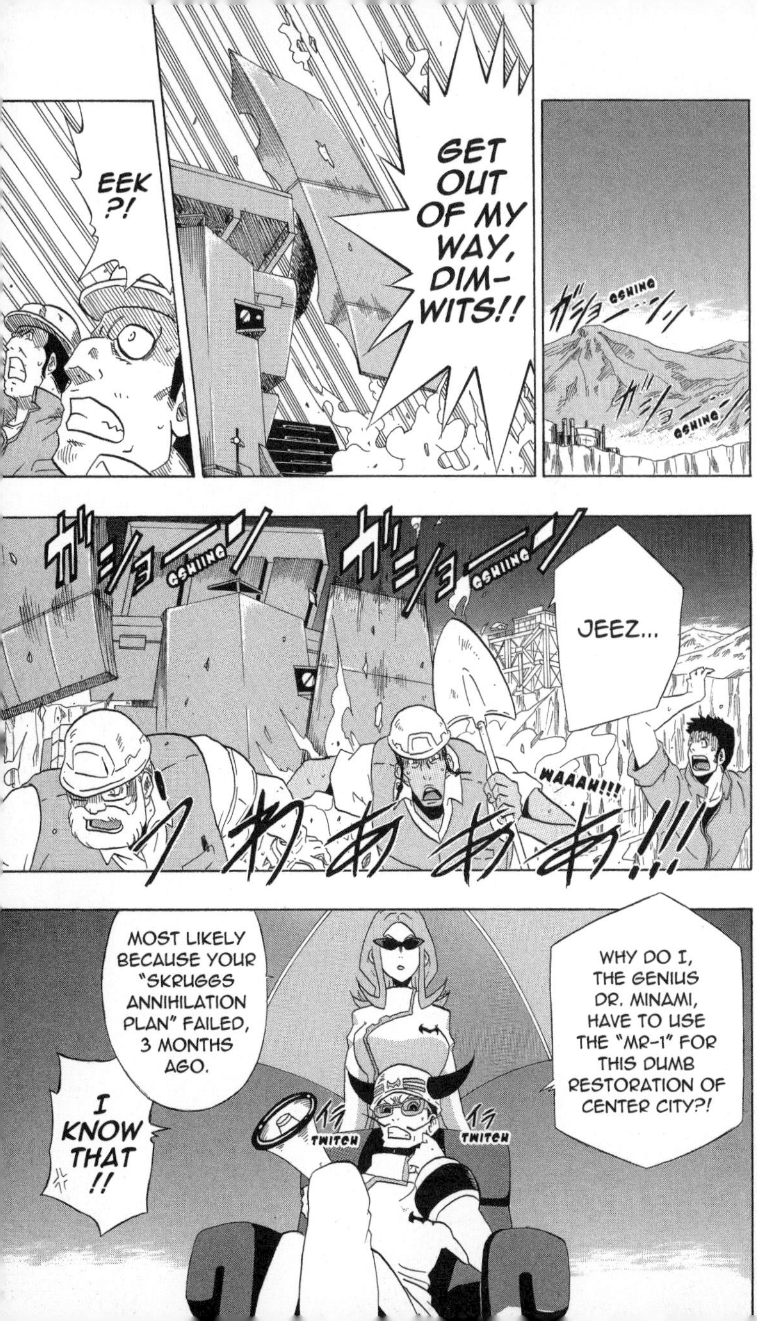

GSHING
GSHING
GET OUT OF MY WAY, DIM-WITS!!
EEK ?!
JEEZ...
GSHIING
GSHIING
WAAAH!!!
WHY DO I, THE GENIUS DR. MINAMI, HAVE TO USE THE "MR-1" FOR THIS DUMB RESTORATION OF CENTER CITY?!
MOST LIKELY BECAUSE YOUR "SKRUGGS ANNIHILATION PLAN" FAILED, 3 MONTHS AGO.
TWITCH
TWITCH
I KNOW THAT !!

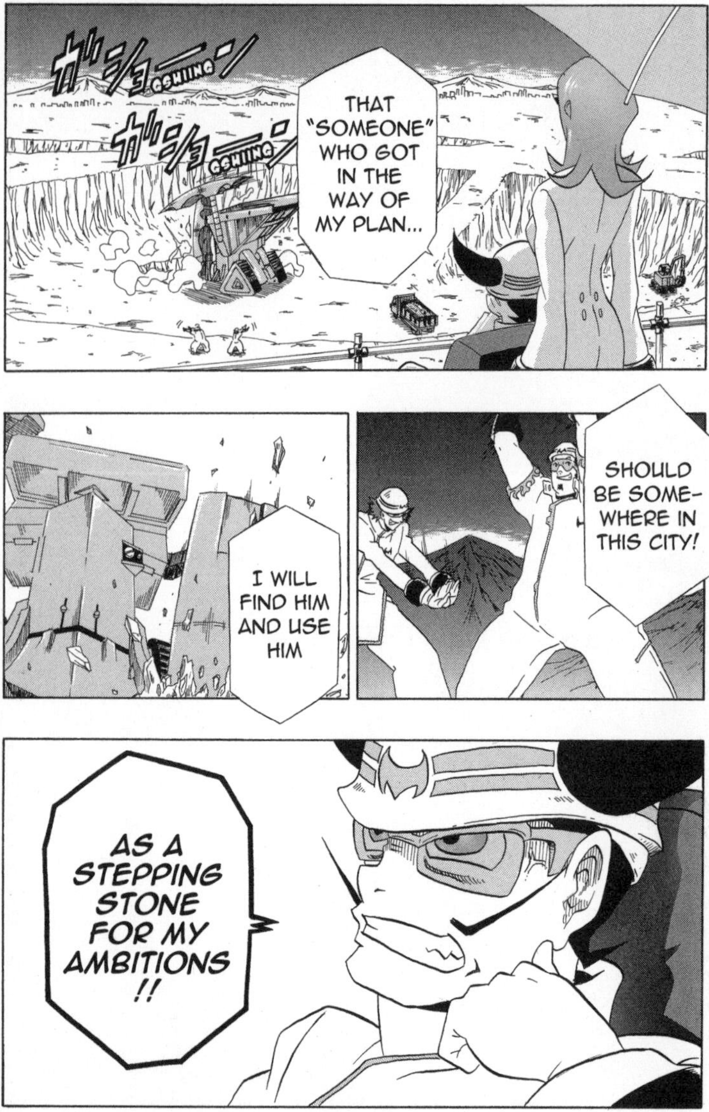
GSHIING
GSHIING
THAT "SOMEONE" WHO GOT IN THE WAY OF MY PLAN...
SHOULD BE SOME-WHERE IN THIS CITY!
I WILL FIND HIM AND USE HIM
AS A STEPPING STONE FOR MY AMBITIONS !!

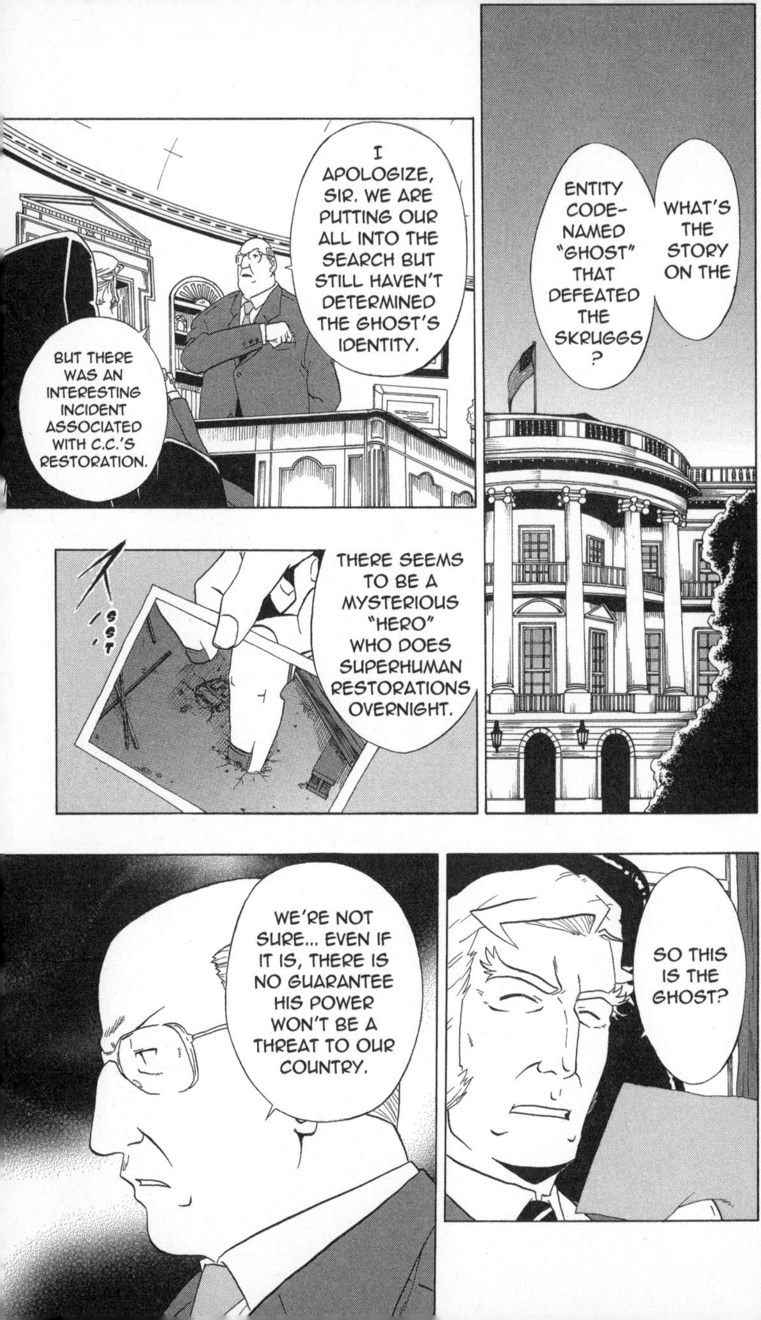
WHAT'S THE STORY ON THE
ENTITY CODE-NAMED "GHOST" THAT DEFEATED THE SKRUGGS?
I APOLOGIZE, SIR. WE ARE PUTTING OUR ALL INTO THE SEARCH BUT STILL HAVEN'T DETERMINED THE GHOST'S IDENTITY.
BUT THERE WAS AN INTERESTING INCIDENT ASSOCIATED WITH C.C.'S RESTORATION.
THERE SEEMS TO BE A MYSTERIOUS "HERO" WHO DOES SUPERHUMAN RESTORATIONS OVERNIGHT.
SST
SO THIS IS THE GHOST?
WE'RE NOT SURE... EVEN IF IT IS, THERE IS NO GUARANTEE HIS POWER WON'T BE A THREAT TO OUR COUNTRY.

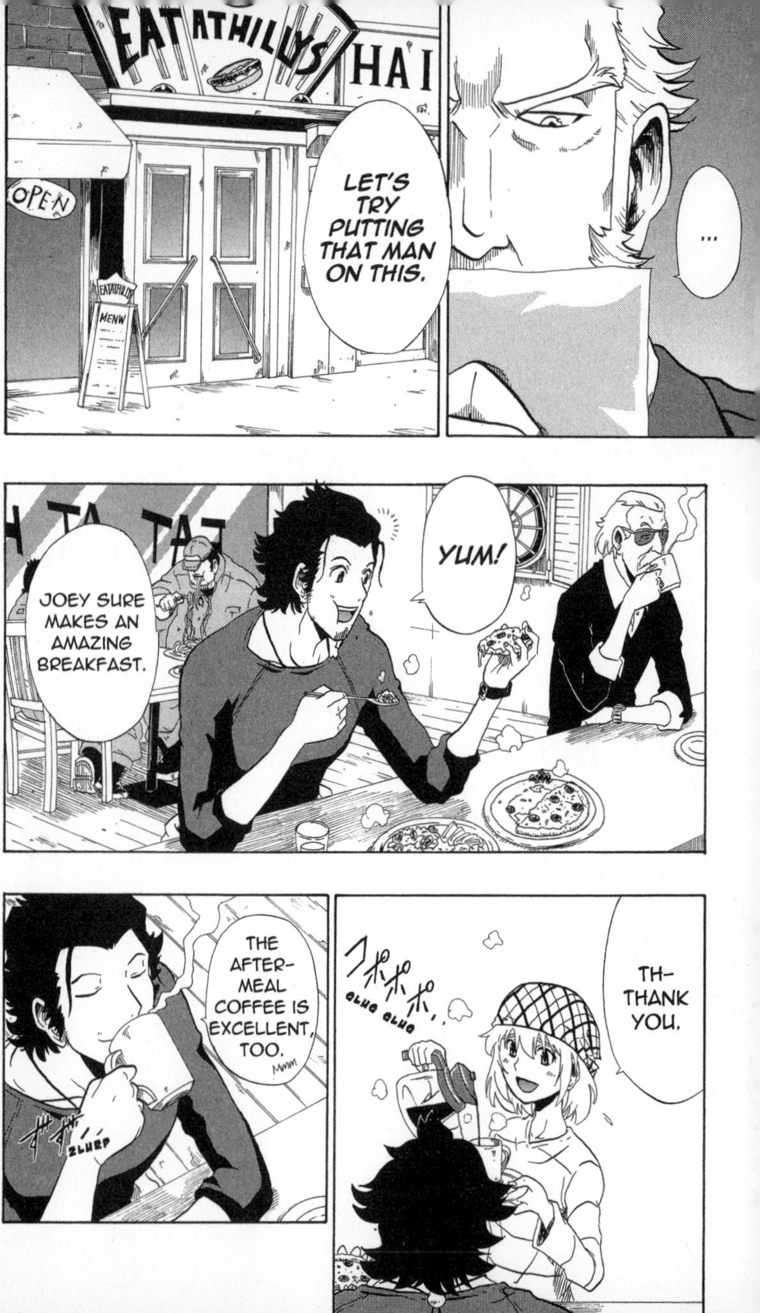
...
EATATHILLY'S
HA I
OPEN
MENW
LET'S TRY PUTTING THAT MAN ON THIS.
YUM!
JOEY SURE MAKES AN AMAZING BREAKFAST.
TH- THANK YOU.
GLUG GLUG
THE AFTER-MEAL COFFEE IS EXCELLENT, TOO.
Mmm
ZLURP

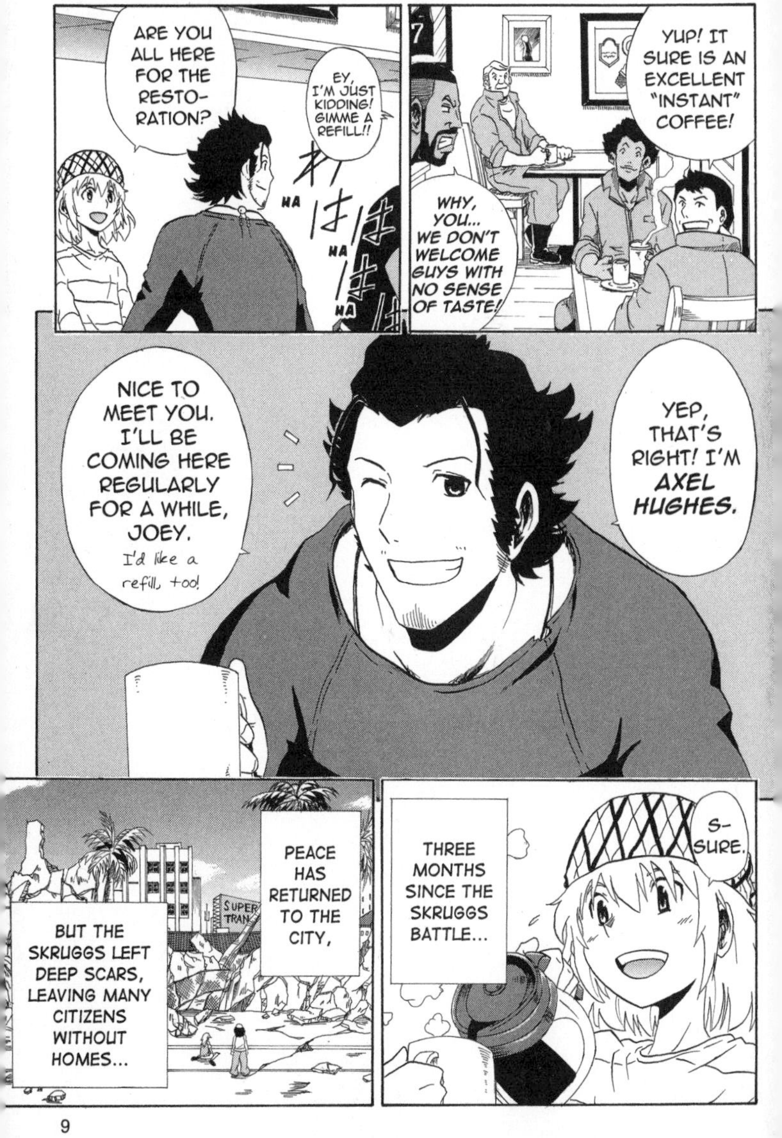
YUP! IT SURE IS AN EXCELLENT "INSTANT" COFFEE!
WHY, YOU... WE DON'T WELCOME GUYS WITH NO SENSE OF TASTE!
EY, I'M JUST KIDDING! GIMME A REFILL!!
HA HA HA
ARE YOU ALL HERE FOR THE RESTO-RATION?
YEP, THAT'S RIGHT! I'M AXEL HUGHES.
NICE TO MEET YOU. I'LL BE COMING HERE REGULARLY FOR A WHILE, JOEY.
I'd like a refill, too!
S-SURE.
THREE MONTHS SINCE THE SKRUGGS BATTLE...
PEACE HAS RETURNED TO THE CITY,
BUT THE SKRUGGS LEFT DEEP SCARS, LEAVING MANY CITIZENS WITHOUT HOMES...

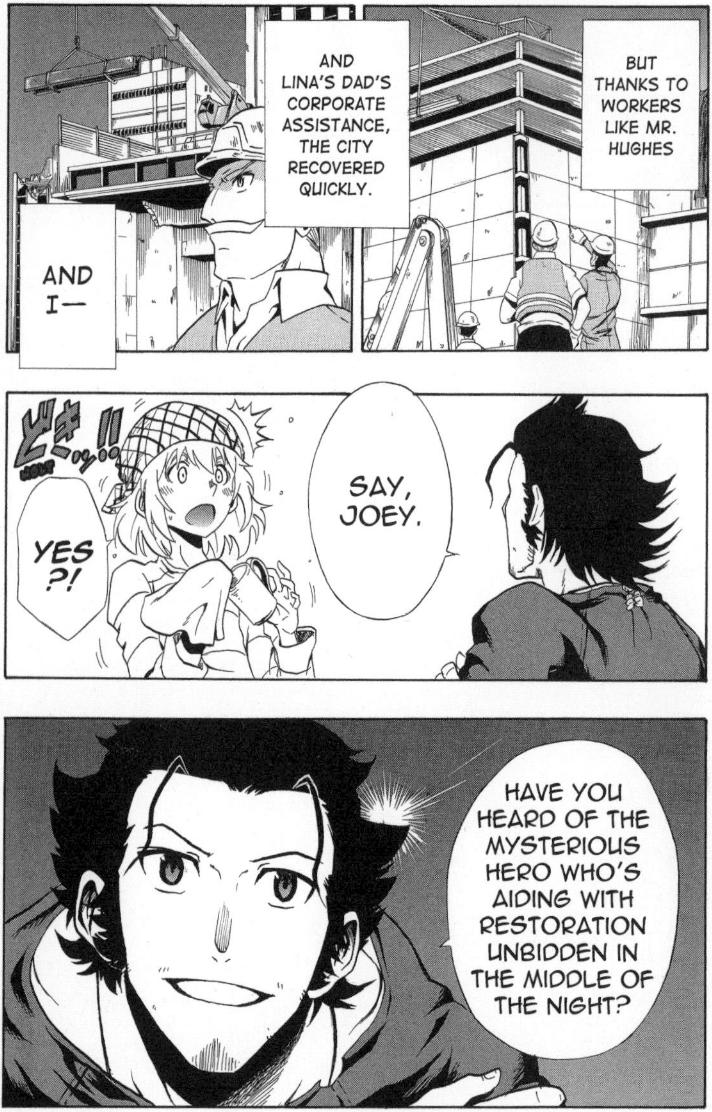
BUT THANKS TO WORKERS LIKE MR. HUGHES
AND LINA'S DAD'S CORPORATE ASSISTANCE, THE CITY RECOVERED QUICKLY.
AND I—
SAY, JOEY.
どきっ!!
YES?!
HAVE YOU HEARD OF THE MYSTERIOUS HERO WHO'S AIDING WITH RESTORATION UNBIDDEN IN THE MIDDLE OF THE NIGHT?

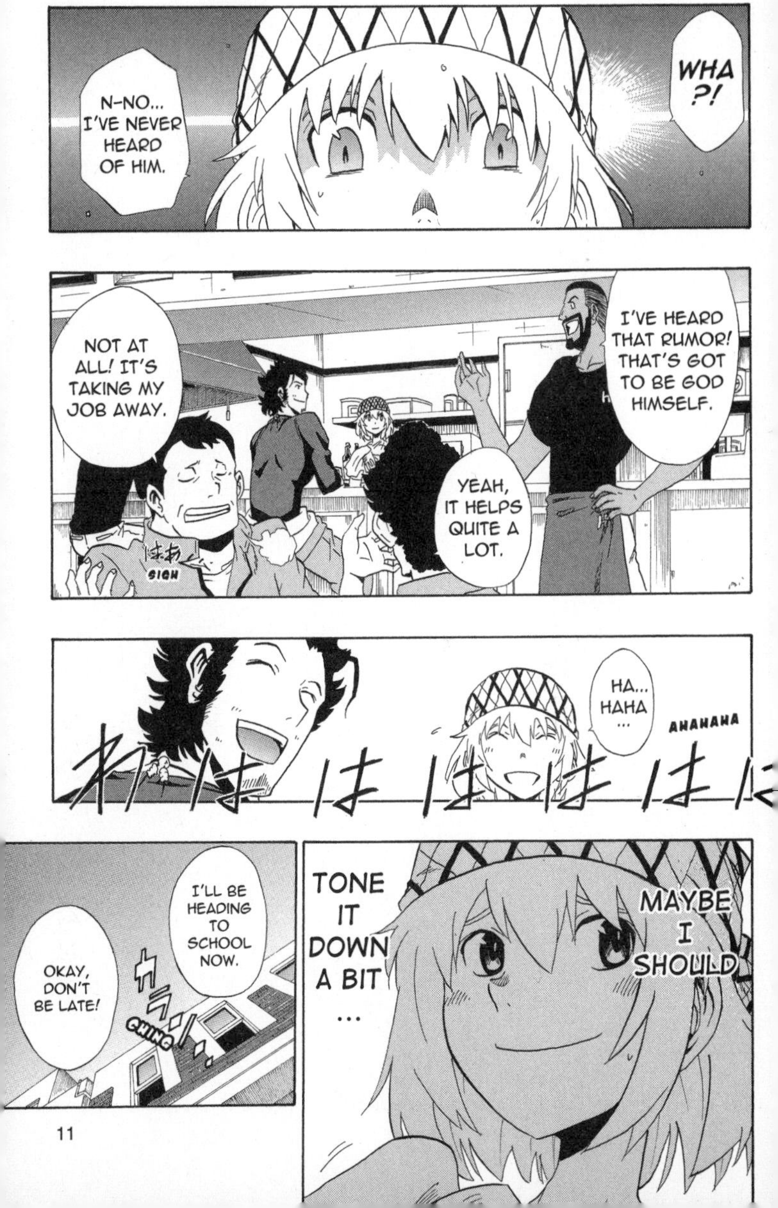
WHA ?!
N-NO... I'VE NEVER HEARD OF HIM.
I'VE HEARD THAT RUMOR! THAT'S GOT TO BE GOD HIMSELF.
YEAH, IT HELPS QUITE A LOT.
NOT AT ALL! IT'S TAKING MY JOB AWAY.
はあ
SIGH
AHAHAHA
HA... HAHA ...
わははははは
MAYBE I SHOULD
TONE IT DOWN A BIT ...
I'LL BE HEADING TO SCHOOL NOW.
カラ
CHING
OKAY, DON'T BE LATE!

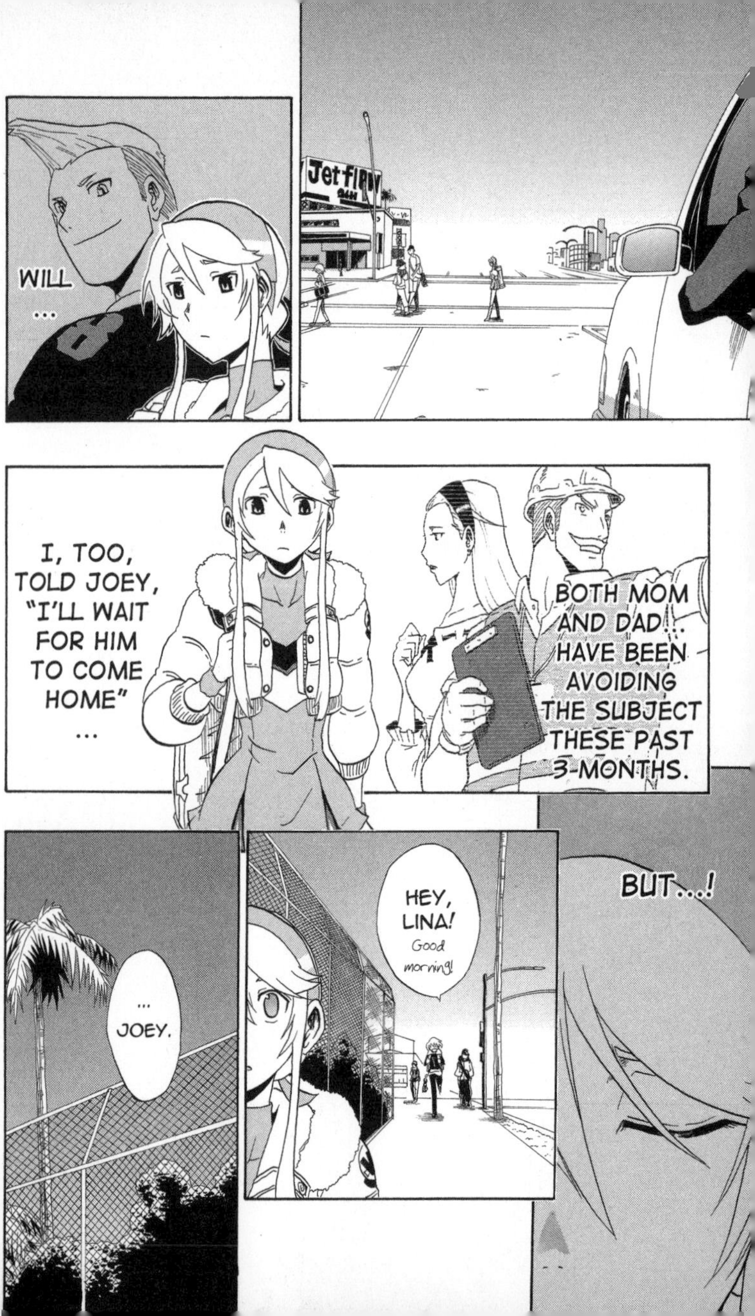
WILL ...
BOTH MOM AND DAD... HAVE BEEN AVOIDING THE SUBJECT THESE PAST 3-MONTHS.
I, TOO, TOLD JOEY, "I'LL WAIT FOR HIM TO COME HOME" ...
BUT...!
HEY, LINA! Good morning!
... JOEY.

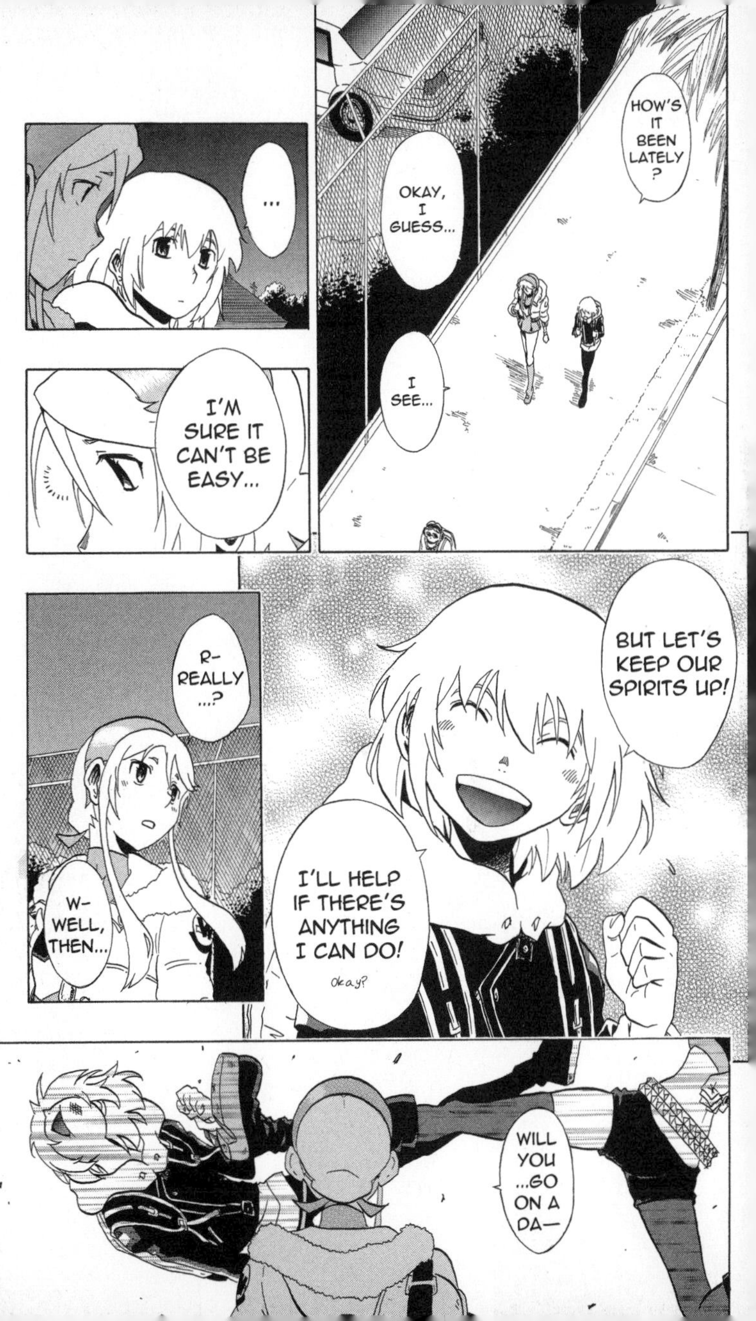
HOW'S IT BEEN LATELY?
OKAY, I GUESS...
I SEE...
...
I'M SURE IT CAN'T BE EASY...
BUT LET'S KEEP OUR SPIRITS UP!
I'LL HELP IF THERE'S ANYTHING I CAN DO!
Okay?
R-REALLY...?
W-WELL, THEN...
WILL YOU ...GO ON A DA—

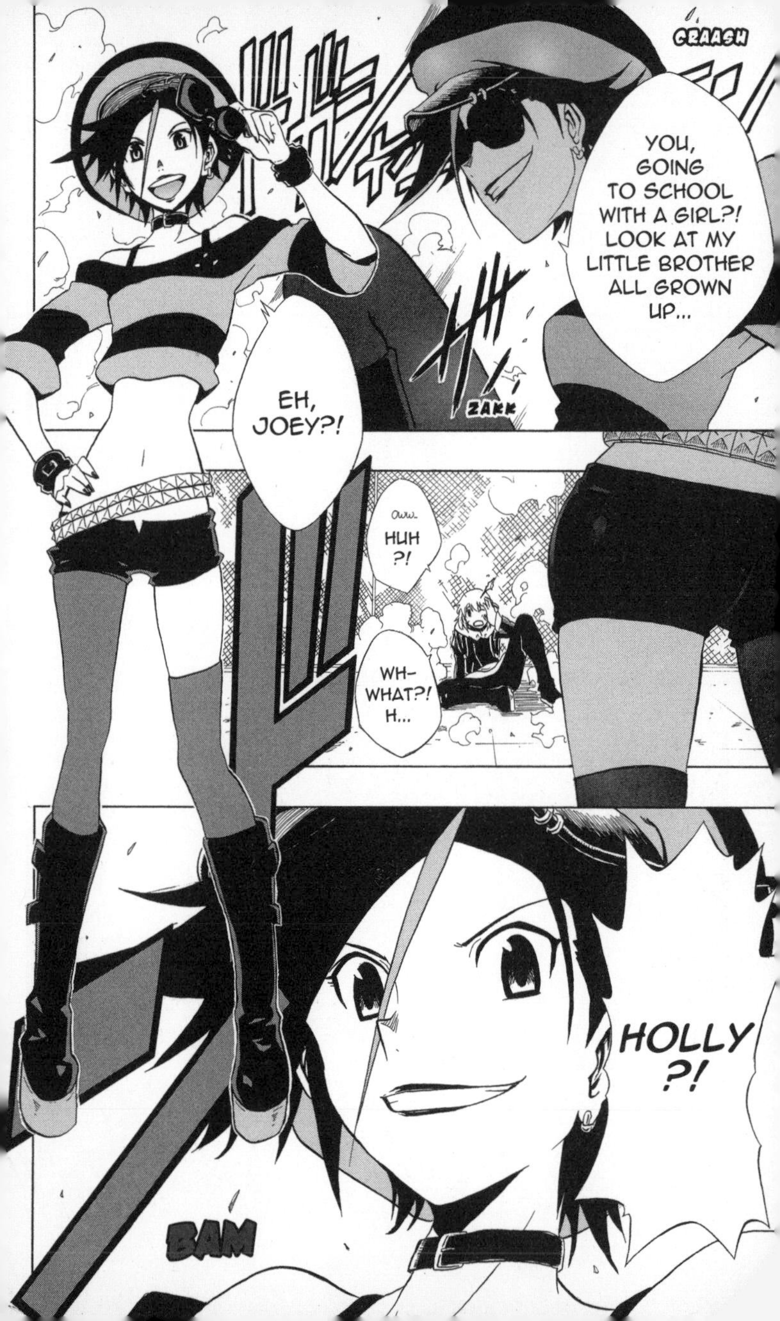
CRAASH
YOU, GOING TO SCHOOL WITH A GIRL?! LOOK AT MY LITTLE BROTHER ALL GROWN UP...
ZAKK
EH, JOEY?!
aww..
HUH ?!
WH- WHAT?! H...
HOLLY ?!
BAM

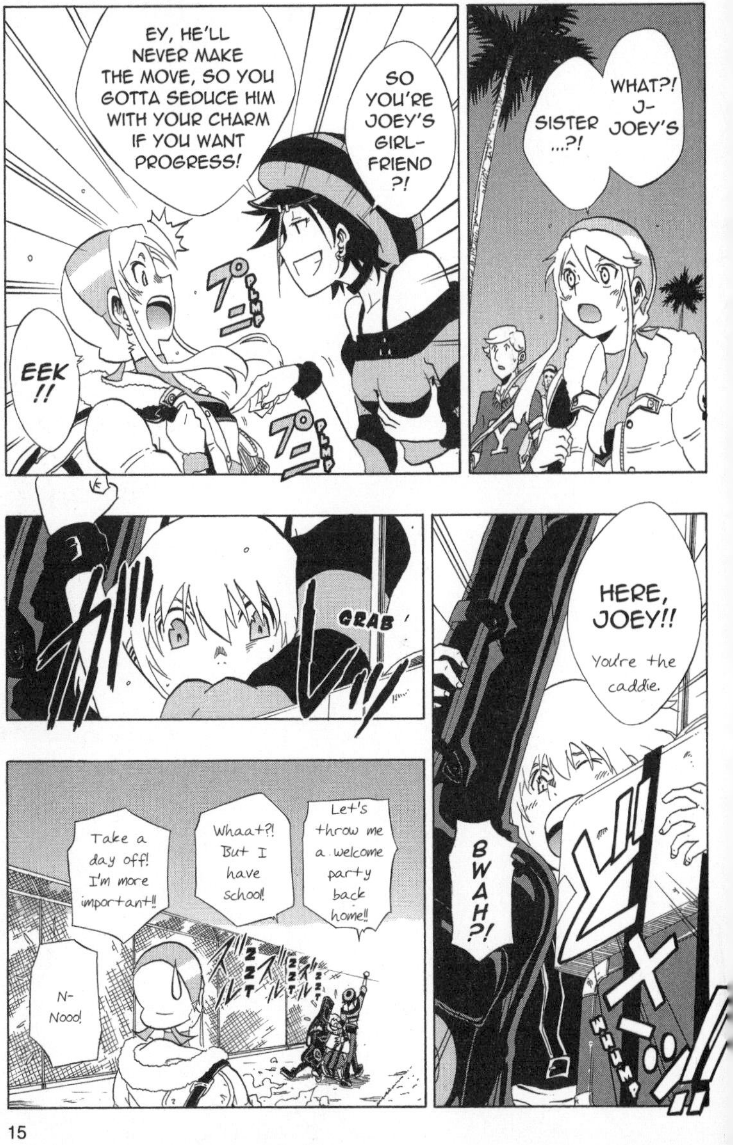
WHAT?! J-JOEY'S SISTER ...?!
SO YOU'RE JOEY'S GIRLFRIEND ?!
EY, HE'LL NEVER MAKE THE MOVE, SO YOU GOTTA SEDUCE HIM WITH YOUR CHARM IF YOU WANT PROGRESS!
PLMP
EEK !!
PLMP
HERE, JOEY!!
You're the caddie.
BWAH?!
WHUMP
GRAB
Let's throw me a welcome party back home!!
Whaat?! But I have school!
Take a day off! I'm more important!!
ZZZT
ZZZT
N-Nooo!

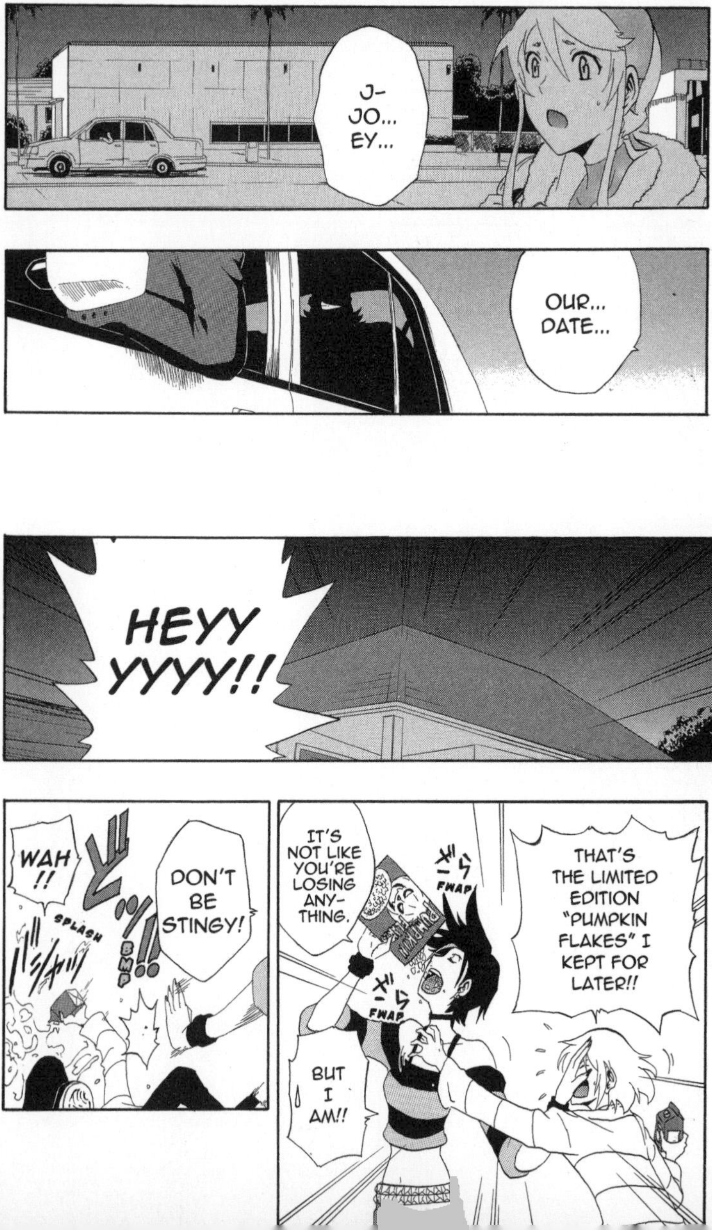

J-
JO...
EY...
OUR...
DATE...
HEYY
YYYY!!
THAT'S THE LIMITED EDITION "PUMPKIN FLAKES" I KEPT FOR LATER!!
IT'S NOT LIKE YOU'RE LOSING ANY-THING.
FWAP
FWAP
BUT I AM!!
DON'T BE STINGY!
BMP
WAH!!
SPLASH

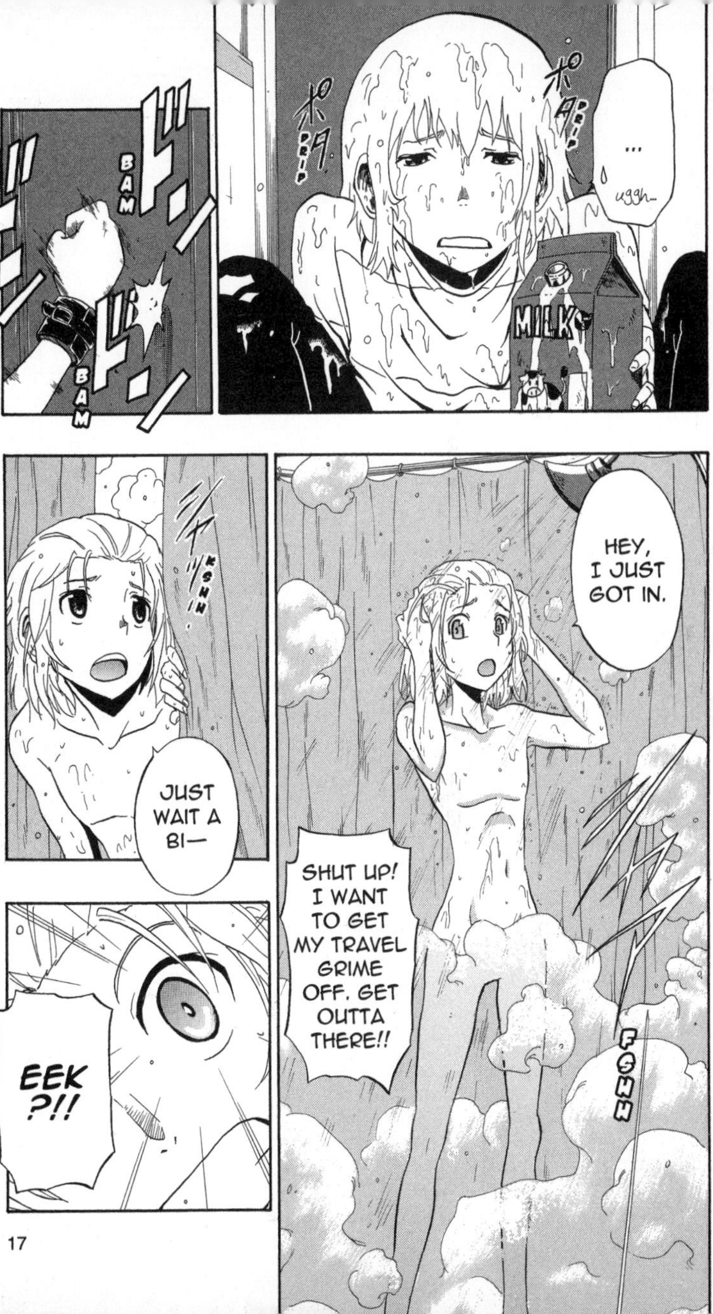

DRIP
DRIP
...
uggh...
MILK
BAM
BAM
BAM
HEY, I JUST GOT IN.
SHUT UP! I WANT TO GET MY TRAVEL GRIME OFF. GET OUTTA THERE!!
FSHH
KSHHH
JUST WAIT A BI—
EEK?!!

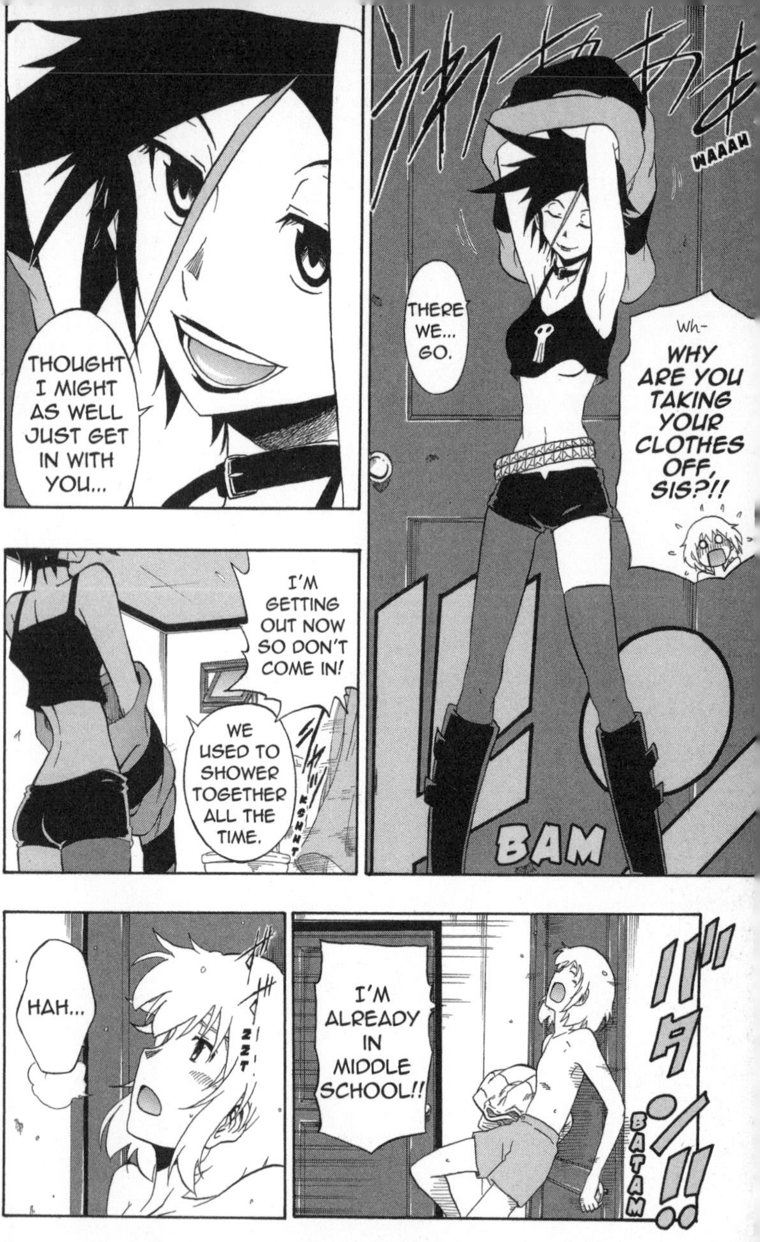
WAAAH
Wh-
WHY ARE YOU TAKING YOUR CLOTHES OFF, SIS?!!
THERE WE... GO.
BAM
THOUGHT I MIGHT AS WELL JUST GET IN WITH YOU...
I'M GETTING OUT NOW SO DON'T COME IN!
KSHHT
WE USED TO SHOWER TOGETHER ALL THE TIME.
BATAM
I'M ALREADY IN MIDDLE SCHOOL!!
ZZT
HAH...

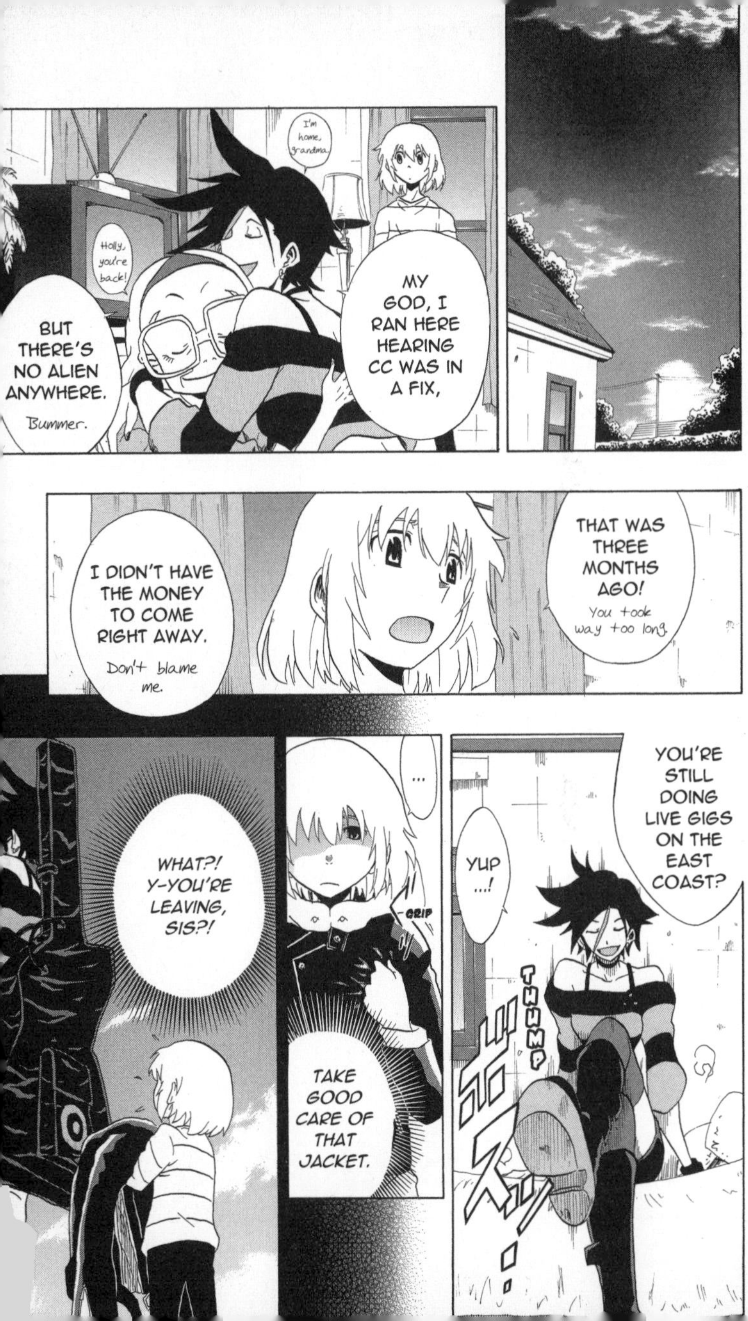
I'm home, grandma.
MY GOD, I RAN HERE HEARING CC WAS IN A FIX,
Holly, you're back!
BUT THERE'S NO ALIEN ANYWHERE.
Bummer.
THAT WAS THREE MONTHS AGO!
You took way too long.
I DIDN'T HAVE THE MONEY TO COME RIGHT AWAY.
Don't blame me.
YOU'RE STILL DOING LIVE GIGS ON THE EAST COAST?
YUP ...!
THUMP
...
GRIP
TAKE GOOD CARE OF THAT JACKET.
WHAT?! Y-YOU'RE LEAVING, SIS?!

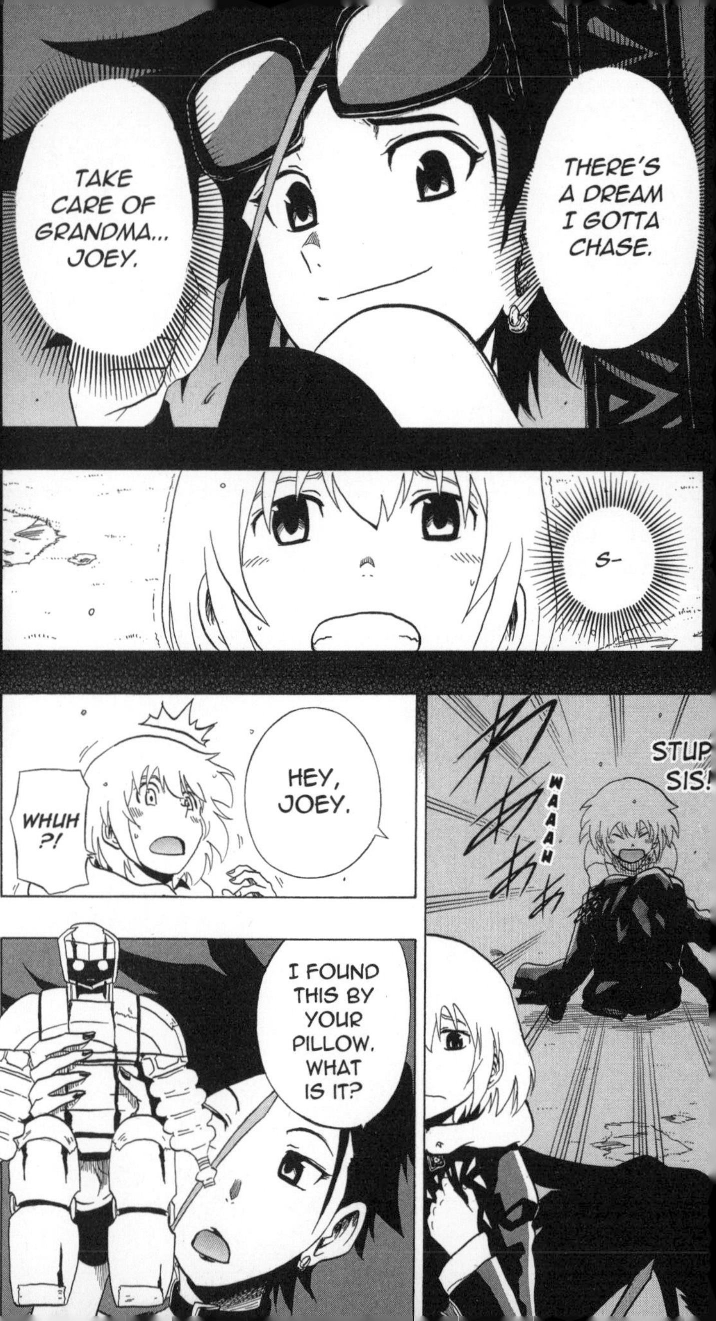
THERE'S A DREAM I GOTTA CHASE.
TAKE CARE OF GRANDMA... JOEY.
S-
STUP SIS!
WAAAAH
HEY, JOEY.
WHUH?!
I FOUND THIS BY YOUR PILLOW. WHAT IS IT?

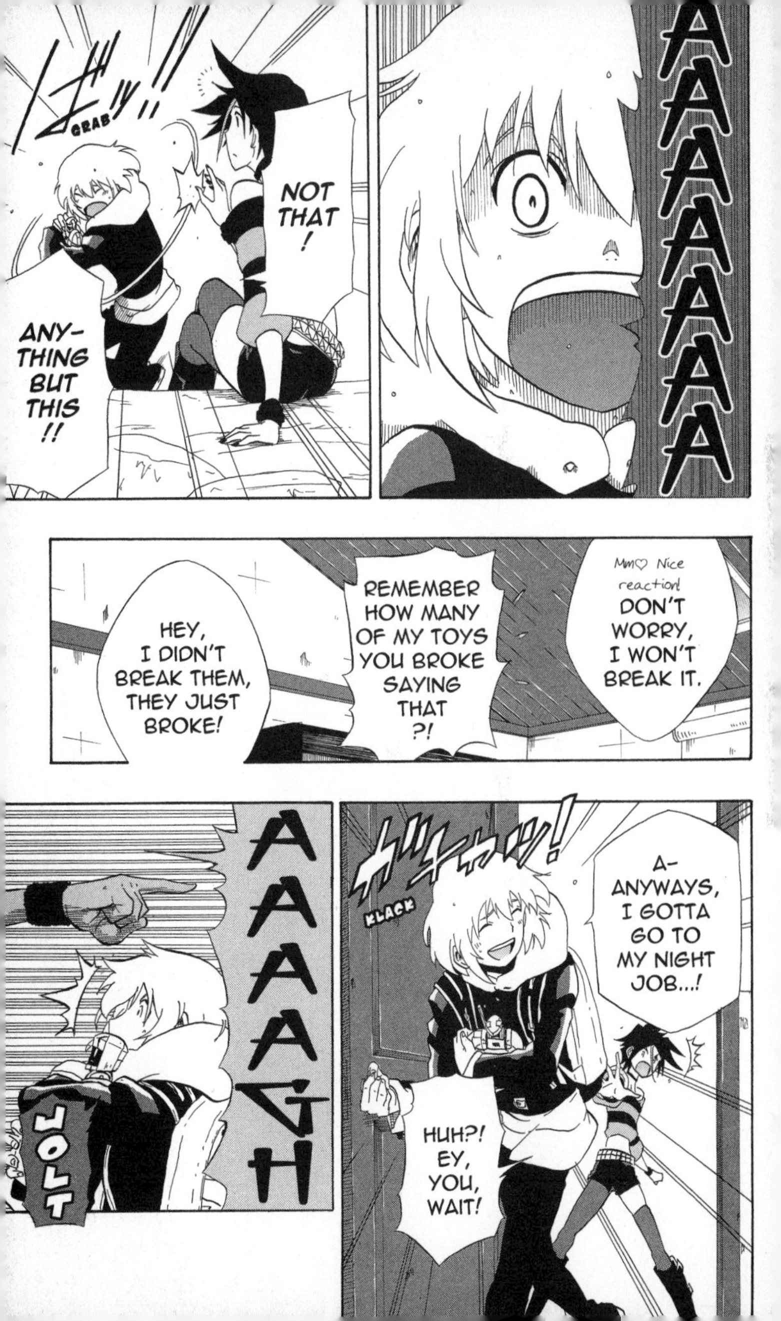
AAAAAAAAA
GRAB
NOT THAT!
ANYTHING BUT THIS!!
Mm♡ Nice reaction!
DON'T WORRY, I WON'T BREAK IT.
REMEMBER HOW MANY OF MY TOYS YOU BROKE SAYING THAT?!
HEY, I DIDN'T BREAK THEM, THEY JUST BROKE!
KLACK
A- ANYWAYS, I GOTTA GO TO MY NIGHT JOB...!
HUH?! EY, YOU, WAIT!
AAAAGH
JOLT

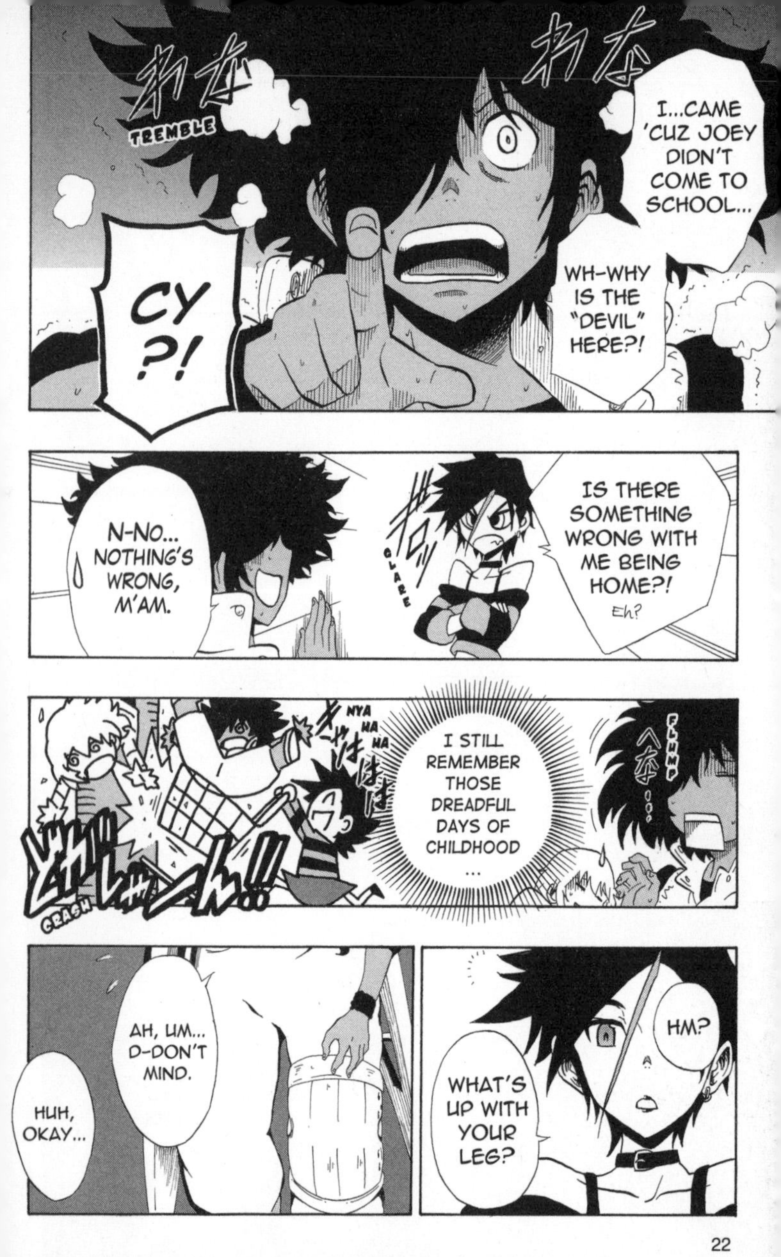
TREMBLE
I...CAME 'CUZ JOEY DIDN'T COME TO SCHOOL...
WH-WHY IS THE "DEVIL" HERE?!
CY ?!
IS THERE SOMETHING WRONG WITH ME BEING HOME?!
Eh?
GLARE
N-NO... NOTHING'S WRONG, M'AM.
FLUMP
I STILL REMEMBER THOSE DREADFUL DAYS OF CHILDHOOD ...
NYA HA HA
CRASH
HM?
WHAT'S UP WITH YOUR LEG?
AH, UM... D-DON'T MIND.
HUH, OKAY...

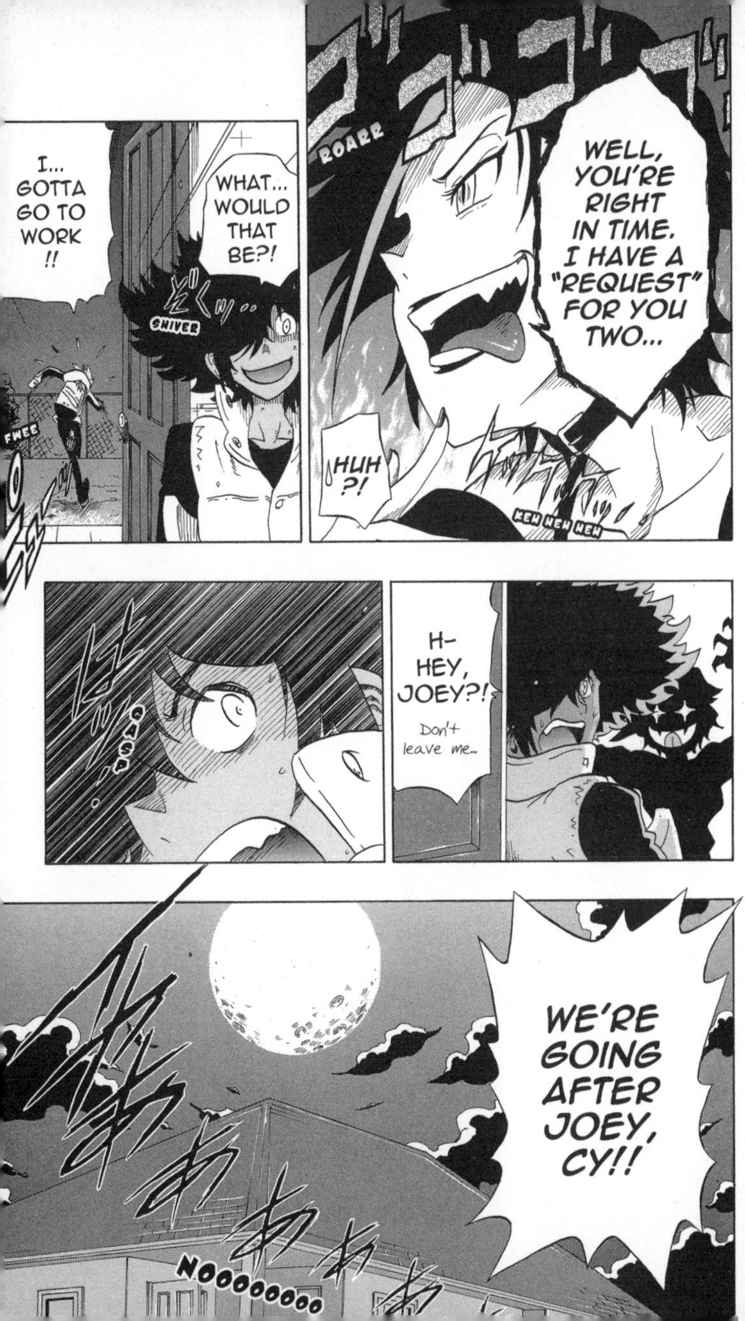
ROARR
WELL, YOU'RE RIGHT IN TIME. I HAVE A "REQUEST" FOR YOU TWO...
HUH ?!
KEH KEH KEH
WHAT... WOULD THAT BE?!
SHIVER
I... GOTTA GO TO WORK !!
FWEE
H- HEY, JOEY?!
Don't leave me...
GASP
WE'RE GOING AFTER JOEY, CY!!
NOOOOOOOOO

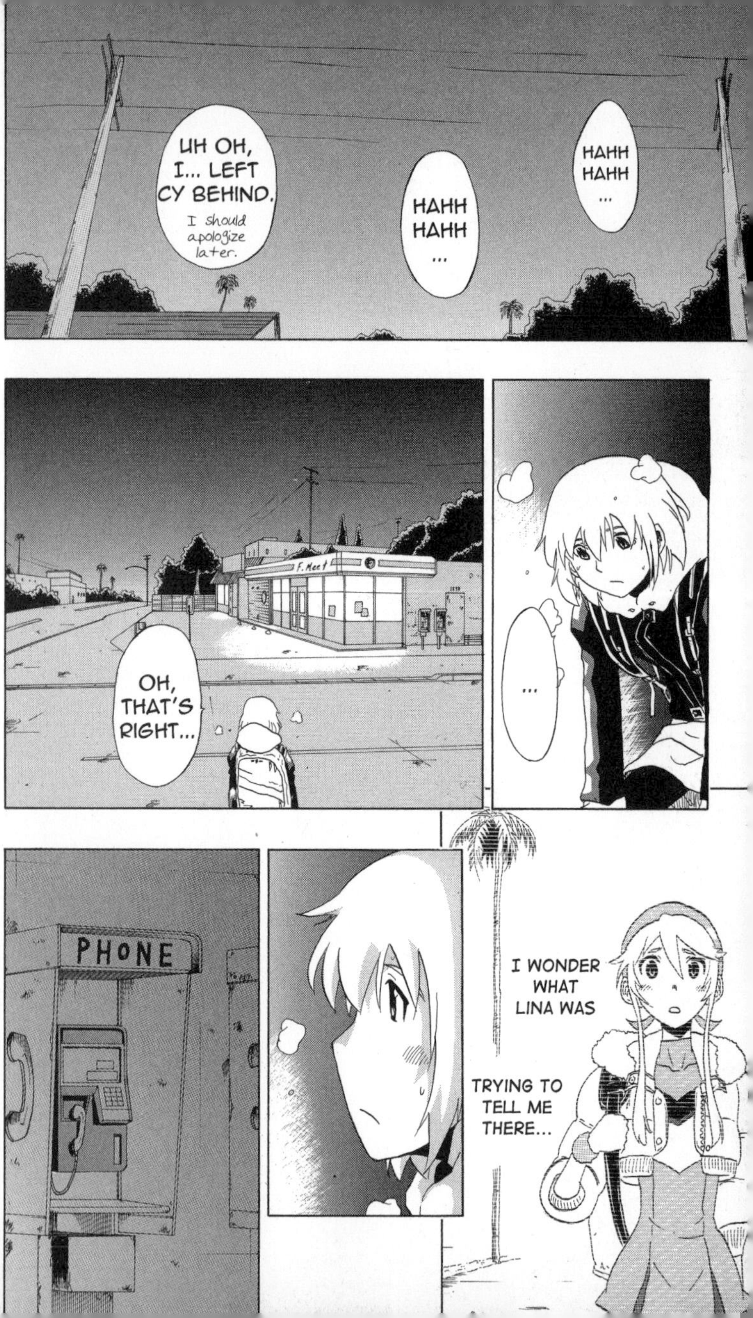
HAHH HAHH ...
HAHH HAHH ...
UH OH, I... LEFT CY BEHIND.
I should apologize later.
...
OH, THAT'S RIGHT...
I WONDER WHAT LINA WAS
TRYING TO TELL ME THERE...
F. Meet
PHONE

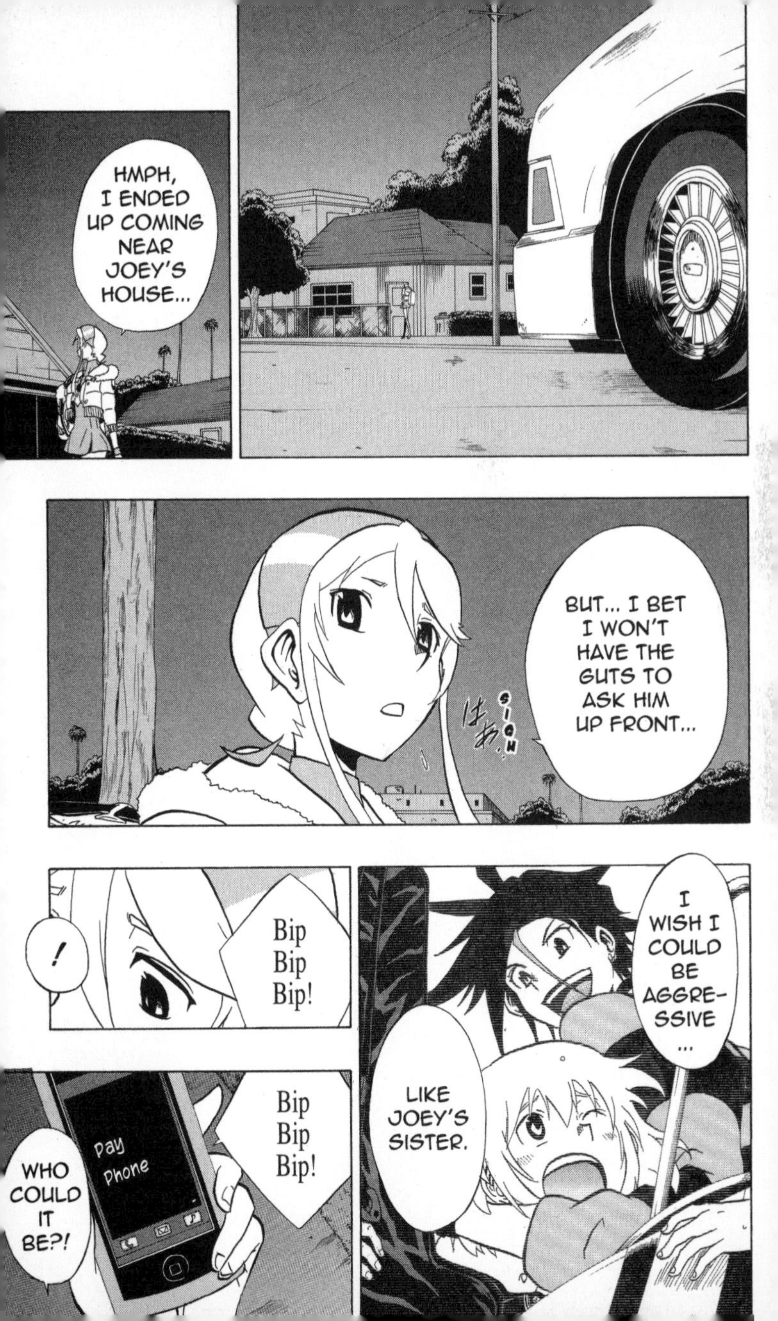
HMPH, I ENDED UP COMING NEAR JOEY'S HOUSE...
BUT... I BET I WON'T HAVE THE GUTS TO ASK HIM UP FRONT...
SIGH
はあ
I WISH I COULD BE AGGRE-SSIVE ...
LIKE JOEY'S SISTER.
Bip Bip Bip!
!
Bip Bip Bip!
Pay Phone
WHO COULD IT BE?!

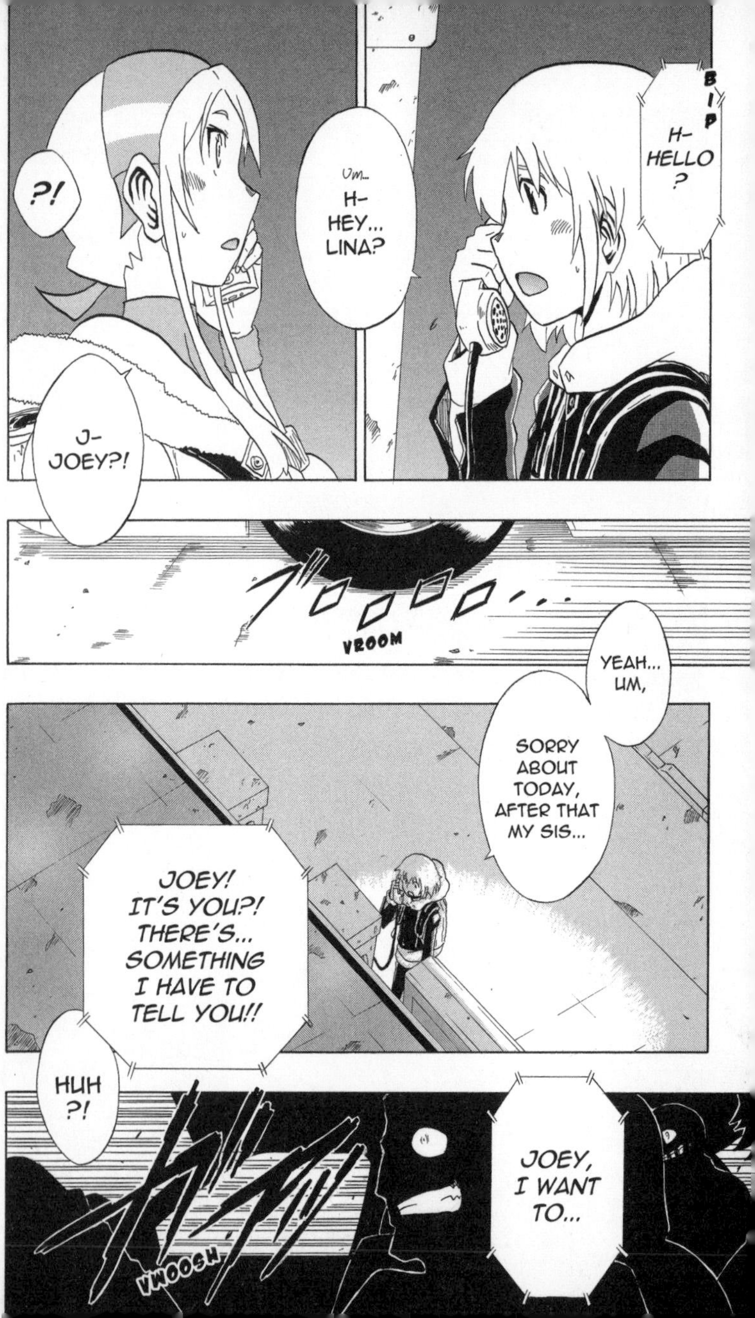
BIP
H- HELLO ?
Um... H- HEY... LINA?
?!
J- JOEY?!
VROOM
YEAH... UM,
SORRY ABOUT TODAY, AFTER THAT MY SIS...
JOEY! IT'S YOU?! THERE'S... SOMETHING I HAVE TO TELL YOU!!
JOEY, I WANT TO...
HUH ?!
VWOOSH

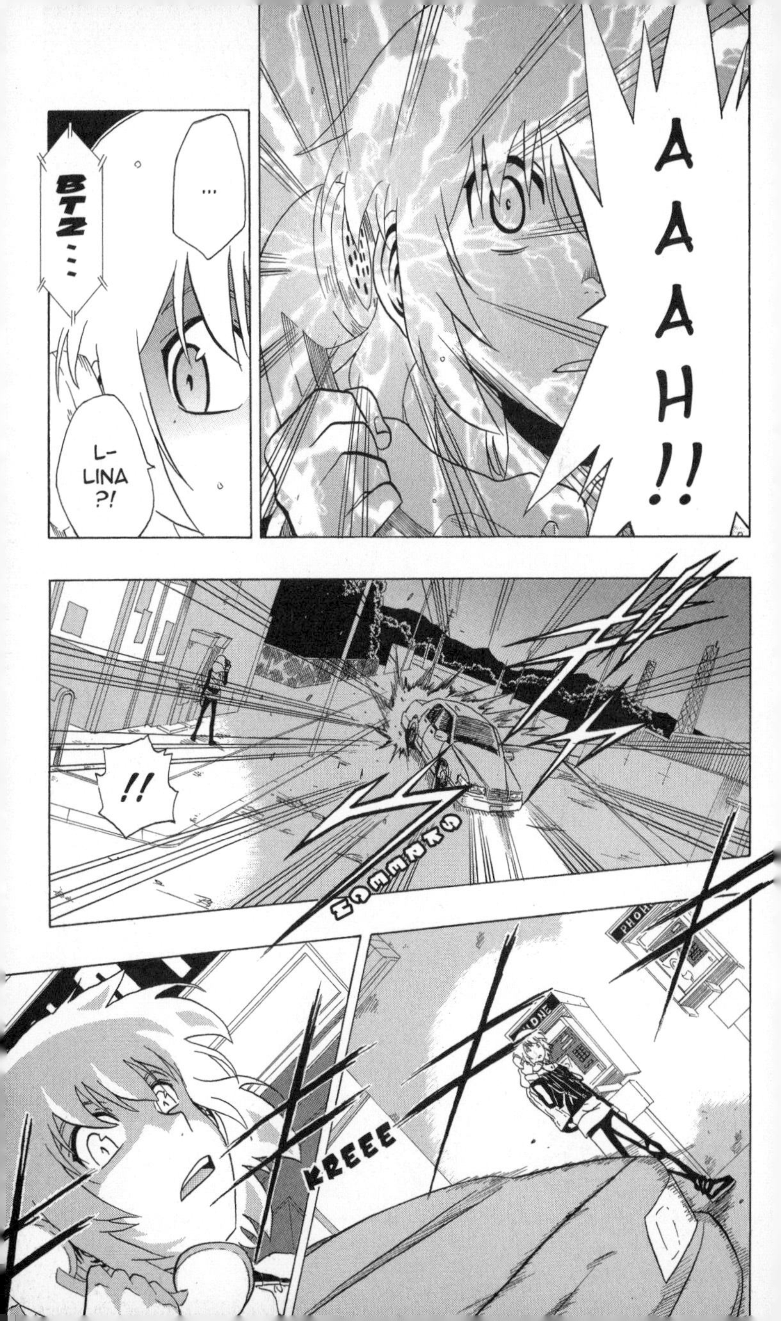
AAAAH!!
BTZ...
...
L-LINA?!
!!
SKREEECH
KREEEE
PHONE

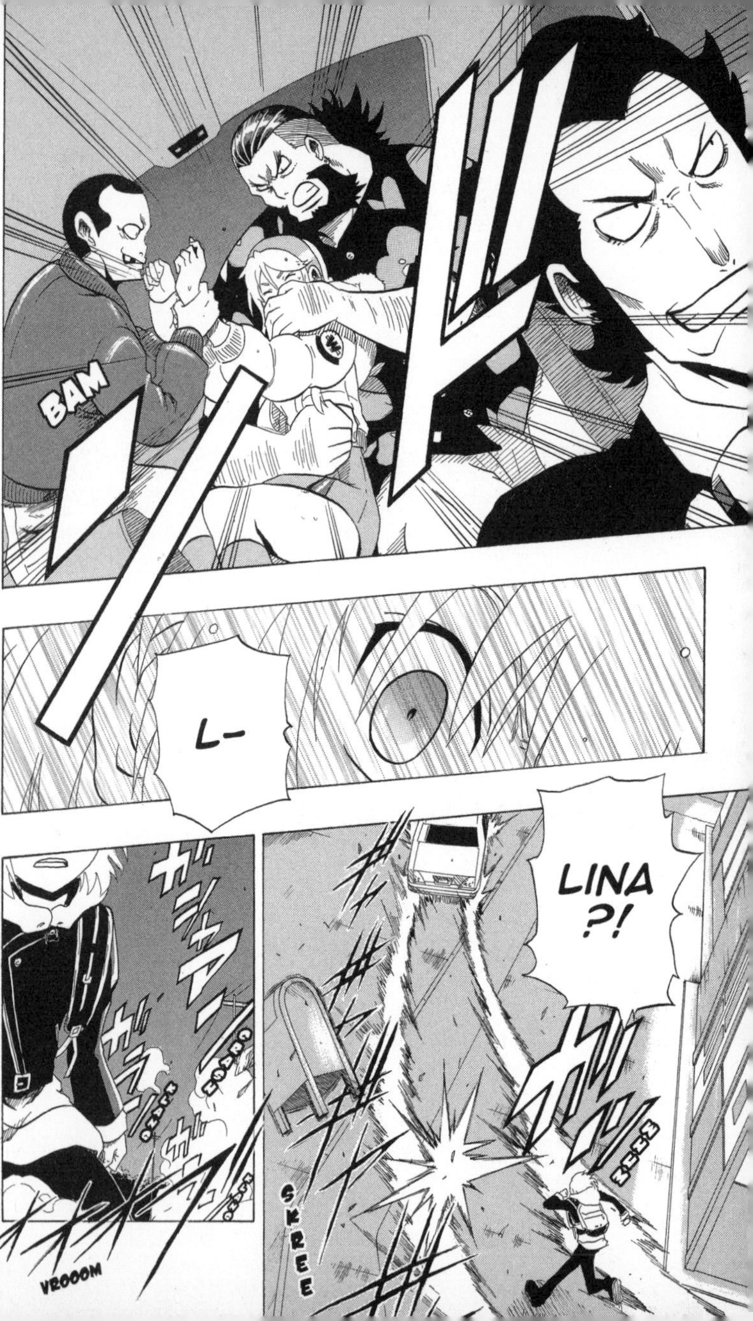
BAM
L–
LINA ?!
SKREE
CRASH
CLANK
KLANG
VROOOM

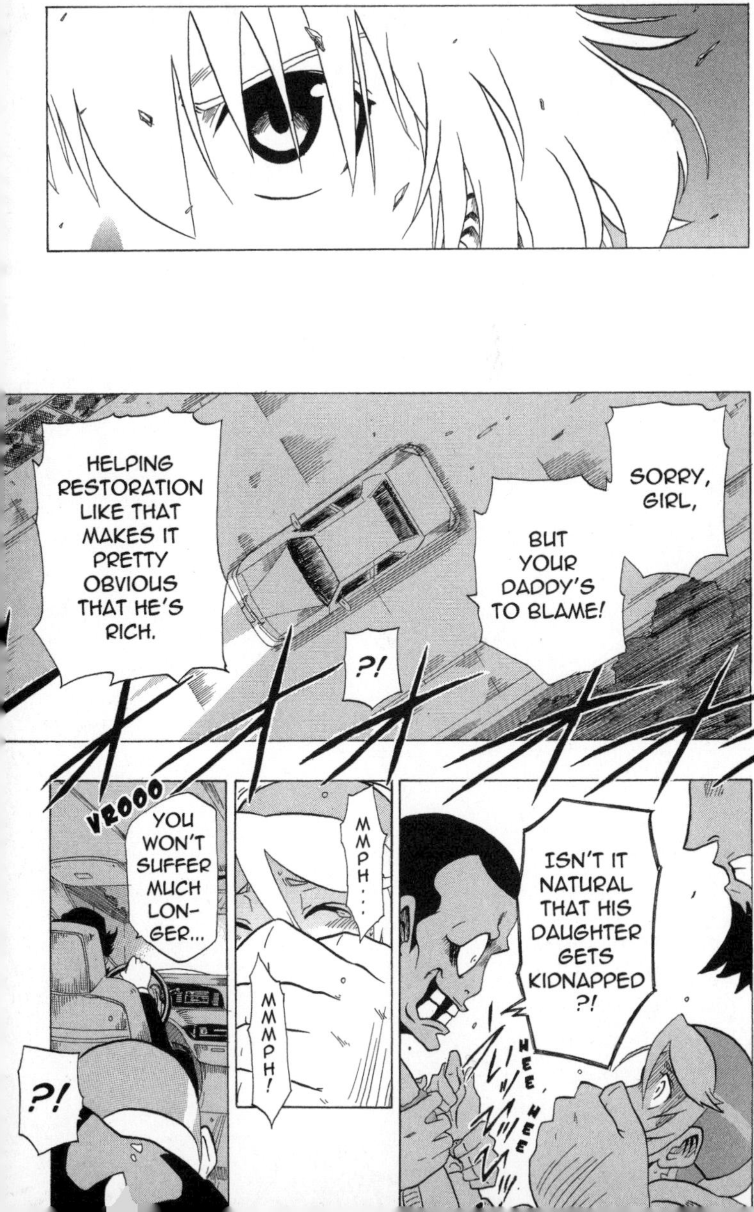
SORRY, GIRL,
BUT YOUR DADDY'S TO BLAME!
HELPING RESTORATION LIKE THAT MAKES IT PRETTY OBVIOUS THAT HE'S RICH.
?!
ISN'T IT NATURAL THAT HIS DAUGHTER GETS KIDNAPPED ?!
HEE HEE HEE
MMPH...
MMMPH!
VROOO
YOU WON'T SUFFER MUCH LONGER...
?!

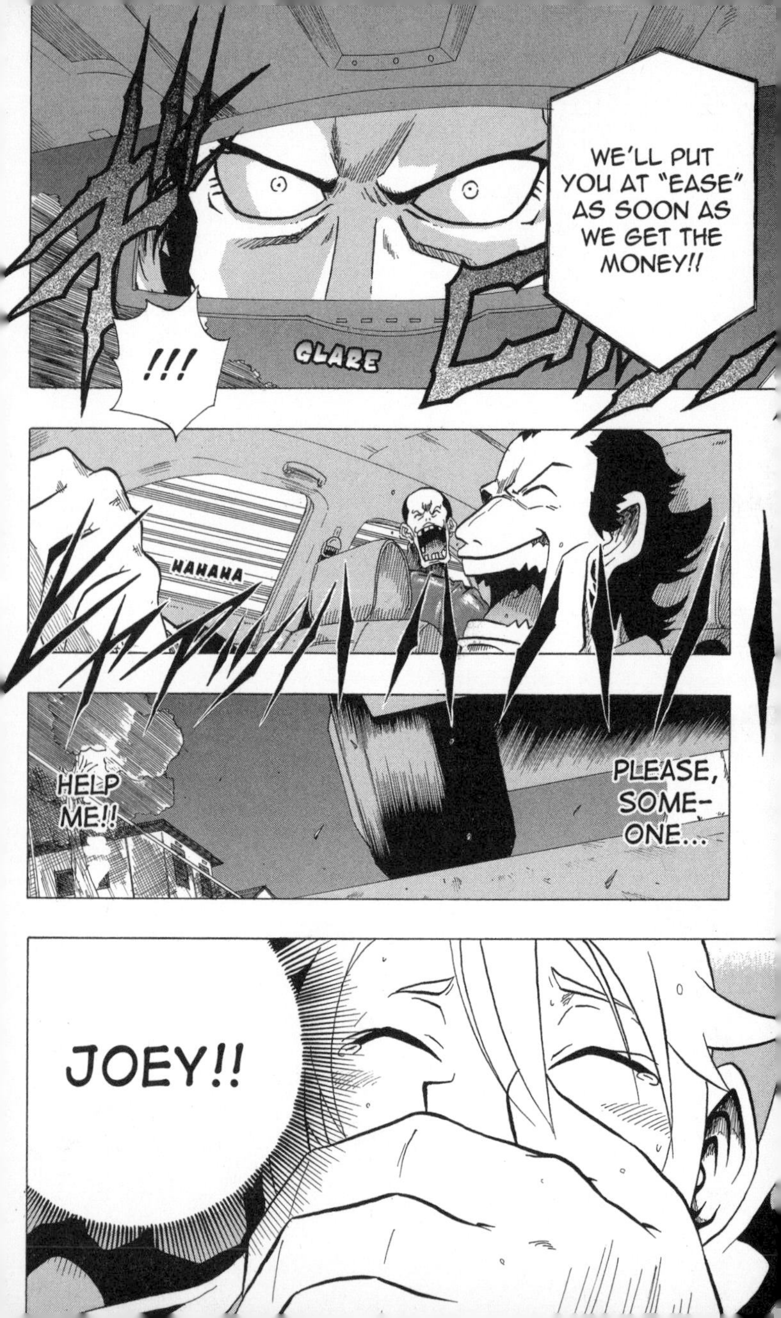
WE'LL PUT YOU AT "EASE" AS SOON AS WE GET THE MONEY!!
GLARE
!!!
HAHAHA
PLEASE, SOME-ONE...
HELP ME!!
JOEY!!

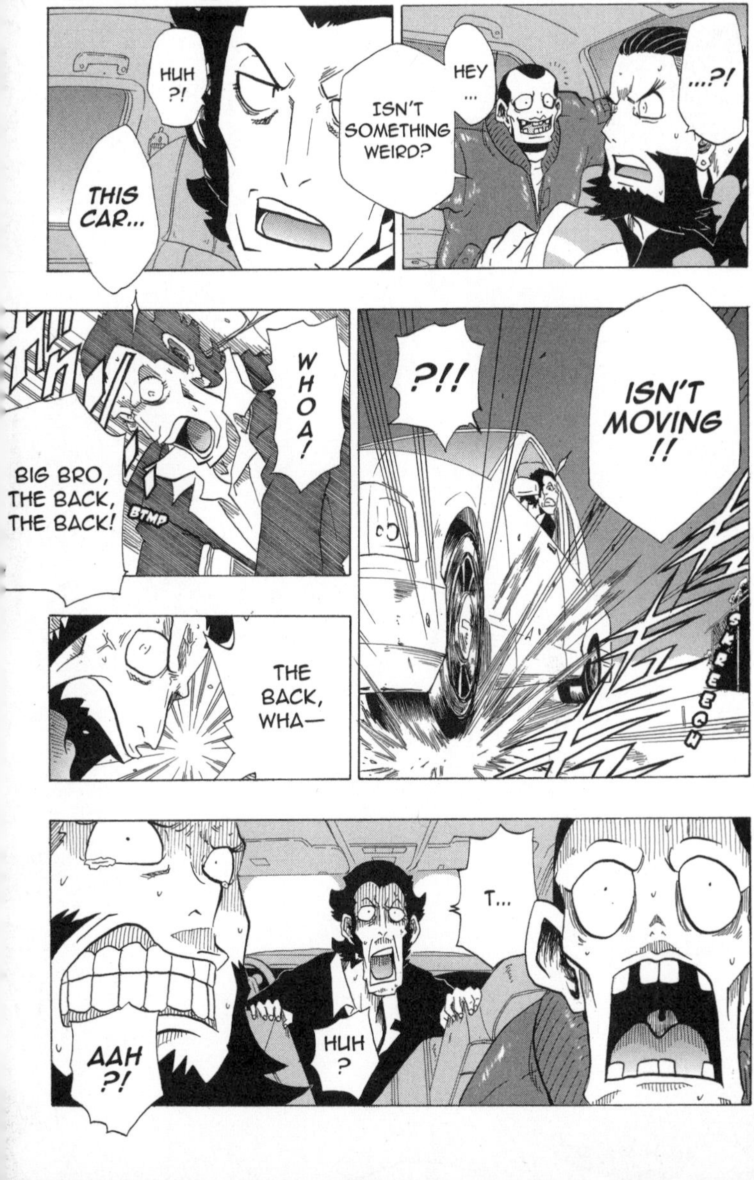
...?!
HEY ...
ISN'T SOMETHING WEIRD?
HUH ?!
THIS CAR...
ISN'T MOVING !!
?!!
SKREECH
WHOA!
BIG BRO, THE BACK, THE BACK!
BTMP
THE BACK, WHA—
T...
HUH ?
AAH ?!

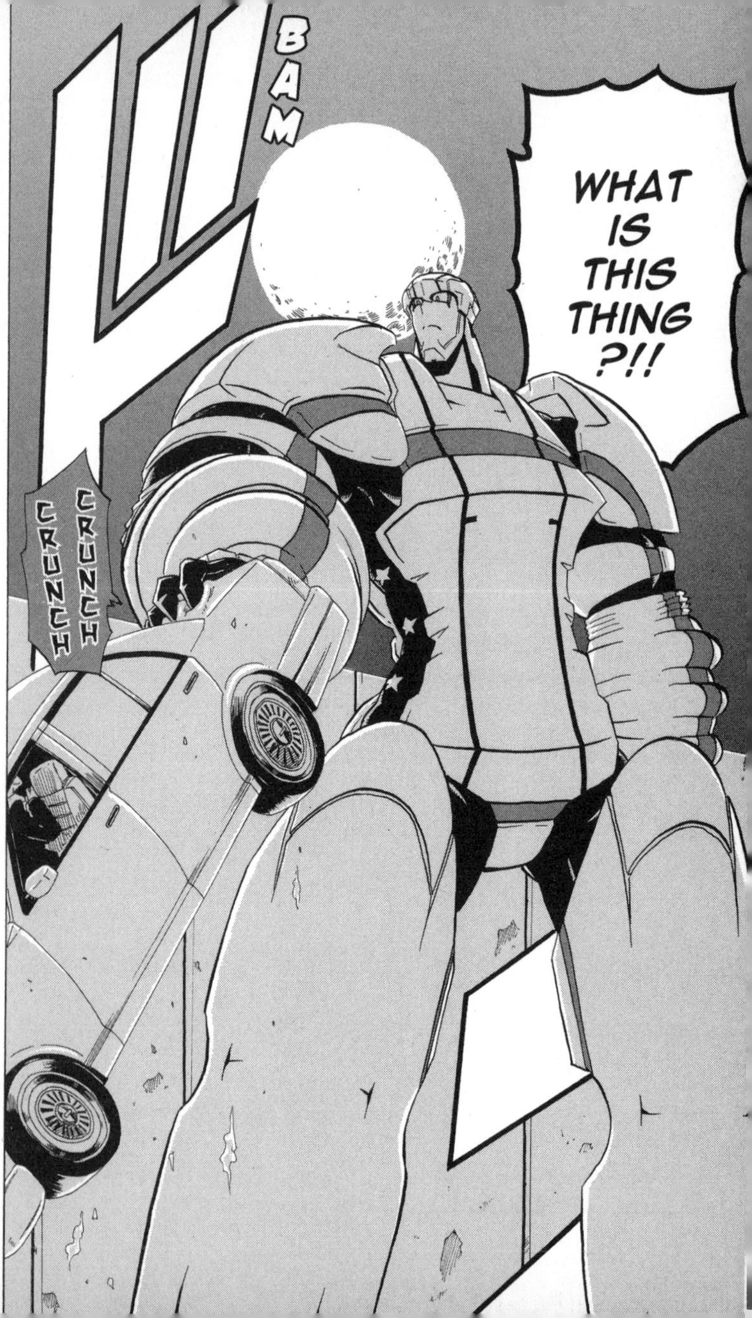
WHAT IS THIS THING?!!
BAM
CRUNCH CRUNCH

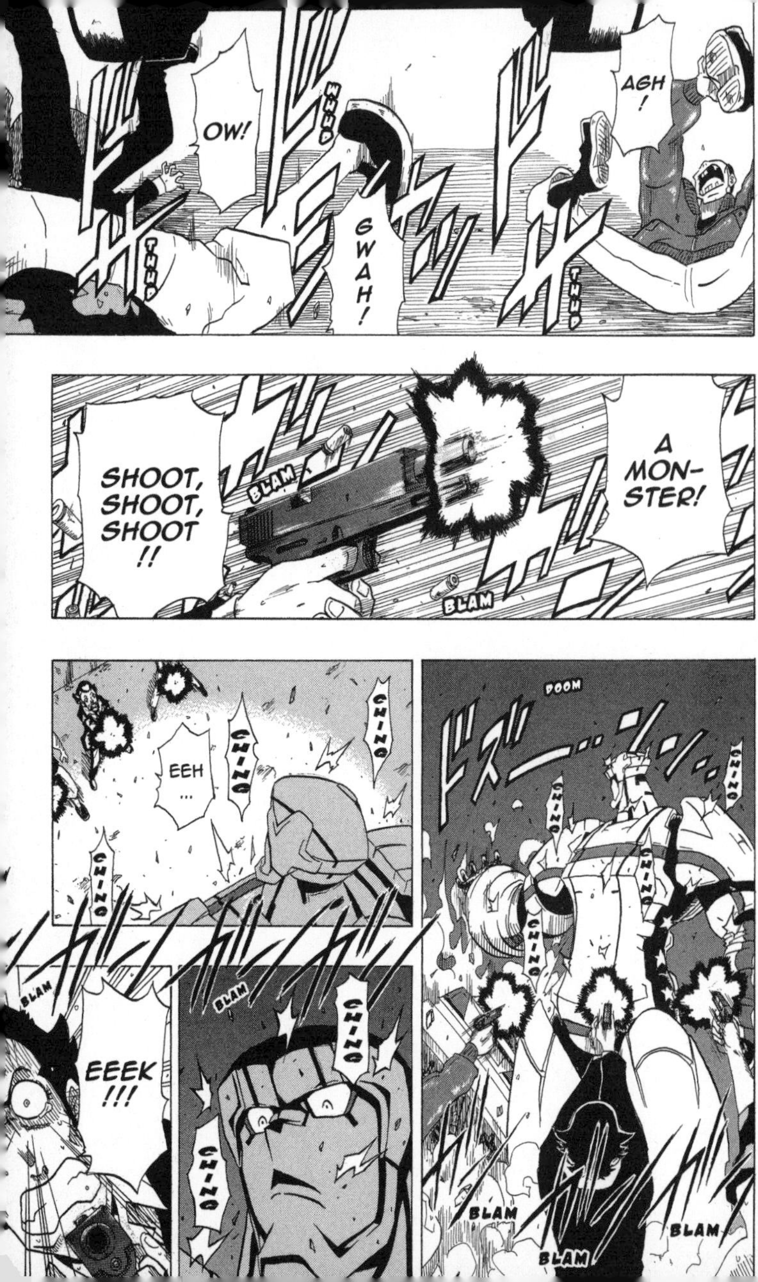
AGH!
THUD
WHUD
GWAH!
OW!
THUD
A MON-STER!
BLAM
SHOOT, SHOOT, SHOOT!!
BLAM
DOOM
CHING
CHING
CHING
CHING
BLAM
BLAM
BLAM
CHING
CHING
EEH...
CHING
BLAM
CHING
CHING
BLAM
EEEK!!!

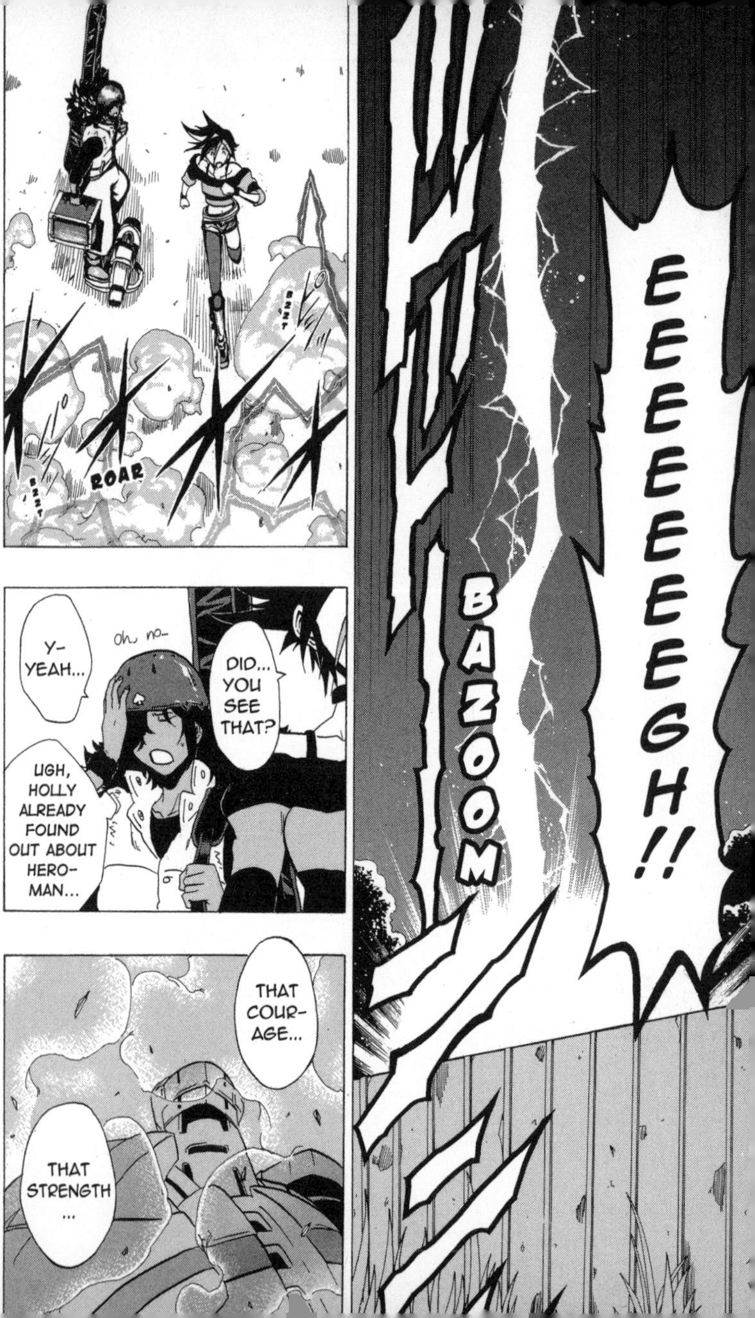
EEEEEEEGH!!
BAZOOM
BZZT
ROAR
BZZT
DID... YOU SEE THAT?
oh, no...
Y-YEAH...
UGH, HOLLY ALREADY FOUND OUT ABOUT HERO-MAN...
THAT COUR-AGE...
THAT STRENGTH ...

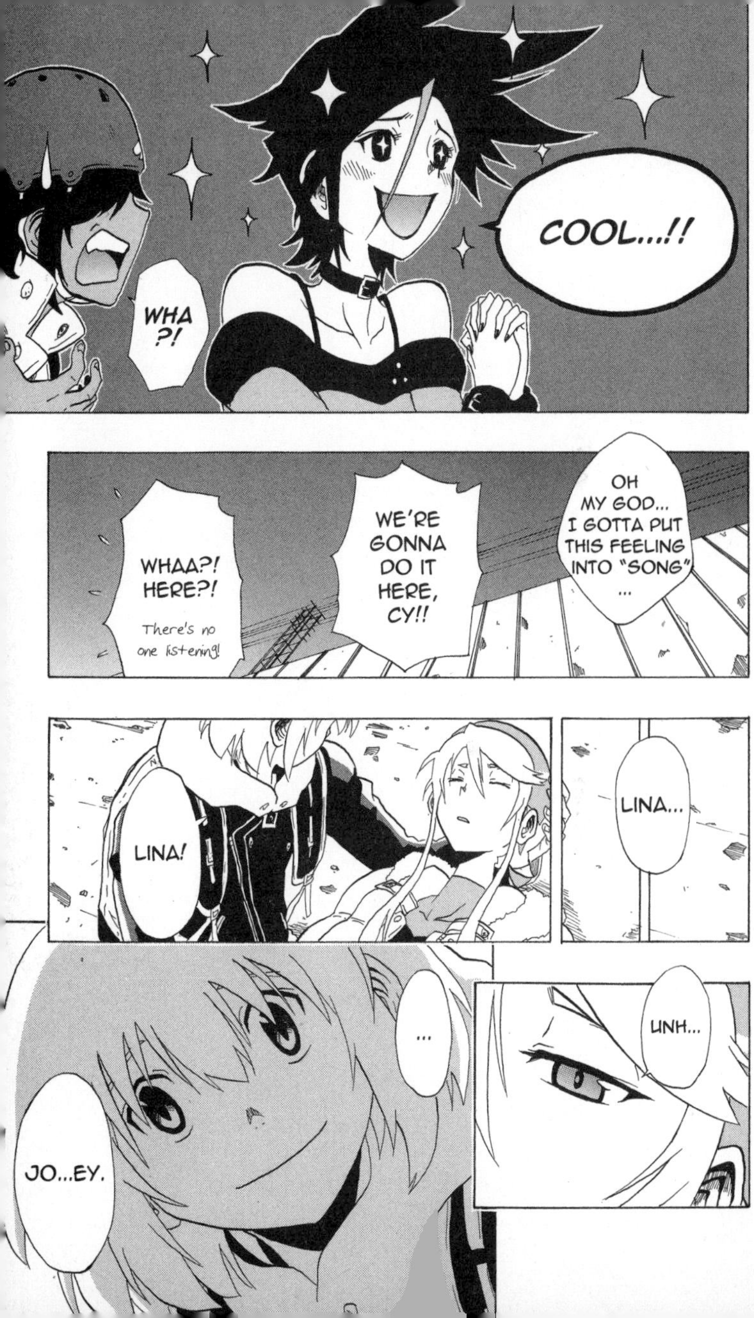
COOL...!!
WHA ?!
OH MY GOD... I GOTTA PUT THIS FEELING INTO "SONG"...
WE'RE GONNA DO IT HERE, CY!!
WHAA?! HERE?!
There's no one listening!
LINA...
LINA!
UNH...
...
JO...EY.

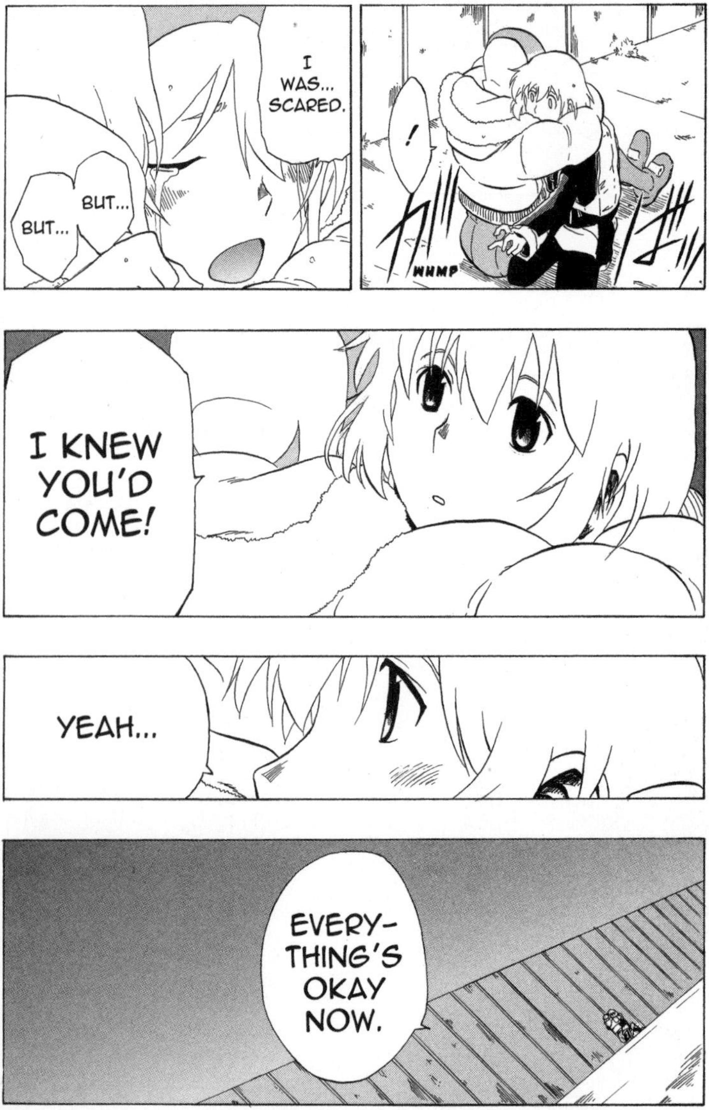
!
WHMP
I WAS... SCARED.
BUT...
BUT...
I KNEW YOU'D COME!
YEAH...
EVERY-THING'S OKAY NOW.

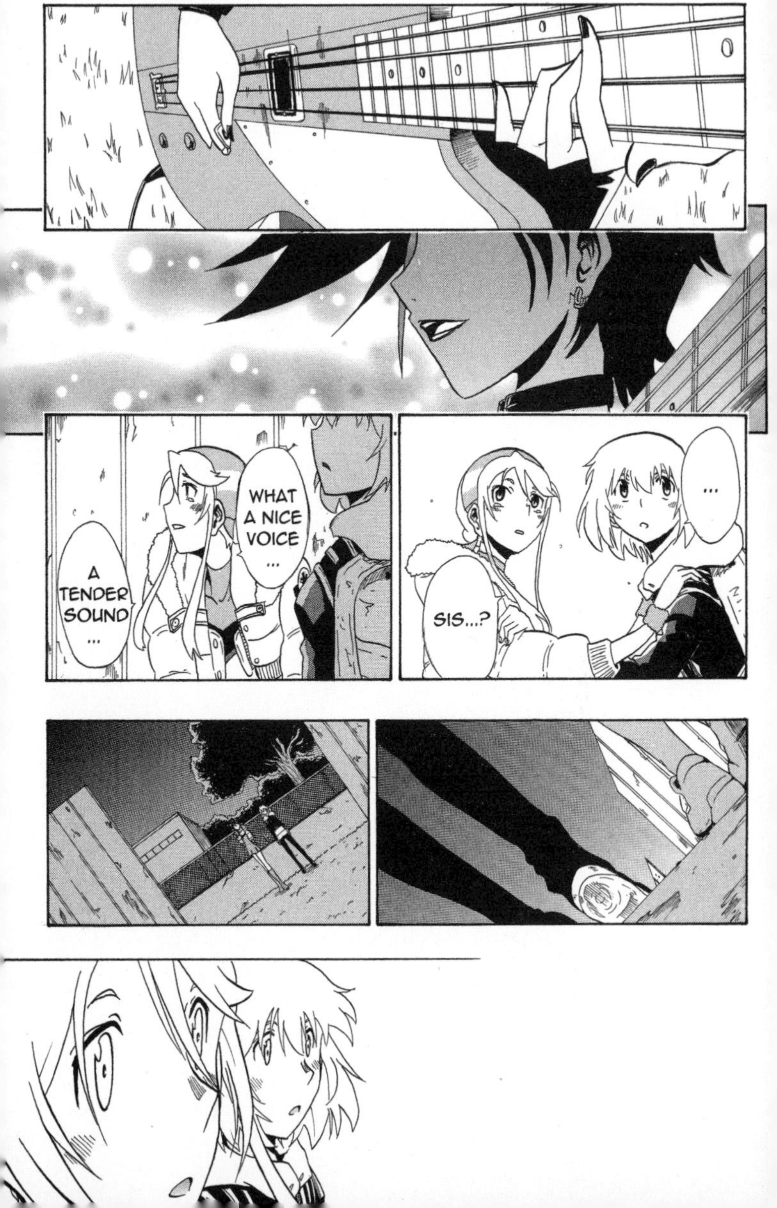
...
SIS...?
WHAT A NICE VOICE ...
A TENDER SOUND ...

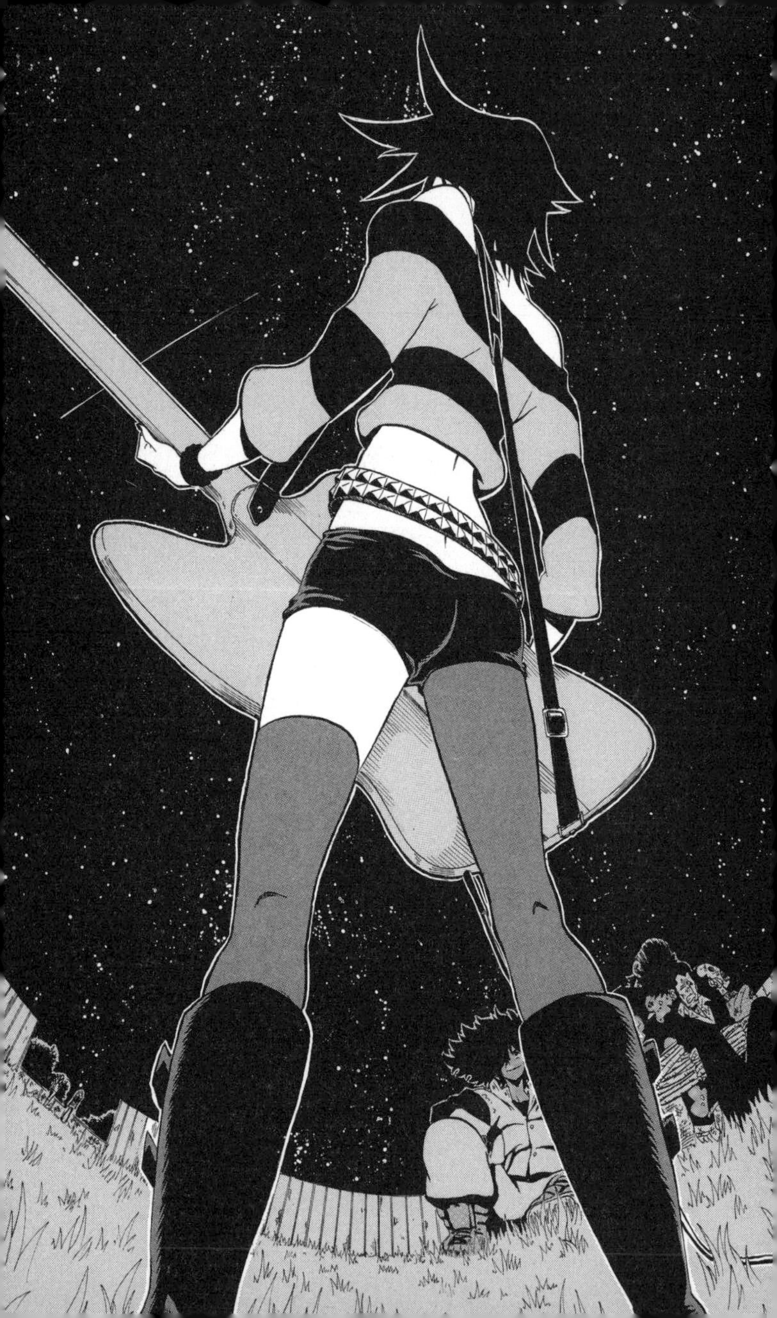

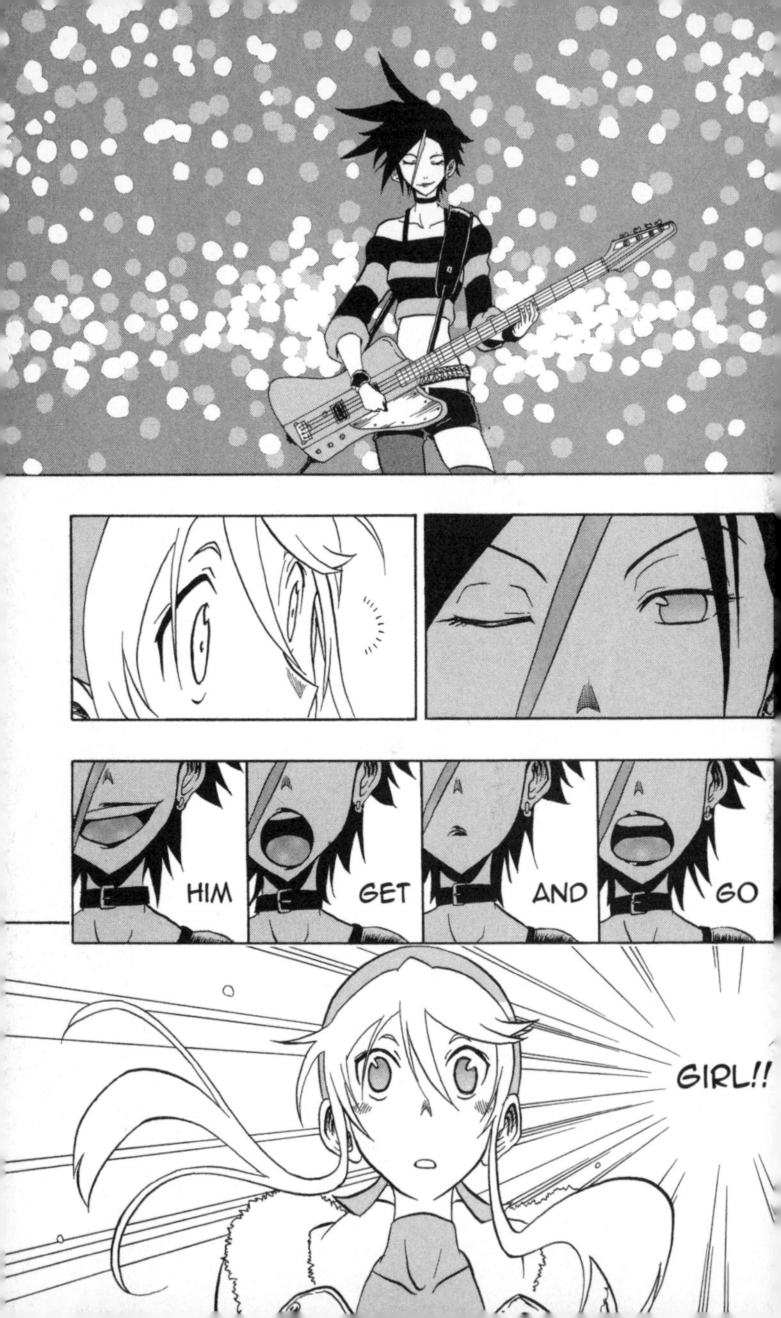
GO
AND
GET
HIM
GIRL!!

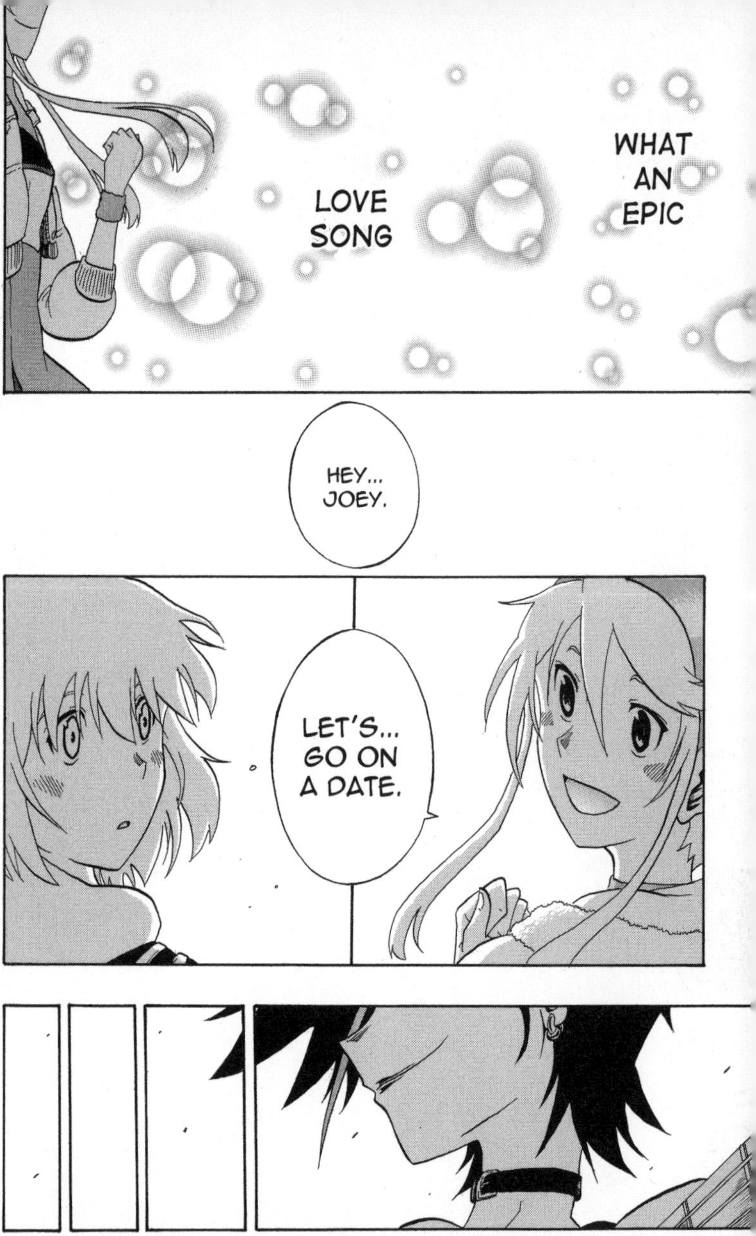
WHAT AN EPIC
LOVE SONG
HEY... JOEY.
LET'S... GO ON A DATE.

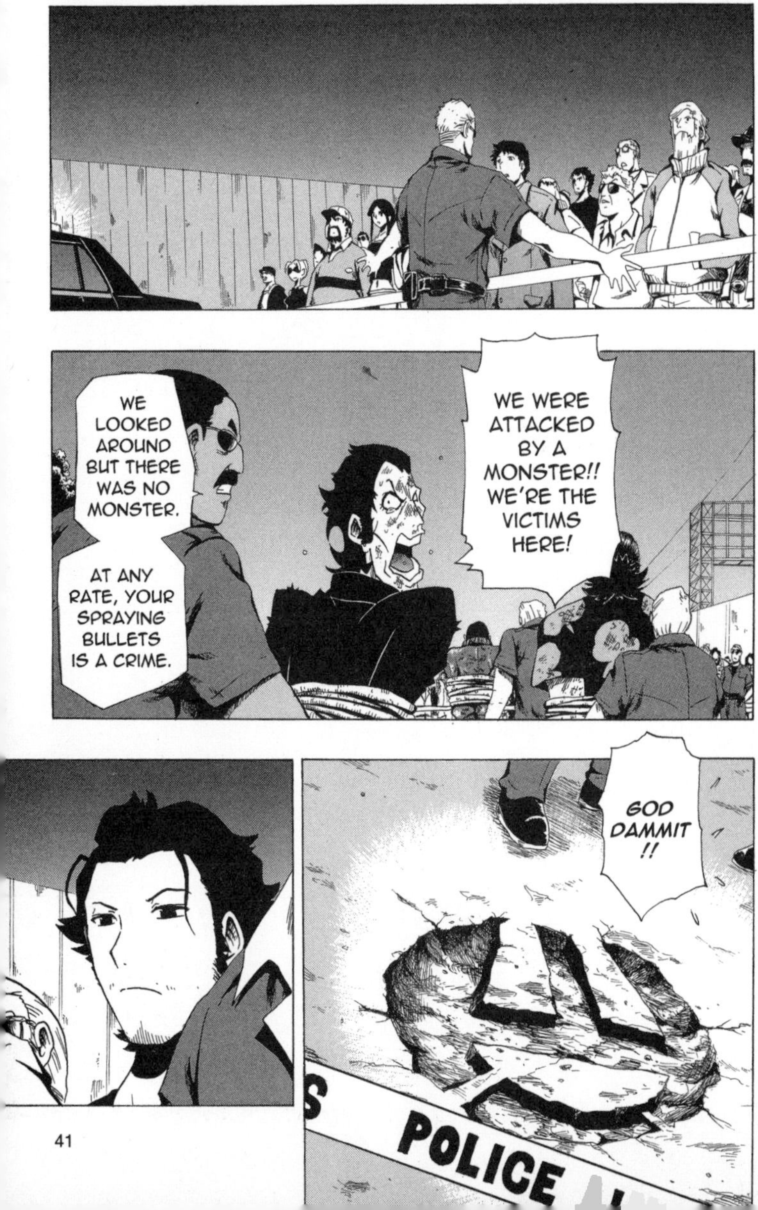
WE WERE ATTACKED BY A MONSTER!! WE'RE THE VICTIMS HERE!
WE LOOKED AROUND BUT THERE WAS NO MONSTER.
AT ANY RATE, YOUR SPRAYING BULLETS IS A CRIME.
GOD DAMMIT !!
POLICE

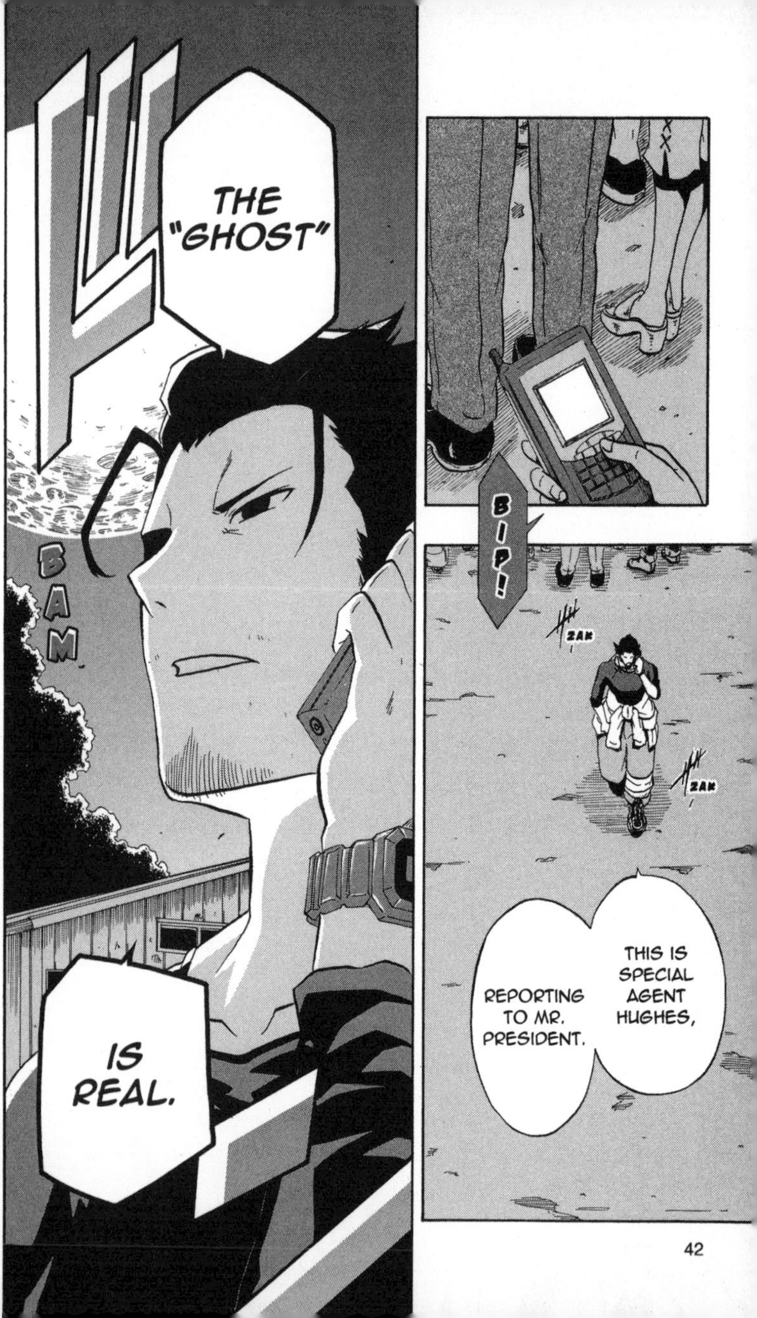
BIP!
ZAK
ZAK
THIS IS SPECIAL AGENT HUGHES,
REPORTING TO MR. PRESIDENT.
THE "GHOST"
BAM
IS REAL.

#16 STALKERS

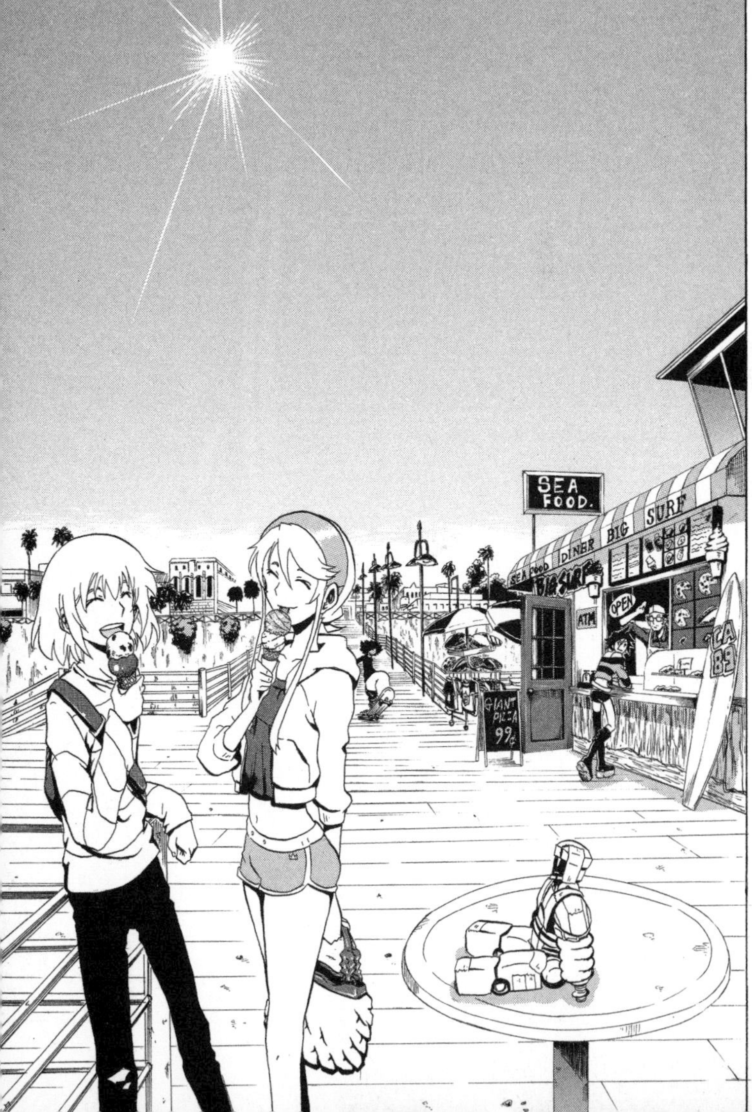

SEA FOOD.
SEA FOOD DINER BIG SURF
BIG SURF
ATM
OPEN
GIANT PIZZA 99¢

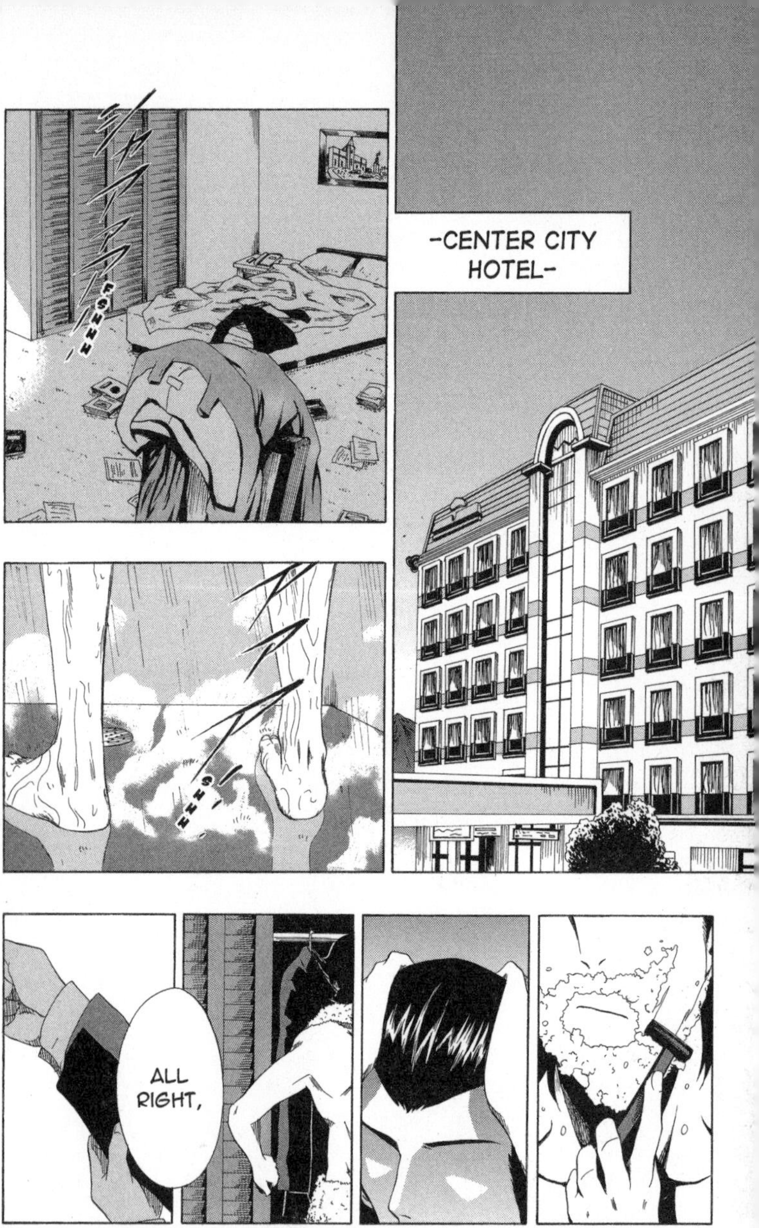
-CENTER CITY HOTEL-
FSHHH
SHHH
ALL RIGHT,

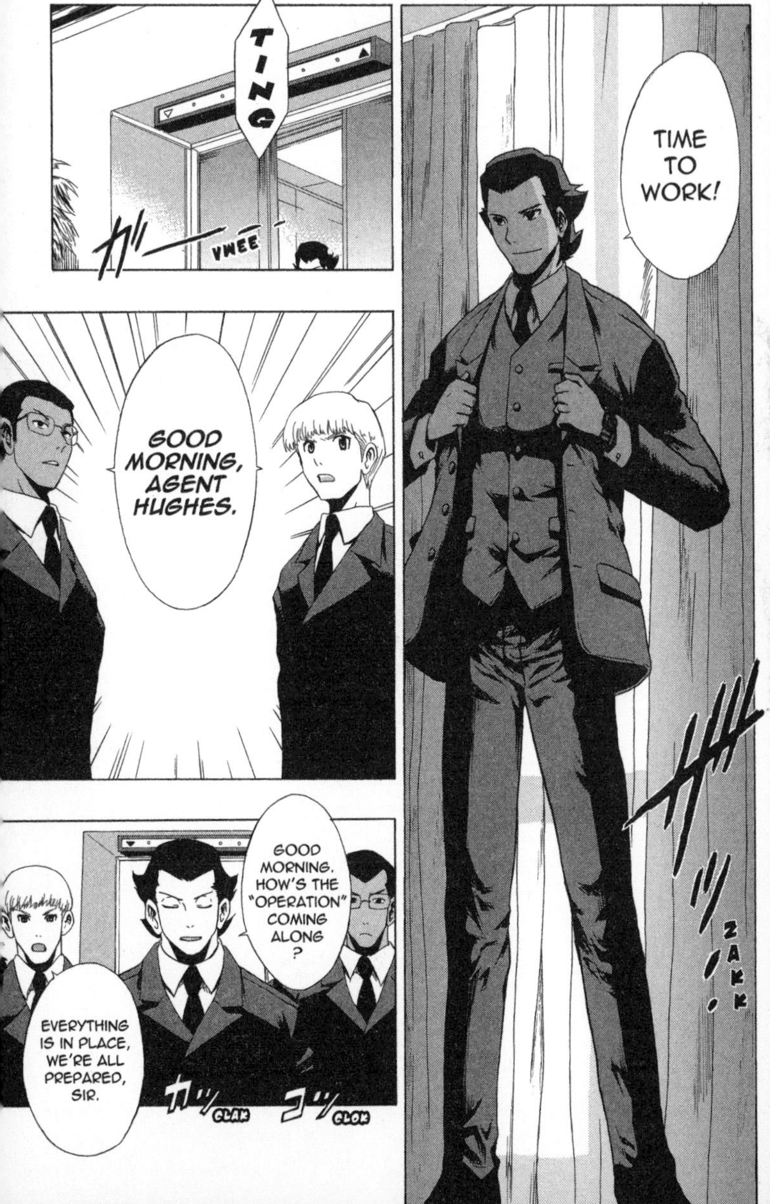
TIME TO WORK!
ZAKK
TING
VWEE
GOOD MORNING, AGENT HUGHES.
GOOD MORNING. HOW'S THE "OPERATION" COMING ALONG ?
EVERYTHING IS IN PLACE, WE'RE ALL PREPARED, SIR.
CLAK
CLOK

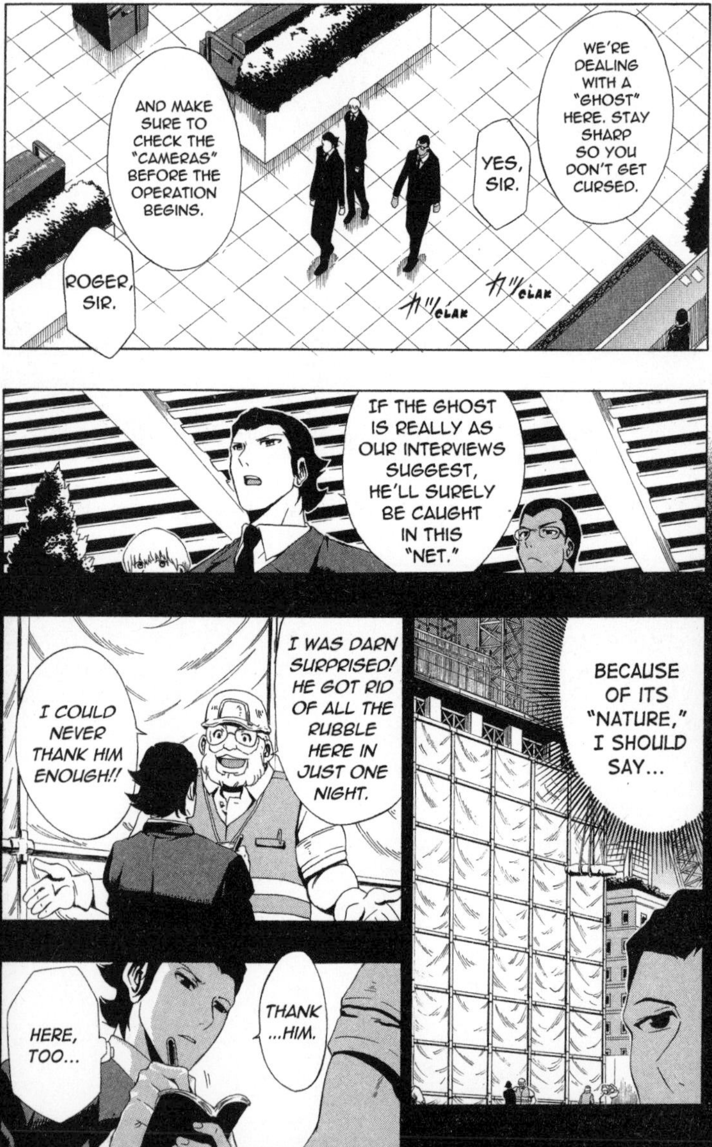
WE'RE DEALING WITH A "GHOST" HERE. STAY SHARP SO YOU DON'T GET CURSED.
YES, SIR.
AND MAKE SURE TO CHECK THE "CAMERAS" BEFORE THE OPERATION BEGINS.
ROGER, SIR.
CLAK
CLAK
IF THE GHOST IS REALLY AS OUR INTERVIEWS SUGGEST, HE'LL SURELY BE CAUGHT IN THIS "NET."
BECAUSE OF ITS "NATURE," I SHOULD SAY...
I WAS DARN SURPRISED! HE GOT RID OF ALL THE RUBBLE HERE IN JUST ONE NIGHT.
I COULD NEVER THANK HIM ENOUGH!!
THANK ...HIM.
HERE, TOO...

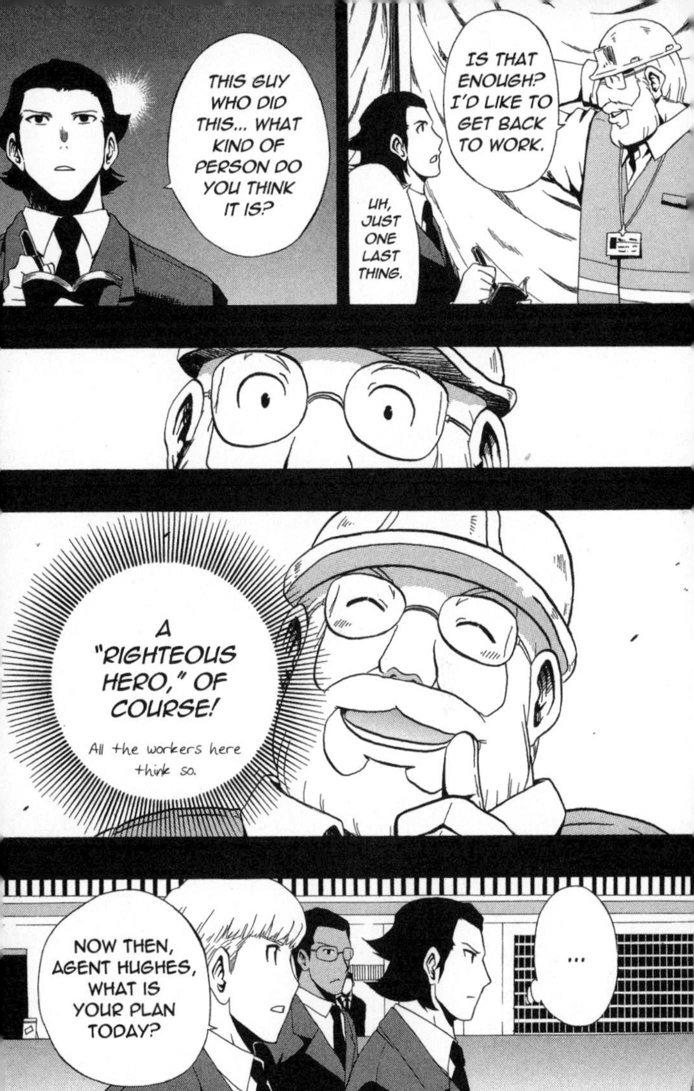
IS THAT ENOUGH? I'D LIKE TO GET BACK TO WORK.
UH, JUST ONE LAST THING.
THIS GUY WHO DID THIS... WHAT KIND OF PERSON DO YOU THINK IT IS?
A "RIGHTEOUS HERO," OF COURSE!
All the workers here think so.
...
NOW THEN, AGENT HUGHES, WHAT IS YOUR PLAN TODAY?

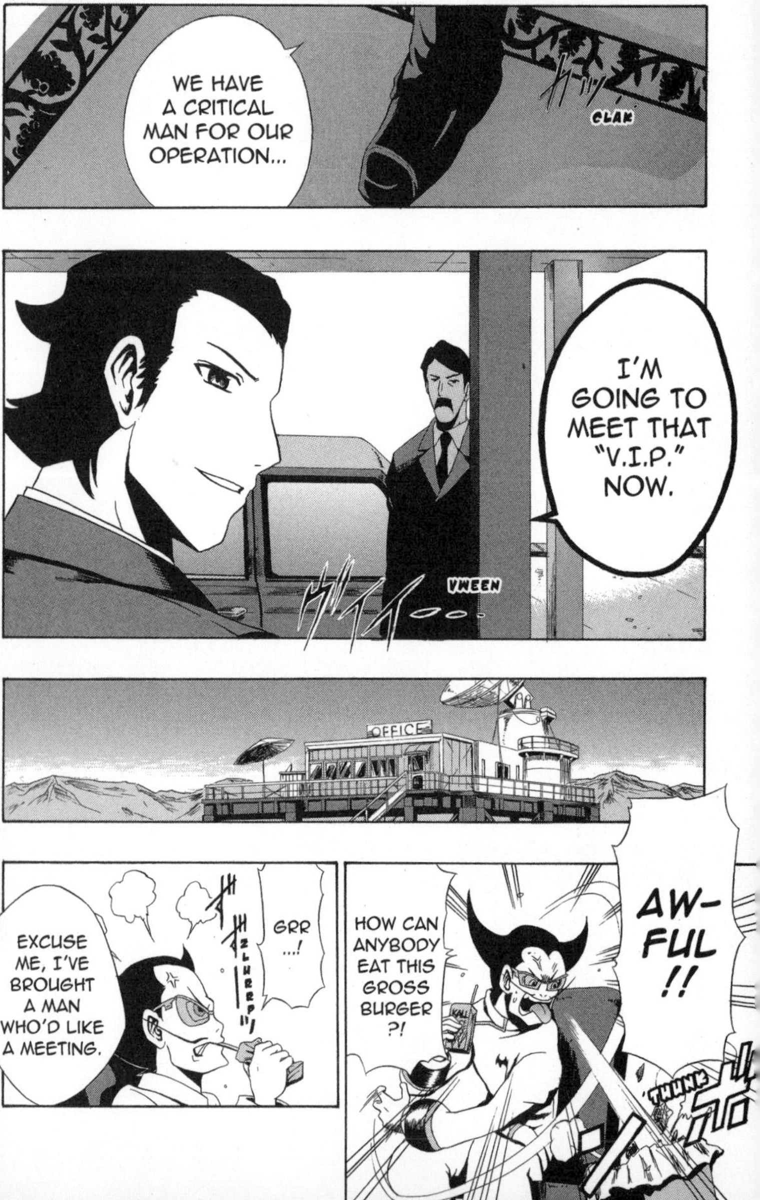
CLAK
WE HAVE A CRITICAL MAN FOR OUR OPERATION...
I'M GOING TO MEET THAT "V.I.P." NOW.
VWEEN
OFFICE
AW-FUL!!
HOW CAN ANYBODY EAT THIS GROSS BURGER?!
THUNK
GRR...!
ZLURRP
EXCUSE ME, I'VE BROUGHT A MAN WHO'D LIKE A MEETING.

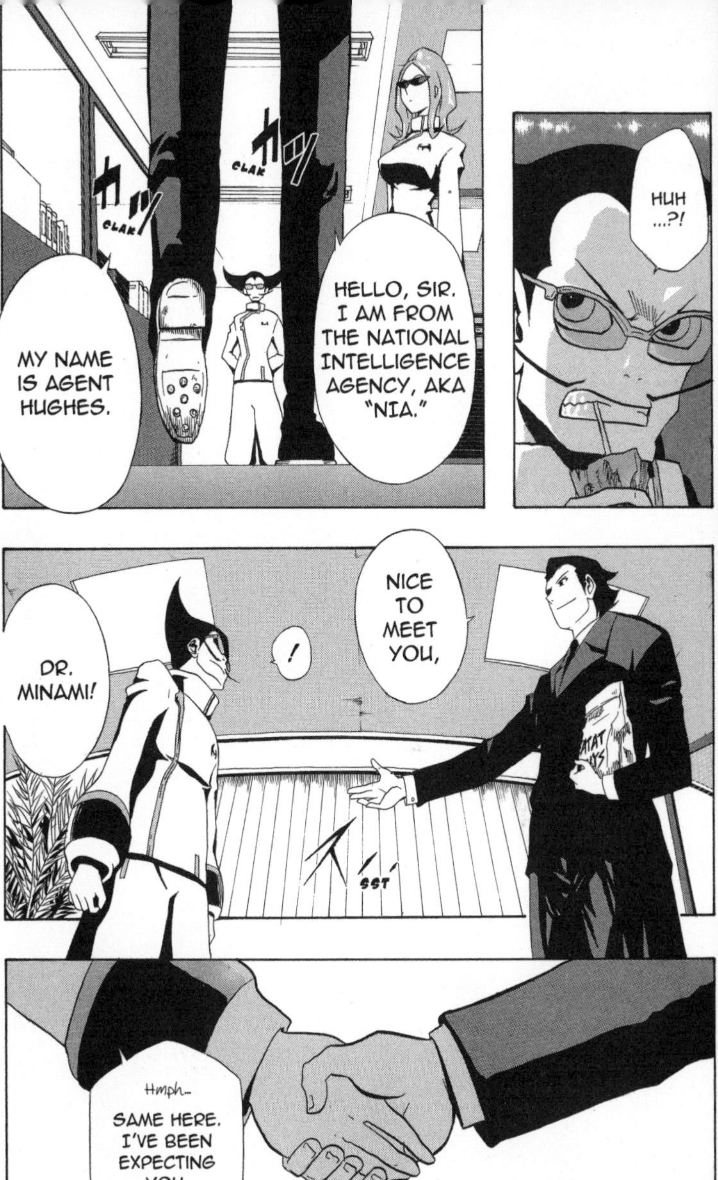
HUH ...?!
CLAK
CLAK
HELLO, SIR. I AM FROM THE NATIONAL INTELLIGENCE AGENCY, AKA "NIA."
MY NAME IS AGENT HUGHES.
NICE TO MEET YOU,
!
DR. MINAMI!
SST
Hmph...
SAME HERE. I'VE BEEN EXPECTING YOU.

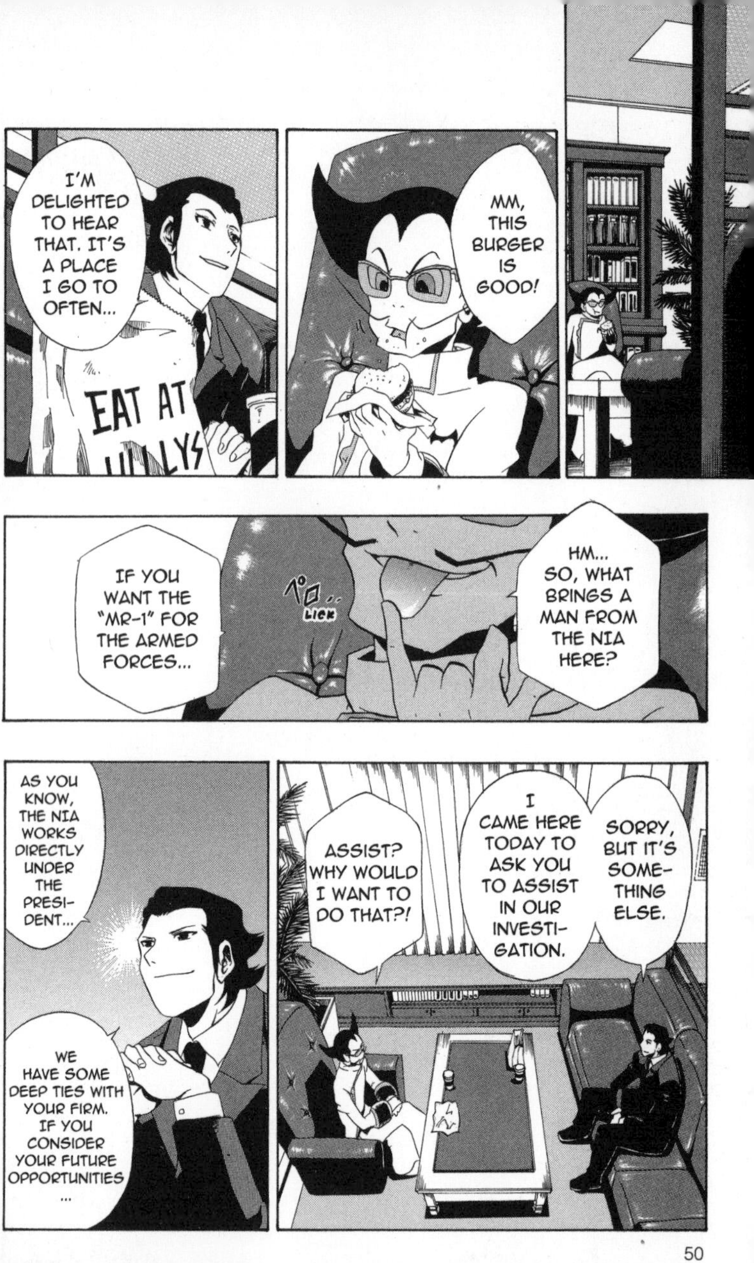
MM, THIS BURGER IS GOOD!
I'M DELIGHTED TO HEAR THAT. IT'S A PLACE I GO TO OFTEN...
EAT AT
HM... SO, WHAT BRINGS A MAN FROM THE NIA HERE?
ペロ LICK
IF YOU WANT THE "MR-1" FOR THE ARMED FORCES...
SORRY, BUT IT'S SOMETHING ELSE.
I CAME HERE TODAY TO ASK YOU TO ASSIST IN OUR INVESTIGATION.
ASSIST? WHY WOULD I WANT TO DO THAT?!
AS YOU KNOW, THE NIA WORKS DIRECTLY UNDER THE PRESIDENT...
WE HAVE SOME DEEP TIES WITH YOUR FIRM. IF YOU CONSIDER YOUR FUTURE OPPORTUNITIES ...

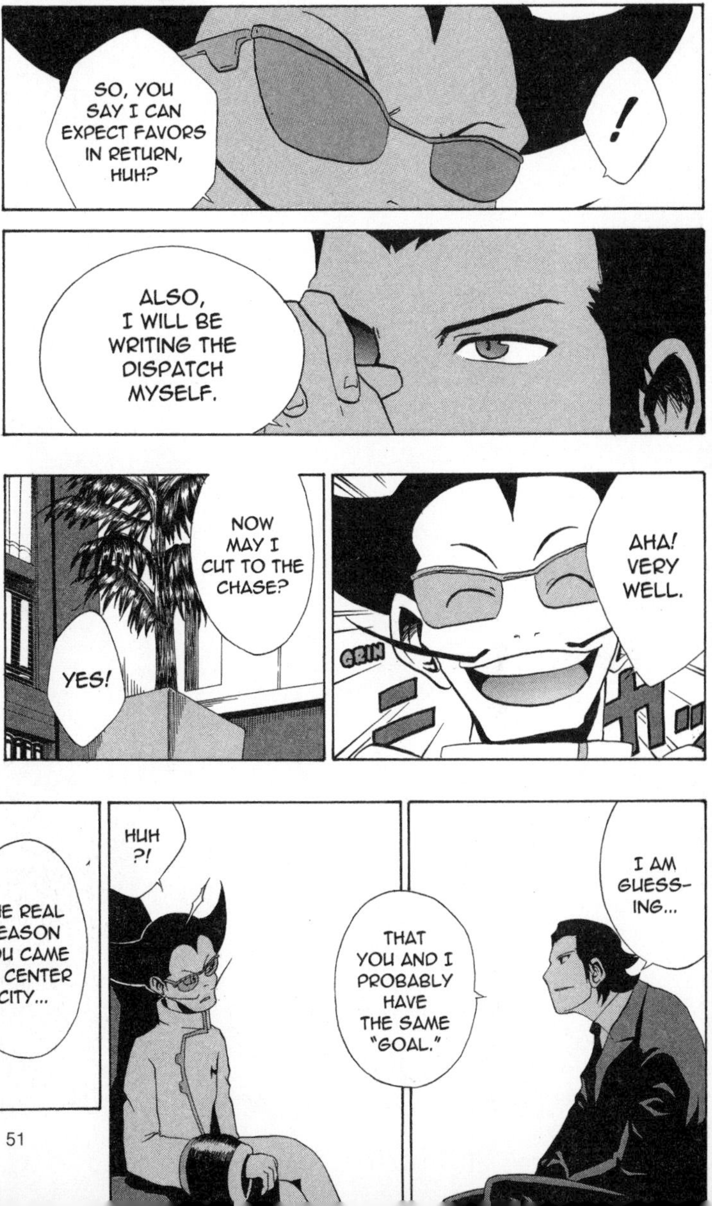
!
SO, YOU SAY I CAN EXPECT FAVORS IN RETURN, HUH?
ALSO, I WILL BE WRITING THE DISPATCH MYSELF.
AHA! VERY WELL.
GRIN
NOW MAY I CUT TO THE CHASE?
YES!
I AM GUESSING...
THAT YOU AND I PROBABLY HAVE THE SAME "GOAL."
HUH ?!
THE REAL REASON YOU CAME TO CENTER CITY...

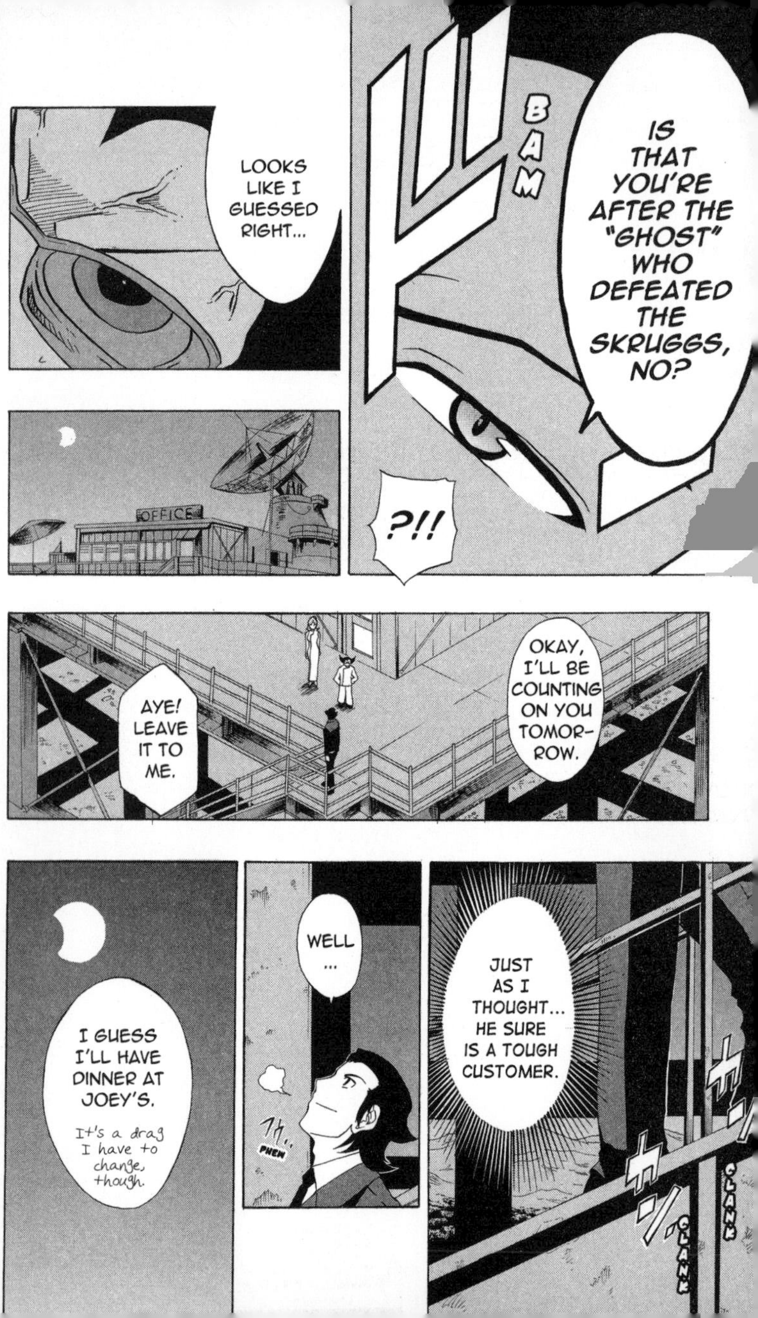
IS THAT YOU'RE AFTER THE "GHOST" WHO DEFEATED THE SKRUGGS, NO?
BAM
?!!
LOOKS LIKE I GUESSED RIGHT...
OFFICE
OKAY, I'LL BE COUNTING ON YOU TOMORROW.
AYE! LEAVE IT TO ME.
JUST AS I THOUGHT... HE SURE IS A TOUGH CUSTOMER.
CLANK
CLANK
WELL ...
PHEW
I GUESS I'LL HAVE DINNER AT JOEY'S.
It's a drag I have to change, though.

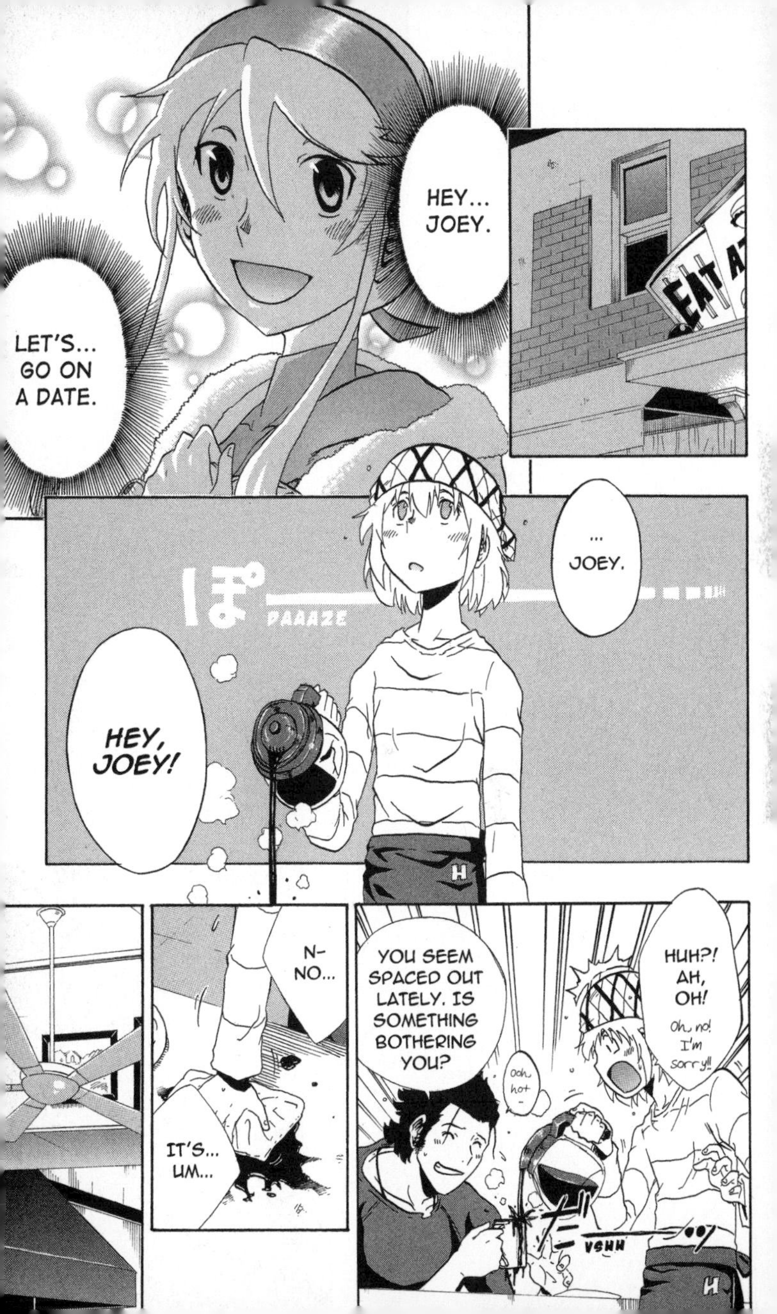
HEY... JOEY.
LET'S... GO ON A DATE.
... JOEY.
ぽ—
PAAAZE
HEY, JOEY!
HUH?! AH, OH!
Oh, no! I'm sorry!!
YOU SEEM SPACED OUT LATELY. IS SOMETHING BOTHERING YOU?
Ooh, hot
VSHH
N- NO...
IT'S... UM...

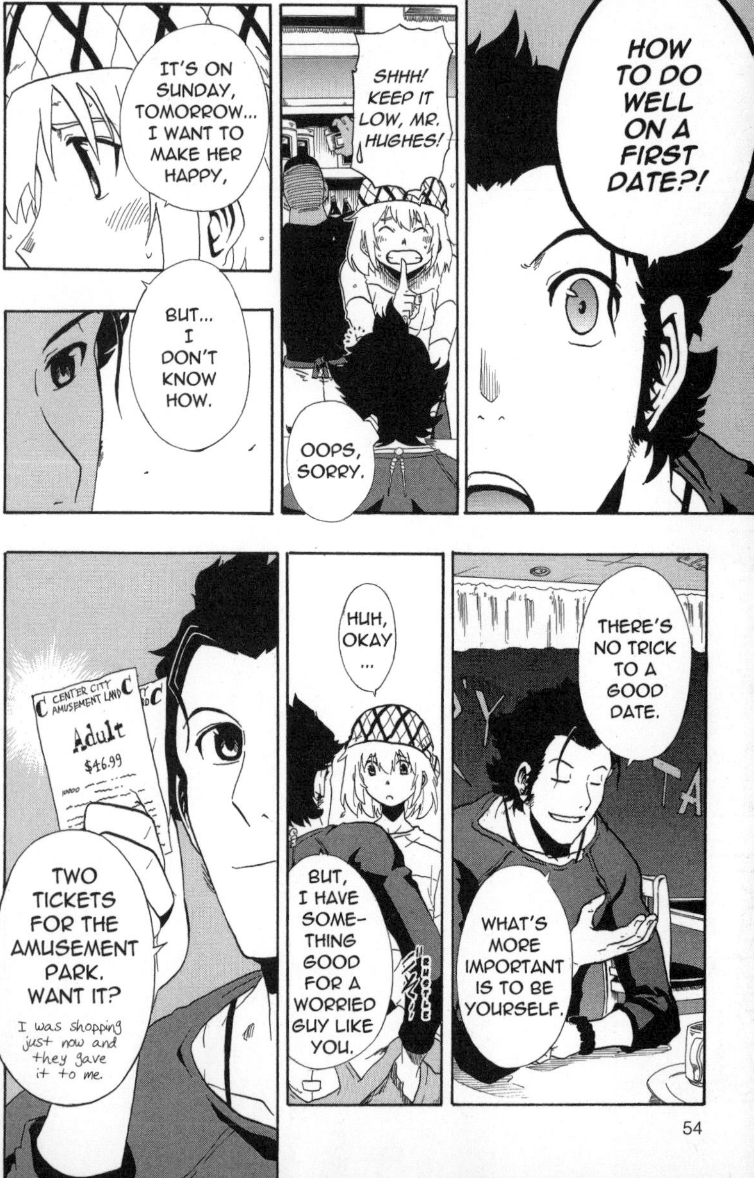
HOW TO DO WELL ON A FIRST DATE?!
SHHH! KEEP IT LOW, MR. HUGHES!
OOPS, SORRY.
IT'S ON SUNDAY, TOMORROW... I WANT TO MAKE HER HAPPY,
BUT... I DON'T KNOW HOW.
THERE'S NO TRICK TO A GOOD DATE.
WHAT'S MORE IMPORTANT IS TO BE YOURSELF.
HUH, OKAY ...
BUT, I HAVE SOME-THING GOOD FOR A WORRIED GUY LIKE YOU.
RUSTLE
CENTER CITY AMUSEMENT LAND
Adult
$46.99
TWO TICKETS FOR THE AMUSEMENT PARK. WANT IT?
I was shopping just now and they gave it to me.

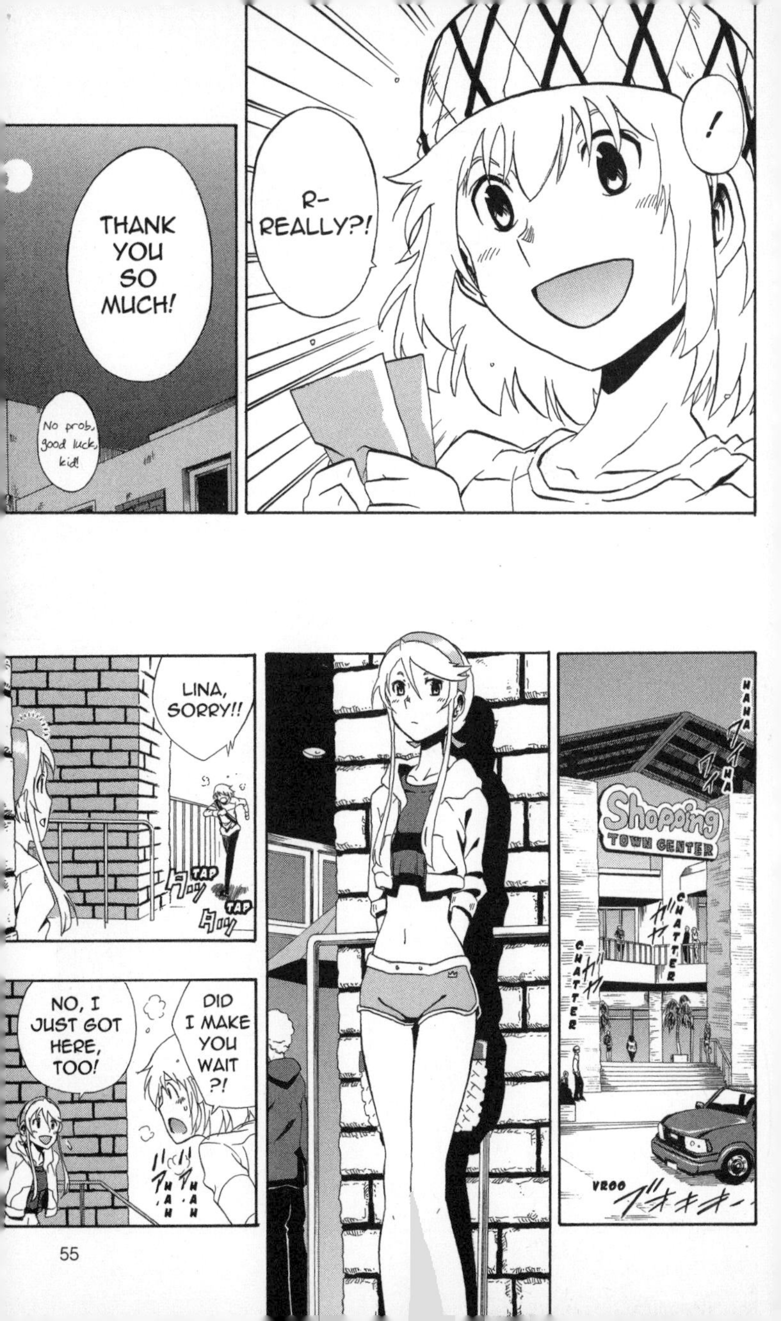
!
R-REALLY?!
THANK YOU SO MUCH!
No prob, good luck, kid!
HAHA
HA
Shopping
TOWN CENTER
CHATTER
CHATTER
VROO
LINA, SORRY!!
TAP
TAP
DID I MAKE YOU WAIT ?!
NO, I JUST GOT HERE, TOO!
HAH
HAH

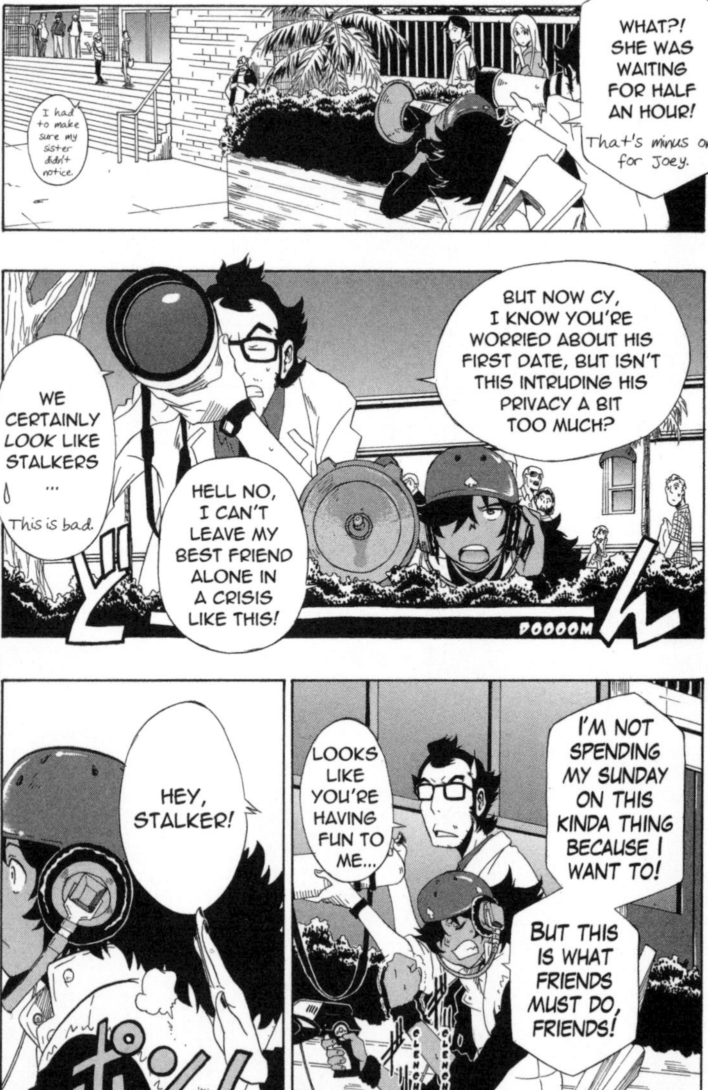
WHAT?! SHE WAS WAITING FOR HALF AN HOUR!
That's minus one for Joey.
I had to make sure my sister didn't notice.
BUT NOW CY, I KNOW YOU'RE WORRIED ABOUT HIS FIRST DATE, BUT ISN'T THIS INTRUDING HIS PRIVACY A BIT TOO MUCH?
HELL NO, I CAN'T LEAVE MY BEST FRIEND ALONE IN A CRISIS LIKE THIS!
WE CERTAINLY *LOOK* LIKE STALKERS ...
This is bad.
DOOOOM
LOOKS LIKE YOU'RE HAVING FUN TO ME...
I'M NOT SPENDING MY SUNDAY ON THIS KINDA THING BECAUSE I WANT TO!
BUT THIS IS WHAT FRIENDS MUST DO, FRIENDS!
CLENCH
CLENCH
HEY, STALKER!
POFF

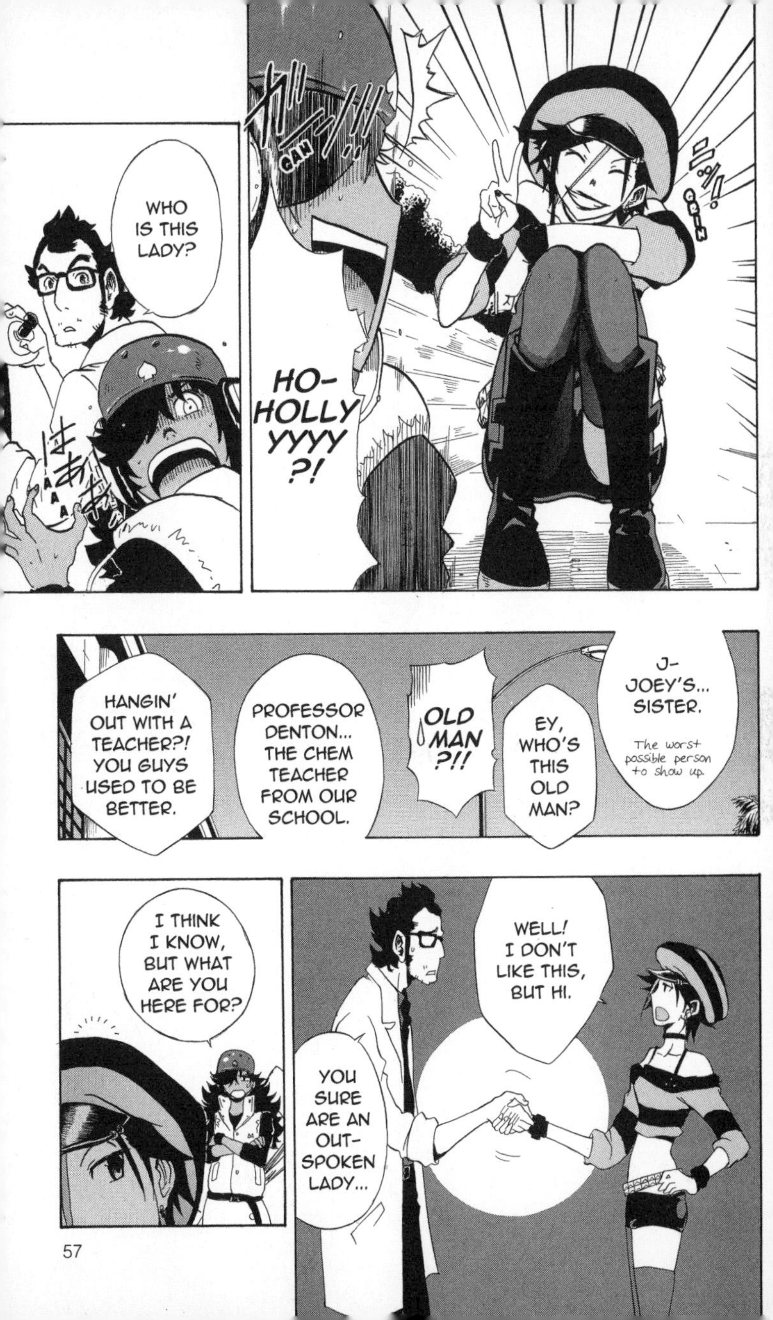
GRIN
GAW
HO-HOLLY YYYY?!
WHO IS THIS LADY?
AAA
J-JOEY'S... SISTER.
The worst possible person to show up.
EY, WHO'S THIS OLD MAN?
OLD MAN?!!
PROFESSOR DENTON... THE CHEM TEACHER FROM OUR SCHOOL.
HANGIN' OUT WITH A TEACHER?! YOU GUYS USED TO BE BETTER.
WELL! I DON'T LIKE THIS, BUT HI.
YOU SURE ARE AN OUT-SPOKEN LADY...
I THINK I KNOW, BUT WHAT ARE YOU HERE FOR?

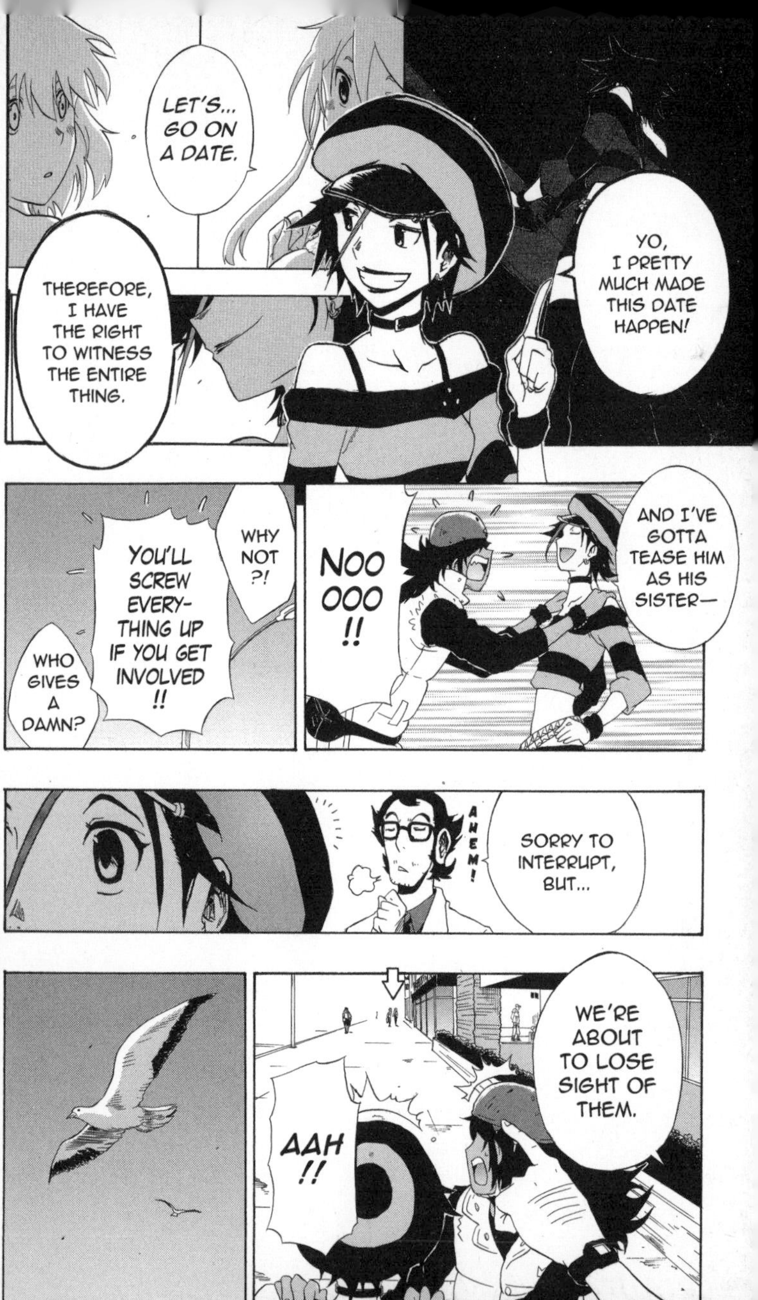
YO, I PRETTY MUCH MADE THIS DATE HAPPEN!
LET'S... GO ON A DATE.
THEREFORE, I HAVE THE RIGHT TO WITNESS THE ENTIRE THING.
AND I'VE GOTTA TEASE HIM AS HIS SISTER—
NOOOOO!!
WHY NOT?!
YOU'LL SCREW EVERY-THING UP IF YOU GET INVOLVED!!
WHO GIVES A DAMN?
AHEM!
SORRY TO INTERRUPT, BUT...
WE'RE ABOUT TO LOSE SIGHT OF THEM.
AAH!!

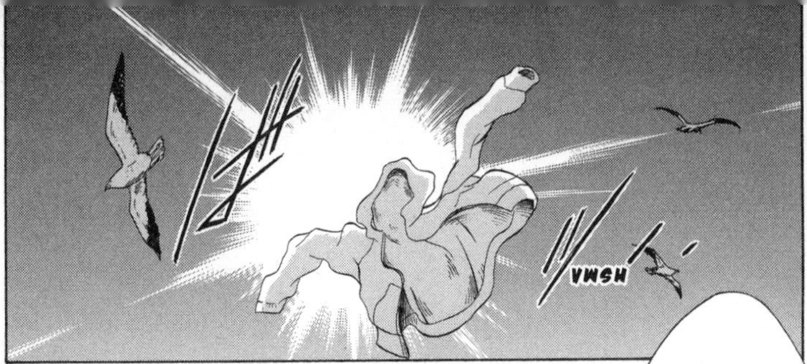
VWSH

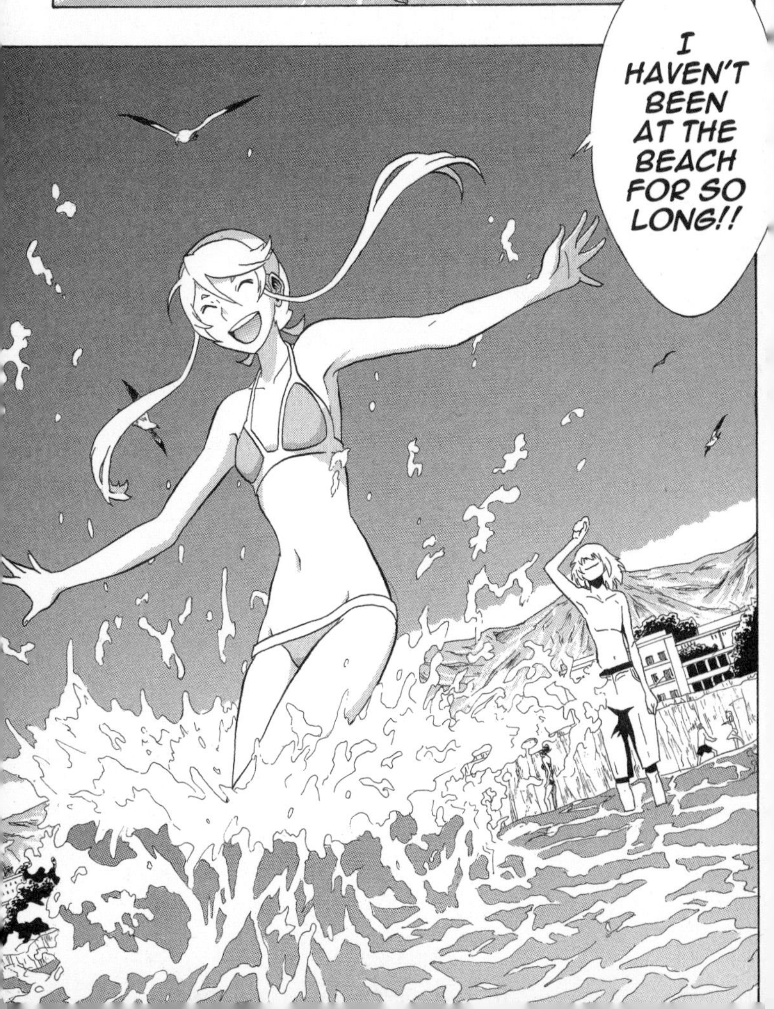
I HAVEN'T BEEN AT THE BEACH FOR SO LONG!!

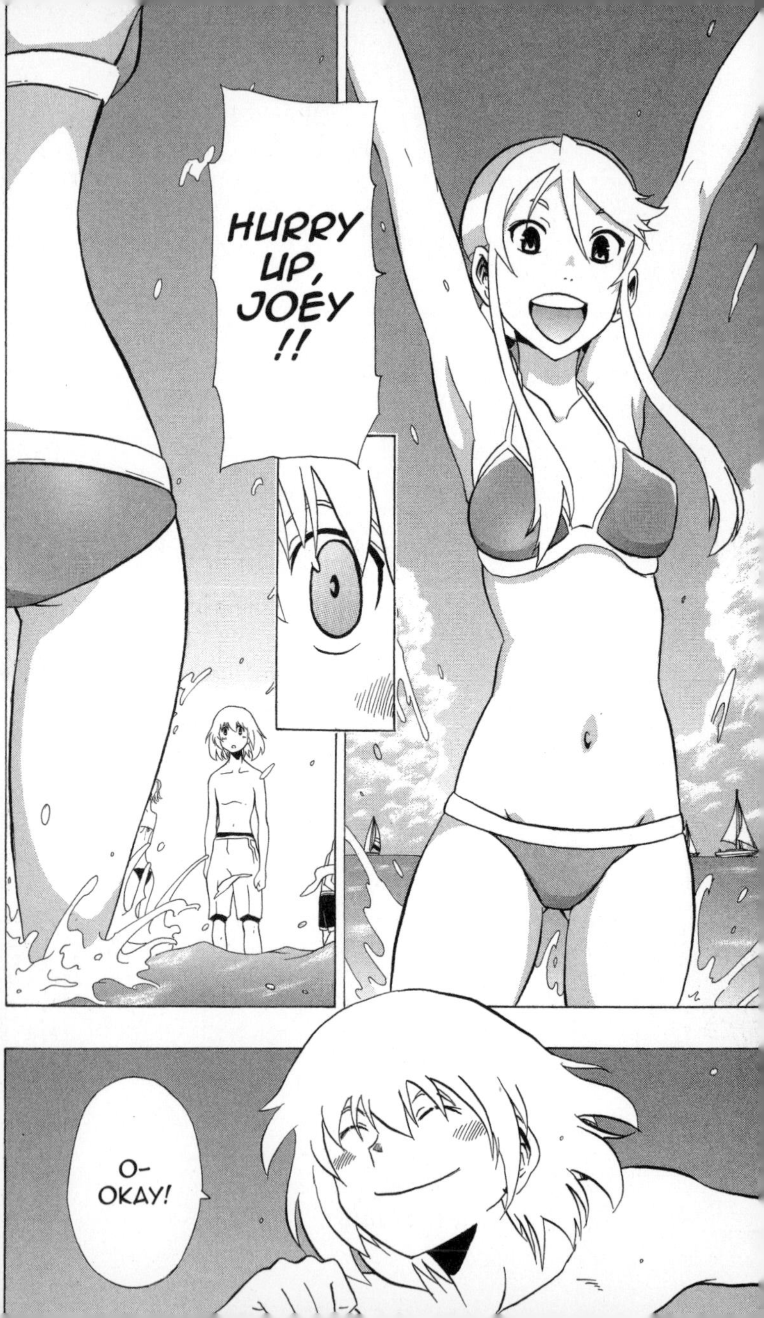
HURRY UP, JOEY !!
O-OKAY!

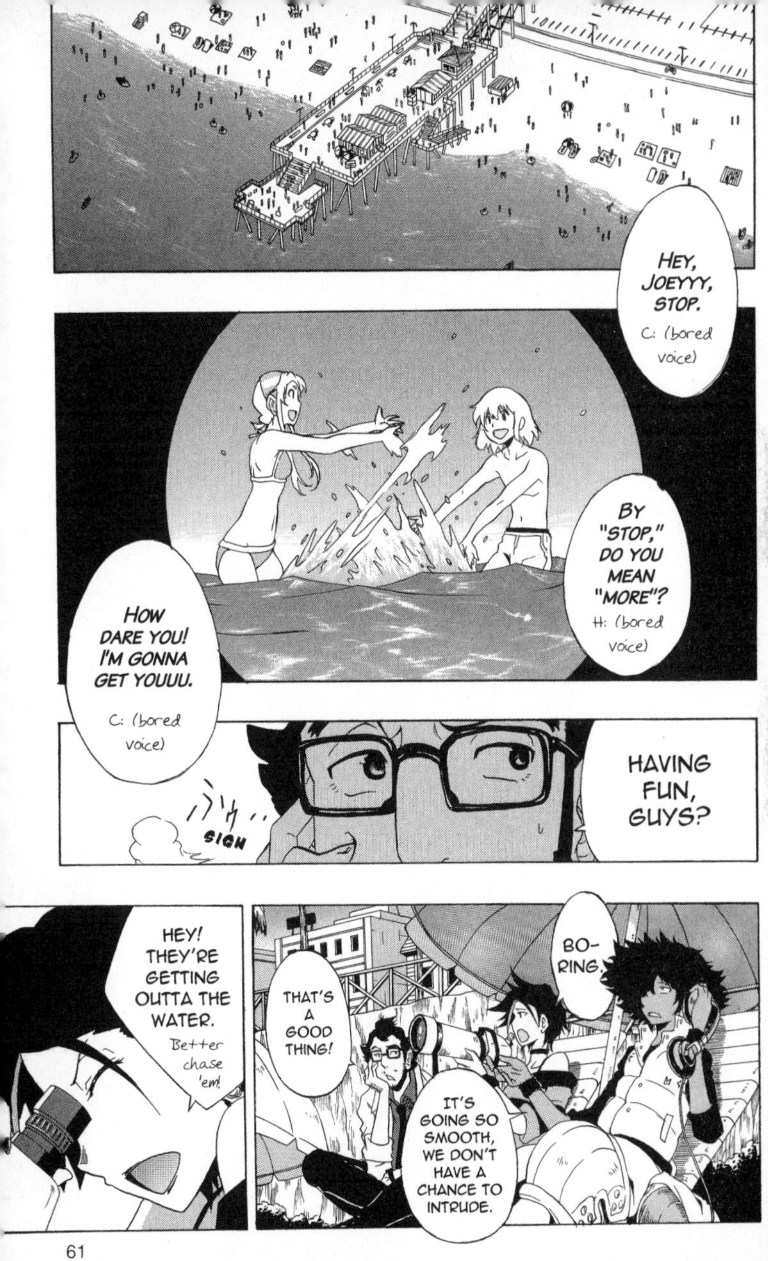
HEY, JOEYYY, STOP.
C: (bored voice)
BY "STOP," DO YOU MEAN "MORE"?
H: (bored voice)
HOW DARE YOU! I'M GONNA GET YOUUU.
C: (bored voice)
HAVING FUN, GUYS?
SIGH
BO-RING.
THAT'S A GOOD THING!
IT'S GOING SO SMOOTH, WE DON'T HAVE A CHANCE TO INTRUDE.
HEY! THEY'RE GETTING OUTTA THE WATER.
Better chase 'em!

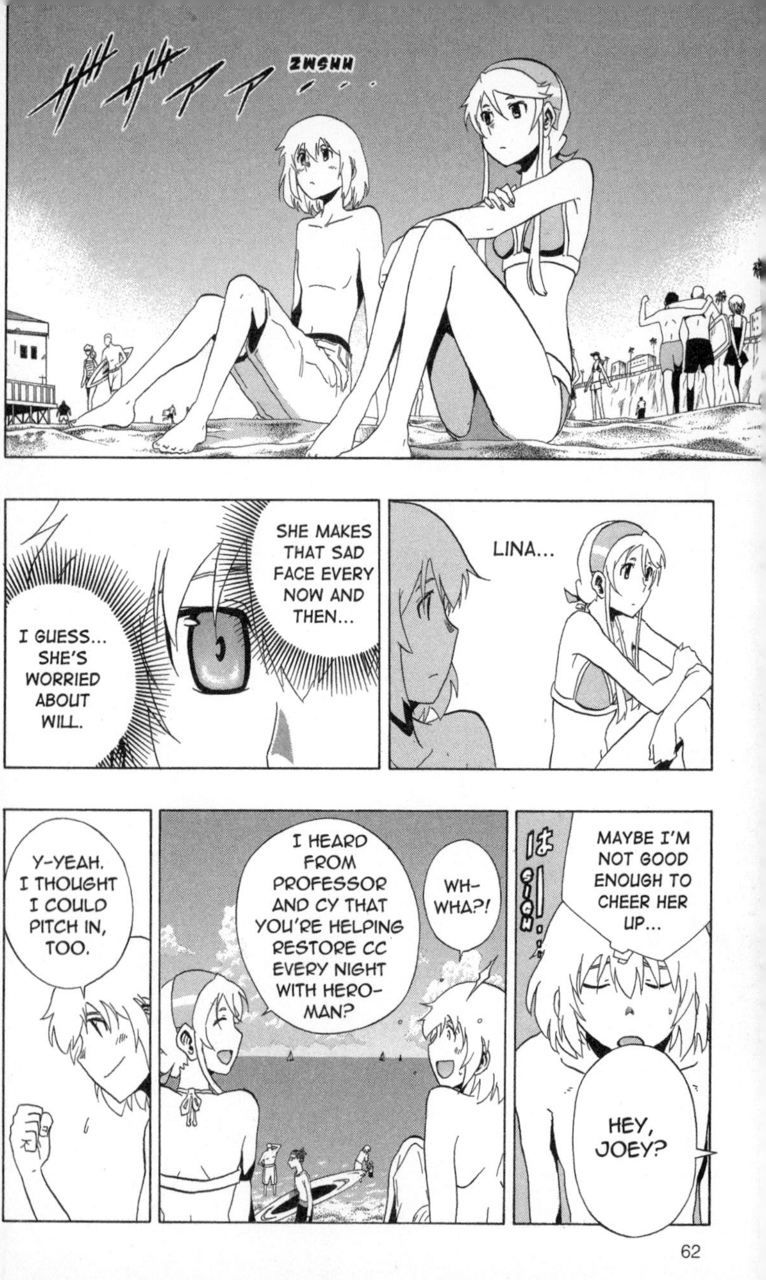
ザザアア
ZWSHH...
LINA...
SHE MAKES THAT SAD FACE EVERY NOW AND THEN...
I GUESS... SHE'S WORRIED ABOUT WILL.
MAYBE I'M NOT GOOD ENOUGH TO CHEER HER UP...
は SIGH...
HEY, JOEY?
I HEARD FROM PROFESSOR AND CY THAT YOU'RE HELPING RESTORE CC EVERY NIGHT WITH HERO-MAN?
WH-WHA?!
Y-YEAH. I THOUGHT I COULD PITCH IN, TOO.

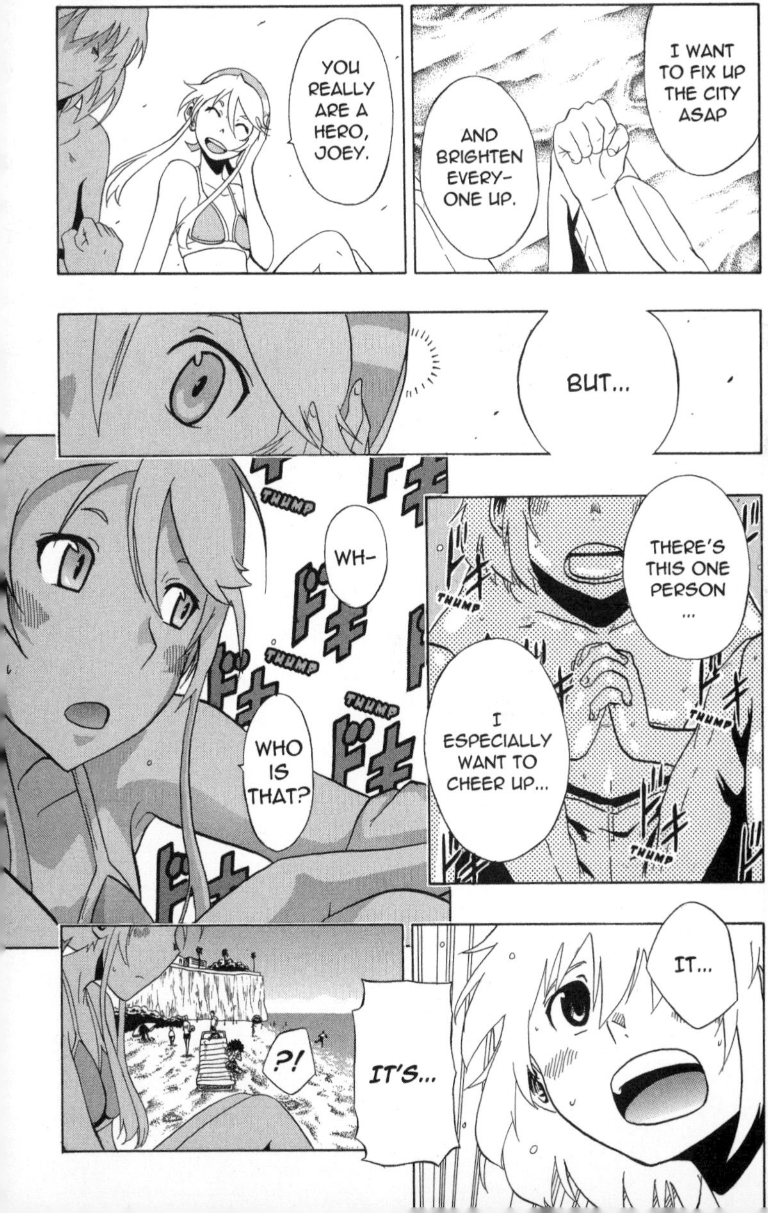
I WANT TO FIX UP THE CITY ASAP
AND BRIGHTEN EVERY-ONE UP.
YOU REALLY ARE A HERO, JOEY.
BUT...
THERE'S THIS ONE PERSON ...
I ESPECIALLY WANT TO CHEER UP...
THUMP
THUMP
WH-
THUMP
THUMP
THUMP
WHO IS THAT?
IT...
IT'S...
?!

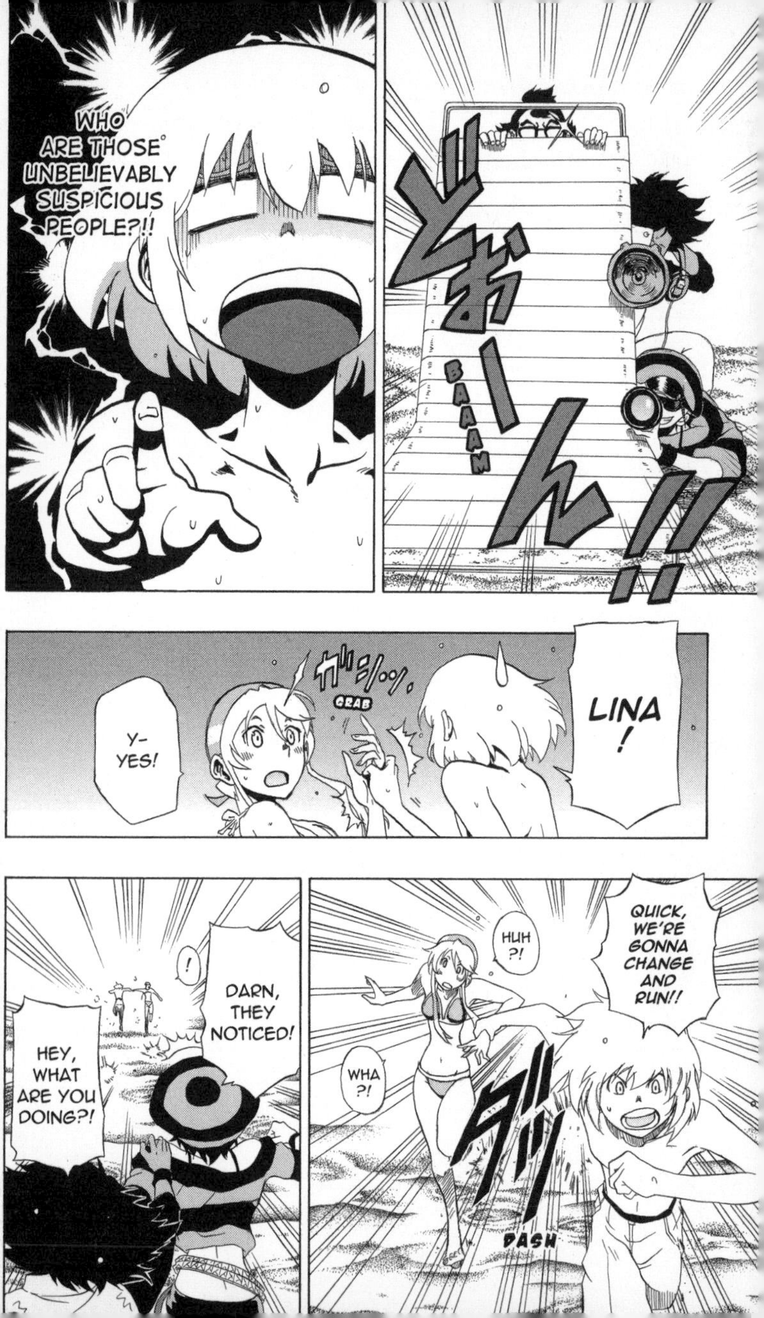
どぉーん!!
BAAAAM
WHO ARE THOSE UNBELIEVABLY SUSPICIOUS PEOPLE?!!
LINA!
GRAB
Y-YES!
QUICK, WE'RE GONNA CHANGE AND RUN!!
HUH?!
WHA?!
DASH
!
DARN, THEY NOTICED!
HEY, WHAT ARE YOU DOING?!

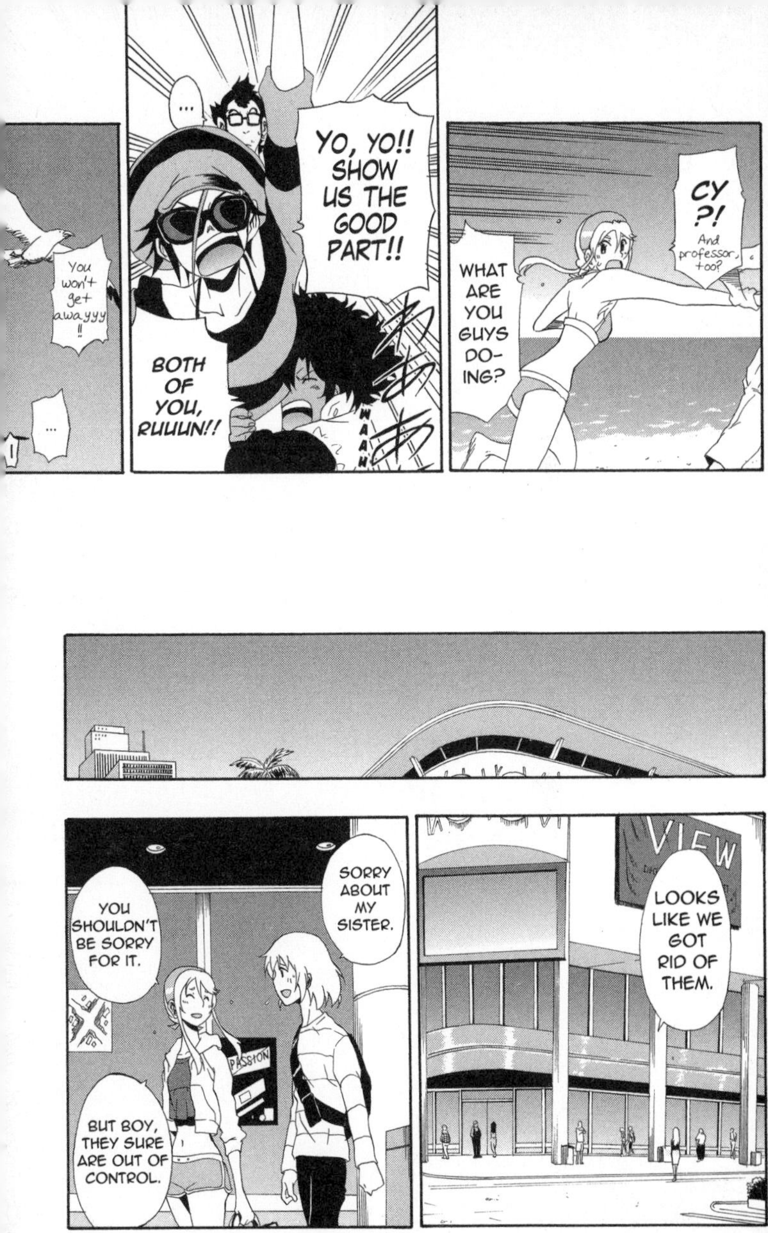
CY ?!
And professor, too?
WHAT ARE YOU GUYS DO-ING?
...
YO, YO!! SHOW US THE GOOD PART!!
BOTH OF YOU, RUUUN!!
WAAAH
あああ
You won't get awayyy !!
...
VIEW
LOOKS LIKE WE GOT RID OF THEM.
SORRY ABOUT MY SISTER.
YOU SHOULDN'T BE SORRY FOR IT.
PASSION
BUT BOY, THEY SURE ARE OUT OF CONTROL.

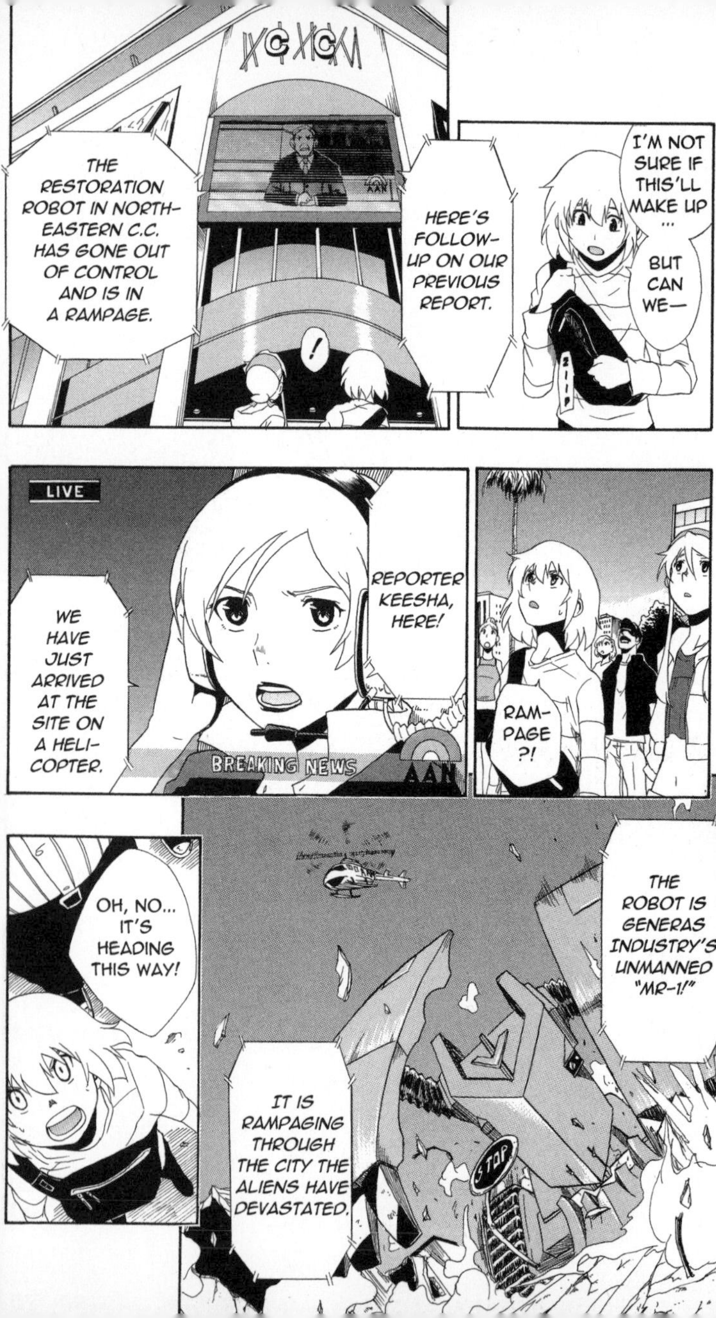
I'M NOT SURE IF THIS'LL MAKE UP ...
BUT CAN WE—
HERE'S FOLLOW-UP ON OUR PREVIOUS REPORT.
THE RESTORATION ROBOT IN NORTH-EASTERN C.C. HAS GONE OUT OF CONTROL AND IS IN A RAMPAGE.
!
RAM-PAGE ?!
REPORTER KEESHA, HERE!
LIVE
WE HAVE JUST ARRIVED AT THE SITE ON A HELI-COPTER.
BREAKING NEWS
AAN
THE ROBOT IS GENERAS INDUSTRY'S UNMANNED "MR-1!"
IT IS RAMPAGING THROUGH THE CITY THE ALIENS HAVE DEVASTATED.
STOP
OH, NO... IT'S HEADING THIS WAY!

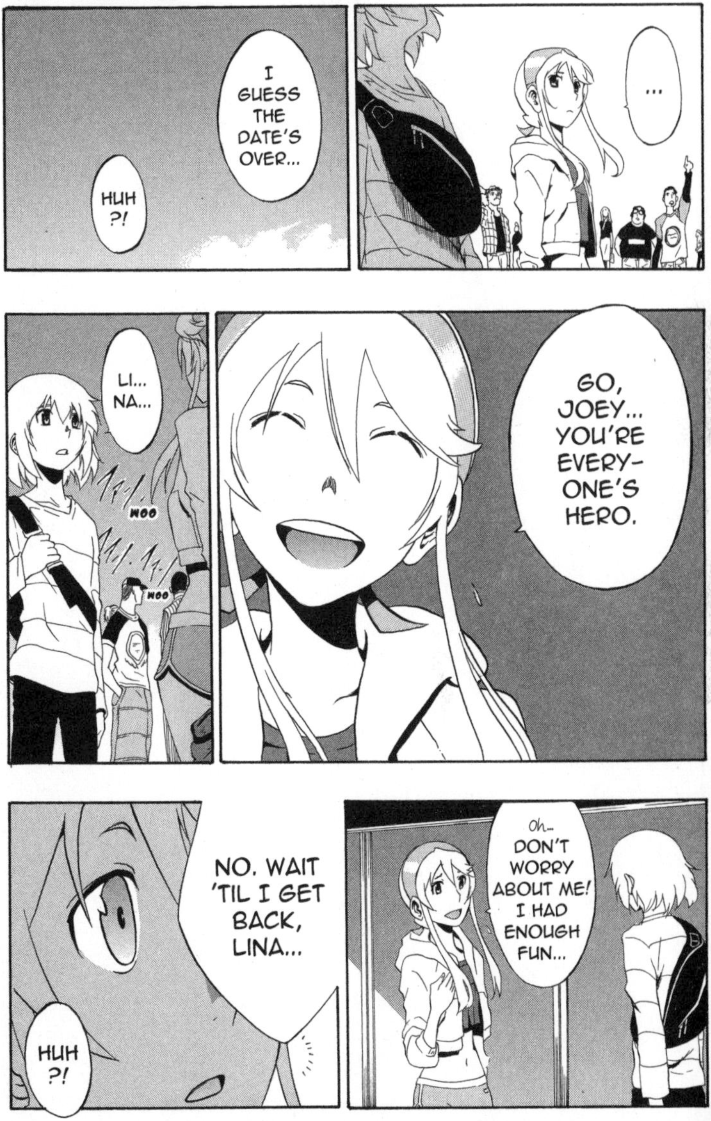
...
I GUESS THE DATE'S OVER...
HUH ?!
GO, JOEY... YOU'RE EVERY-ONE'S HERO.
LI... NA...
WOO
WOO
Oh... DON'T WORRY ABOUT ME! I HAD ENOUGH FUN...
NO. WAIT 'TIL I GET BACK, LINA...
HUH ?!

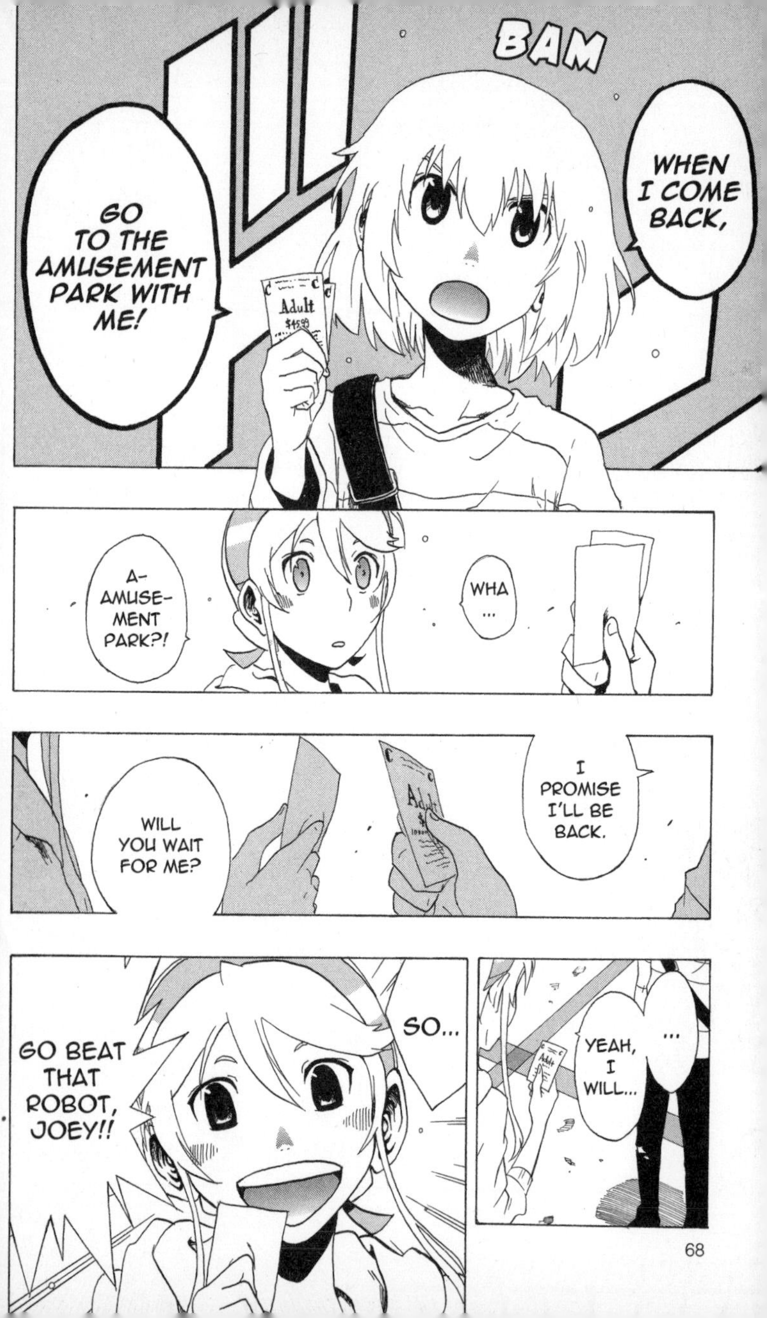
BAM
WHEN I COME BACK,
GO TO THE AMUSEMENT PARK WITH ME!
WHA ...
A- AMUSE- MENT PARK?!
I PROMISE I'LL BE BACK.
WILL YOU WAIT FOR ME?
...
YEAH, I WILL...
SO...
GO BEAT THAT ROBOT, JOEY!!

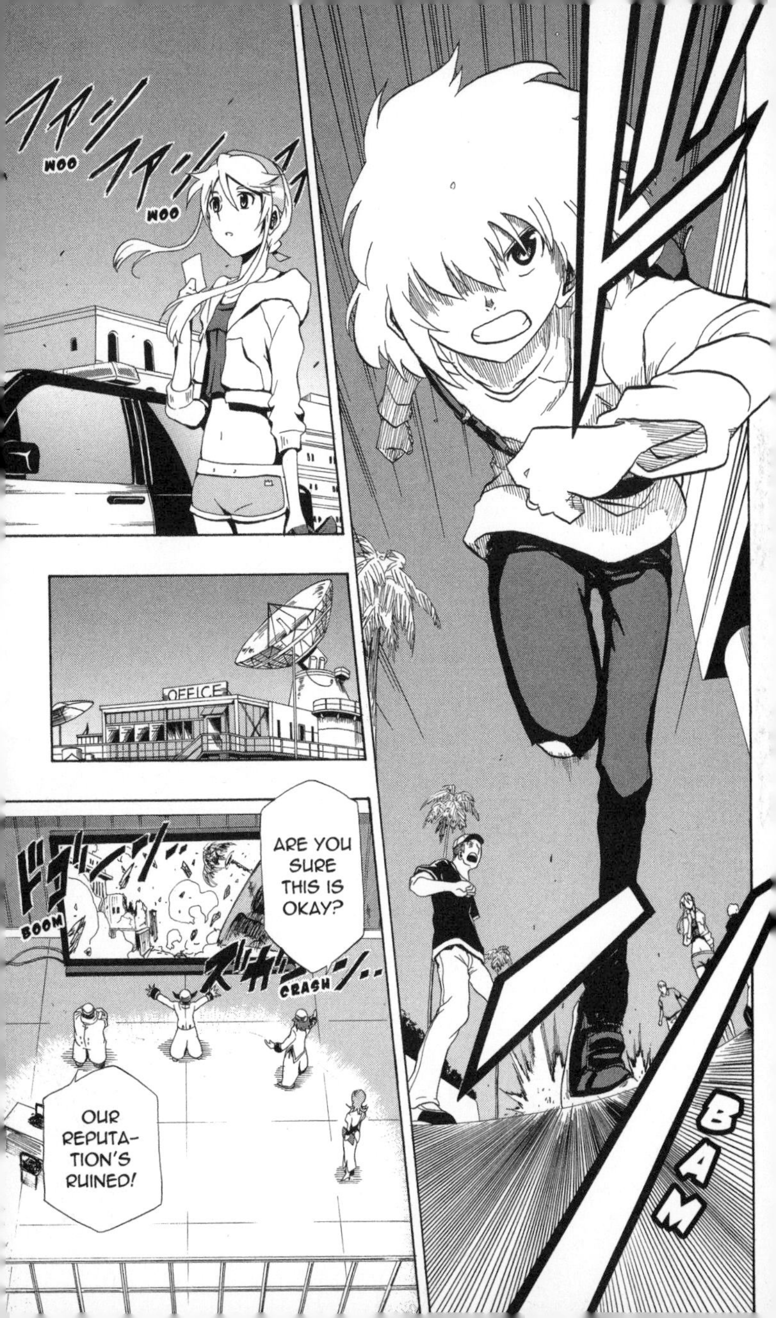
BAM
WOO
WOO
OFFICE
ARE YOU SURE THIS IS OKAY?
BOOM
CRASH
OUR REPUTATION'S RUINED!

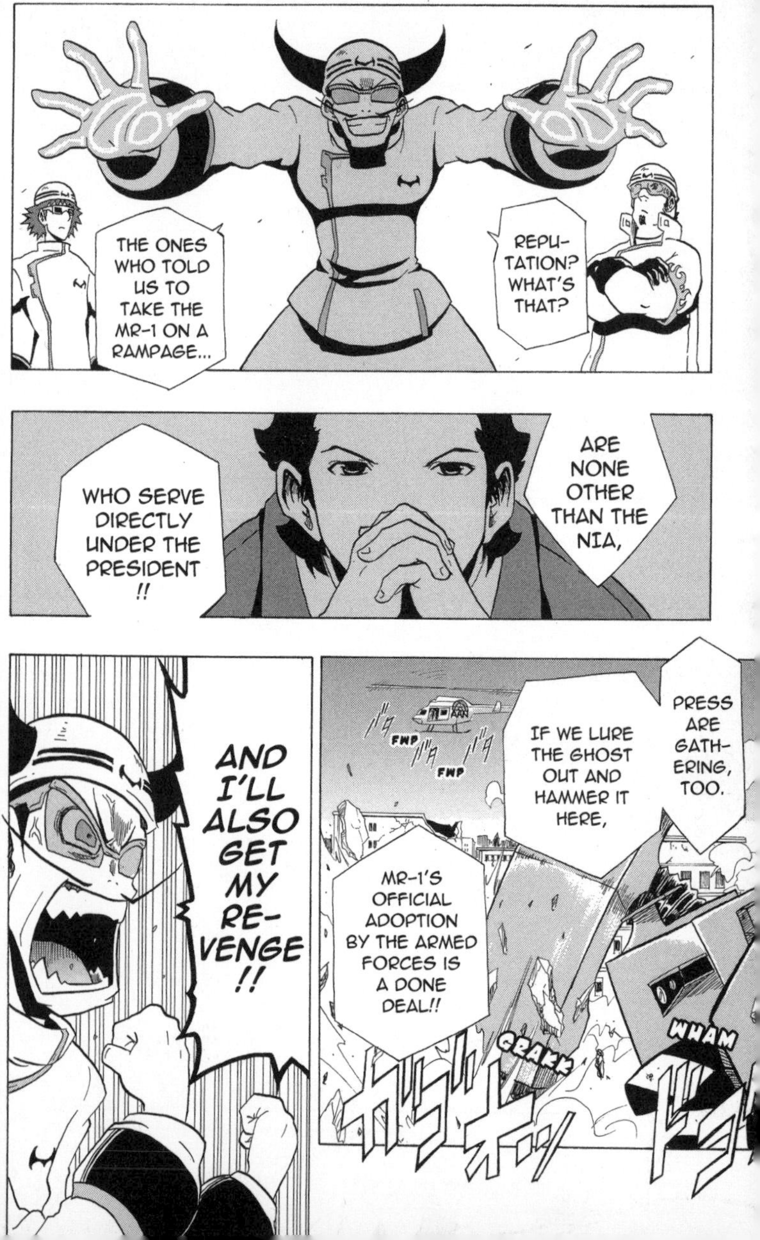
REPU-TATION? WHAT'S THAT?
THE ONES WHO TOLD US TO TAKE THE MR-1 ON A RAMPAGE...
ARE NONE OTHER THAN THE NIA,
WHO SERVE DIRECTLY UNDER THE PRESIDENT !!
PRESS ARE GATH-ERING, TOO.
FWP
FWP
IF WE LURE THE GHOST OUT AND HAMMER IT HERE,
MR-1'S OFFICIAL ADOPTION BY THE ARMED FORCES IS A DONE DEAL!!
WHAM
GRAKK
AND I'LL ALSO GET MY RE-VENGE !!

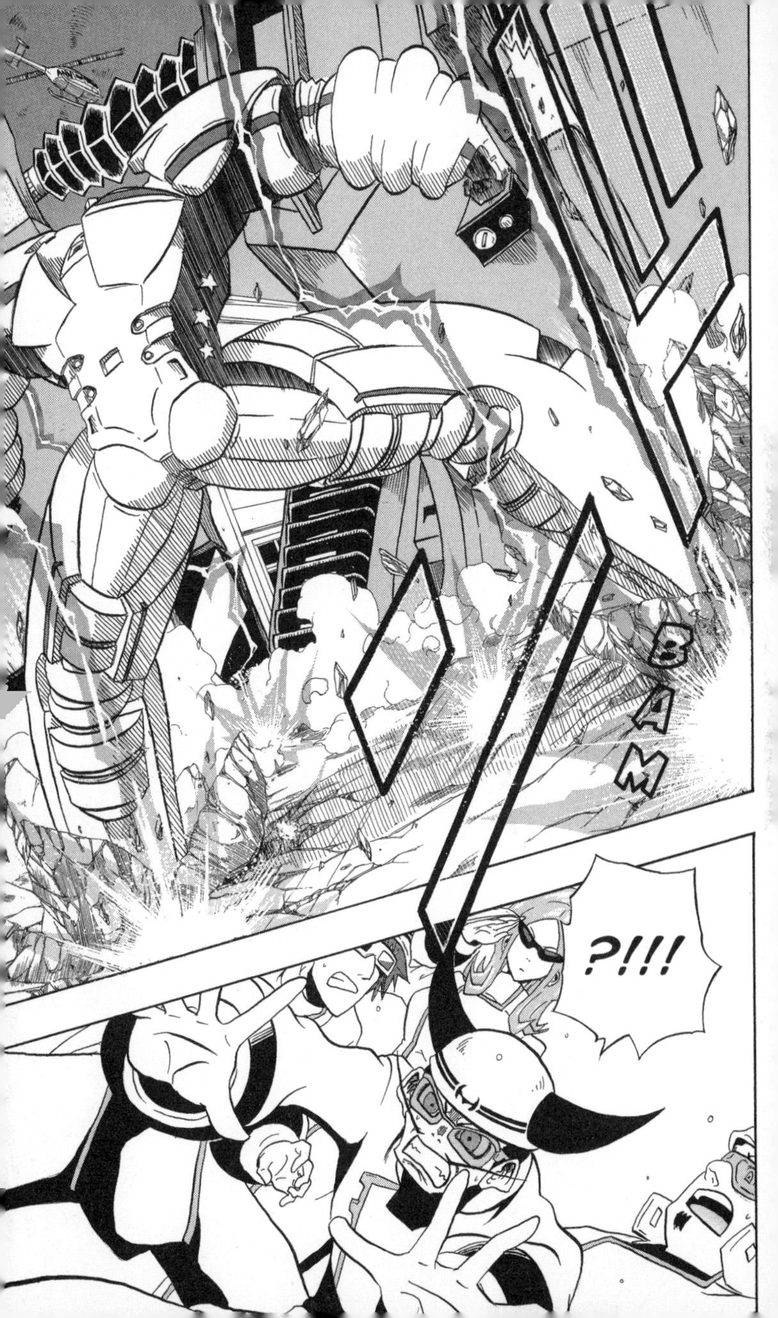
BAM
?!!!

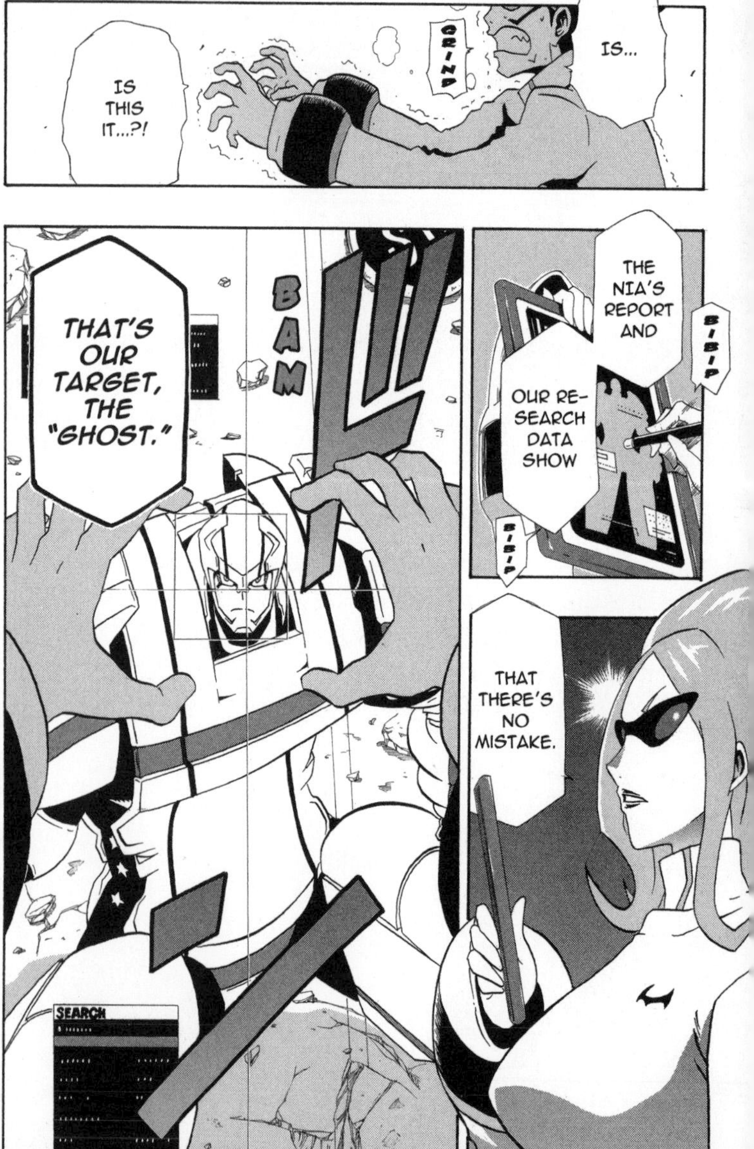
IS...
GRIND
IS THIS IT...?!
THE NIA'S REPORT AND
BIBIP
OUR RE-SEARCH DATA SHOW
BIBIP
THAT THERE'S NO MISTAKE.
BAM
THAT'S OUR TARGET, THE "GHOST."
SEARCH

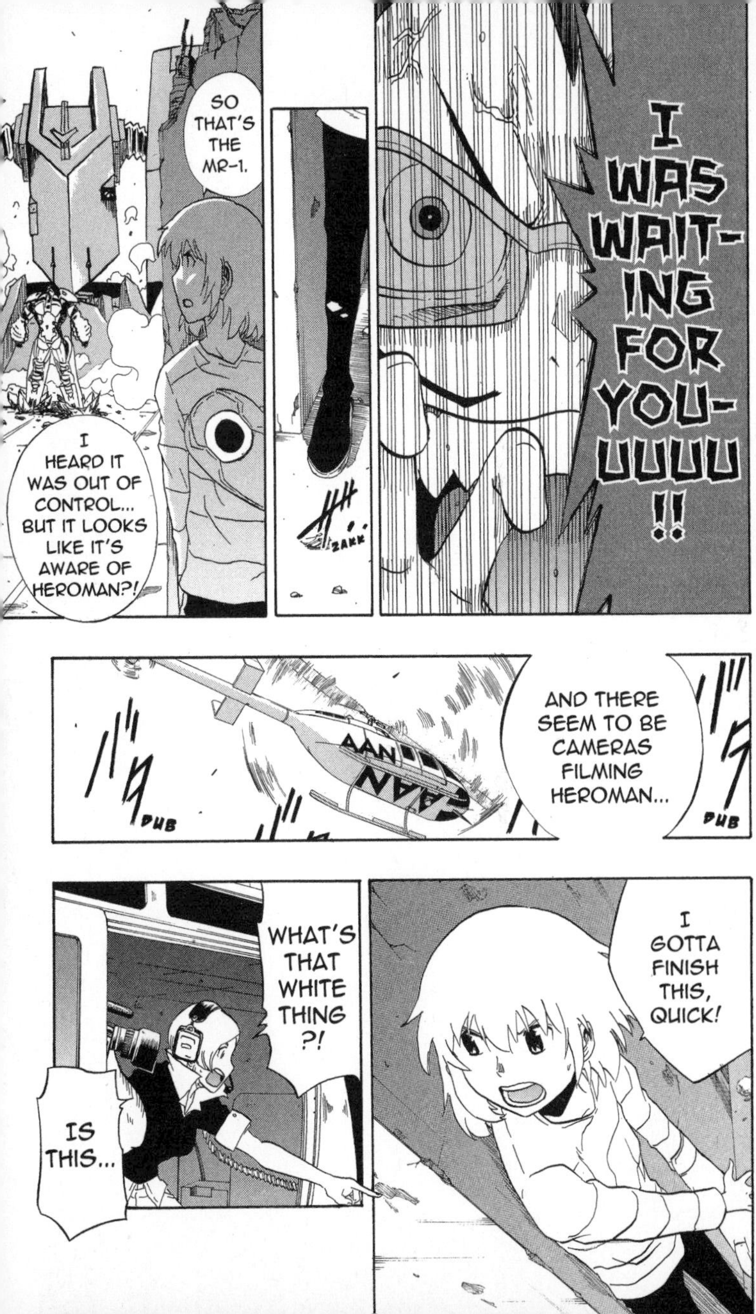
I WAS WAIT-ING FOR YOU-UUUU!!
ZAKK
SO THAT'S THE MR-1.
I HEARD IT WAS OUT OF CONTROL... BUT IT LOOKS LIKE IT'S AWARE OF HEROMAN?!
DUB
AND THERE SEEM TO BE CAMERAS FILMING HEROMAN...
DUB
I GOTTA FINISH THIS, QUICK!
WHAT'S THAT WHITE THING?!
IS THIS...

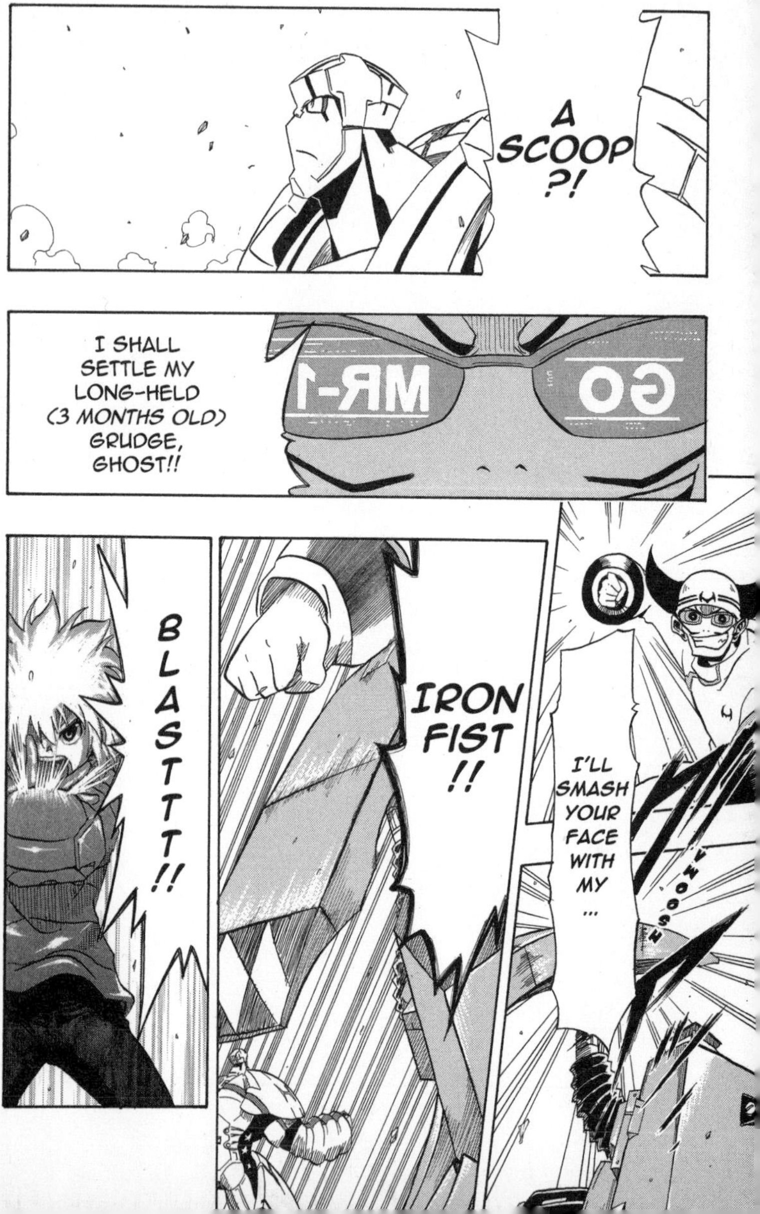
A SCOOP ?!
I SHALL SETTLE MY LONG-HELD (3 MONTHS OLD) GRUDGE, GHOST!!
I'LL SMASH YOUR FACE WITH MY ...
WHOOSH
IRON FIST !!
BLASTTTT!!

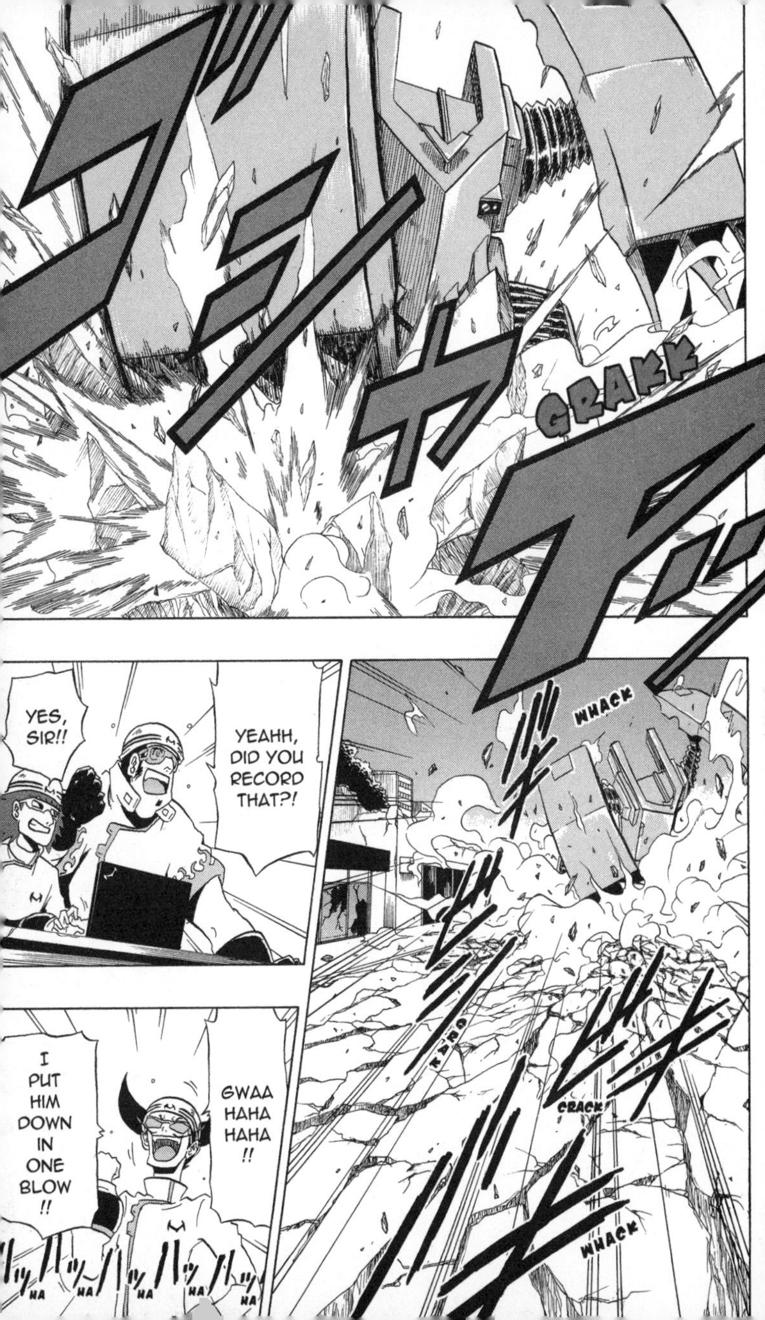
GRAKK
WHACK
CRACK
WHACK
YEAHH, DID YOU RECORD THAT?!
YES, SIR!!
GWAA HAHA HAHA !!
I PUT HIM DOWN IN ONE BLOW !!
HA HA HA HA HA HA

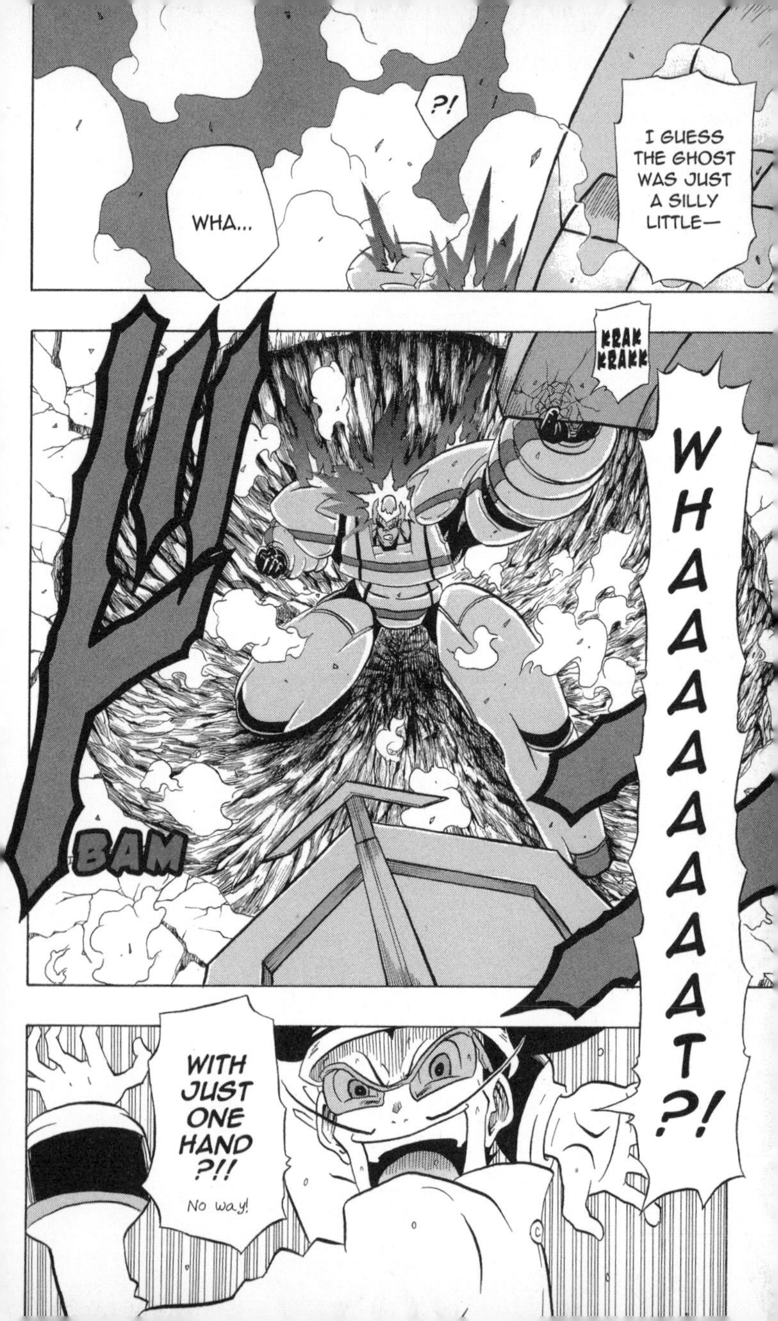
I GUESS THE GHOST WAS JUST A SILLY LITTLE—
?!
WHA...
KRAK KRAKK
WHAAAAAAAAAT?!
BAM
WITH JUST ONE HAND?!!
No way!

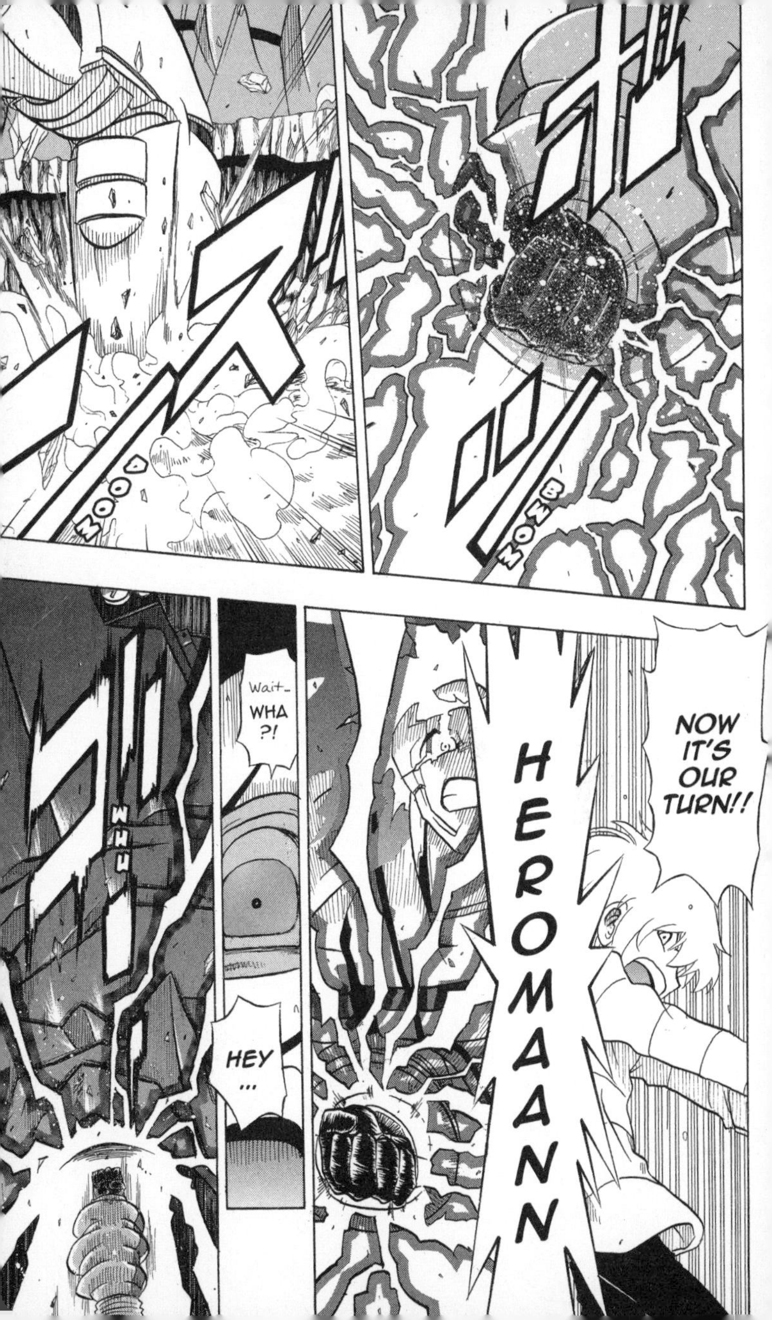
BWOM
DOOM
NOW IT'S OUR TURN!!
HEROMANN
Wait... WHA ?!
HEY ...
WHU

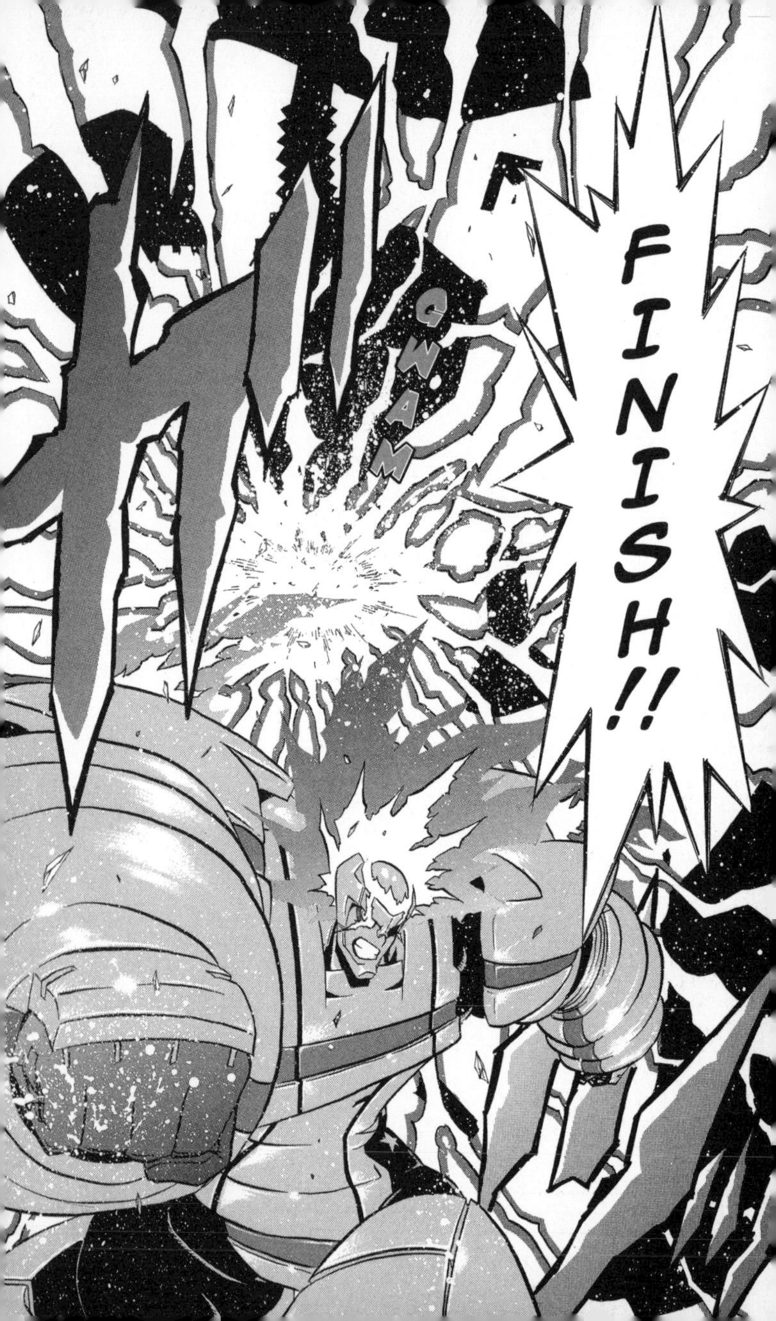
GWAM
FINISH!!

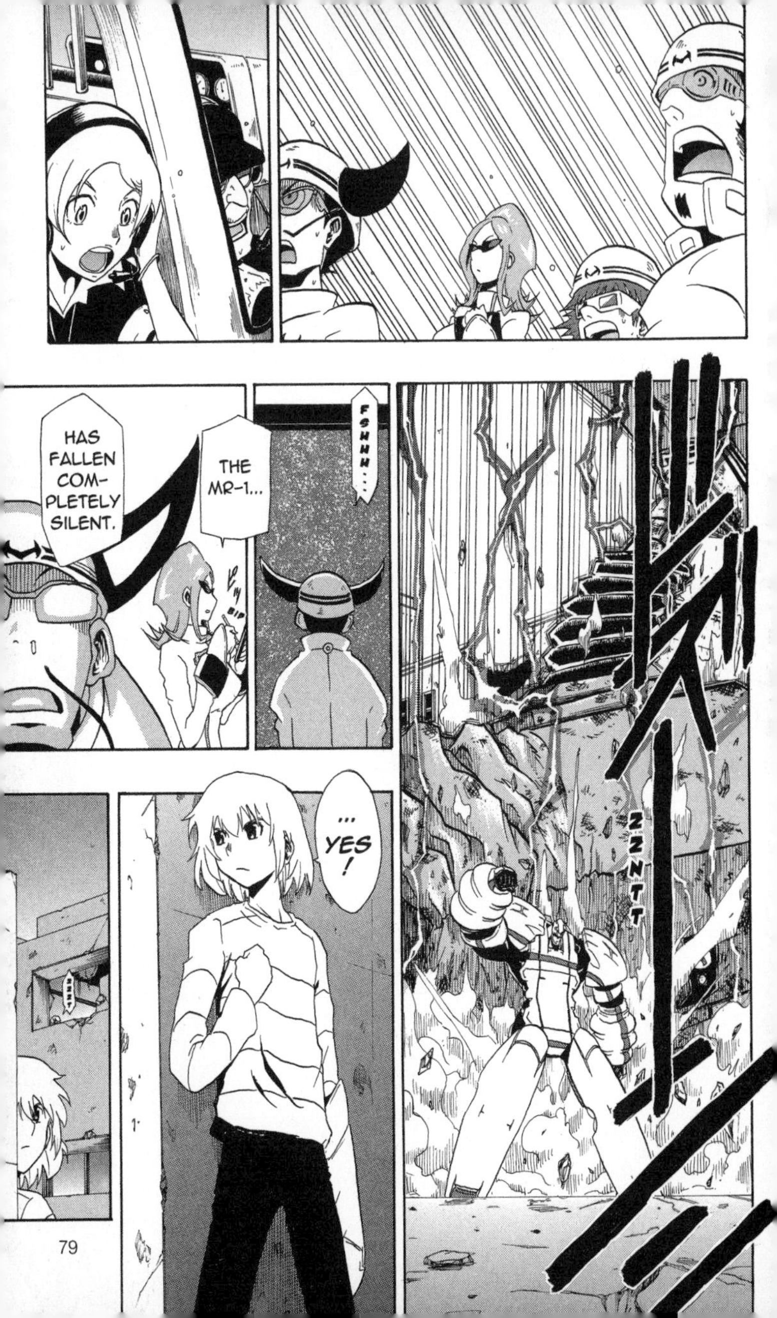
ZZNTT
FSHHH...
THE MR-1...
BIP
HAS FALLEN COM-PLETELY SILENT.
...YES!

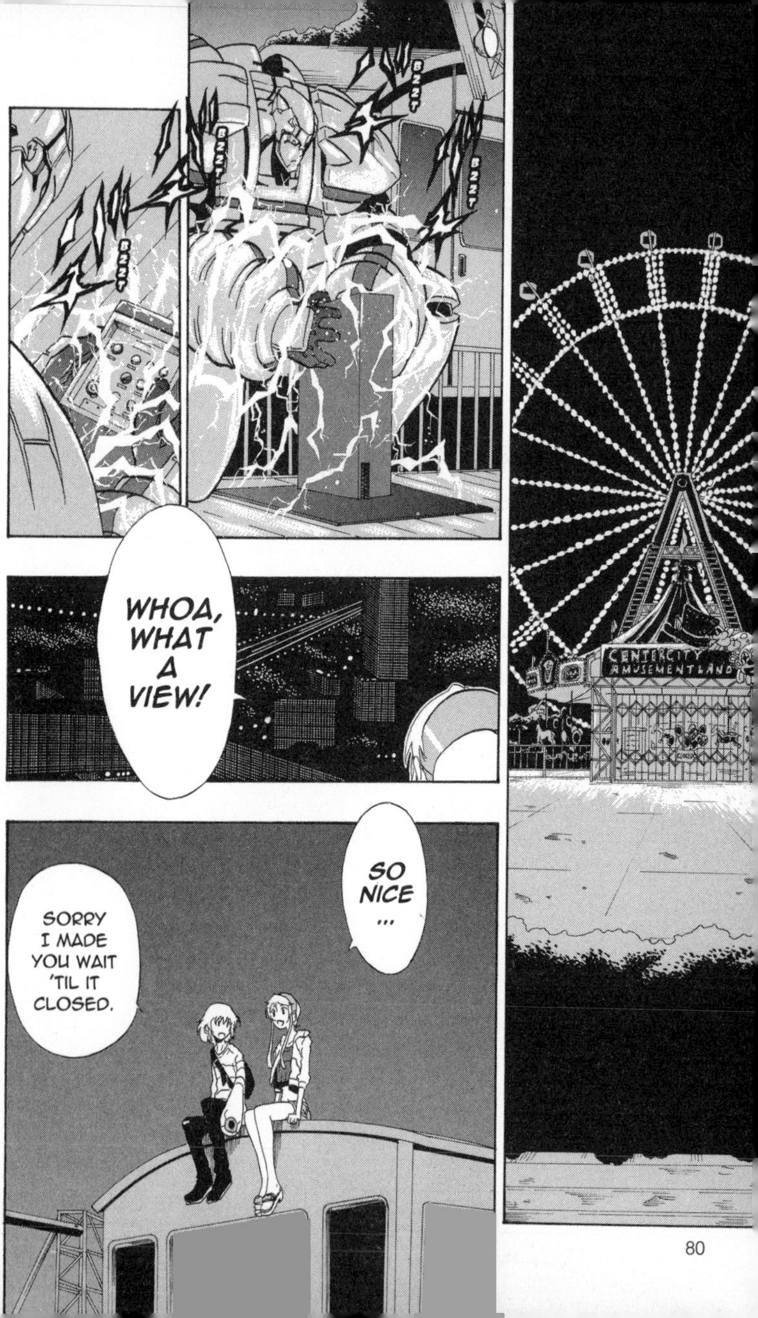
CENTERCITY AMUSEMENTLAND
BZZT
BZZT
BZZT
WHOA, WHAT A VIEW!
SO NICE ...
SORRY I MADE YOU WAIT 'TIL IT CLOSED.

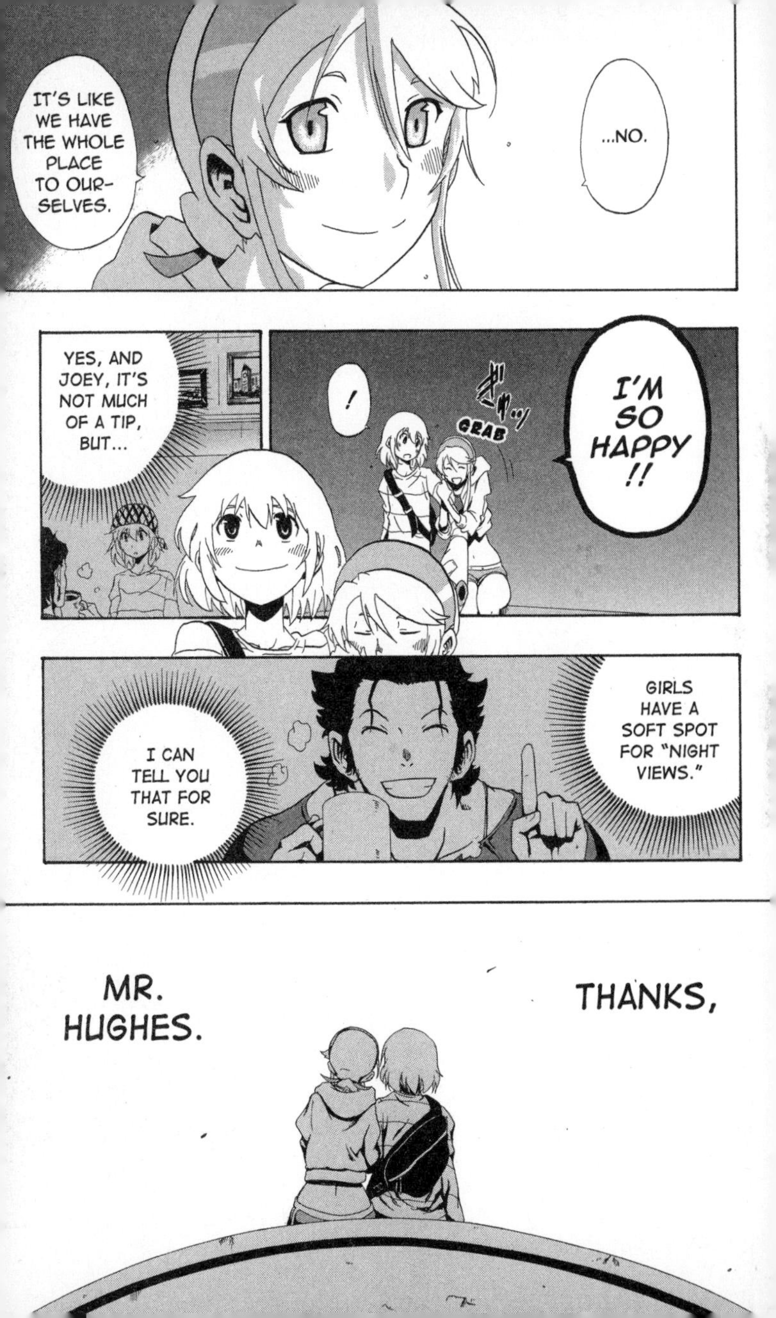
...NO.
IT'S LIKE WE HAVE THE WHOLE PLACE TO OUR-SELVES.
I'M SO HAPPY!!
GRAB
!
YES, AND JOEY, IT'S NOT MUCH OF A TIP, BUT...
GIRLS HAVE A SOFT SPOT FOR "NIGHT VIEWS."
I CAN TELL YOU THAT FOR SURE.
THANKS,
MR. HUGHES.

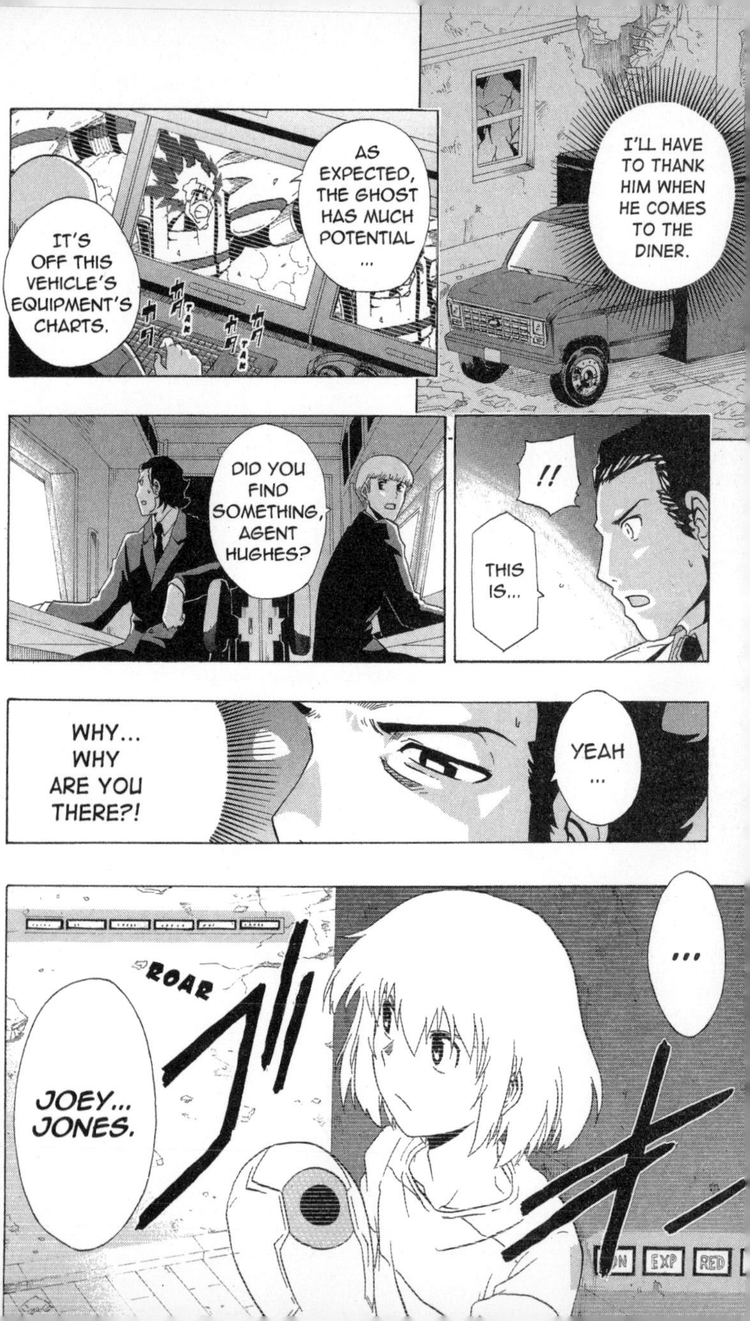
I'LL HAVE TO THANK HIM WHEN HE COMES TO THE DINER.
AS EXPECTED, THE GHOST HAS MUCH POTENTIAL ...
IT'S OFF THIS VEHICLE'S EQUIPMENT'S CHARTS.
TAK
TAK
!!
THIS IS...
DID YOU FIND SOMETHING, AGENT HUGHES?
YEAH ...
WHY... WHY ARE YOU THERE?!
...
ROAR
JOEY... JONES.
EXP
RED

#17 GETAWAY

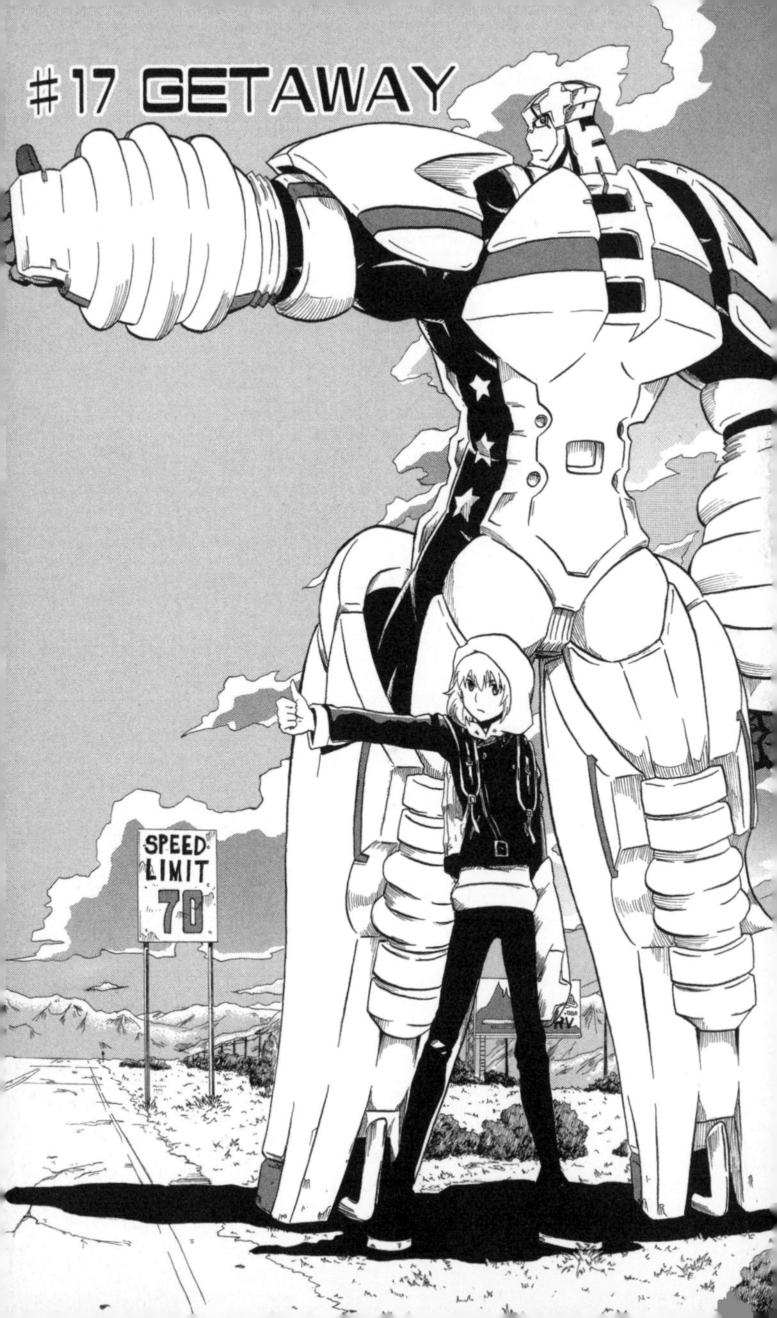
SPEED LIMIT
70

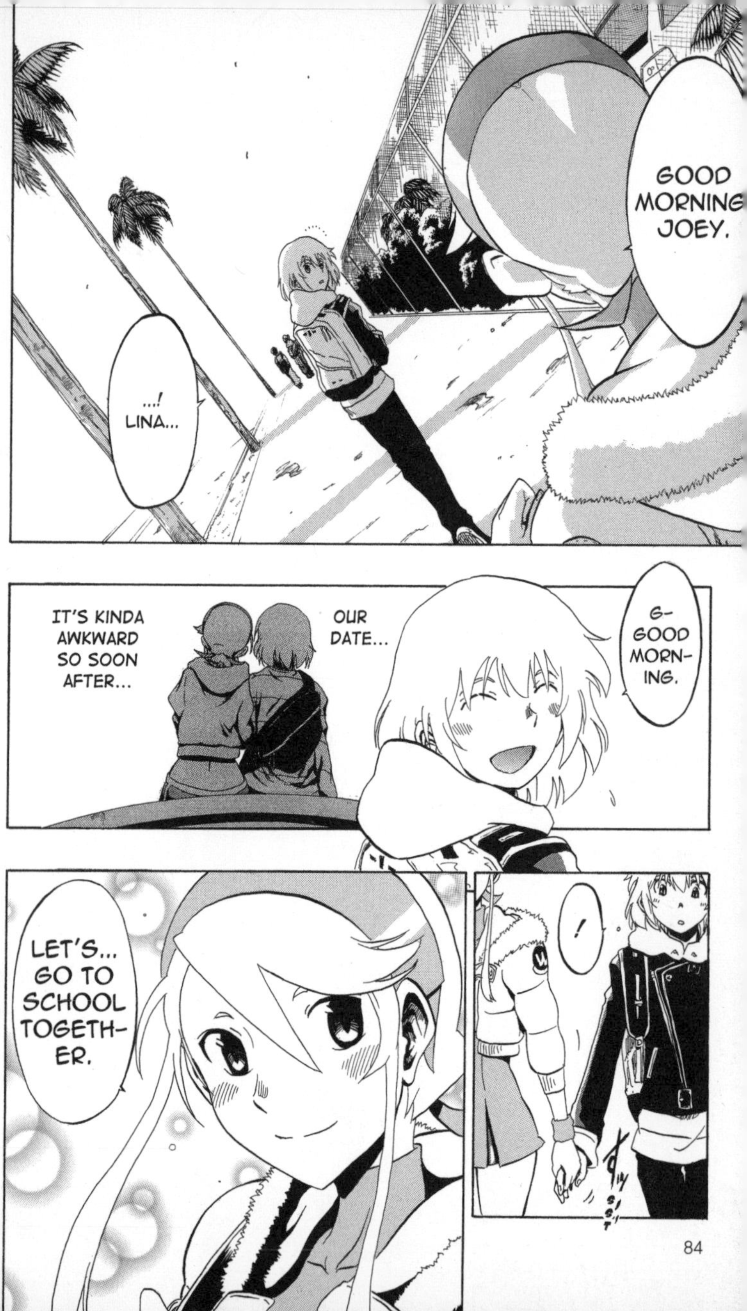
GOOD MORNING JOEY.
...! LINA...
G-GOOD MORN-ING.
OUR DATE...
IT'S KINDA AWKWARD SO SOON AFTER...
!
LET'S... GO TO SCHOOL TOGETH-ER.

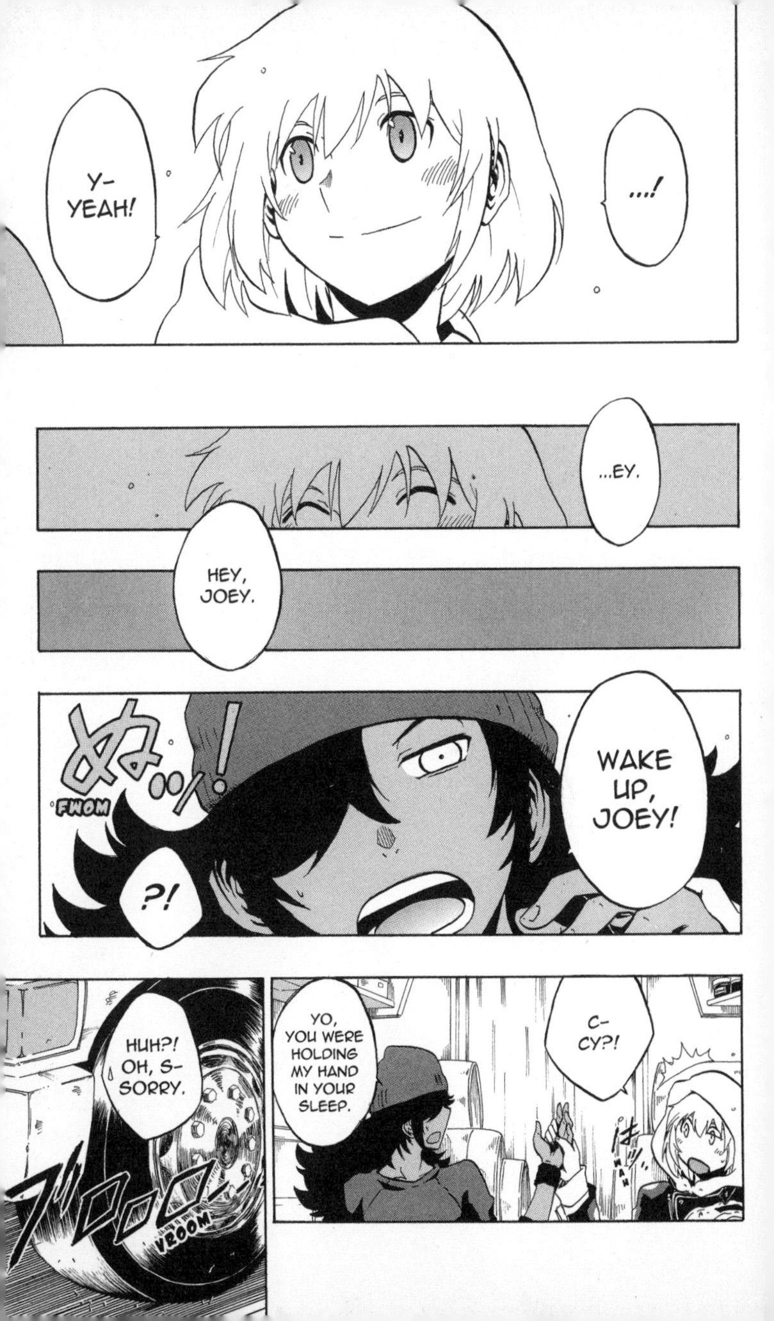

...!
Y-YEAH!
...EY.
HEY, JOEY.
WAKE UP, JOEY!
FWOM
?!
C-CY?!
WAH
YO, YOU WERE HOLDING MY HAND IN YOUR SLEEP.
HUH?! OH, S-SORRY.
VROOM

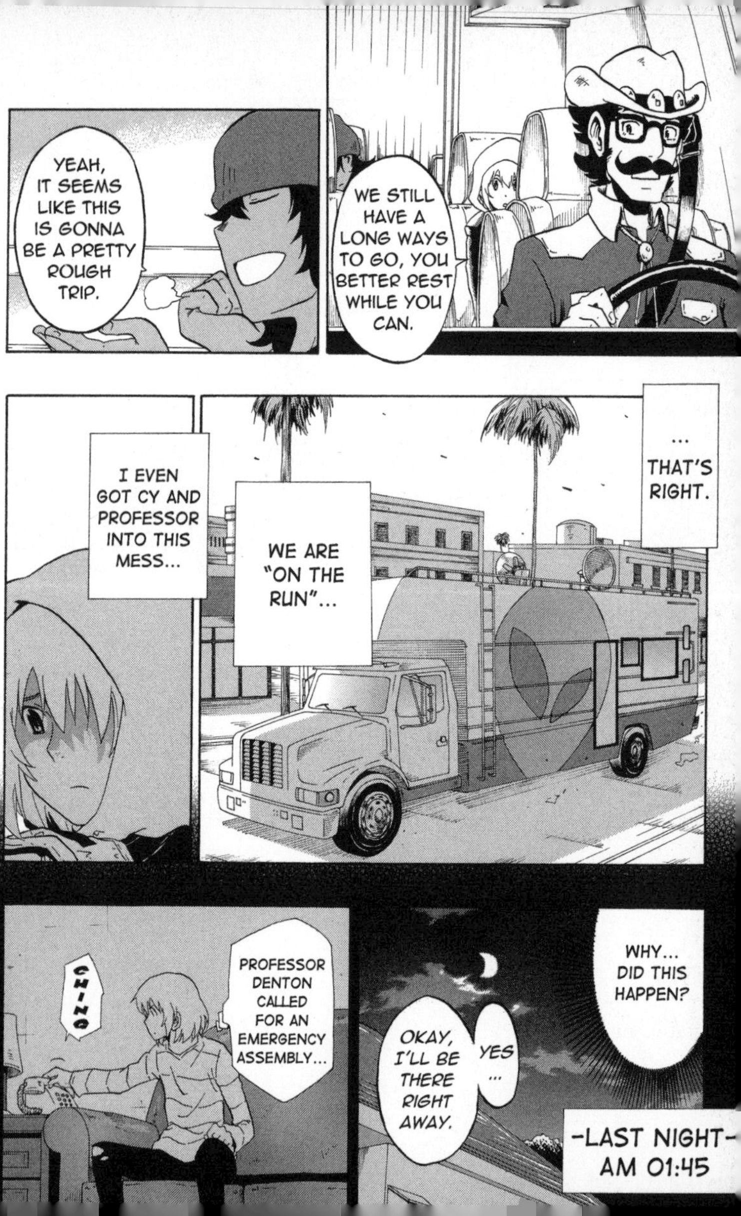
WE STILL HAVE A LONG WAYS TO GO, YOU BETTER REST WHILE YOU CAN.
YEAH, IT SEEMS LIKE THIS IS GONNA BE A PRETTY ROUGH TRIP.
... THAT'S RIGHT.
WE ARE "ON THE RUN"...
I EVEN GOT CY AND PROFESSOR INTO THIS MESS...
WHY... DID THIS HAPPEN?
-LAST NIGHT- AM 01:45
YES...
OKAY, I'LL BE THERE RIGHT AWAY.
PROFESSOR DENTON CALLED FOR AN EMERGENCY ASSEMBLY...
CHING

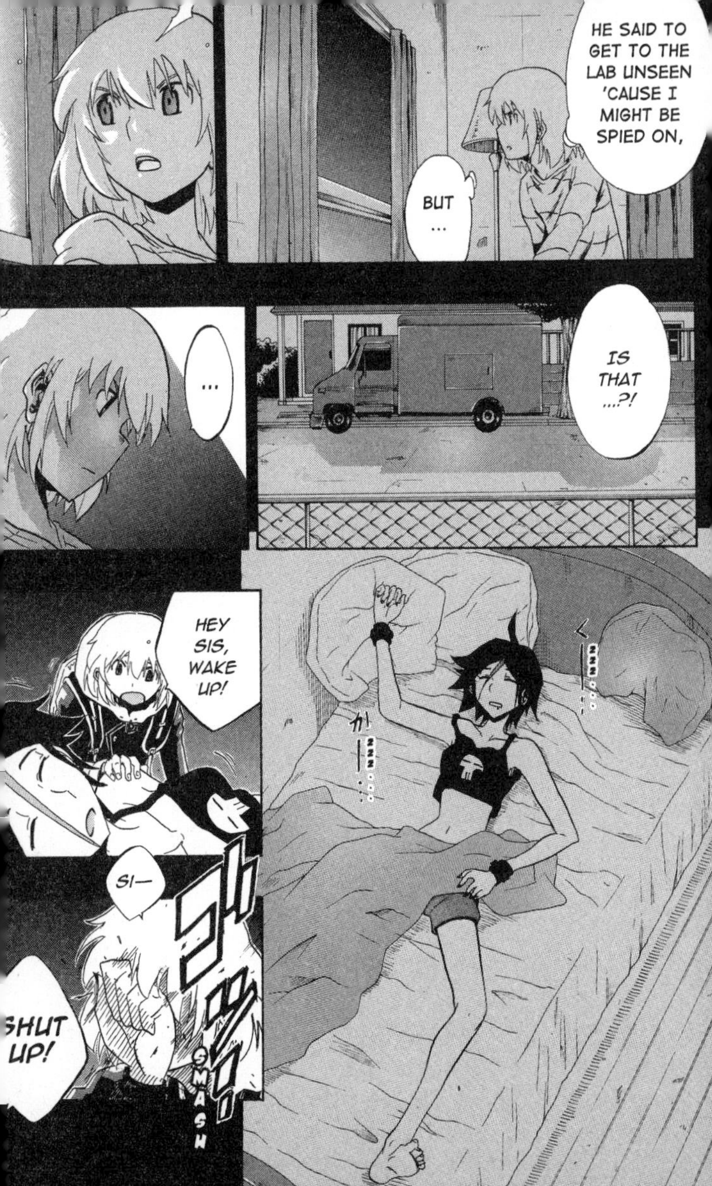
HE SAID TO GET TO THE LAB UNSEEN 'CAUSE I MIGHT BE SPIED ON,
BUT ...
IS THAT ...?!
...
ZZZ...
ZZZ...
HEY SIS, WAKE UP!
SI—
SHUT UP!
SMASH

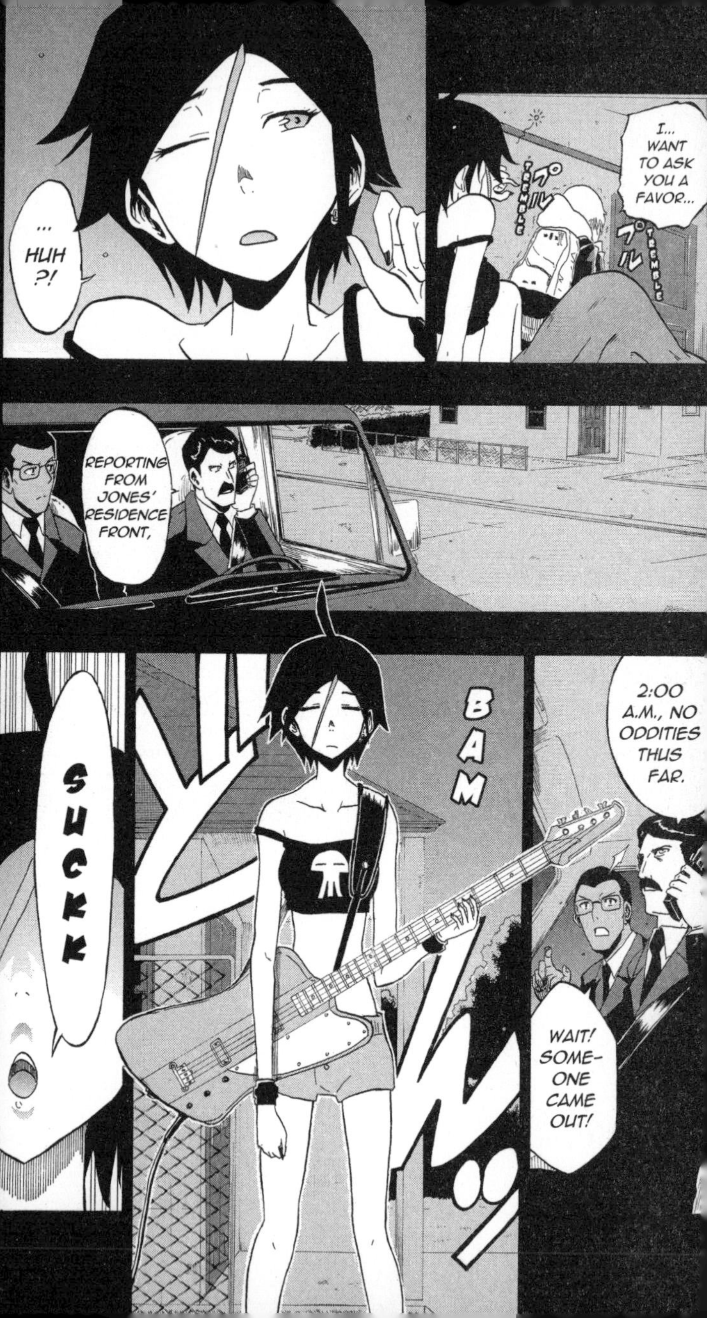
I... WANT TO ASK YOU A FAVOR...
TREMBLE
TREMBLE
... HUH ?!
REPORTING FROM JONES' RESIDENCE FRONT,
2:00 A.M., NO ODDITIES THUS FAR.
WAIT! SOME-ONE CAME OUT!
BAM
SUCKK

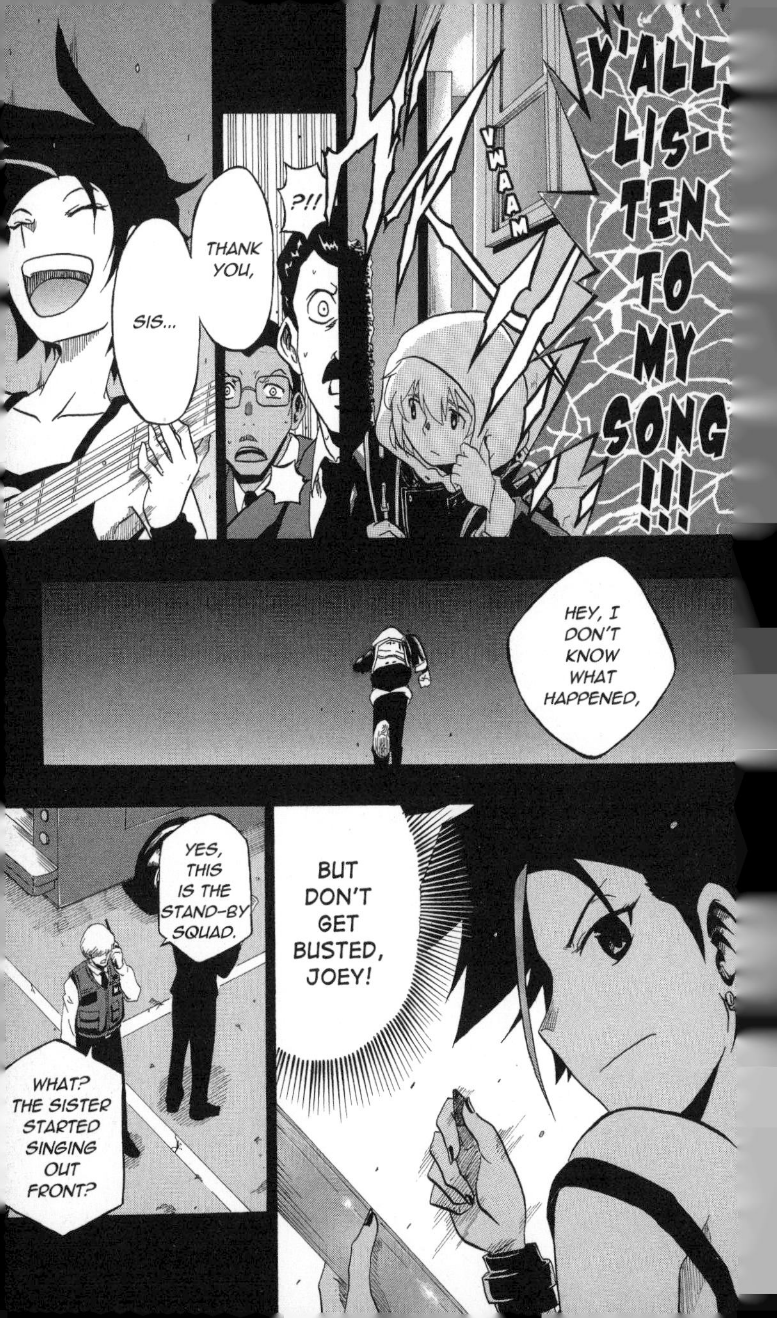
Y'ALL LIS-TEN TO MY SONG!!!
VWAAM
?!!
THANK YOU, SIS...
HEY, I DON'T KNOW WHAT HAPPENED,
BUT DON'T GET BUSTED, JOEY!
YES, THIS IS THE STAND-BY SQUAD.
WHAT? THE SISTER STARTED SINGING OUT FRONT?

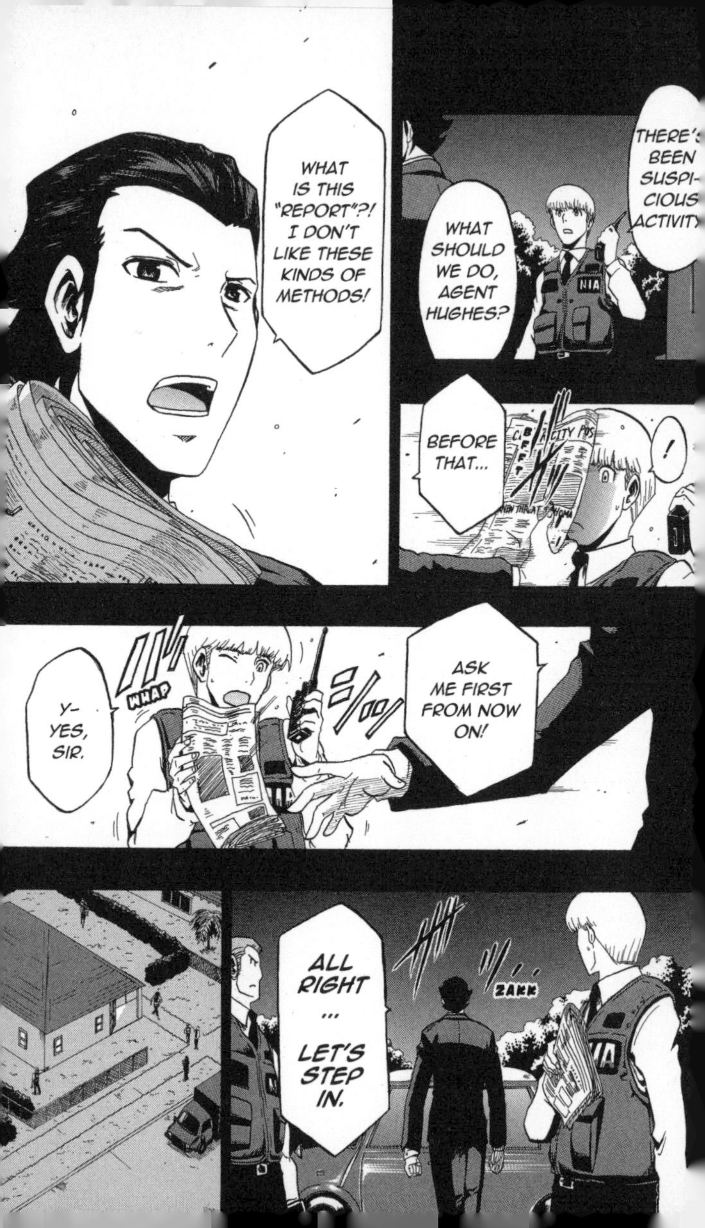
THERE'S BEEN SUSPICIOUS ACTIVITY
WHAT SHOULD WE DO, AGENT HUGHES?
!
BEFORE THAT...
WHAT IS THIS "REPORT"?! I DON'T LIKE THESE KINDS OF METHODS!
ASK ME FIRST FROM NOW ON!
WHAP
Y-YES, SIR.
ZAKK
ALL RIGHT ... LET'S STEP IN.

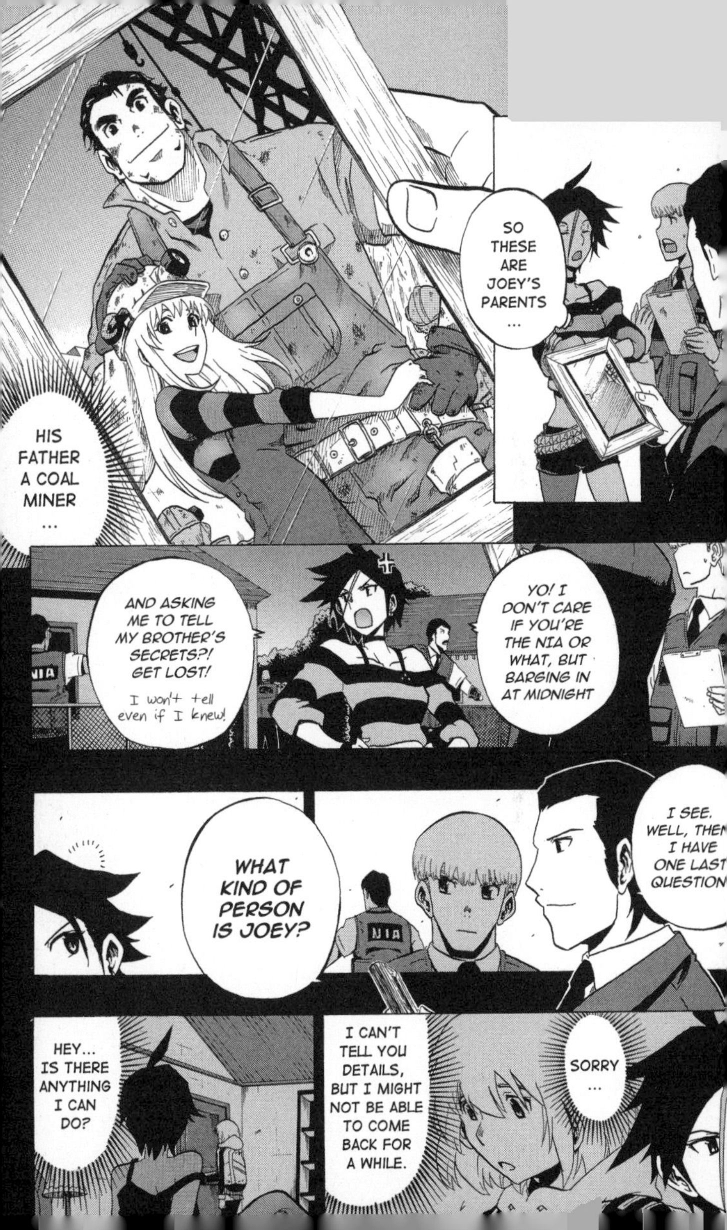
SO THESE ARE JOEY'S PARENTS...
HIS FATHER A COAL MINER...
YO! I DON'T CARE IF YOU'RE THE NIA OR WHAT, BUT BARGING IN AT MIDNIGHT
AND ASKING ME TO TELL MY BROTHER'S SECRETS?! GET LOST!
I won't tell even if I knew!
I SEE. WELL, THEN I HAVE ONE LAST QUESTION
WHAT KIND OF PERSON IS JOEY?
SORRY...
I CAN'T TELL YOU DETAILS, BUT I MIGHT NOT BE ABLE TO COME BACK FOR A WHILE.
HEY... IS THERE ANYTHING I CAN DO?

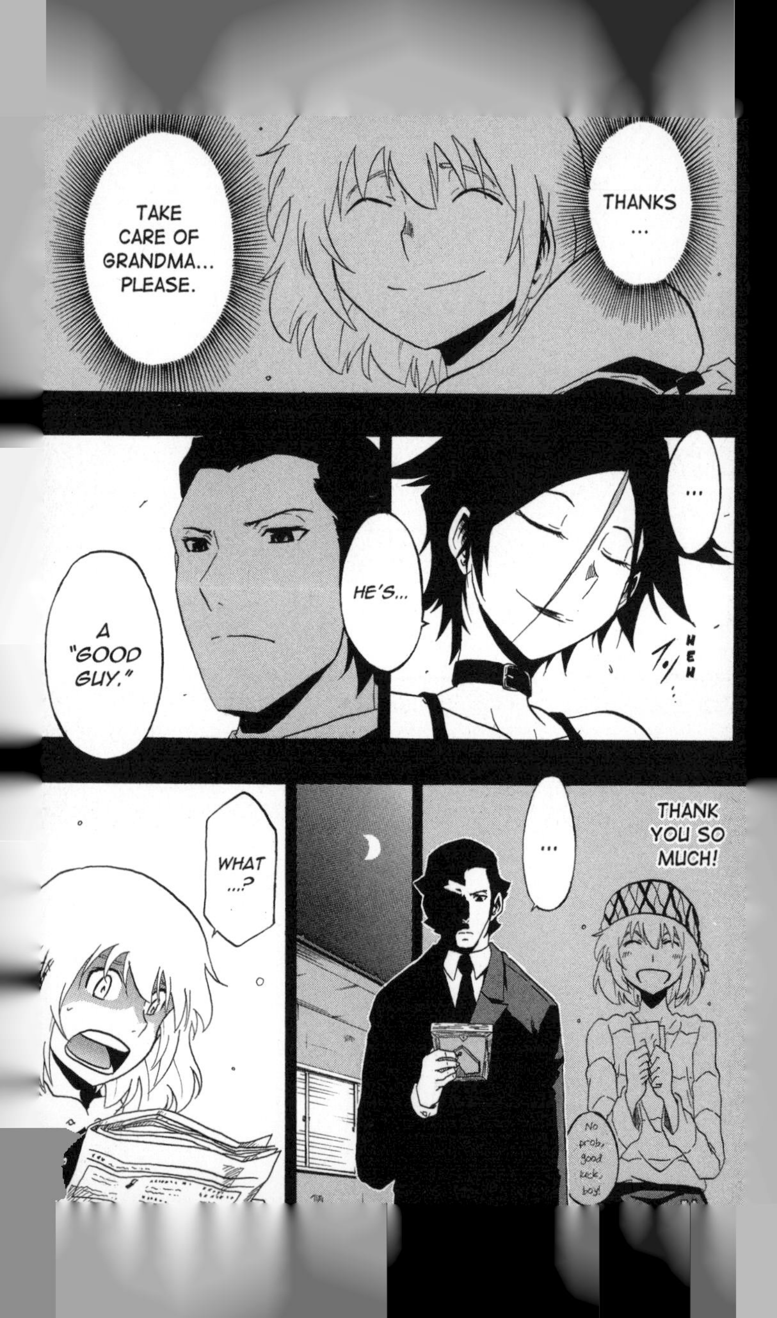
THANKS ...
TAKE CARE OF GRANDMA... PLEASE.
...
HE'S...
HEH
A "GOOD GUY."
THANK YOU SO MUCH!
...
No prob, good luck, boy!
WHAT ...?

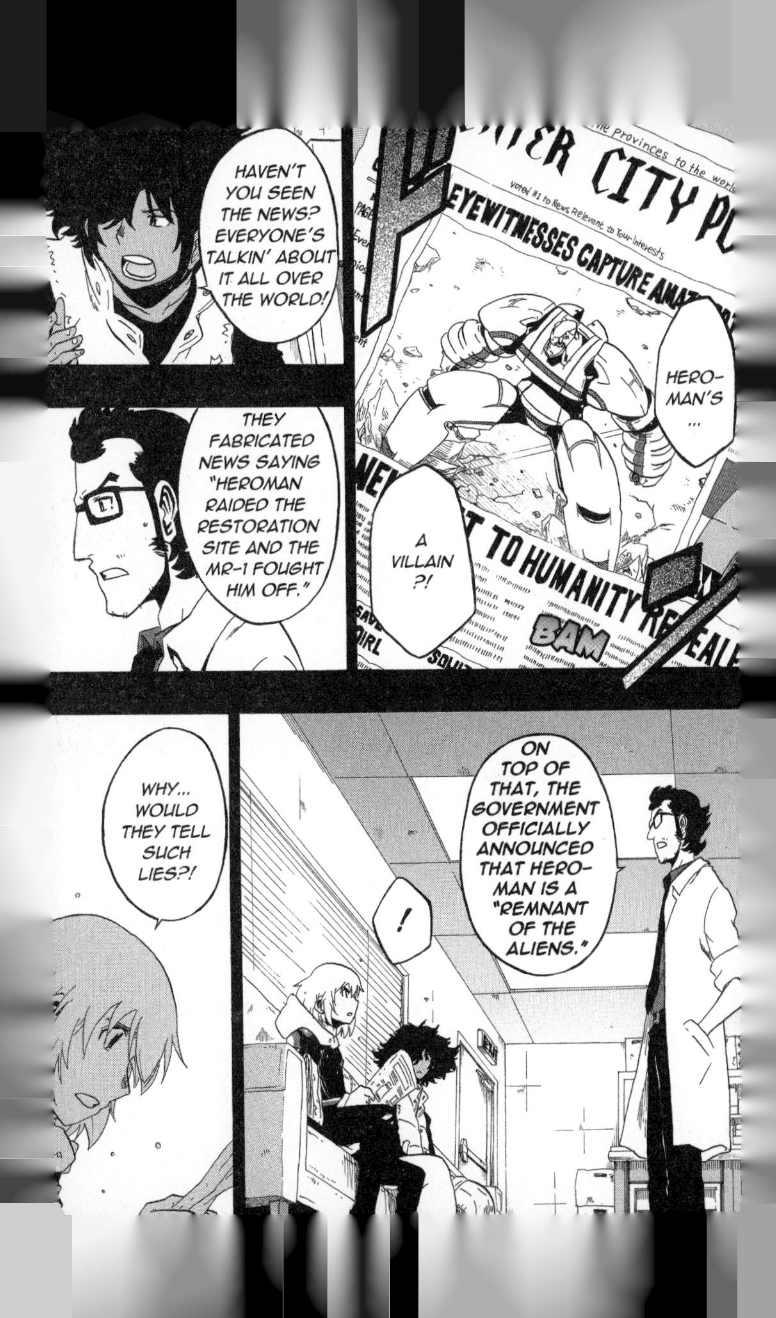
CITY
Voted #1 to News Relevant to Your Interests
EYEWITNESSES CAPTURE
TO HUMANITY
BAM
HERO-MAN'S ...
A VILLAIN ?!
HAVEN'T YOU SEEN THE NEWS? EVERYONE'S TALKIN' ABOUT IT ALL OVER THE WORLD!
THEY FABRICATED NEWS SAYING "HEROMAN RAIDED THE RESTORATION SITE AND THE MR-1 FOUGHT HIM OFF."
ON TOP OF THAT, THE GOVERNMENT OFFICIALLY ANNOUNCED THAT HERO-MAN IS A "REMNANT OF THE ALIENS."
!
WHY... WOULD THEY TELL SUCH LIES?!

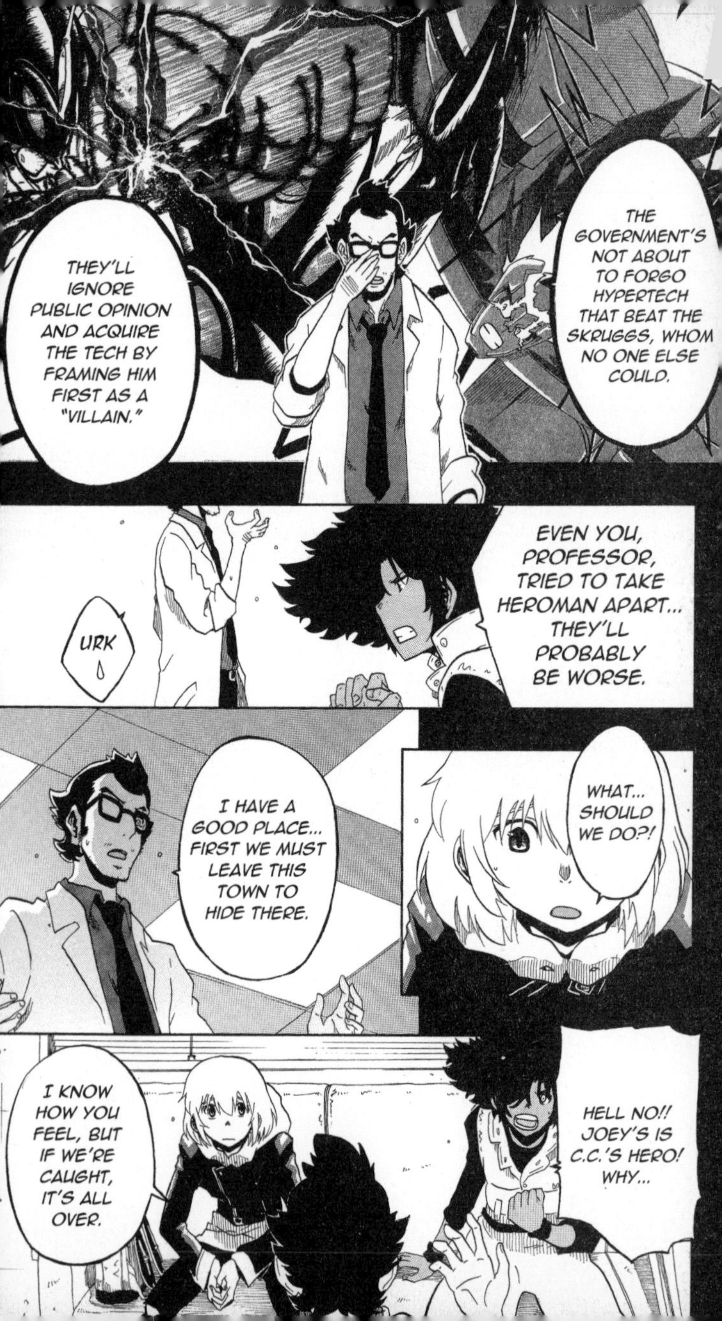
THE GOVERNMENT'S NOT ABOUT TO FORGO HYPERTECH THAT BEAT THE SKRUGGS, WHOM NO ONE ELSE COULD.
THEY'LL IGNORE PUBLIC OPINION AND ACQUIRE THE TECH BY FRAMING HIM FIRST AS A "VILLAIN."
EVEN YOU, PROFESSOR, TRIED TO TAKE HEROMAN APART... THEY'LL PROBABLY BE WORSE.
URK
WHAT... SHOULD WE DO?!
I HAVE A GOOD PLACE... FIRST WE MUST LEAVE THIS TOWN TO HIDE THERE.
HELL NO!! JOEY'S IS C.C.'S HERO! WHY...
I KNOW HOW YOU FEEL, BUT IF WE'RE CAUGHT, IT'S ALL OVER.

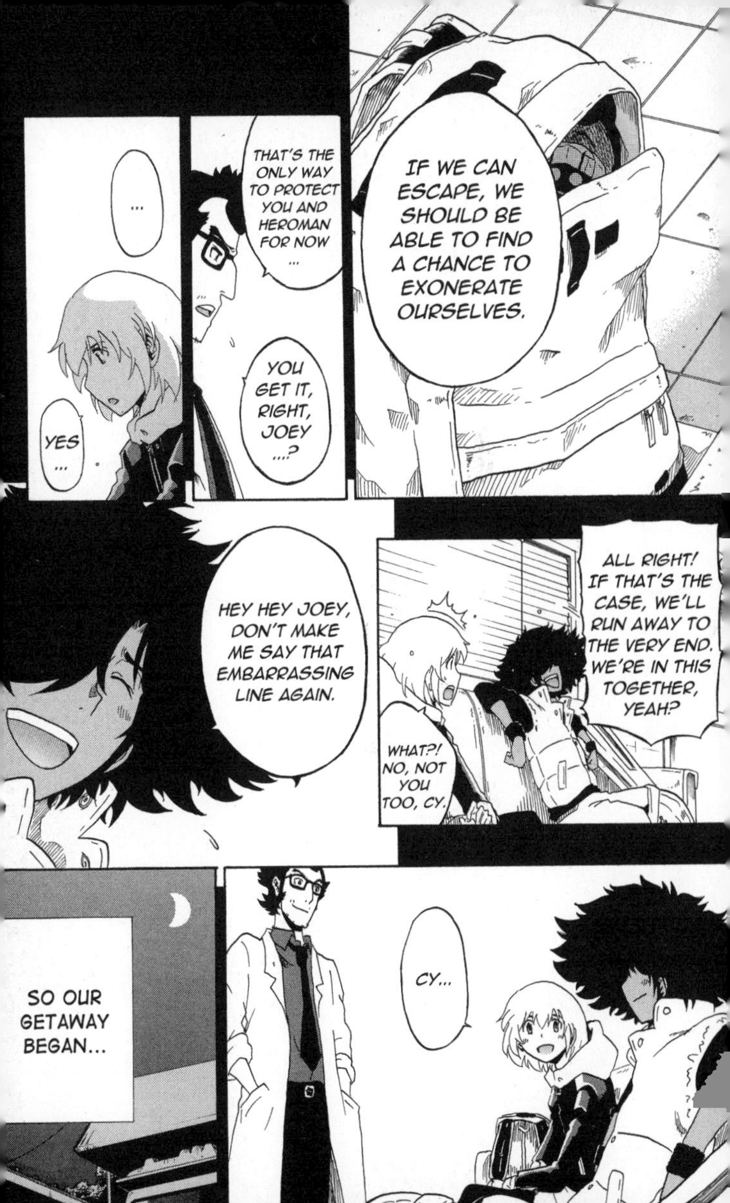
IF WE CAN ESCAPE, WE SHOULD BE ABLE TO FIND A CHANCE TO EXONERATE OURSELVES.
THAT'S THE ONLY WAY TO PROTECT YOU AND HEROMAN FOR NOW ...
YOU GET IT, RIGHT, JOEY ...?
...
YES ...
ALL RIGHT! IF THAT'S THE CASE, WE'LL RUN AWAY TO THE VERY END. WE'RE IN THIS TOGETHER, YEAH?
WHAT?! NO, NOT YOU TOO, CY.
HEY HEY JOEY, DON'T MAKE ME SAY THAT EMBARRASSING LINE AGAIN.
CY...
SO OUR GETAWAY BEGAN...

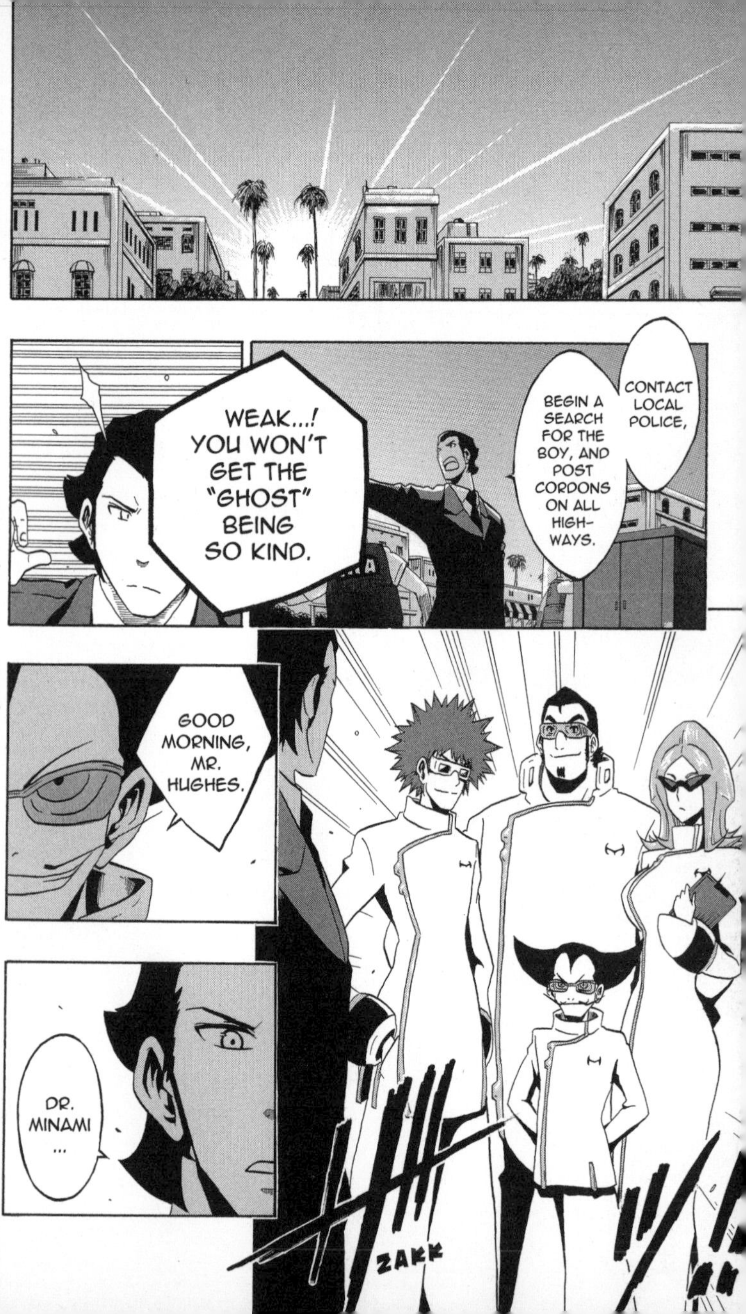
CONTACT LOCAL POLICE,
BEGIN A SEARCH FOR THE BOY, AND POST CORDONS ON ALL HIGH-WAYS.
WEAK...! YOU WON'T GET THE "GHOST" BEING SO KIND.
ZAKK
GOOD MORNING, MR. HUGHES.
DR. MINAMI ...

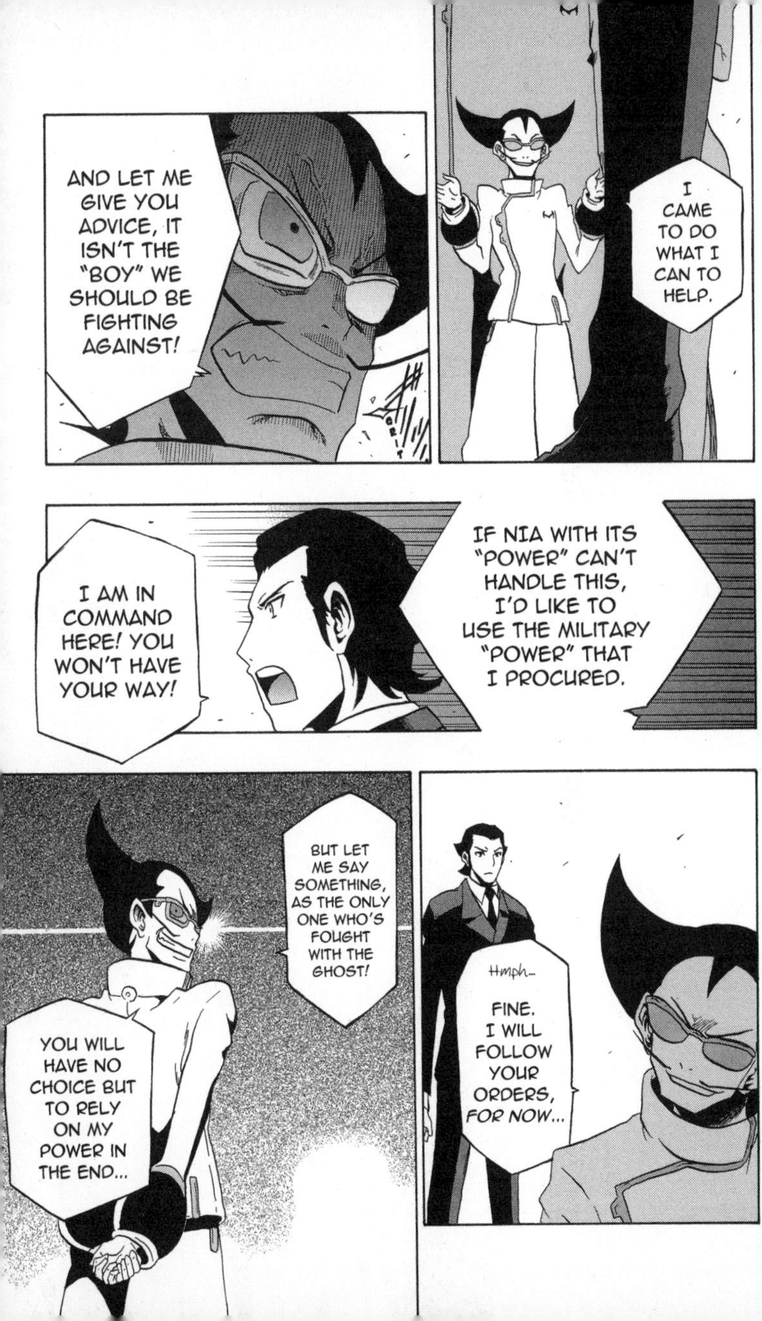
I CAME TO DO WHAT I CAN TO HELP.
AND LET ME GIVE YOU ADVICE, IT ISN'T THE "BOY" WE SHOULD BE FIGHTING AGAINST!
GRIT
IF NIA WITH ITS "POWER" CAN'T HANDLE THIS, I'D LIKE TO USE THE MILITARY "POWER" THAT I PROCURED.
I AM IN COMMAND HERE! YOU WON'T HAVE YOUR WAY!
Hmph...
FINE. I WILL FOLLOW YOUR ORDERS, FOR NOW...
BUT LET ME SAY SOMETHING, AS THE ONLY ONE WHO'S FOUGHT WITH THE GHOST!
YOU WILL HAVE NO CHOICE BUT TO RELY ON MY POWER IN THE END...

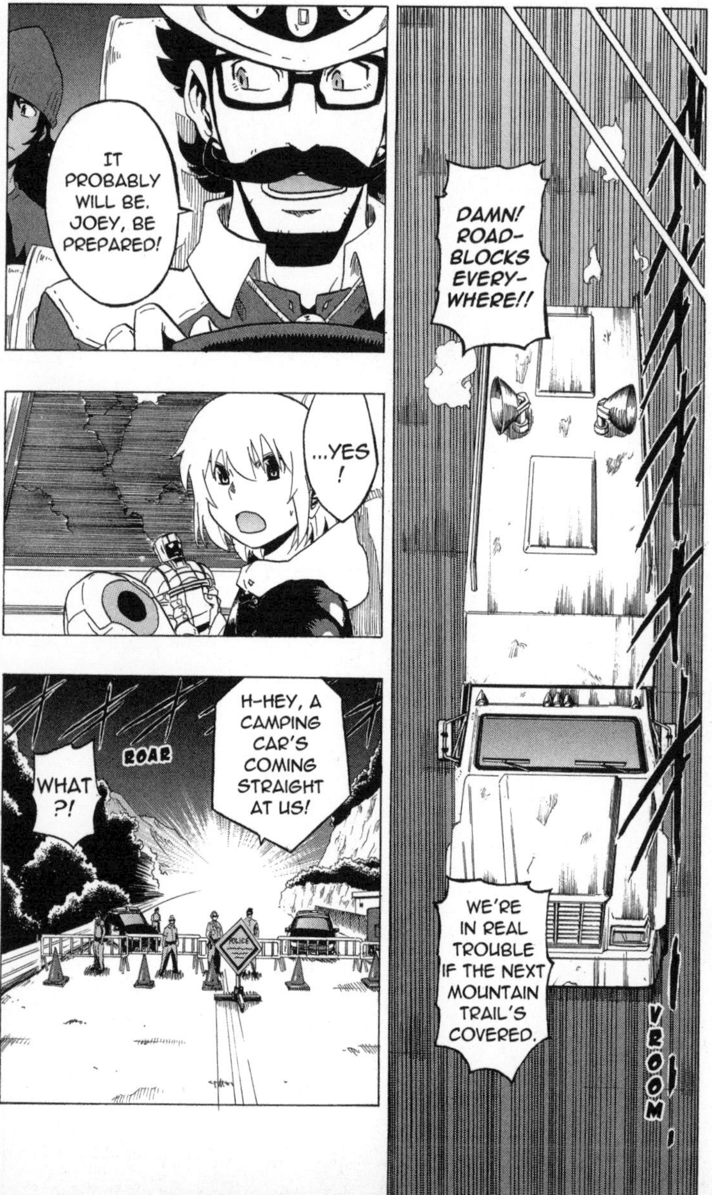
DAMN! ROAD-BLOCKS EVERY-WHERE!!
WE'RE IN REAL TROUBLE IF THE NEXT MOUNTAIN TRAIL'S COVERED.
VROOM.
IT PROBABLY WILL BE. JOEY, BE PREPARED!
...YES!
H-HEY, A CAMPING CAR'S COMING STRAIGHT AT US!
ROAR
WHAT?!

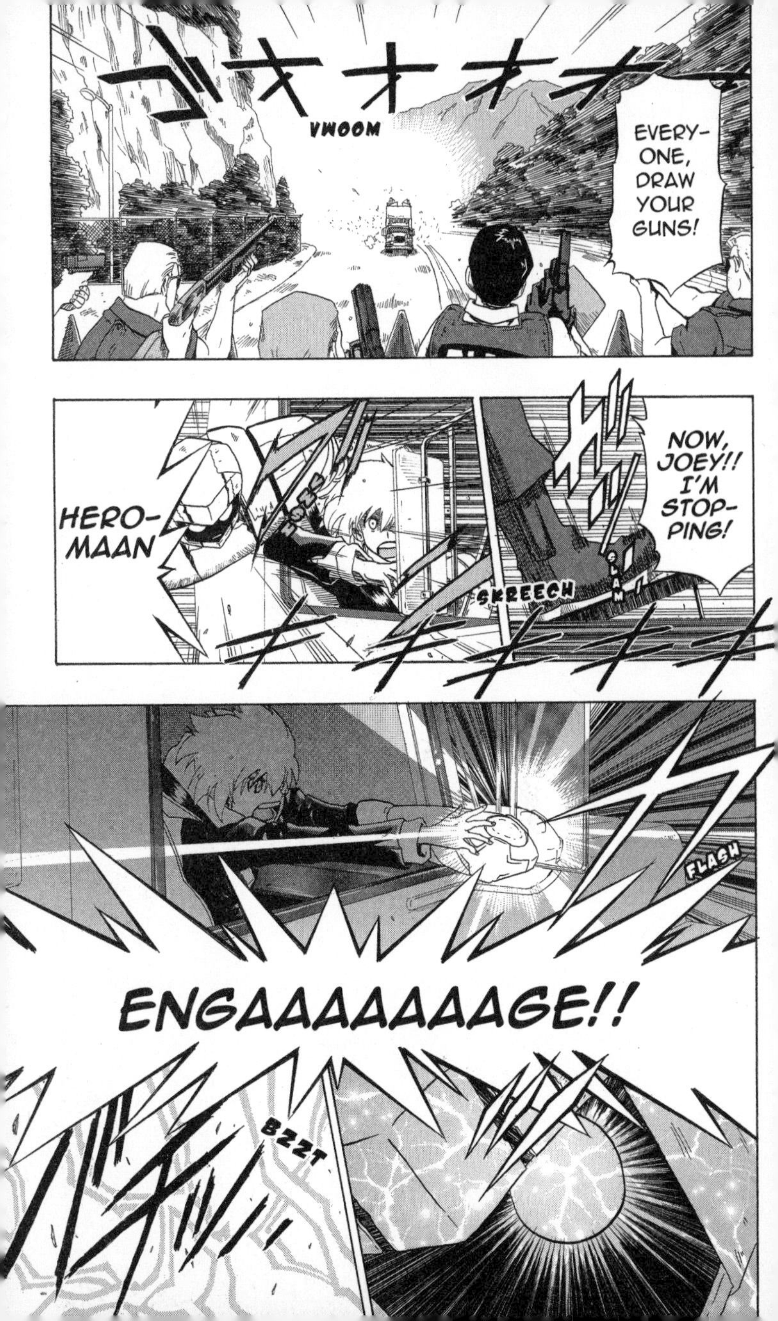
EVERY-ONE, DRAW YOUR GUNS!
VWOOM
NOW, JOEY!! I'M STOP-PING!
SLAM!
SKREECH
VWSH
HERO-MAAN
FLASH
ENGAAAAAAAGE!!
BZZT

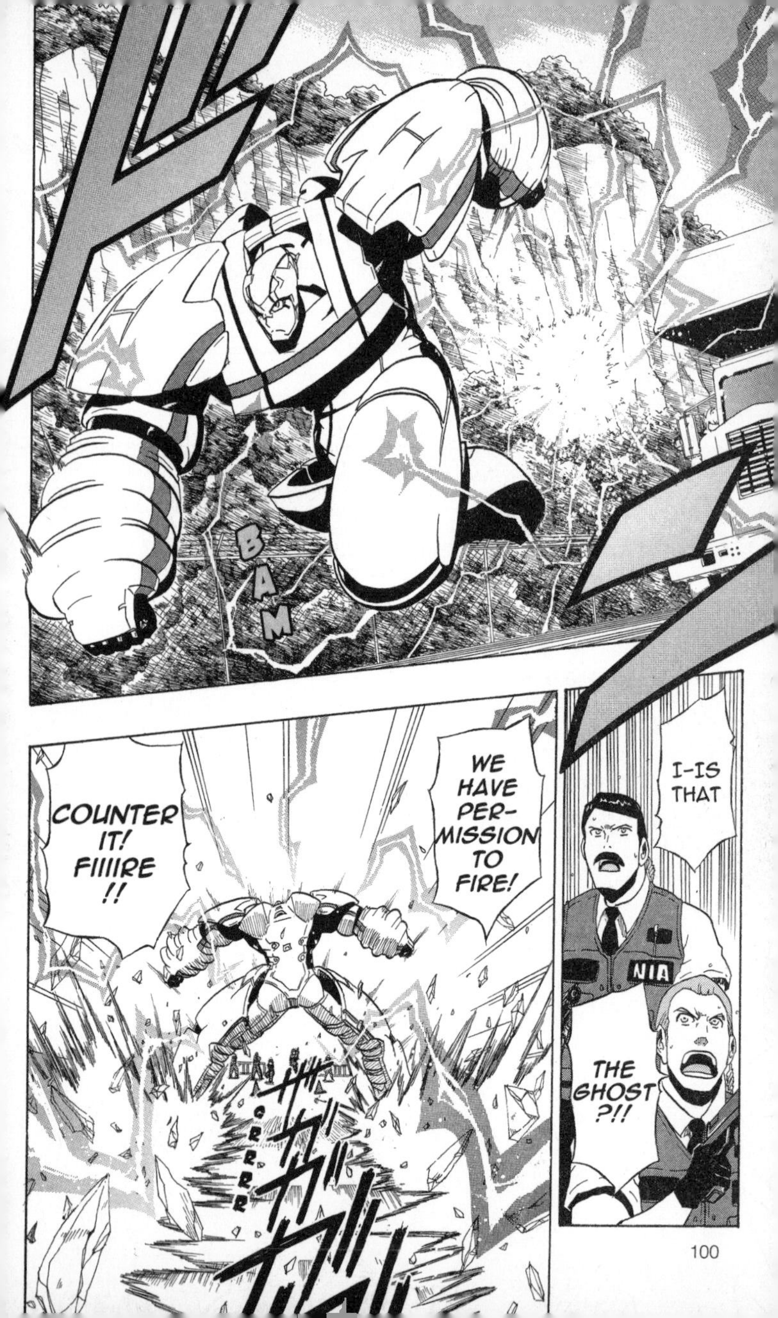
BAM
I-IS THAT
THE GHOST ?!!
WE HAVE PER-MISSION TO FIRE!
COUNTER IT! FIIIIRE !!
GRRRRR

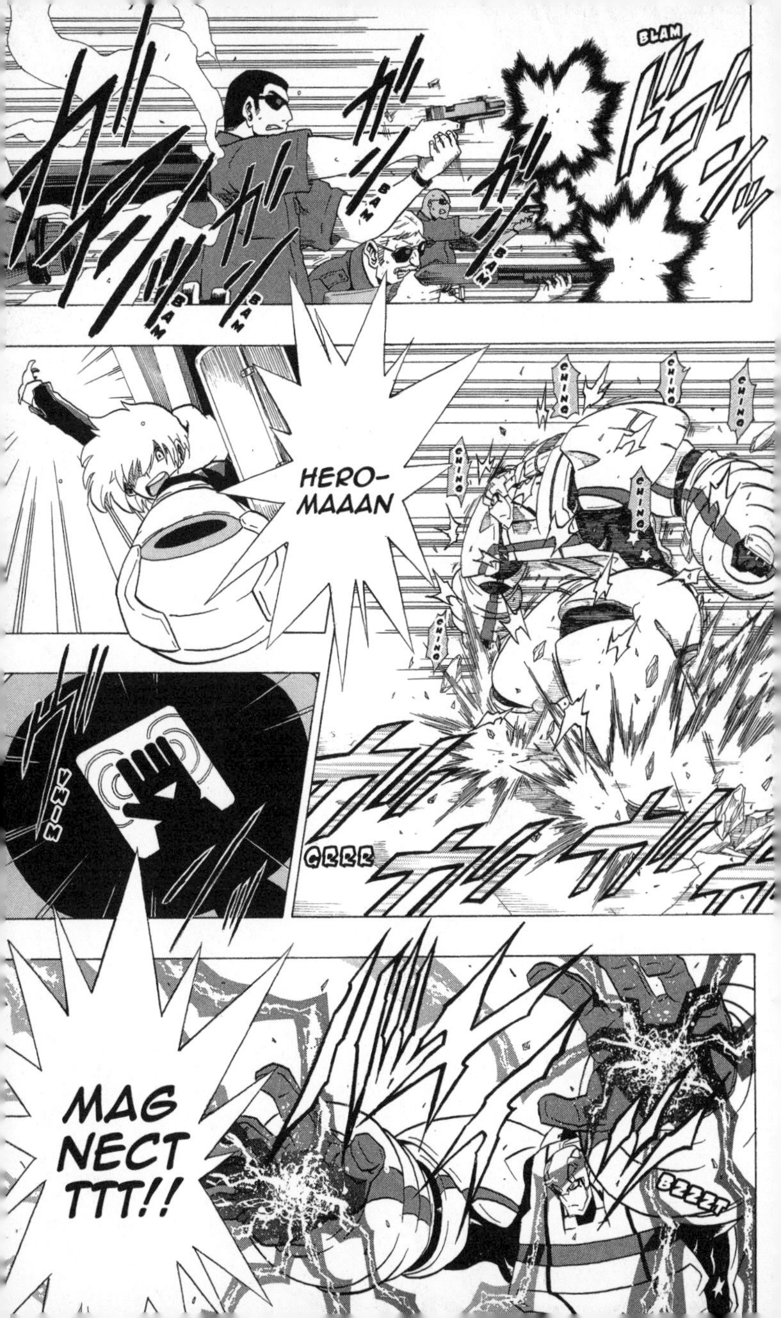
BLAM
BAM
BAM
BAM
BAM
CHING
CHING
CHING
CHING
CHING
CHING
HERO-
MAAAN
GRRR
MAG
NECT
TTT!!
BZZZT

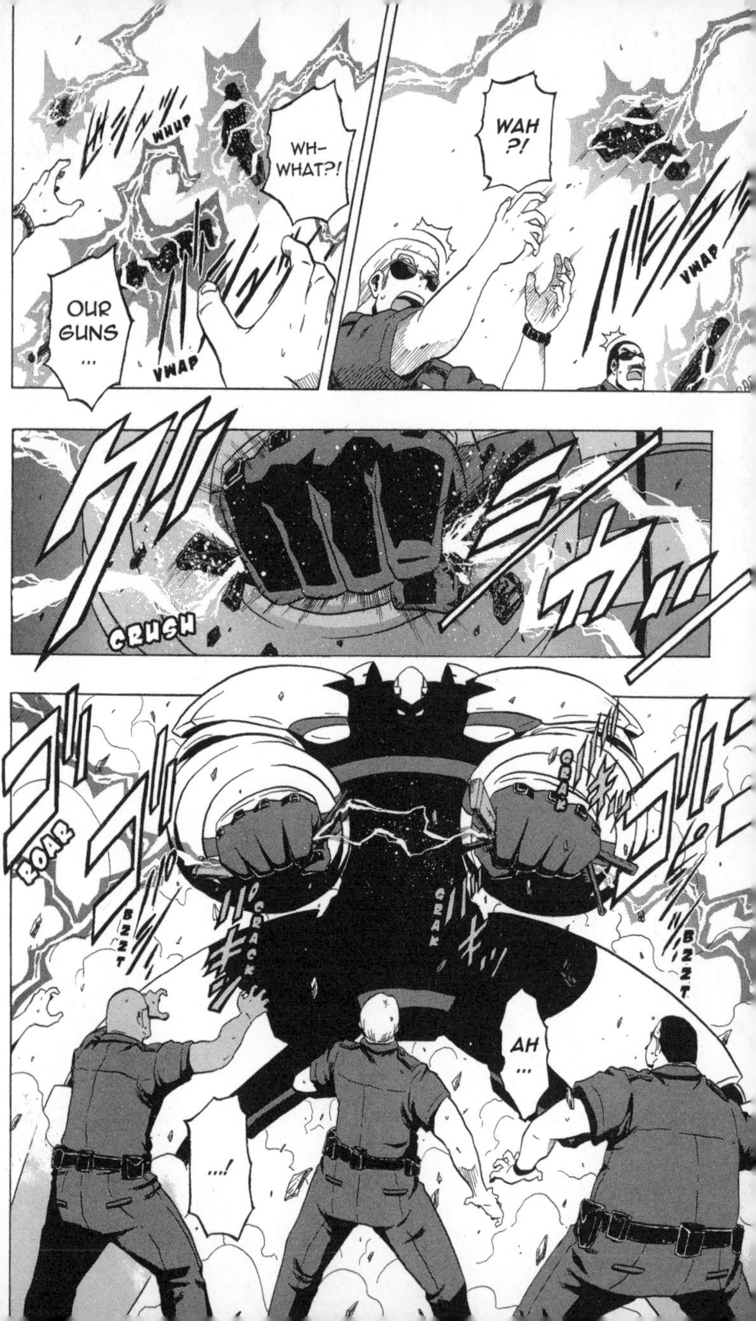
WAH ?!
VWAP
WH- WHAT?!
WHUP
OUR GUNS ...
VWAP
CRUSH
CRAK
BZZT
GRAK
AH ...
...!
CRACK
BZZT
ROAR

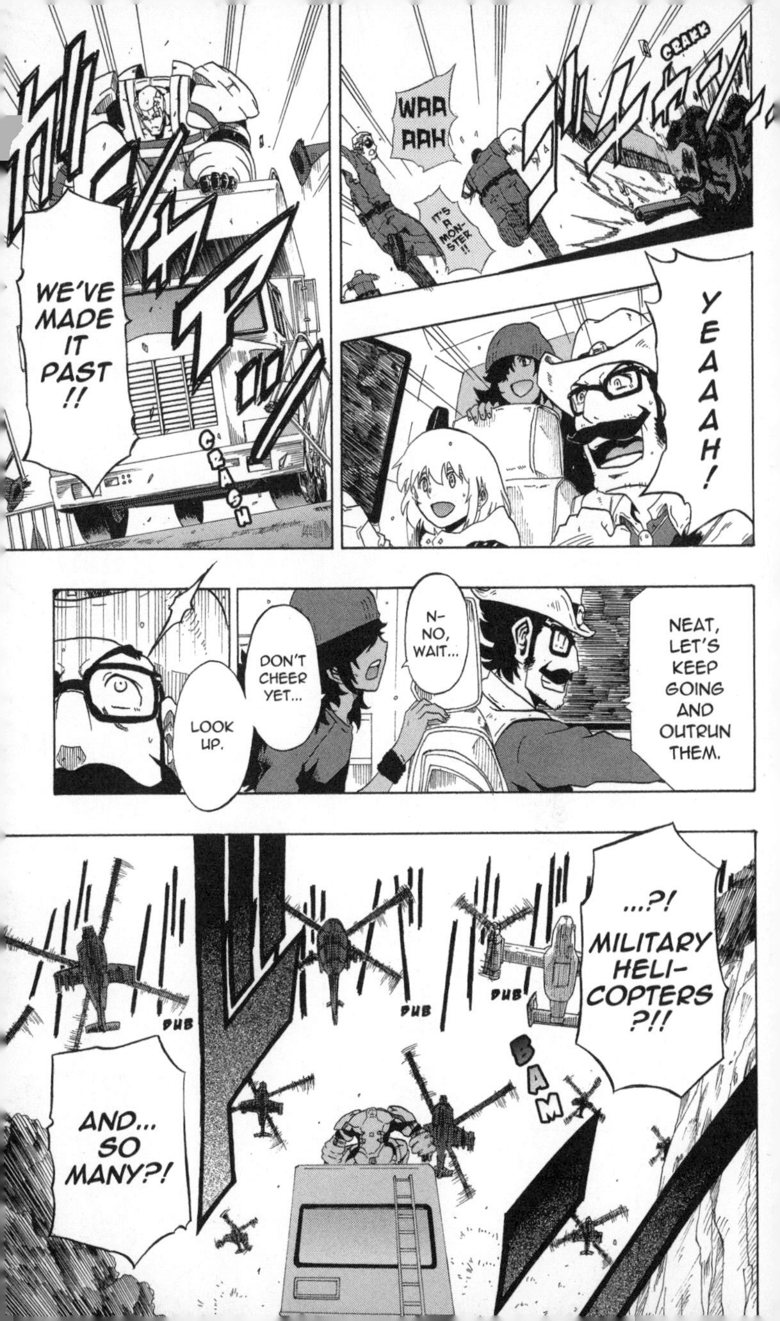
CRAKK
WAA AAH
IT'S A MON-STER!!
YEAAAAH!
WE'VE MADE IT PAST!!
CRASH
NEAT, LET'S KEEP GOING AND OUTRUN THEM.
N-NO, WAIT...
DON'T CHEER YET...
LOOK UP.
...?! MILITARY HELI-COPTERS?!!
DUB
DUB
DUB
BAM
AND... SO MANY?!

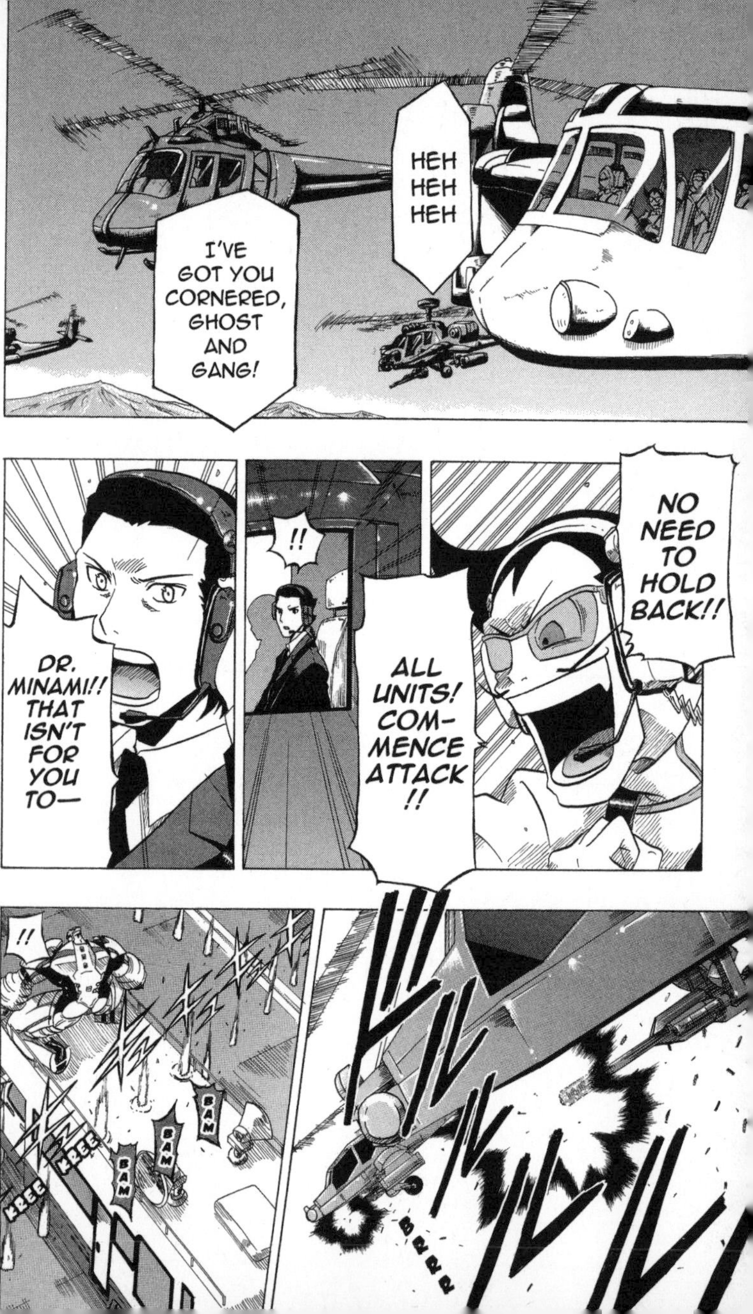
HEH HEH HEH
I'VE GOT YOU CORNERED, GHOST AND GANG!
NO NEED TO HOLD BACK!!
ALL UNITS! COM-MENCE ATTACK!!
!!
DR. MINAMI!! THAT ISN'T FOR YOU TO—
BRRRR
!!
BAM
BAM
BAM
KREE
KREE

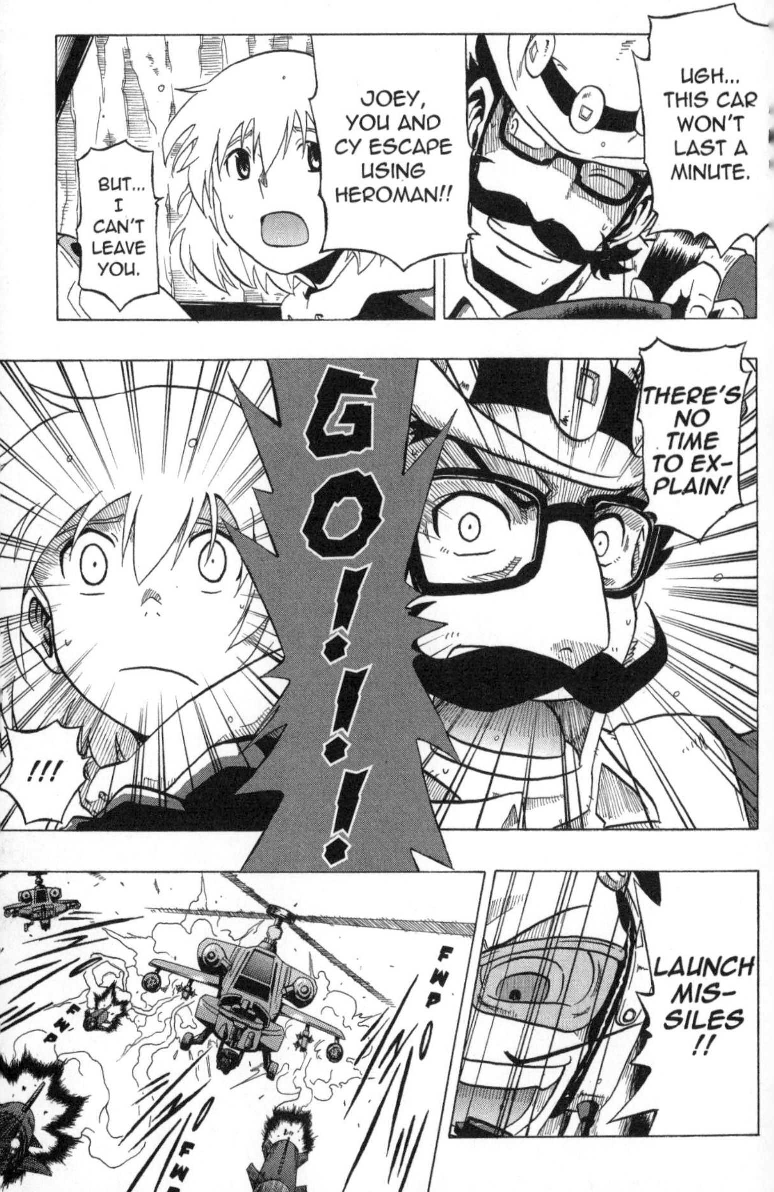
UGH... THIS CAR WON'T LAST A MINUTE.
JOEY, YOU AND CY ESCAPE USING HEROMAN!!
BUT... I CAN'T LEAVE YOU.
THERE'S NO TIME TO EX-PLAIN!
GO!!!!
!!!
LAUNCH MIS-SILES!!
FWP
FWP
FWP

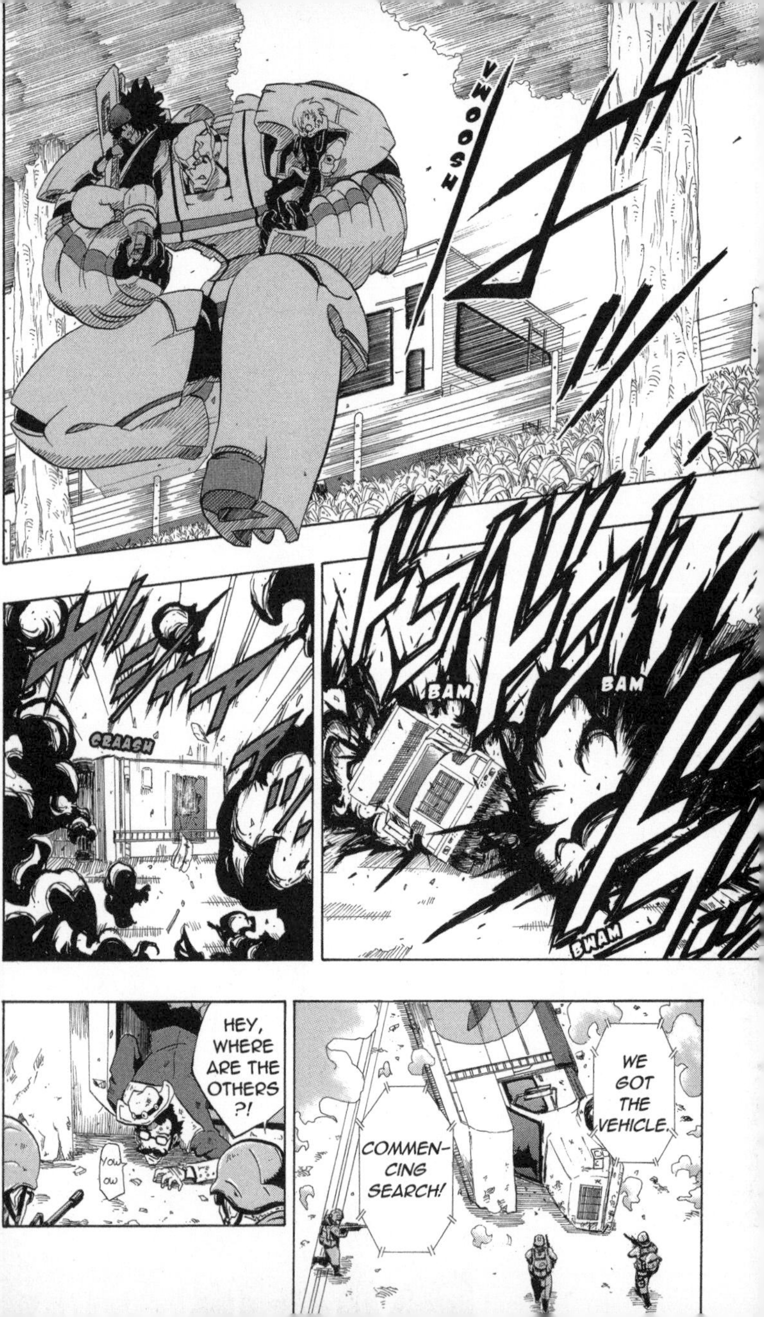
VWOOSH
BAM
BAM
BWAM
CRAASH
WE GOT THE VEHICLE.
COMMEN-CING SEARCH!
HEY, WHERE ARE THE OTHERS ?!
YOW OW

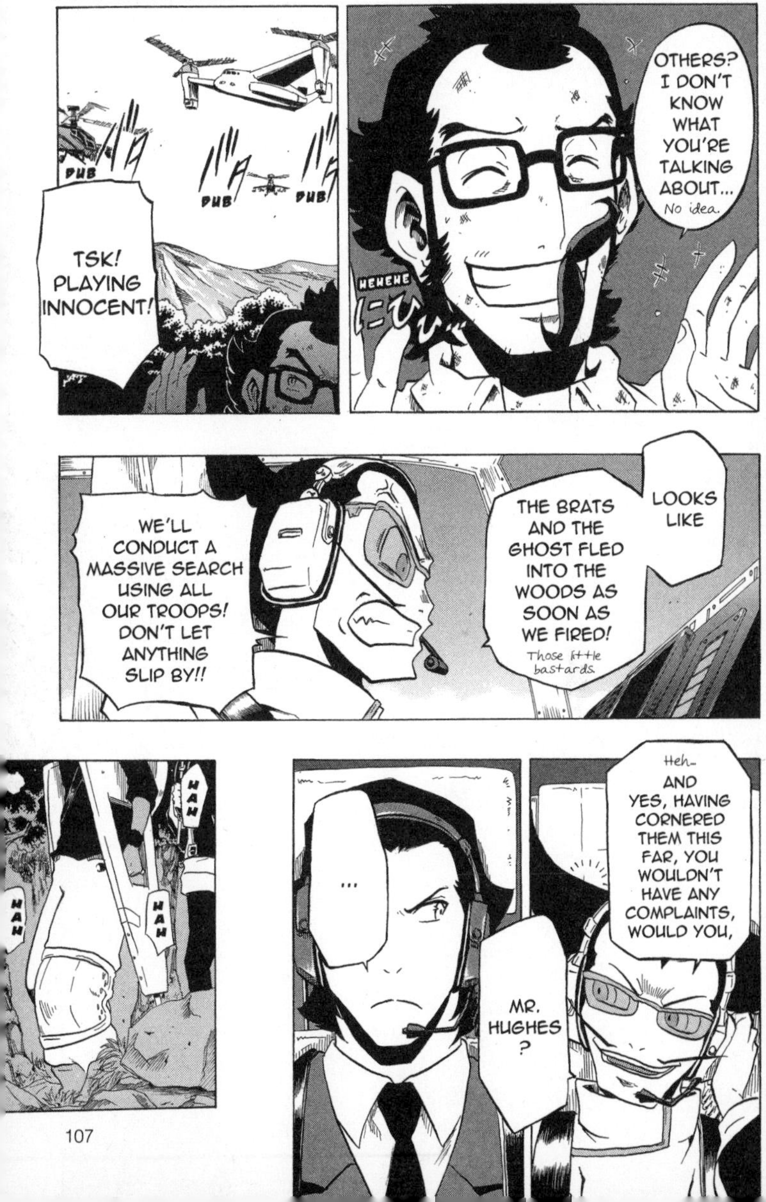
OTHERS? I DON'T KNOW WHAT YOU'RE TALKING ABOUT...
No idea.
HEHEHE
DUB
DUB
DUB
TSK! PLAYING INNOCENT!
LOOKS LIKE
THE BRATS AND THE GHOST FLED INTO THE WOODS AS SOON AS WE FIRED!
Those little bastards.
WE'LL CONDUCT A MASSIVE SEARCH USING ALL OUR TROOPS! DON'T LET ANYTHING SLIP BY!!
Heh-
AND YES, HAVING CORNERED THEM THIS FAR, YOU WOULDN'T HAVE ANY COMPLAINTS, WOULD YOU,
MR. HUGHES?
...
HAH
HAH
HAH

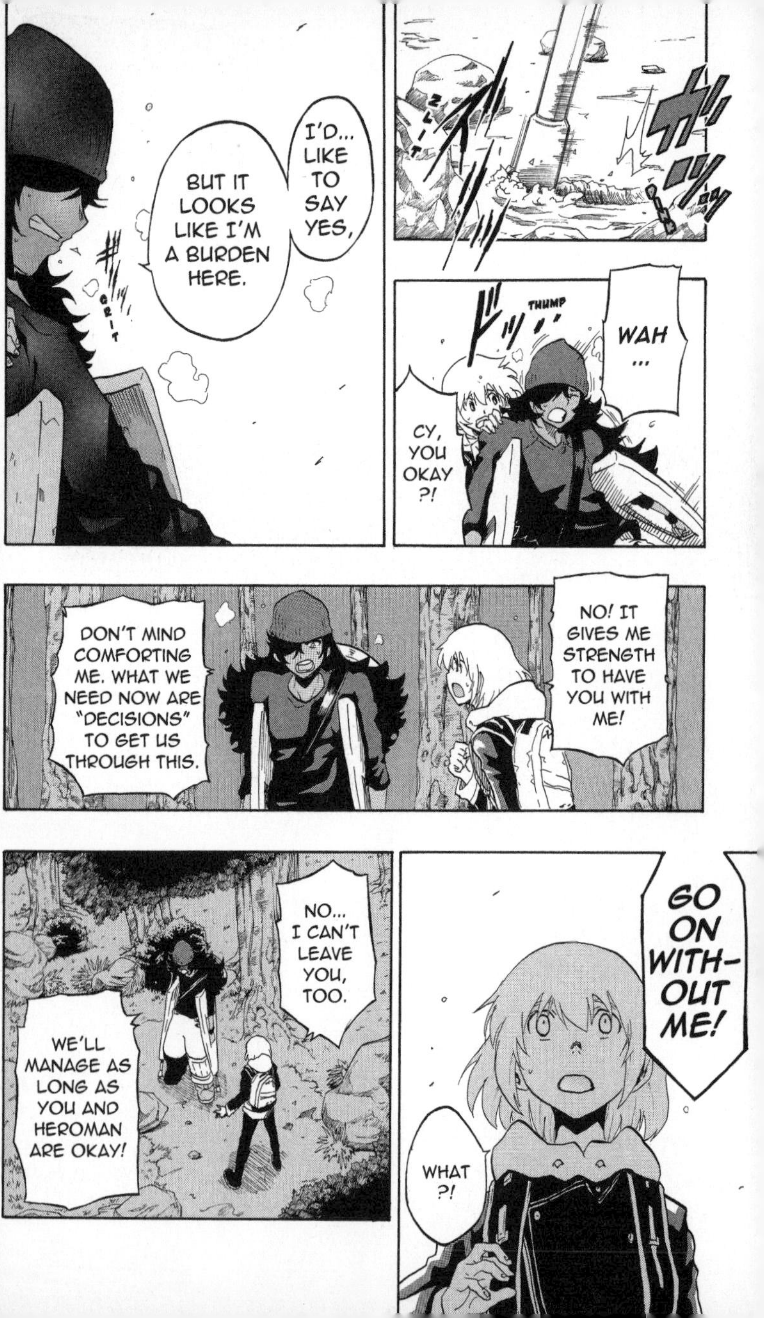
ZLIT
PING
THUMP
WAH ...
CY, YOU OKAY ?!
I'D... LIKE TO SAY YES,
BUT IT LOOKS LIKE I'M A BURDEN HERE.
GRIT
NO! IT GIVES ME STRENGTH TO HAVE YOU WITH ME!
DON'T MIND COMFORTING ME. WHAT WE NEED NOW ARE "DECISIONS" TO GET US THROUGH THIS.
GO ON WITH-OUT ME!
WHAT ?!
NO... I CAN'T LEAVE YOU, TOO.
WE'LL MANAGE AS LONG AS YOU AND HEROMAN ARE OKAY!

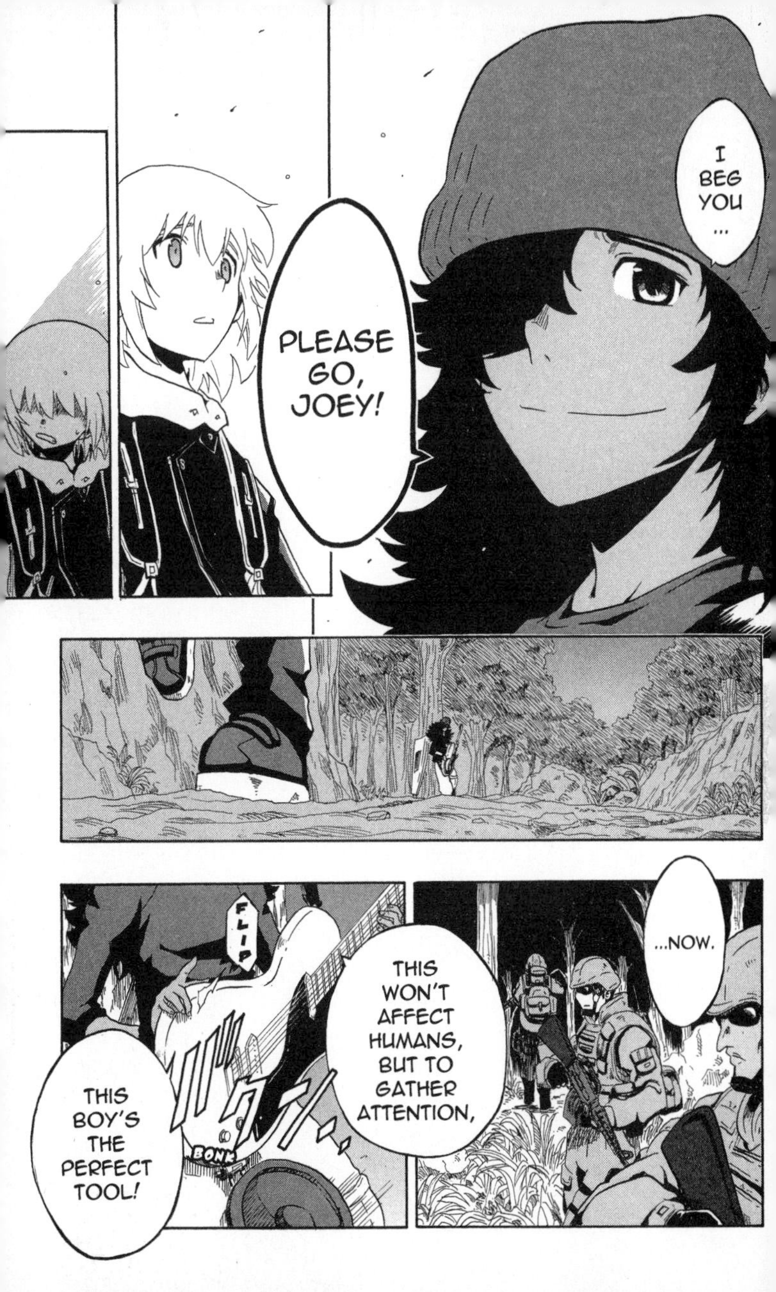
I BEG YOU ...
PLEASE GO, JOEY!
...NOW.
FLIP
THIS WON'T AFFECT HUMANS, BUT TO GATHER ATTENTION,
THIS BOY'S THE PERFECT TOOL!
BONK

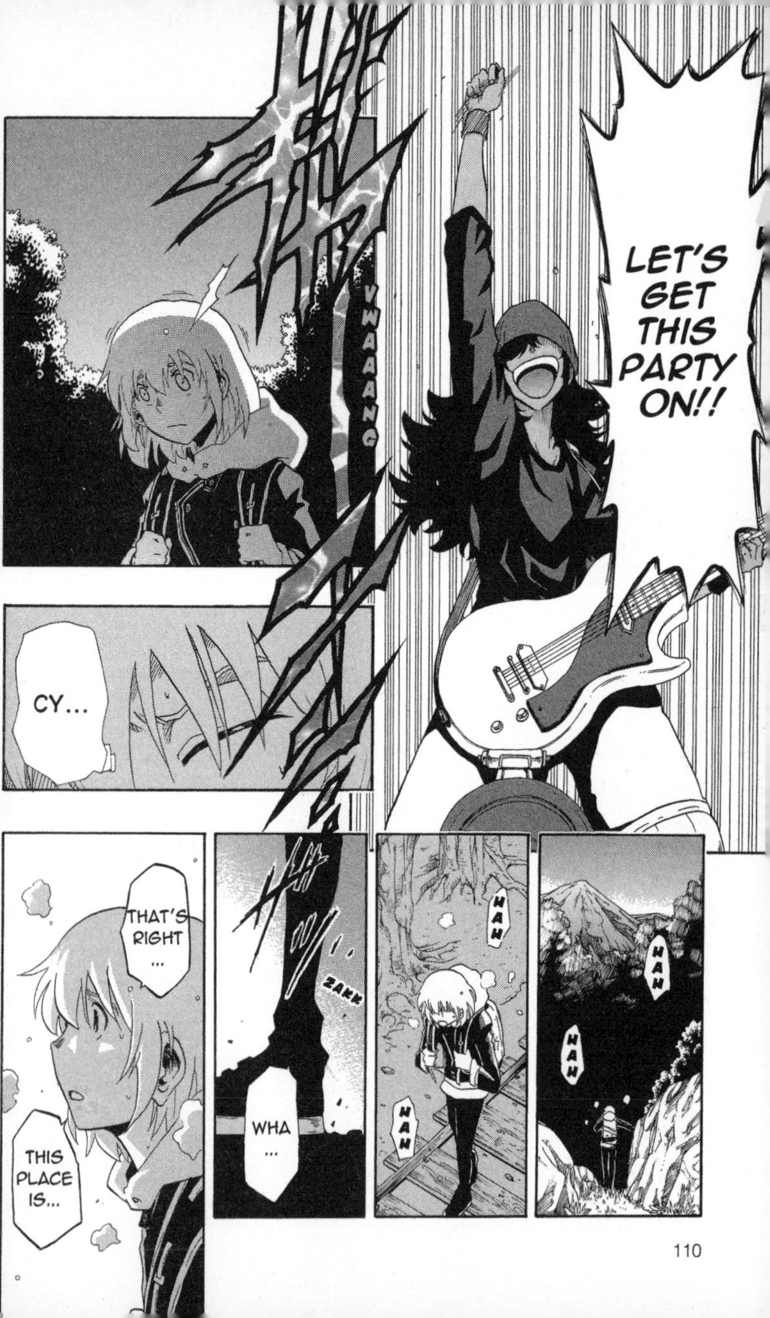
LET'S GET THIS PARTY ON!!
VWAAAANG
CY...
HAH
HAH
HAH
HAH
ZAKK
WHA...
THAT'S RIGHT...
THIS PLACE IS...

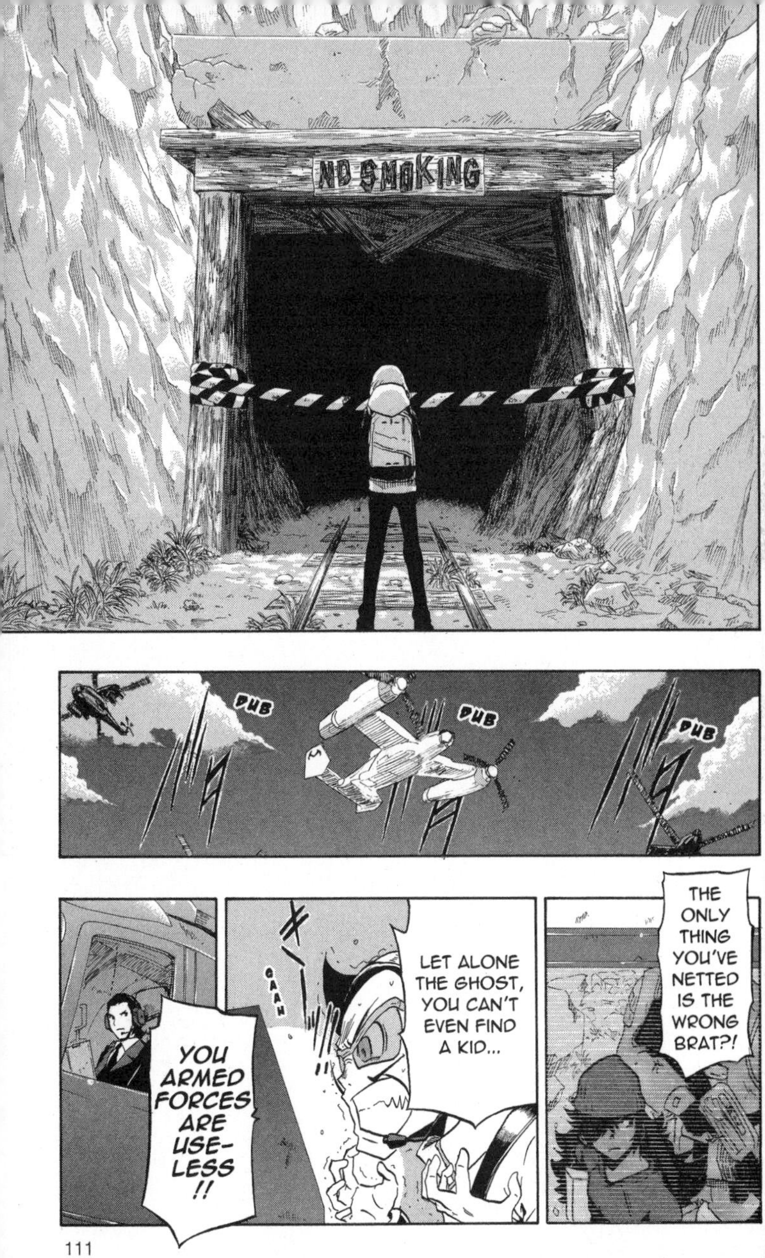
NO SMOKING
DUB
DUB
DUB
THE ONLY THING YOU'VE NETTED IS THE WRONG BRAT?!
LET ALONE THE GHOST, YOU CAN'T EVEN FIND A KID...
GAAH
YOU ARMED FORCES ARE USE-LESS!!

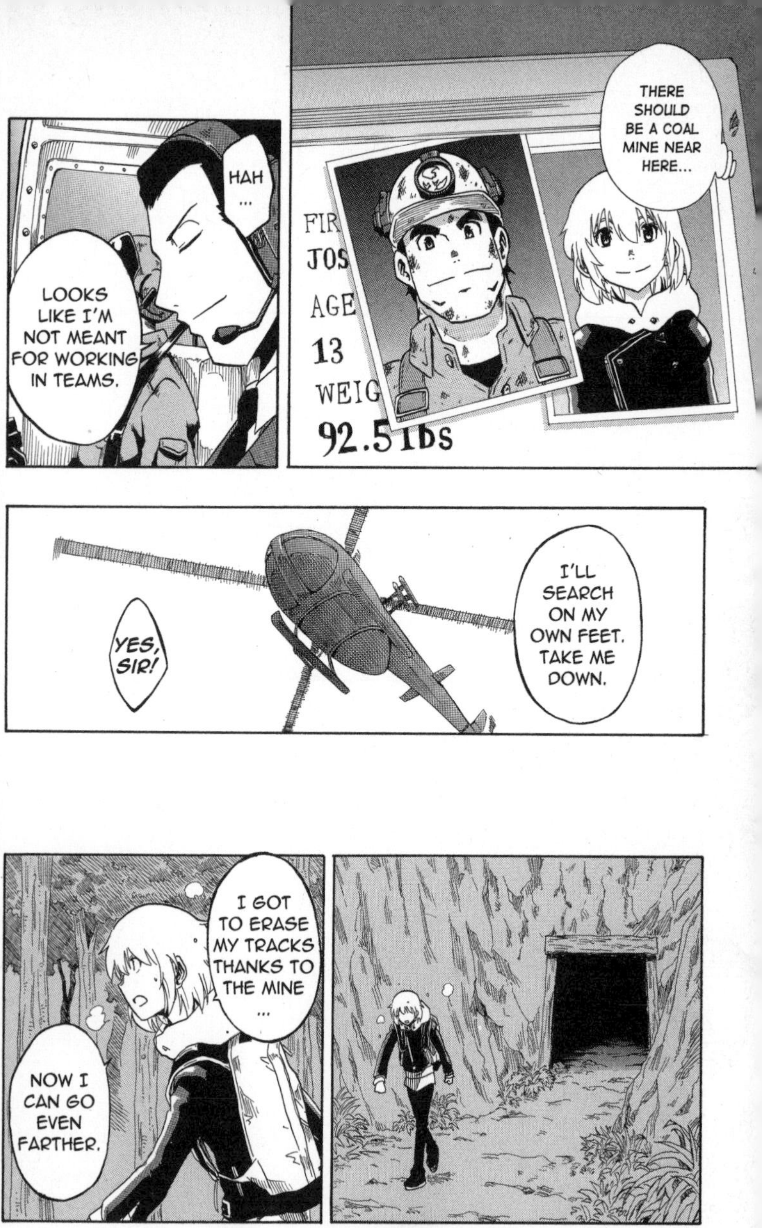
THERE SHOULD BE A COAL MINE NEAR HERE...
FIR
JOS
AGE
13
WEIG
92.5 lbs
HAH ...
LOOKS LIKE I'M NOT MEANT FOR WORKING IN TEAMS.
I'LL SEARCH ON MY OWN FEET. TAKE ME DOWN.
YES, SIR!
I GOT TO ERASE MY TRACKS THANKS TO THE MINE ...
NOW I CAN GO EVEN FARTHER.

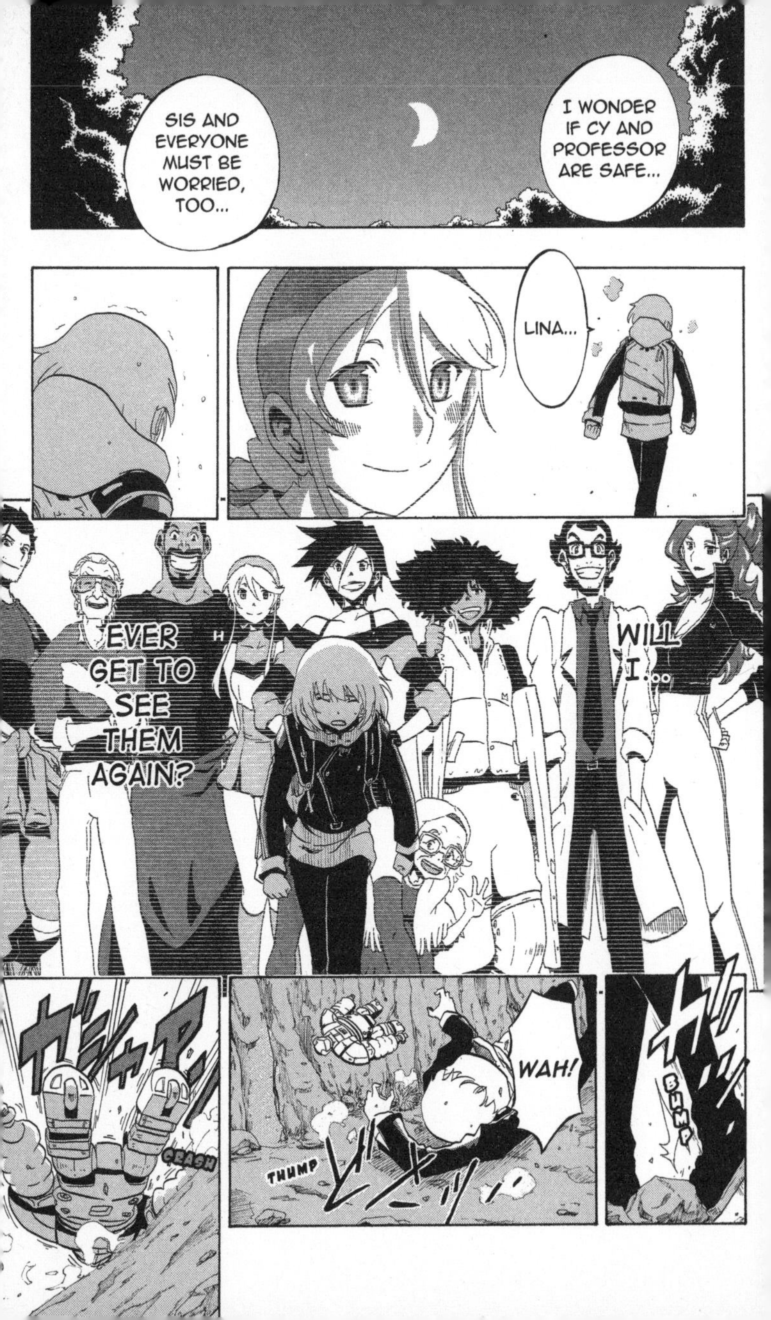
I WONDER IF CY AND PROFESSOR ARE SAFE...
SIS AND EVERYONE MUST BE WORRIED, TOO...
LINA...
WILL I...
EVER GET TO SEE THEM AGAIN?
BUMP
WAH!
THUMP
CRASH

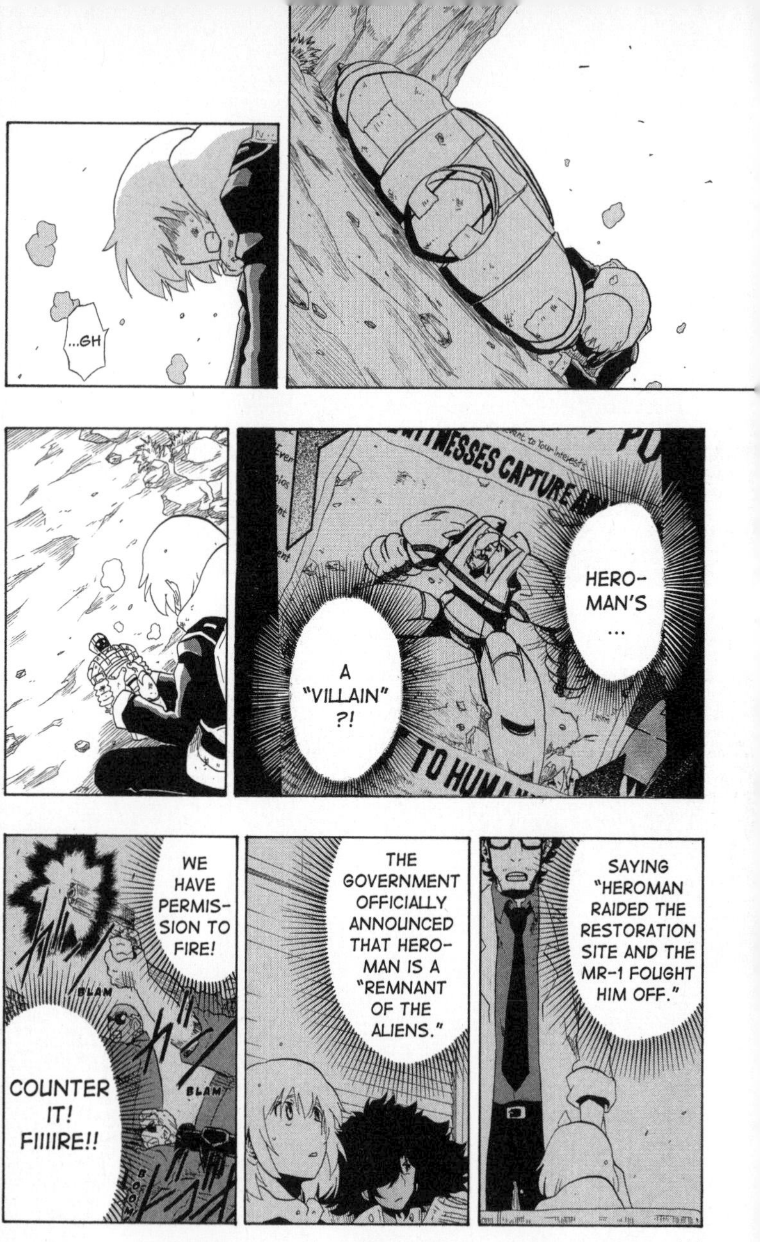
...GH
HERO-MAN'S ...
A "VILLAIN" ?!
SAYING "HEROMAN RAIDED THE RESTORATION SITE AND THE MR-1 FOUGHT HIM OFF."
THE GOVERNMENT OFFICIALLY ANNOUNCED THAT HERO-MAN IS A "REMNANT OF THE ALIENS."
WE HAVE PERMIS-SION TO FIRE!
BLAM
BLAM
COUNTER IT! FIIIRE!!
BOOM

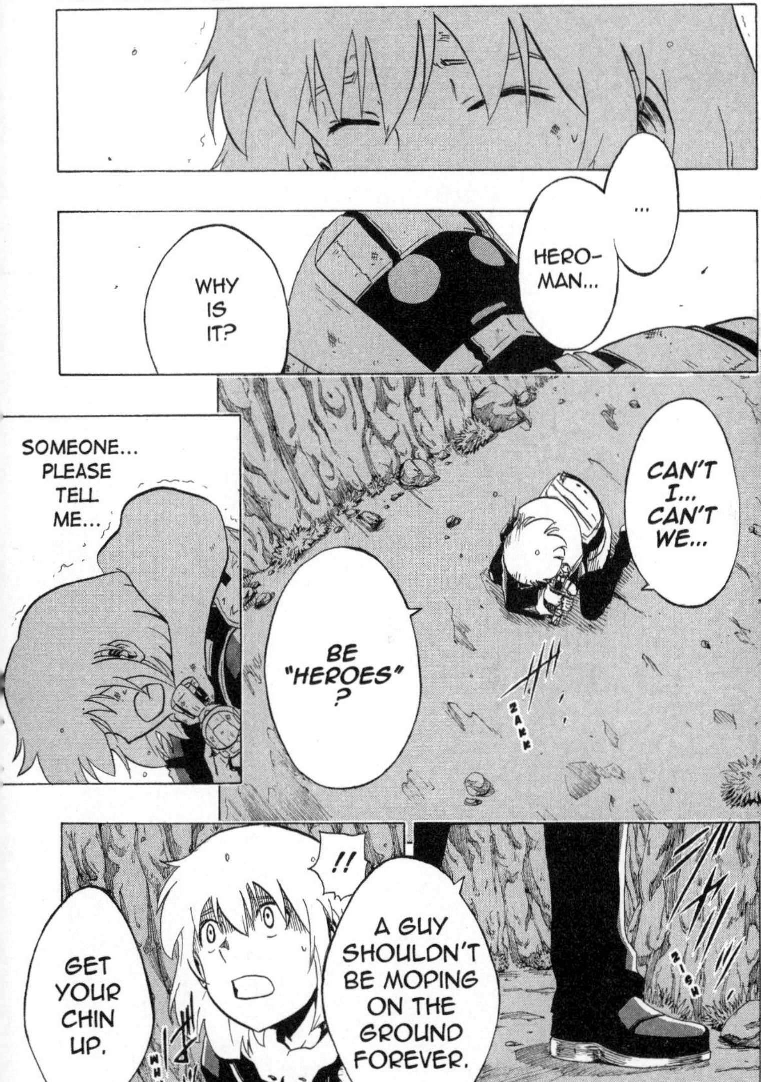
...
HERO-MAN...
WHY IS IT?
CAN'T I... CAN'T WE...
BE "HEROES"?
ZAKK
SOMEONE... PLEASE TELL ME...
ZISH
!!
A GUY SHOULDN'T BE MOPING ON THE GROUND FOREVER.
GET YOUR CHIN UP.
WHUP

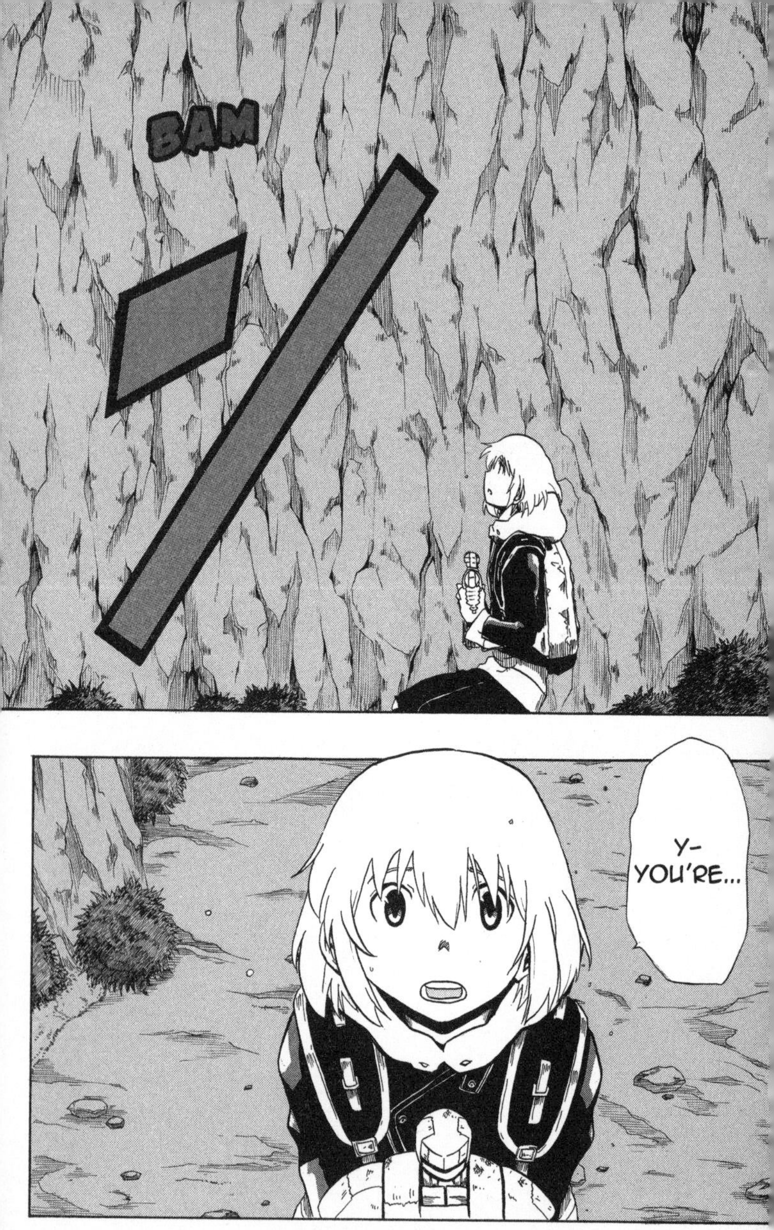
BAM
Y- YOU'RE...

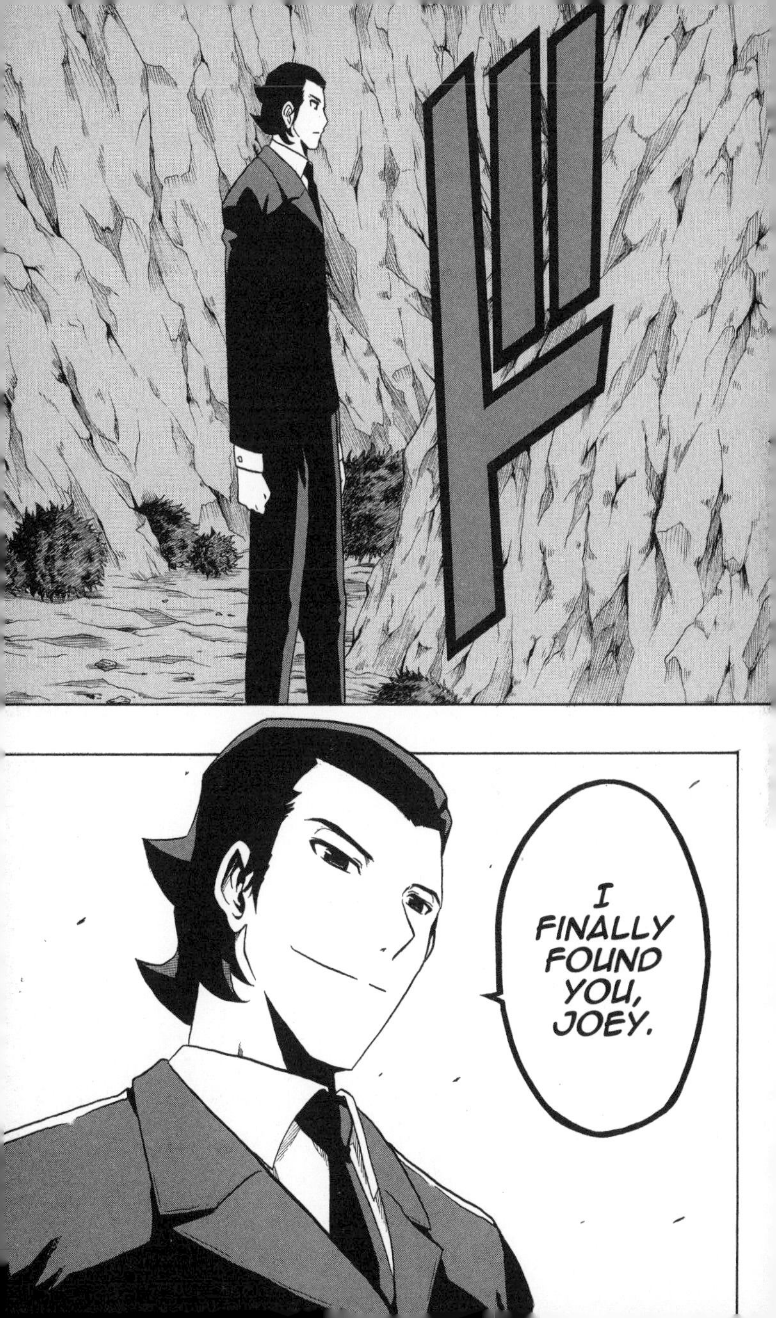
I FINALLY FOUND YOU, JOEY.

HEROMAN·4

⟨ STAFF ⟩

YUKI SUZUKI

MASATO YOSHIOKA

CHITOSHI AOKI

NOBUYUKI YAMAMORI

HIROSHI IWASAKI

TAMAKI SAITO

AYA OHTA

⟨ SPECIAL THANKS ⟩

HITOSHI NANBA

SHIGETO KOYAMA

SHINGO TAKEBA

NAOKI AMANO

Thanks ☆

. . . . .

TO BE CONTINUED

GIRL JOEY & GIRL CY

TAMON.

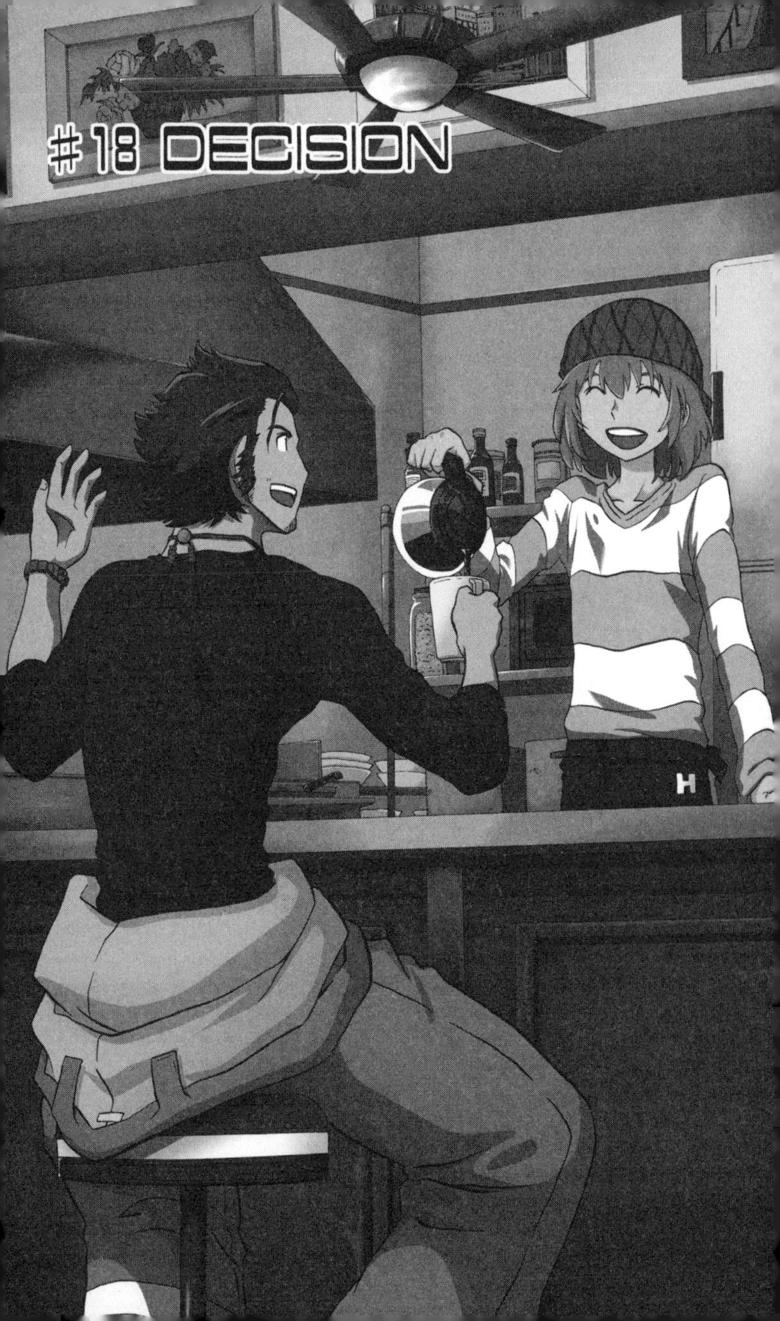
#18 DECISION
H

HEROMAN

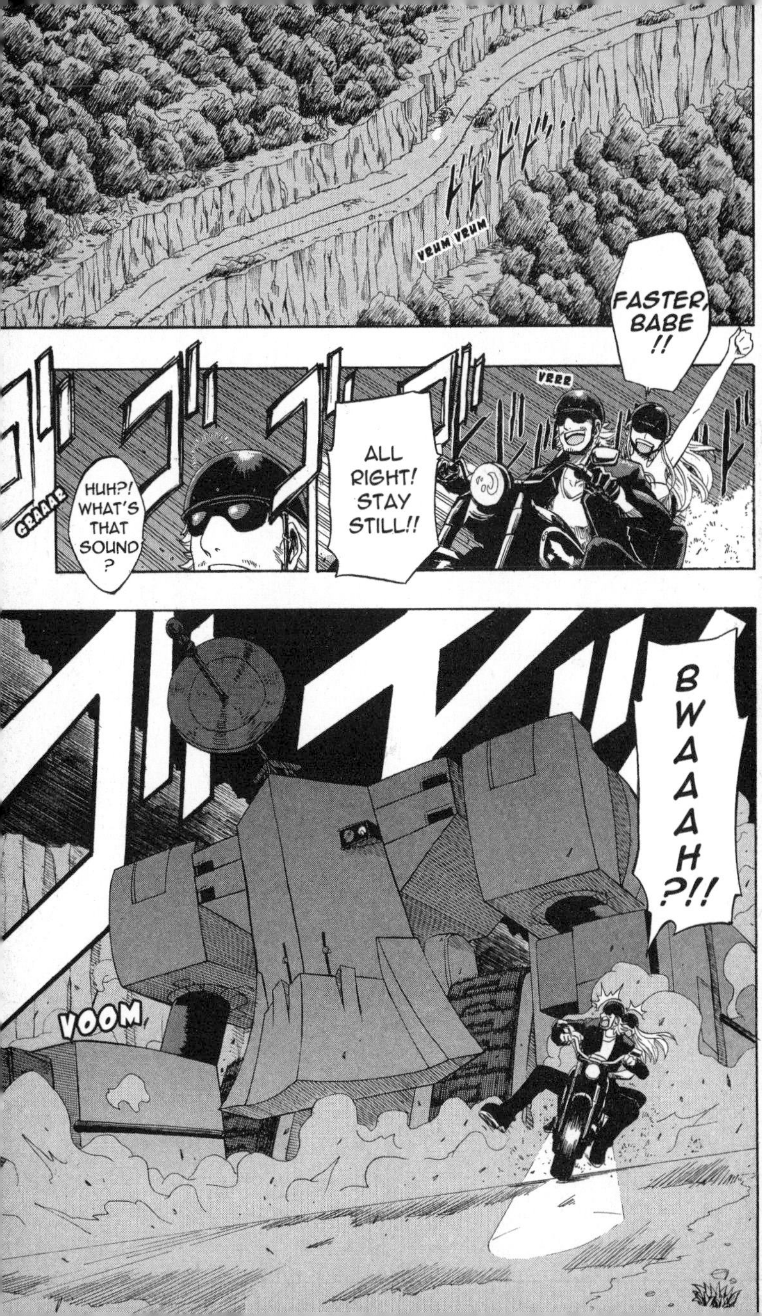
VRUM VRUM
FASTER, BABE!!
VRRR
ALL RIGHT! STAY STILL!!
HUH?! WHAT'S THAT SOUND?
GRAAAR
BWAAAAH?!!
VOOM

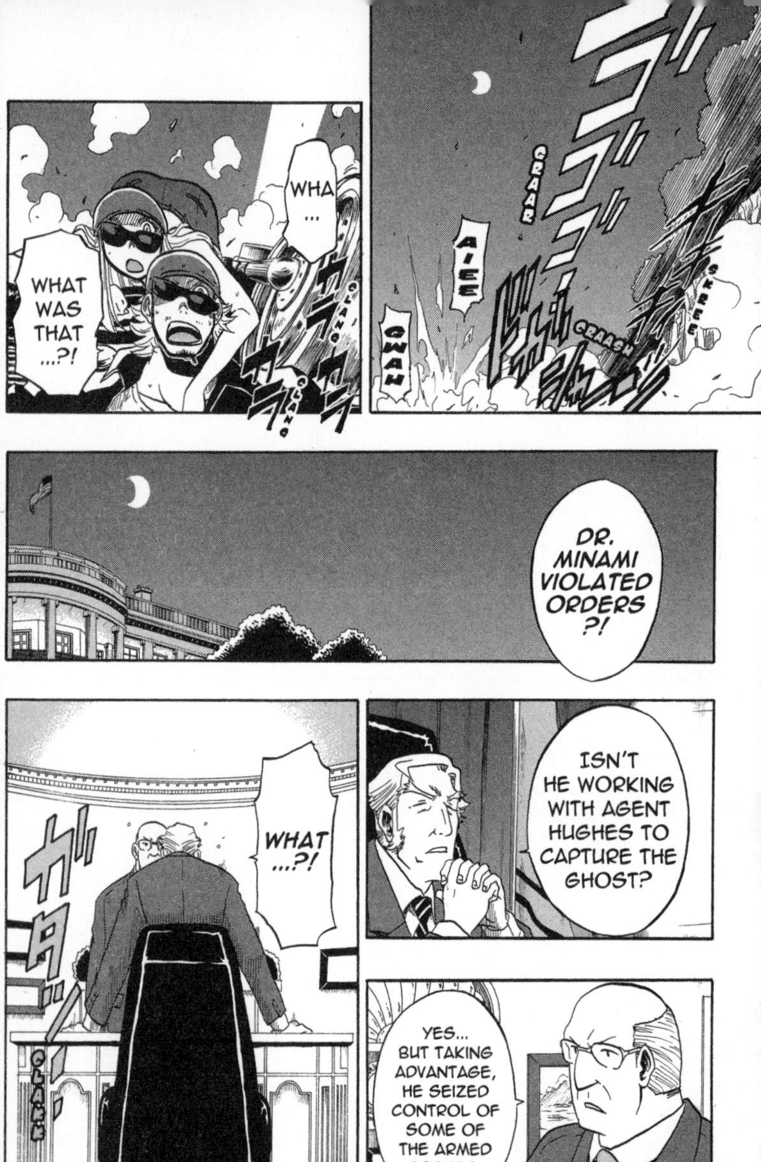
SKREEE
GRAAR
CRAASH
AIEE
GWAH
WHA...
CLANG
CLANG
WHAT WAS THAT...?!
DR. MINAMI VIOLATED ORDERS?!
ISN'T HE WORKING WITH AGENT HUGHES TO CAPTURE THE GHOST?
YES... BUT TAKING ADVANTAGE, HE SEIZED CONTROL OF SOME OF THE ARMED FORCES.
WHAT...?!
CLANK

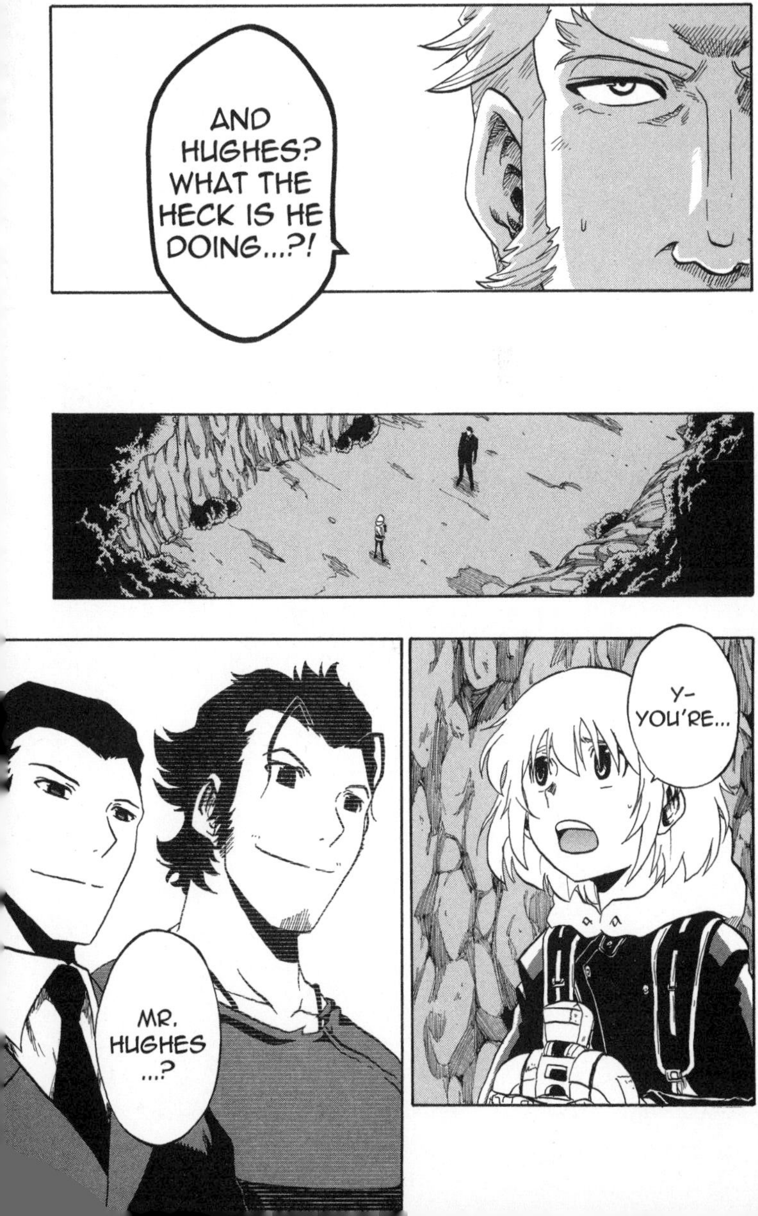
AND HUGHES? WHAT THE HECK IS HE DOING...?!
Y- YOU'RE...
MR. HUGHES ...?

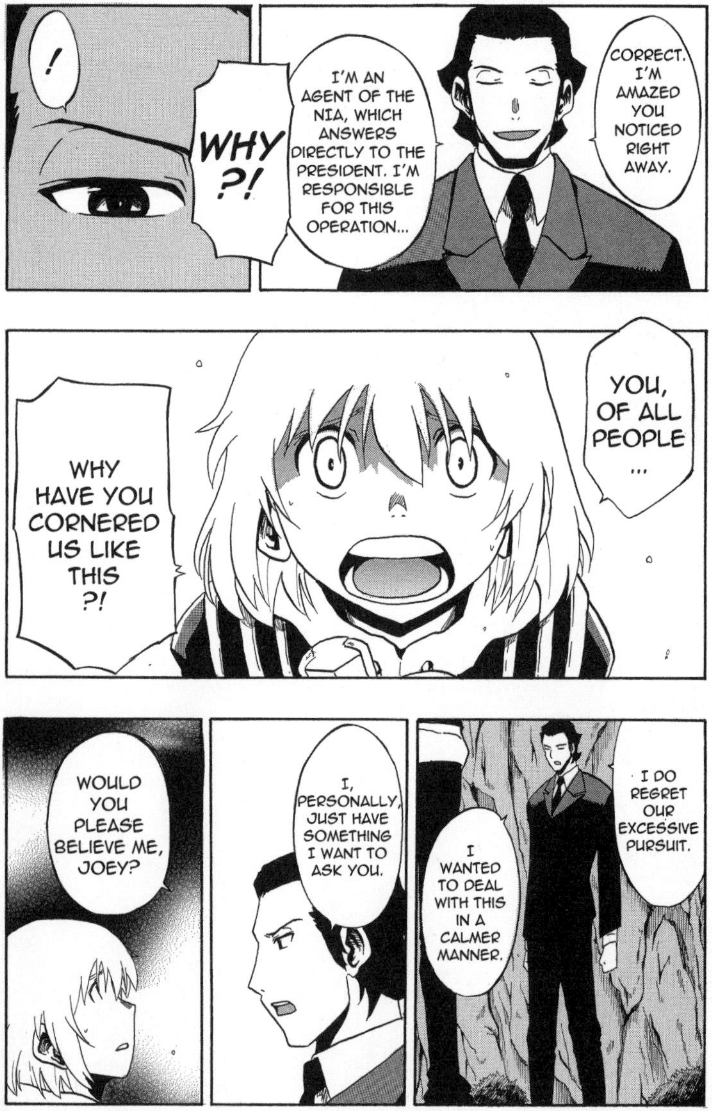
CORRECT. I'M AMAZED YOU NOTICED RIGHT AWAY.
I'M AN AGENT OF THE NIA, WHICH ANSWERS DIRECTLY TO THE PRESIDENT. I'M RESPONSIBLE FOR THIS OPERATION...
!
WHY ?!
YOU, OF ALL PEOPLE ...
WHY HAVE YOU CORNERED US LIKE THIS ?!
I DO REGRET OUR EXCESSIVE PURSUIT.
I WANTED TO DEAL WITH THIS IN A CALMER MANNER.
I, PERSONALLY, JUST HAVE SOMETHING I WANT TO ASK YOU.
WOULD YOU PLEASE BELIEVE ME, JOEY?

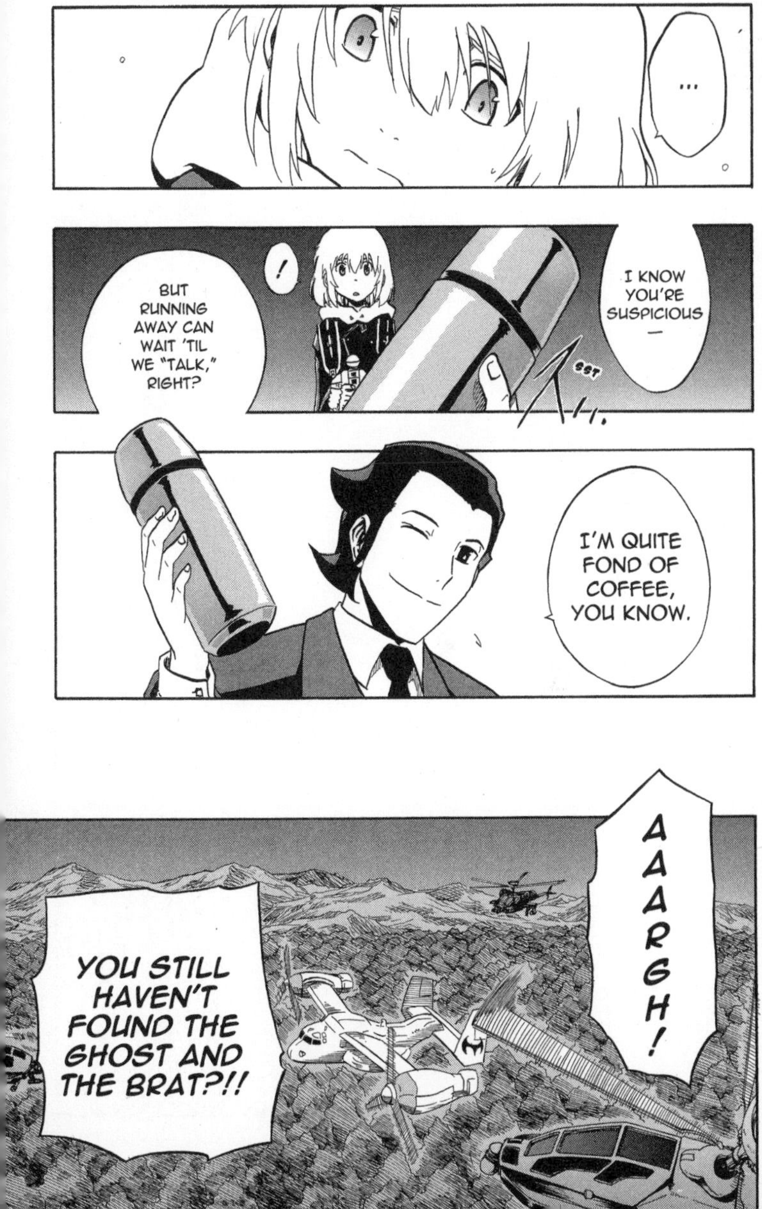
...
I KNOW YOU'RE SUSPICIOUS —
SST
!
BUT RUNNING AWAY CAN WAIT 'TIL WE "TALK," RIGHT?
I'M QUITE FOND OF COFFEE, YOU KNOW.
AAAARGH!
YOU STILL HAVEN'T FOUND THE GHOST AND THE BRAT?!!

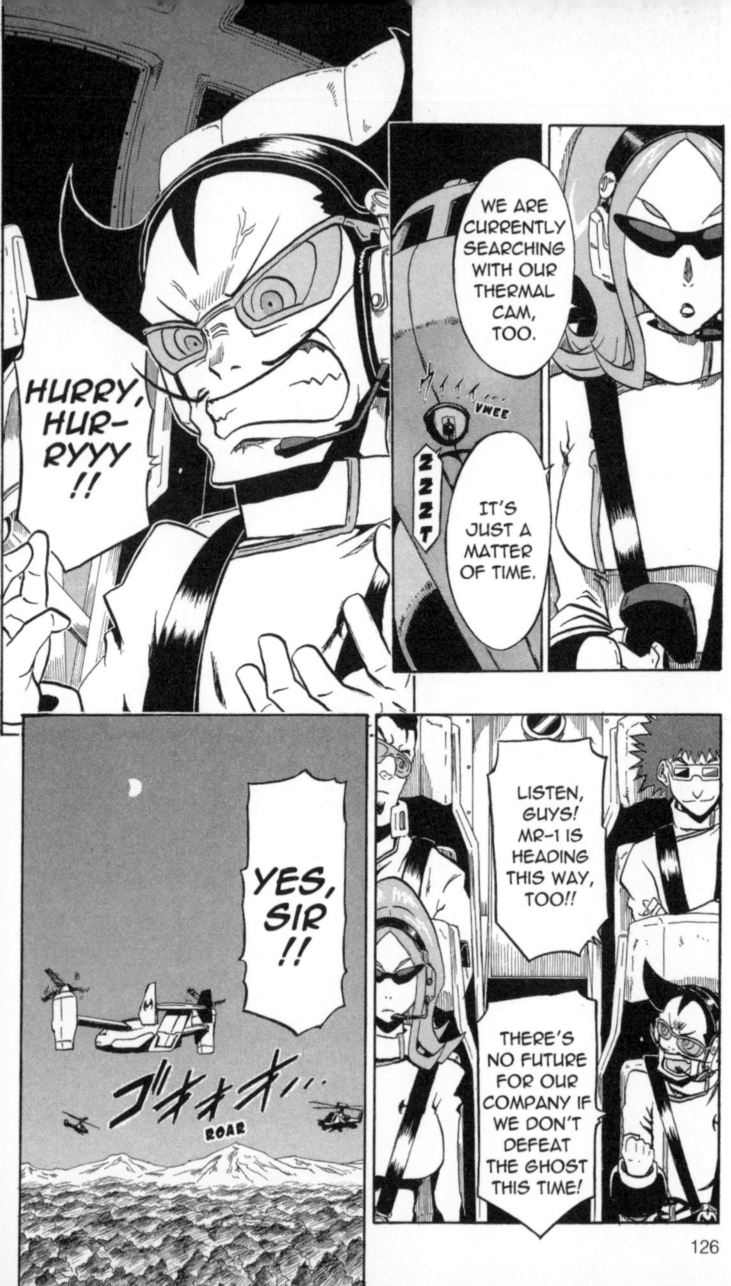
WE ARE CURRENTLY SEARCHING WITH OUR THERMAL CAM, TOO.
VWEE
ZZZT
IT'S JUST A MATTER OF TIME.
HURRY, HUR-RYYY!!
LISTEN, GUYS! MR-1 IS HEADING THIS WAY, TOO!!
THERE'S NO FUTURE FOR OUR COMPANY IF WE DON'T DEFEAT THE GHOST THIS TIME!
YES, SIR!!
ROAR

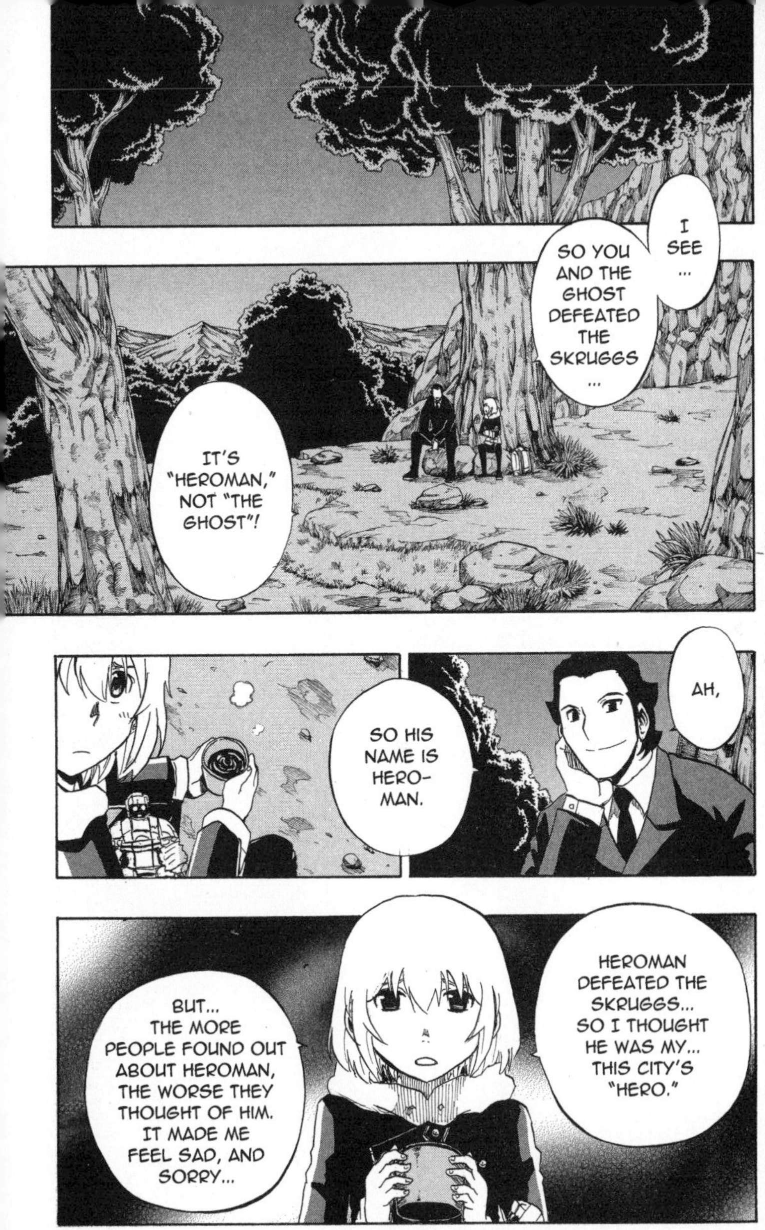

I SEE ...
SO YOU AND THE GHOST DEFEATED THE SKRUGGS ...
IT'S "HEROMAN," NOT "THE GHOST"!
AH,
SO HIS NAME IS HERO-MAN.
HEROMAN DEFEATED THE SKRUGGS... SO I THOUGHT HE WAS MY... THIS CITY'S "HERO."
BUT... THE MORE PEOPLE FOUND OUT ABOUT HEROMAN, THE WORSE THEY THOUGHT OF HIM. IT MADE ME FEEL SAD, AND SORRY...

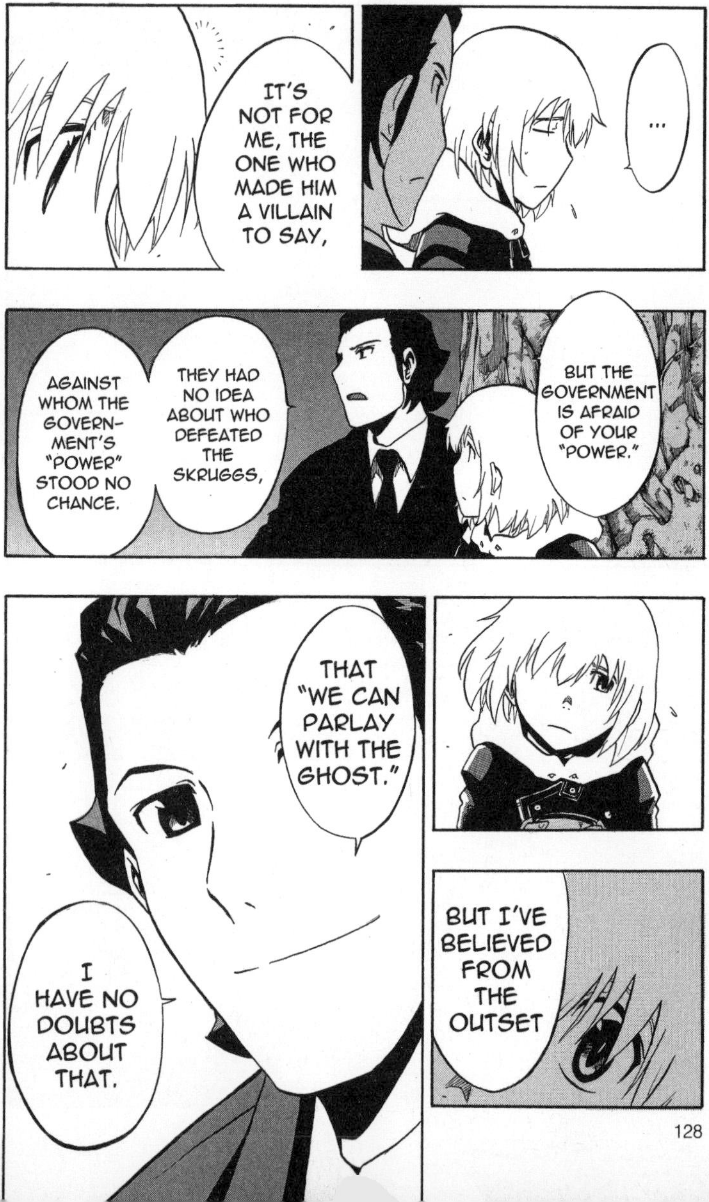
...
IT'S NOT FOR ME, THE ONE WHO MADE HIM A VILLAIN TO SAY,
BUT THE GOVERNMENT IS AFRAID OF YOUR "POWER."
THEY HAD NO IDEA ABOUT WHO DEFEATED THE SKRUGGS,
AGAINST WHOM THE GOVERN-MENT'S "POWER" STOOD NO CHANCE.
BUT I'VE BELIEVED FROM THE OUTSET
THAT "WE CAN PARLAY WITH THE GHOST."
I HAVE NO DOUBTS ABOUT THAT.

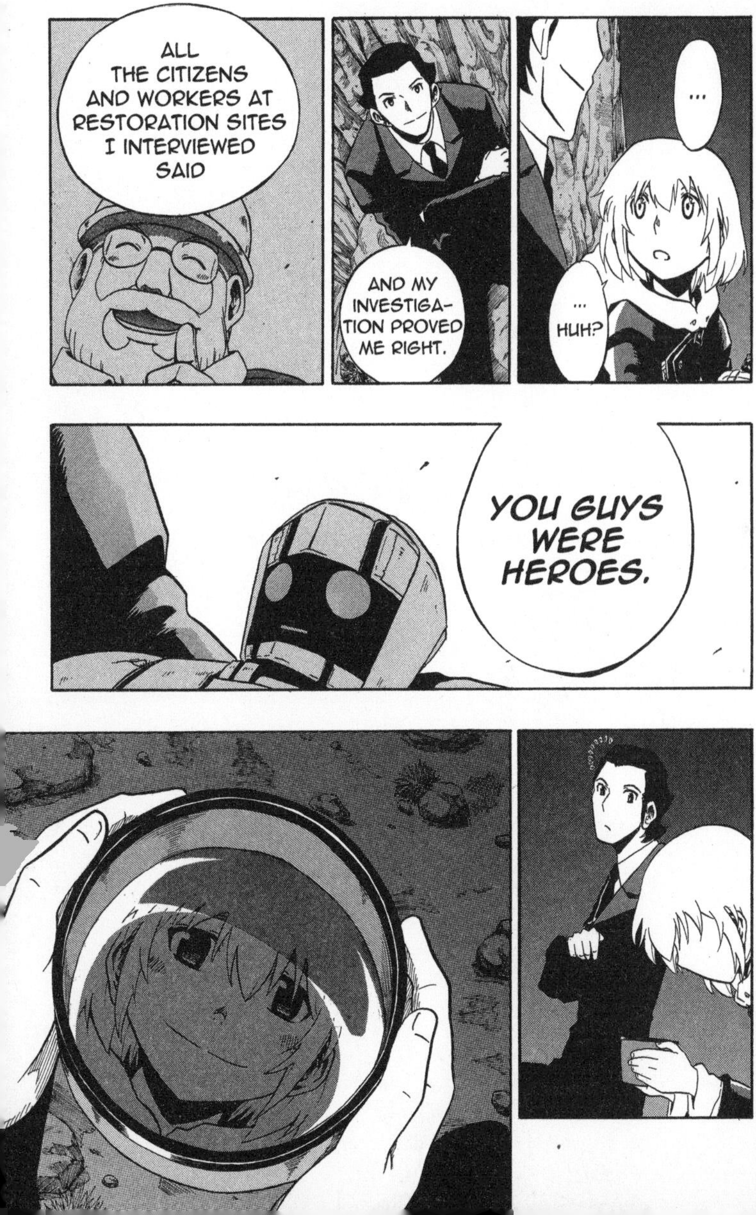
...
...
HUH?
AND MY INVESTIGA-
TION PROVED
ME RIGHT.
ALL
THE CITIZENS
AND WORKERS AT
RESTORATION SITES
I INTERVIEWED
SAID
YOU GUYS
WERE
HEROES.

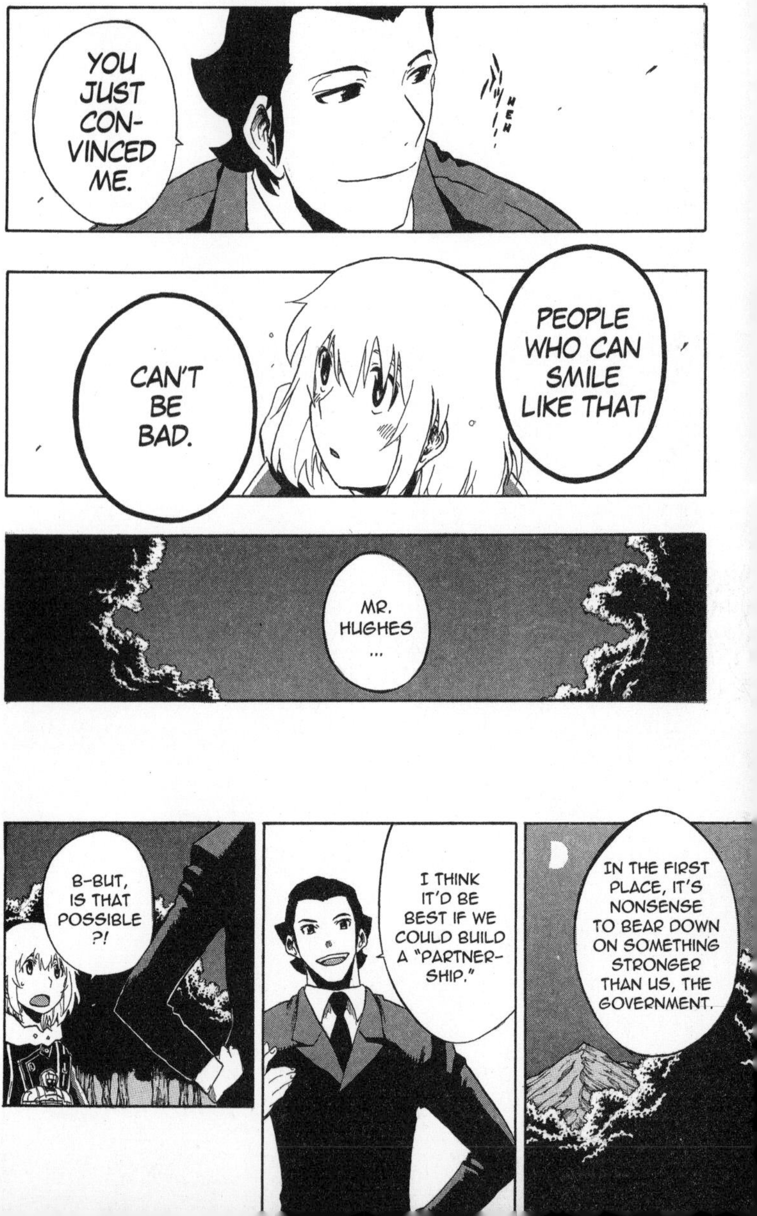
YOU JUST CON-VINCED ME.
HEH
PEOPLE WHO CAN SMILE LIKE THAT
CAN'T BE BAD.
MR. HUGHES ...
IN THE FIRST PLACE, IT'S NONSENSE TO BEAR DOWN ON SOMETHING STRONGER THAN US, THE GOVERNMENT.
I THINK IT'D BE BEST IF WE COULD BUILD A "PARTNER-SHIP."
B-BUT, IS THAT POSSIBLE ?!

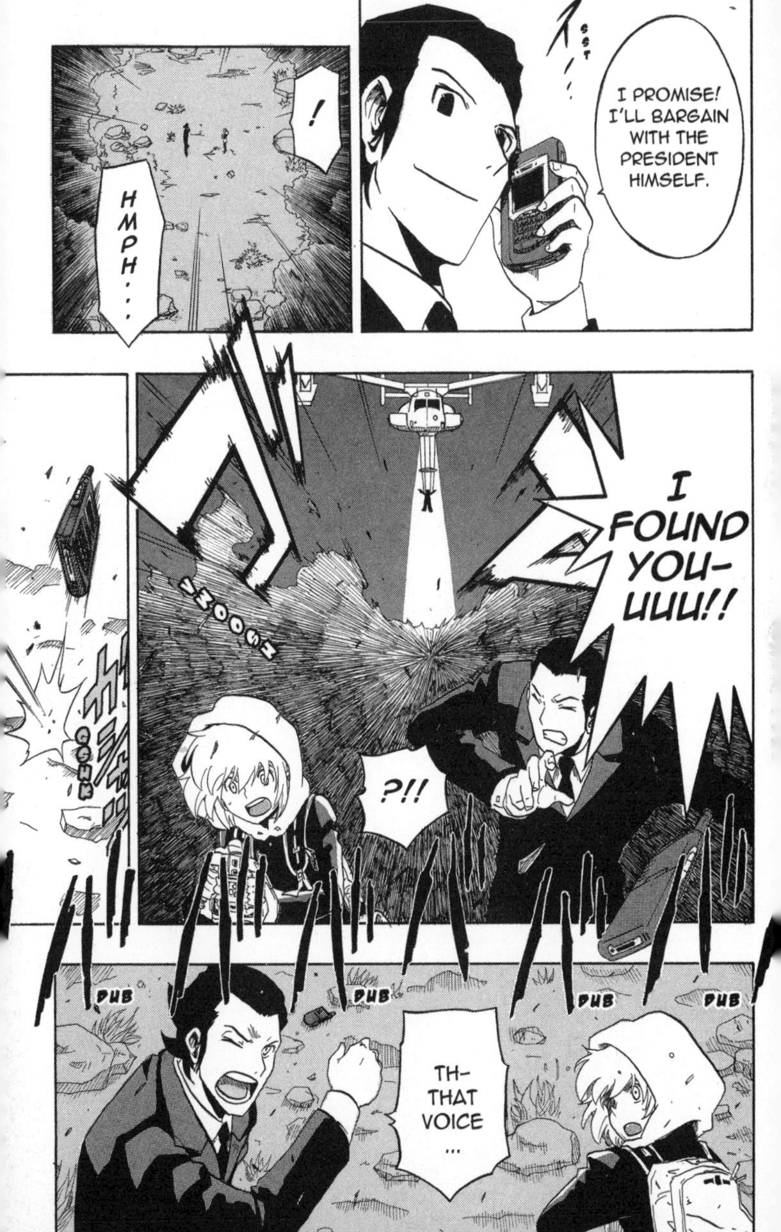
SST
I PROMISE! I'LL BARGAIN WITH THE PRESIDENT HIMSELF.
!
HMPH...
I FOUND YOU-UUU!!
WHOOSH
?!!
GSHK
DUB
DUB
DUB
DUB
TH- THAT VOICE ...

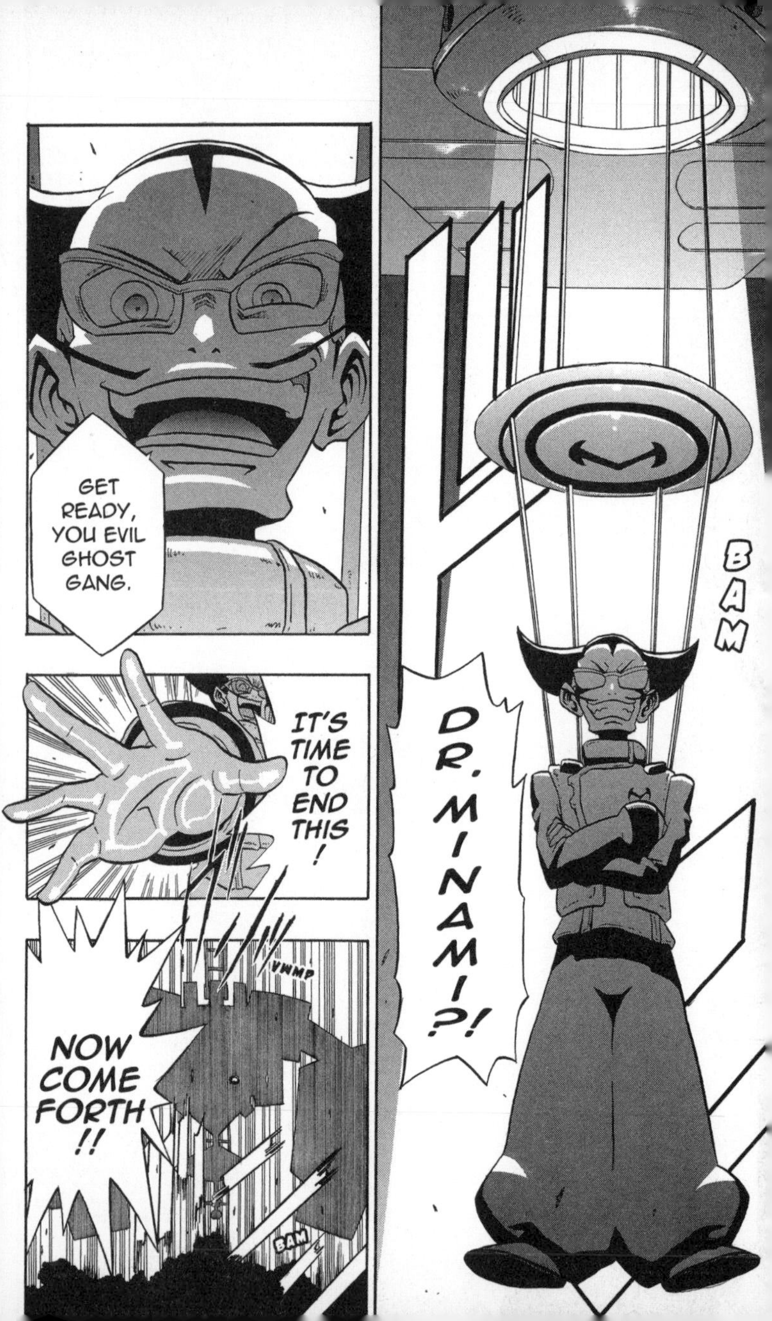
BAM
DR. MINAMI?!
GET READY, YOU EVIL GHOST GANG.
IT'S TIME TO END THIS!
VWMP
NOW COME FORTH!!
BAM

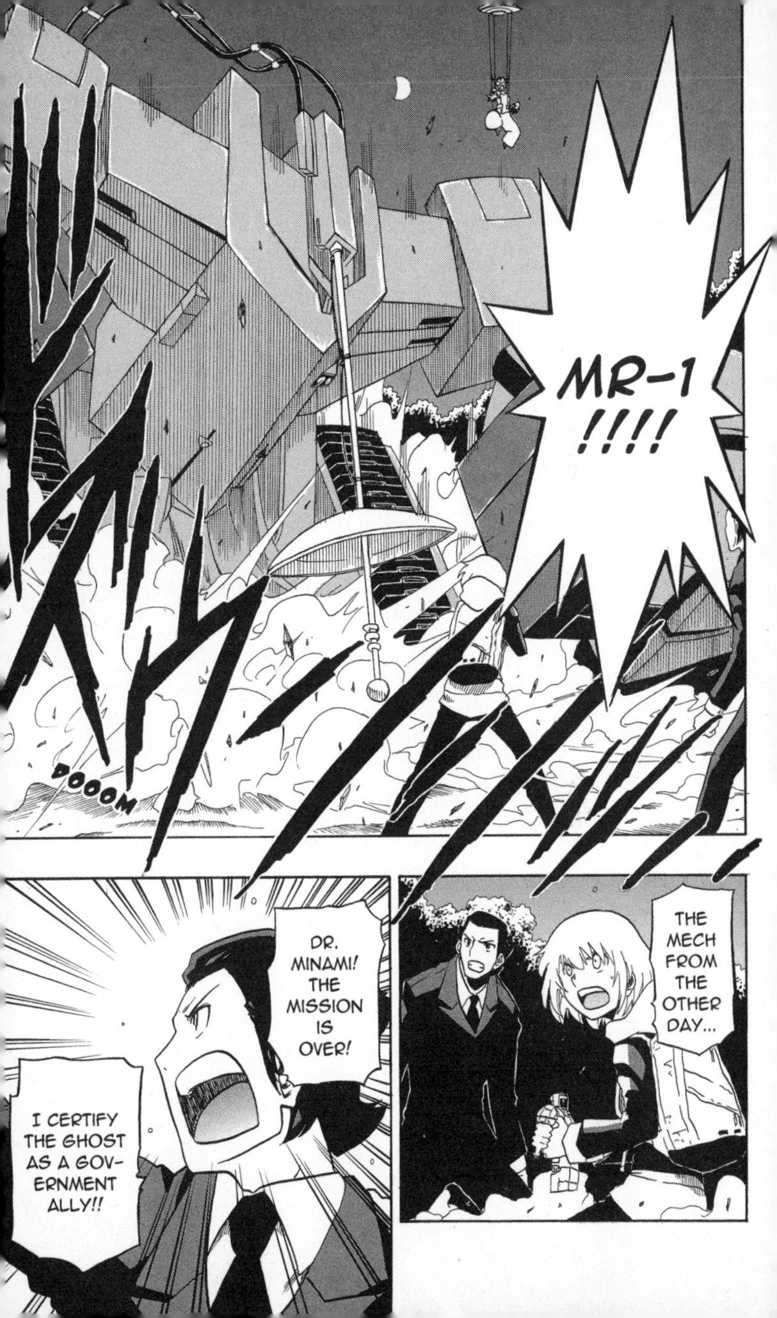
MR-1 !!!!
DOOOM
THE MECH FROM THE OTHER DAY...
DR. MINAMI! THE MISSION IS OVER!
I CERTIFY THE GHOST AS A GOV-ERNMENT ALLY!!

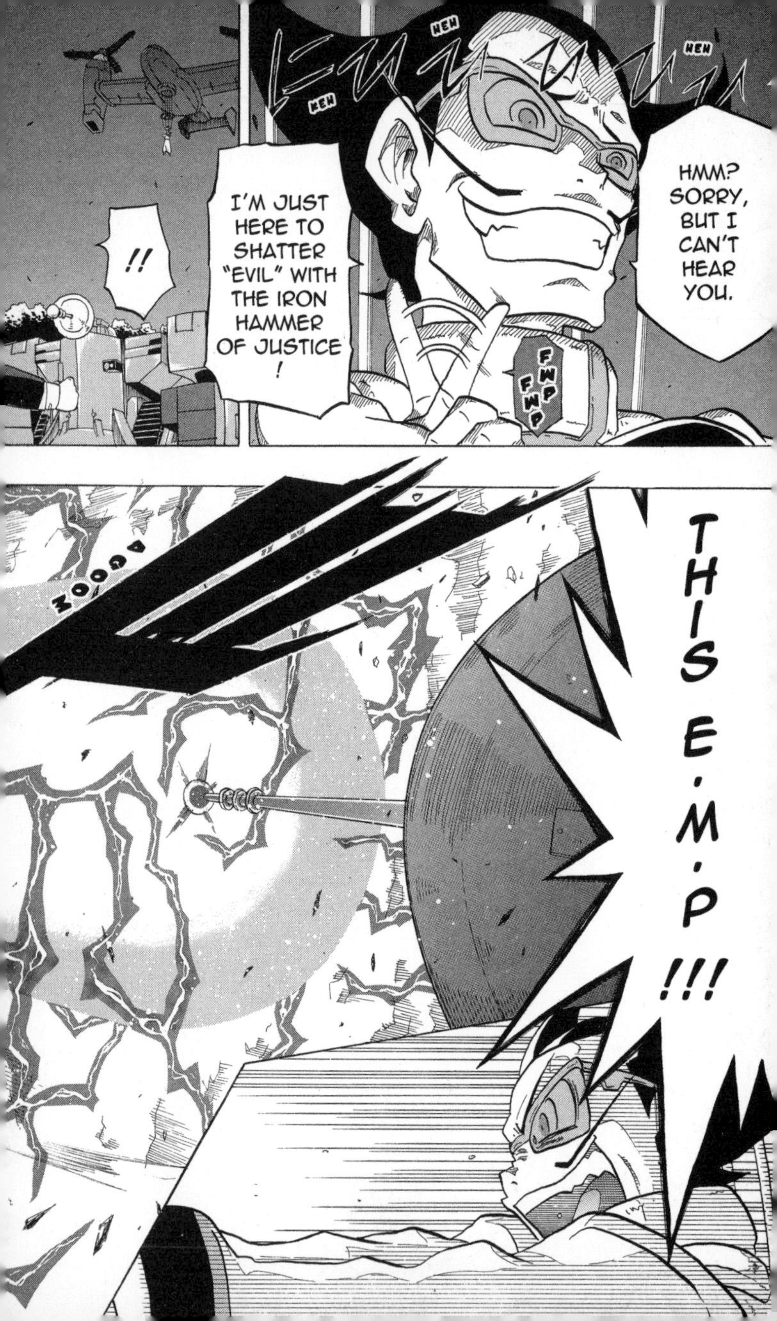
HEH
HEH
HEH
HMM? SORRY, BUT I CAN'T HEAR YOU.
I'M JUST HERE TO SHATTER "EVIL" WITH THE IRON HAMMER OF JUSTICE!
FWP FWP
!!
THIS E.M.P!!!
DOOM

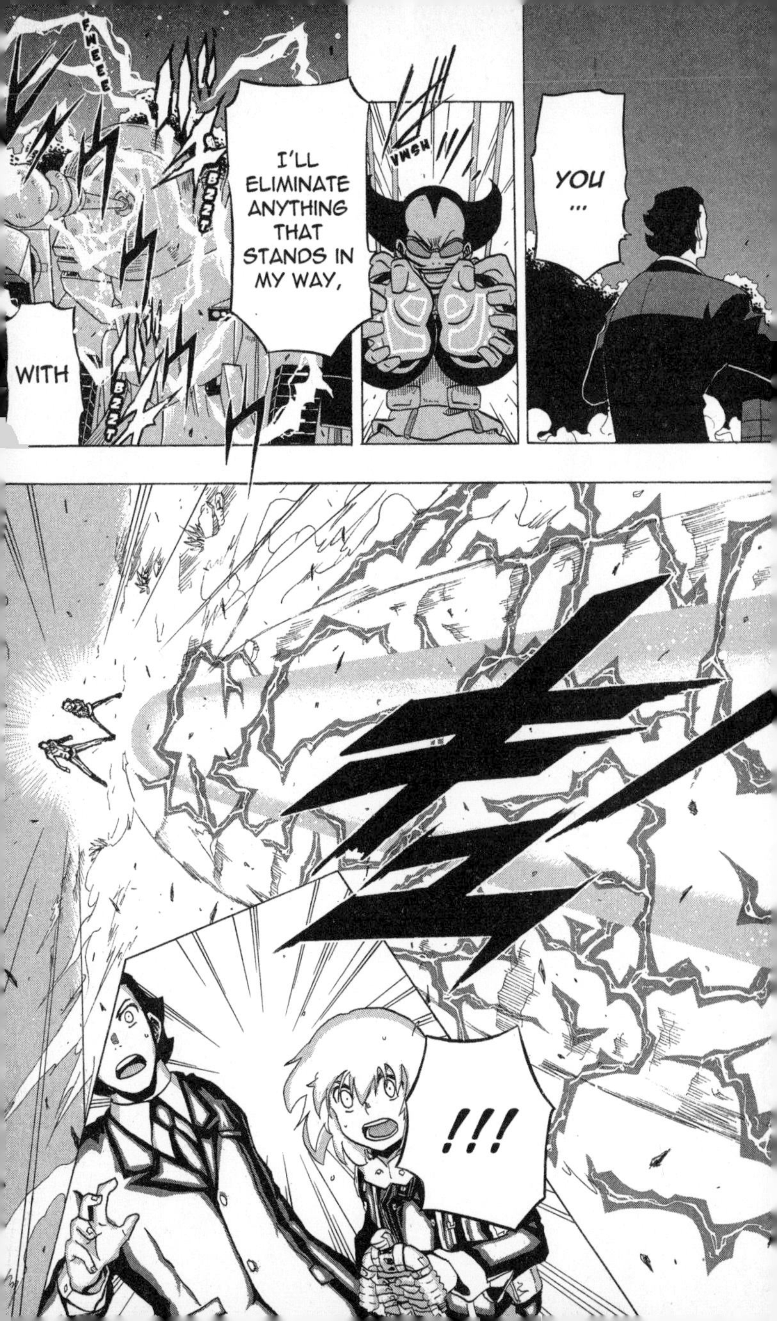

YOU ...
VWSH
I'LL ELIMINATE ANYTHING THAT STANDS IN MY WAY,
FWEEE
BZZT
BZZT
WITH
!!!

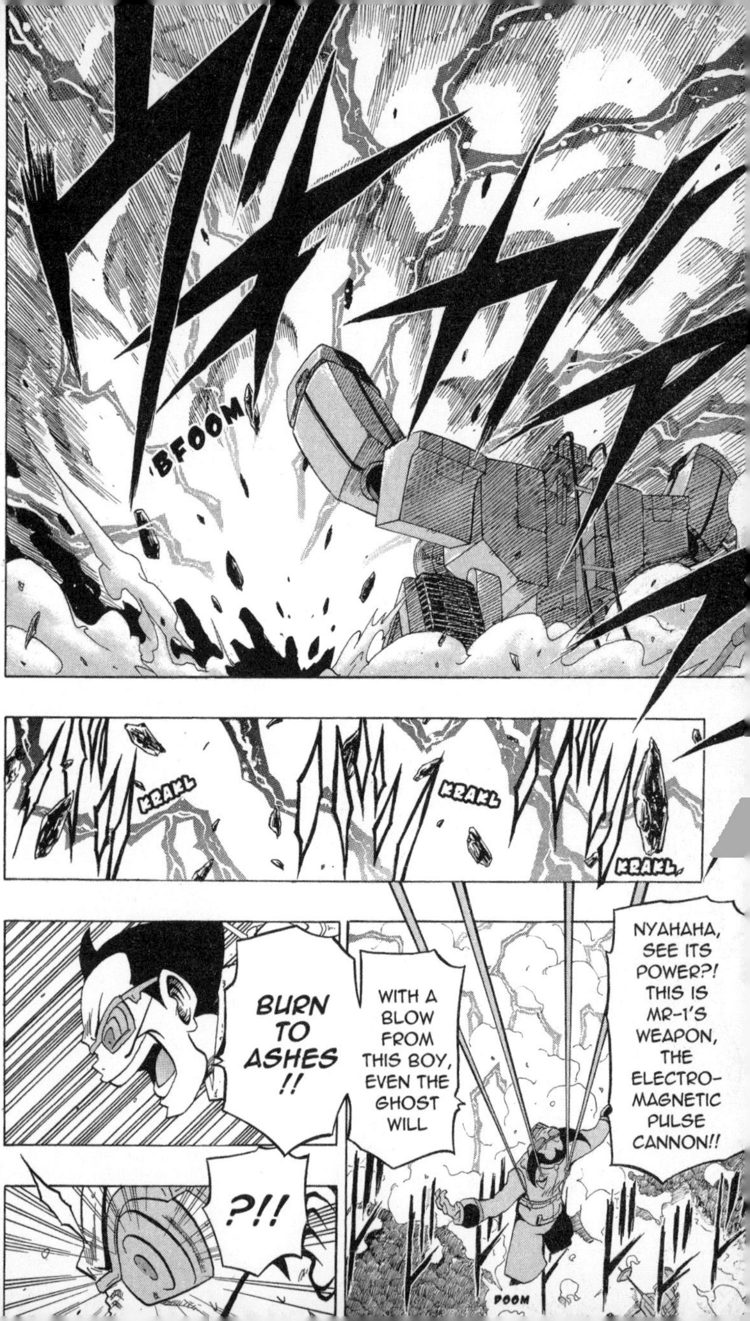
BFOOM
KRAKL
KRAKL
KRAKL
NYAHAHA, SEE ITS POWER?! THIS IS MR-1'S WEAPON, THE ELECTRO-MAGNETIC PULSE CANNON!!
WITH A BLOW FROM THIS BOY, EVEN THE GHOST WILL
DOOM
BURN TO ASHES !!
?!!

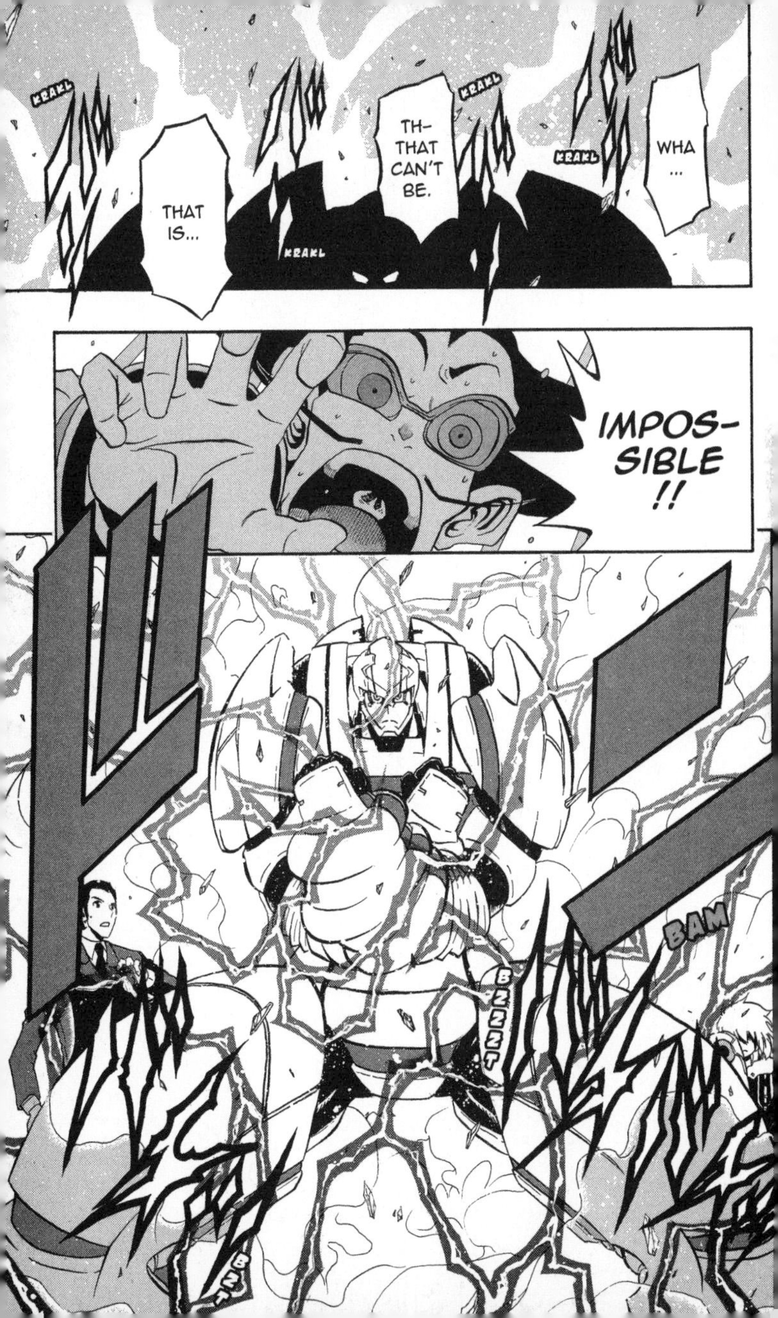
KRAKL
WHA ...
KRAKL
TH- THAT CAN'T BE.
KRAKL
THAT IS...
KRAKL
IMPOSSIBLE!!
BAM
BZZZT
BZT

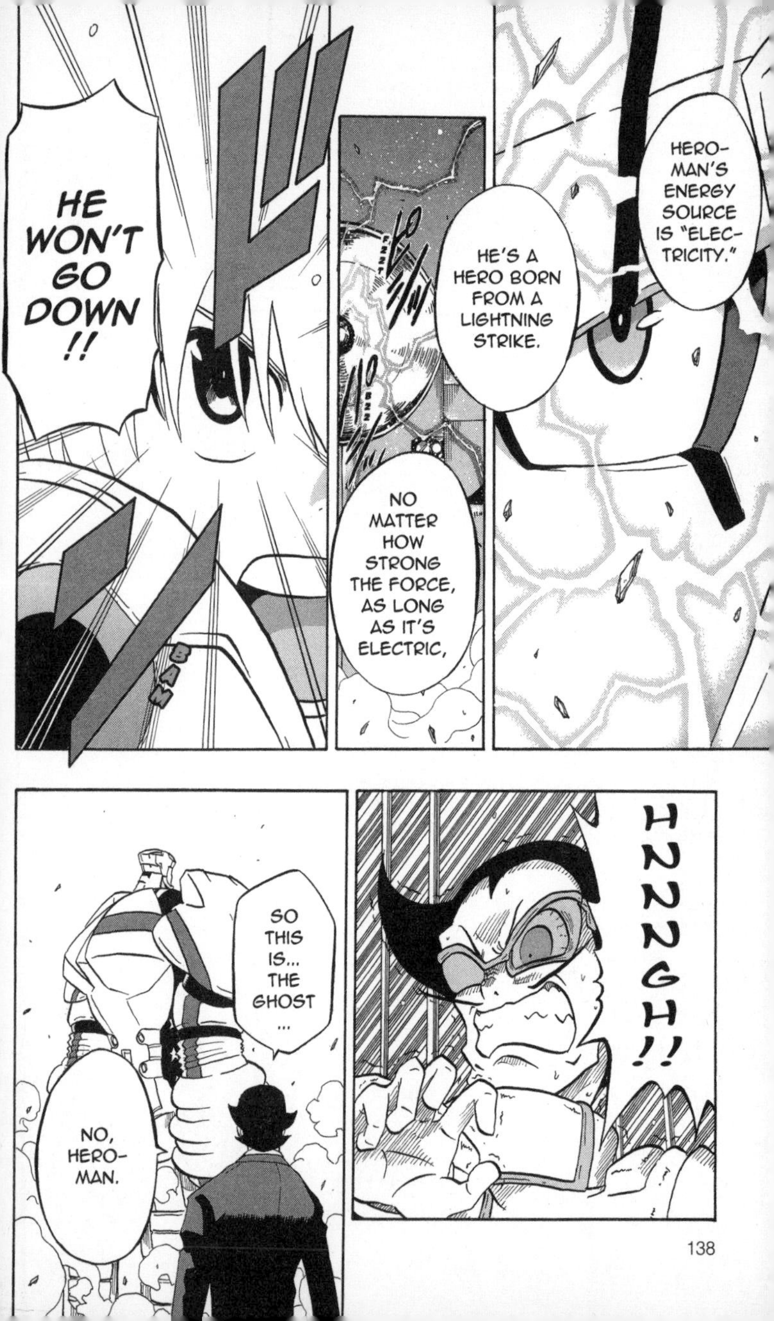
HERO-MAN'S ENERGY SOURCE IS "ELECTRICITY."
HE'S A HERO BORN FROM A LIGHTNING STRIKE.
FZZT
NO MATTER HOW STRONG THE FORCE, AS LONG AS IT'S ELECTRIC,
HE WON'T GO DOWN!!
BAM
HNNNGH!!
SO THIS IS... THE GHOST...
NO, HERO-MAN.

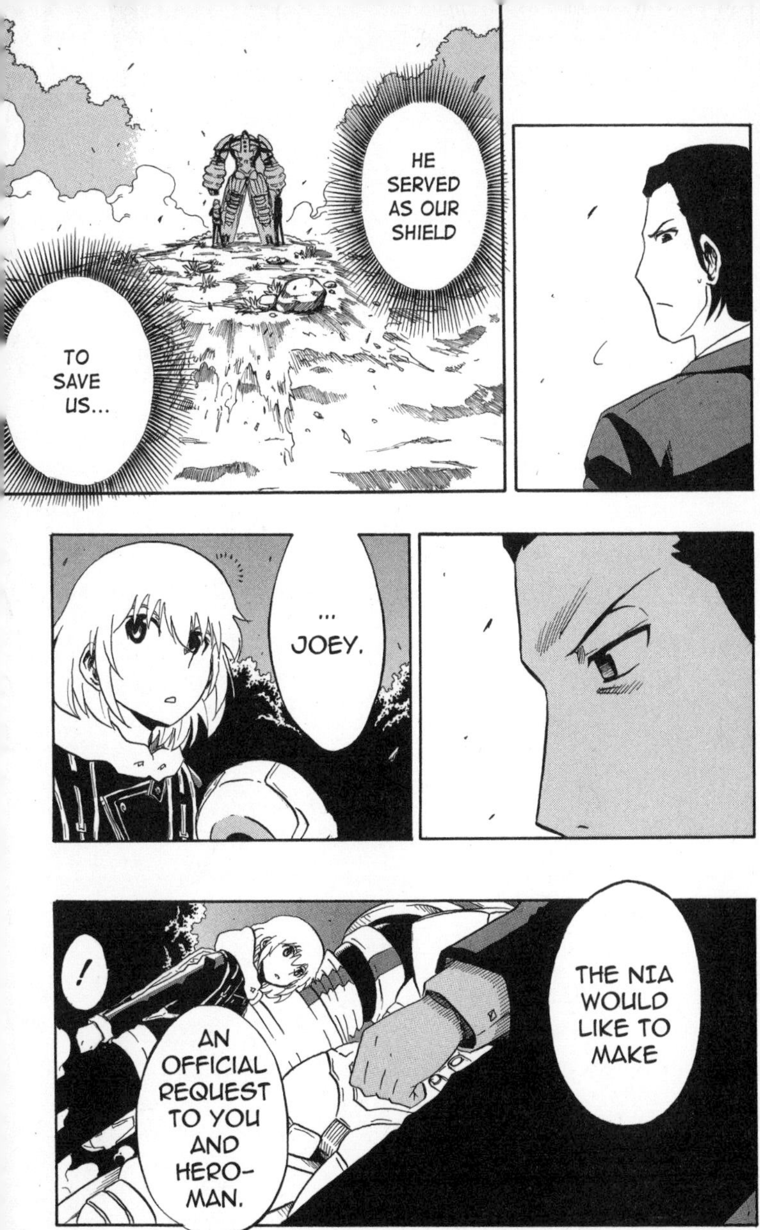
HE SERVED AS OUR SHIELD
TO SAVE US...
... JOEY.
THE NIA WOULD LIKE TO MAKE
!
AN OFFICIAL REQUEST TO YOU AND HERO-MAN.

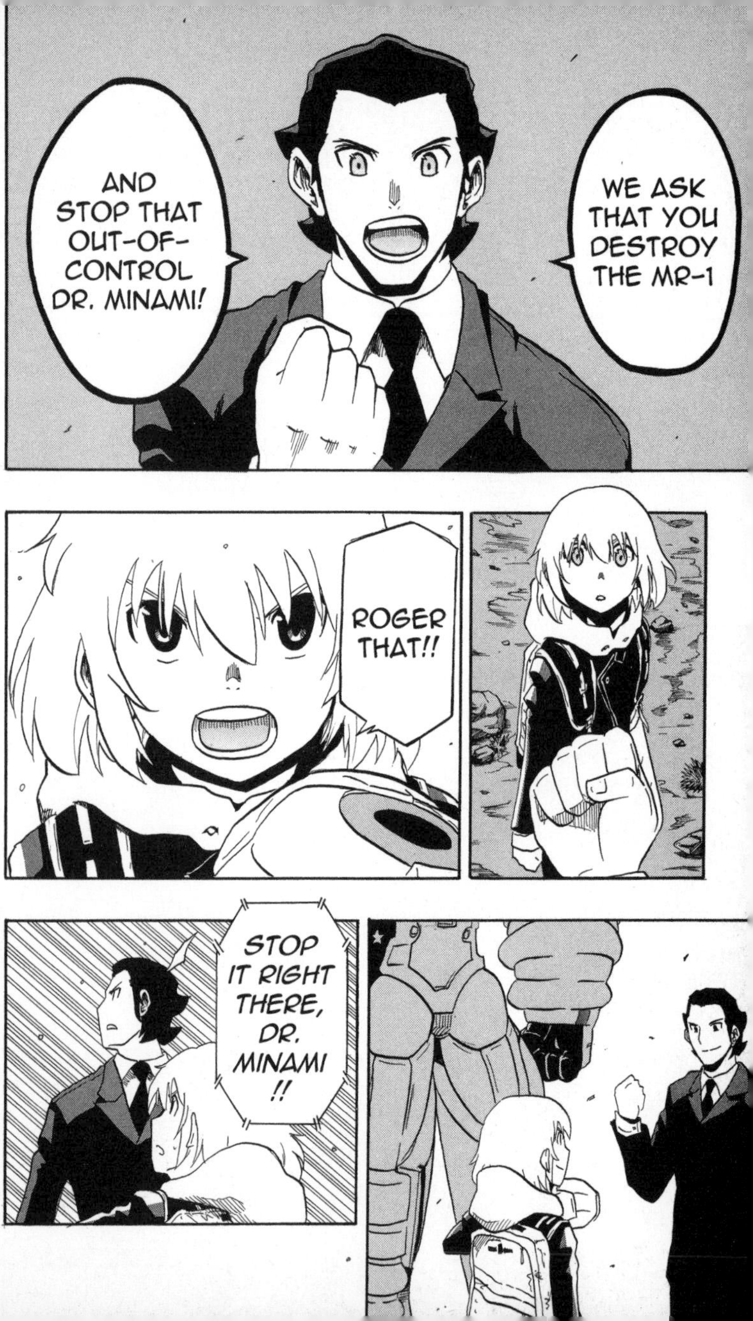
WE ASK THAT YOU DESTROY THE MR-1
AND STOP THAT OUT-OF-CONTROL DR. MINAMI!
ROGER THAT!!
STOP IT RIGHT THERE, DR. MINAMI!!

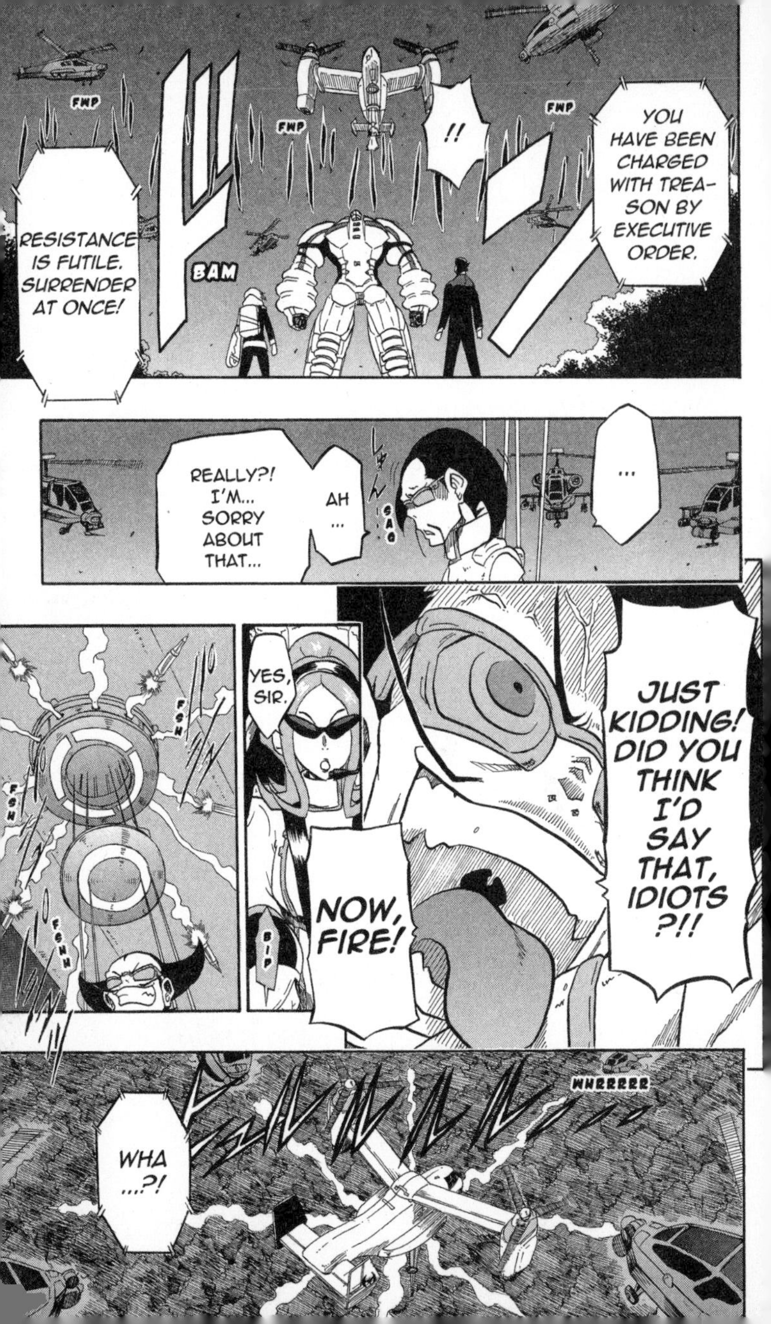
YOU HAVE BEEN CHARGED WITH TREASON BY EXECUTIVE ORDER.
FWP
!!
FWP
FWP
BAM
RESISTANCE IS FUTILE. SURRENDER AT ONCE!
...
SAG
AH ...
REALLY?! I'M... SORRY ABOUT THAT...
JUST KIDDING! DID YOU THINK I'D SAY THAT, IDIOTS?!!
NOW, FIRE!
YES, SIR.
BIP
FSH
FSH
FSHH
WHRRRRR
WHA ...?!

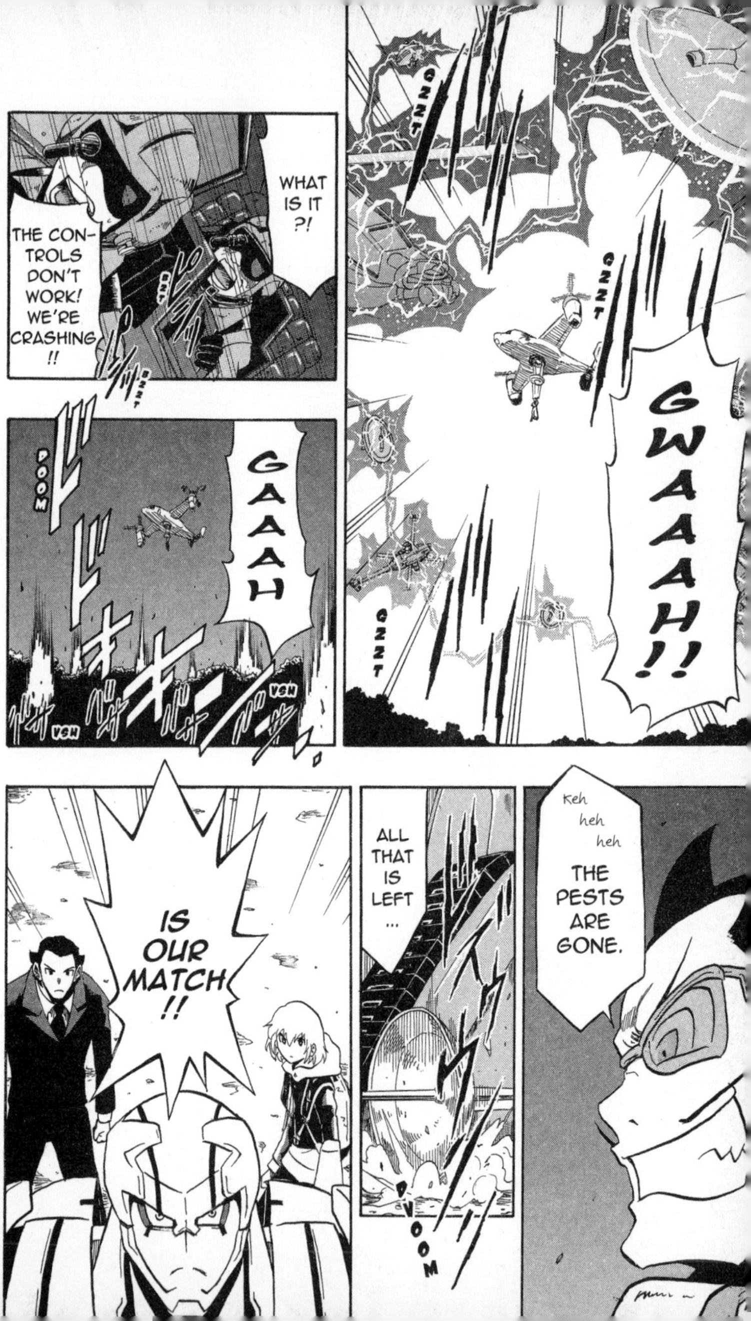
GZZT
GZZT
GWAAAAH!!
GZZT
WHAT IS IT ?!
THE CON-TROLS DON'T WORK! WE'RE CRASHING !!
BZZT
GAAAH
DOOM
VSH
VSH
Keh heh heh
THE PESTS ARE GONE.
ALL THAT IS LEFT ...
DVOOM
IS OUR MATCH !!

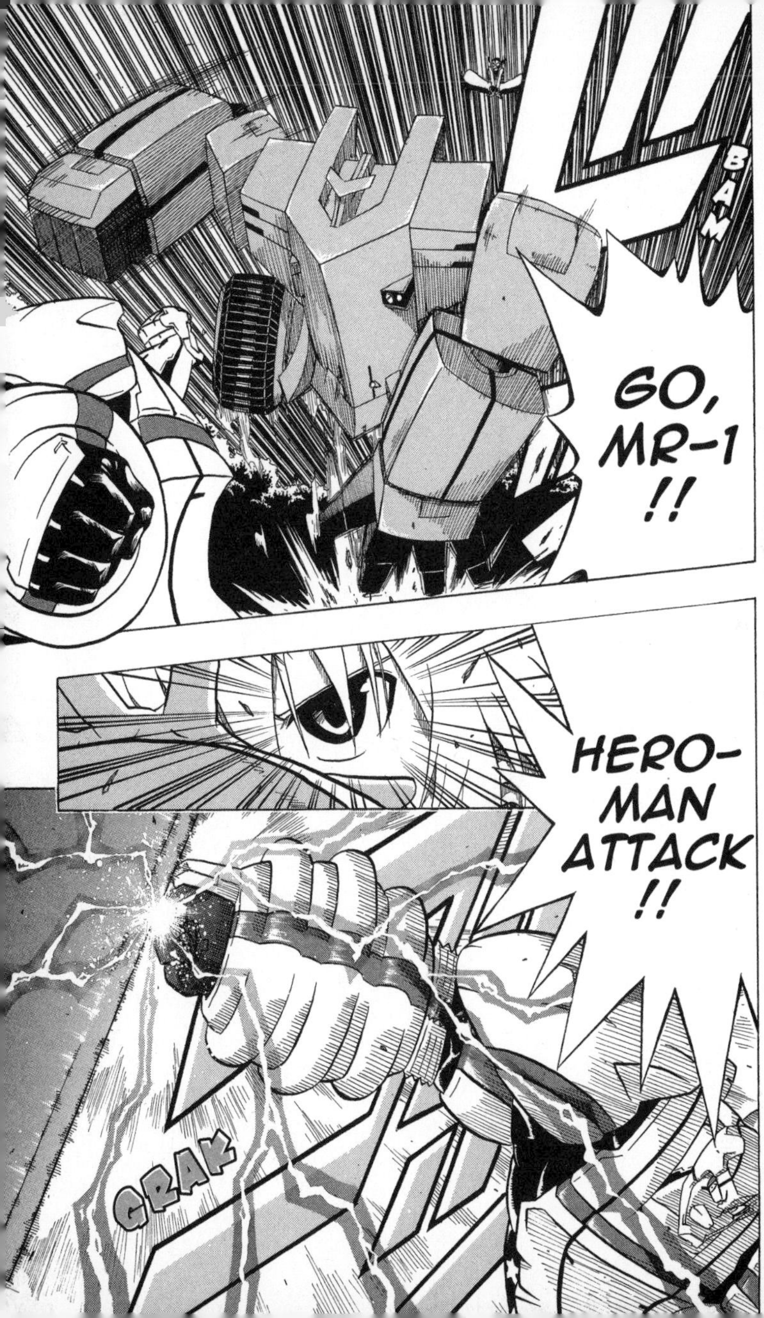
BAM
GO, MR-1!!
HERO-MAN ATTACK!!
GRAK

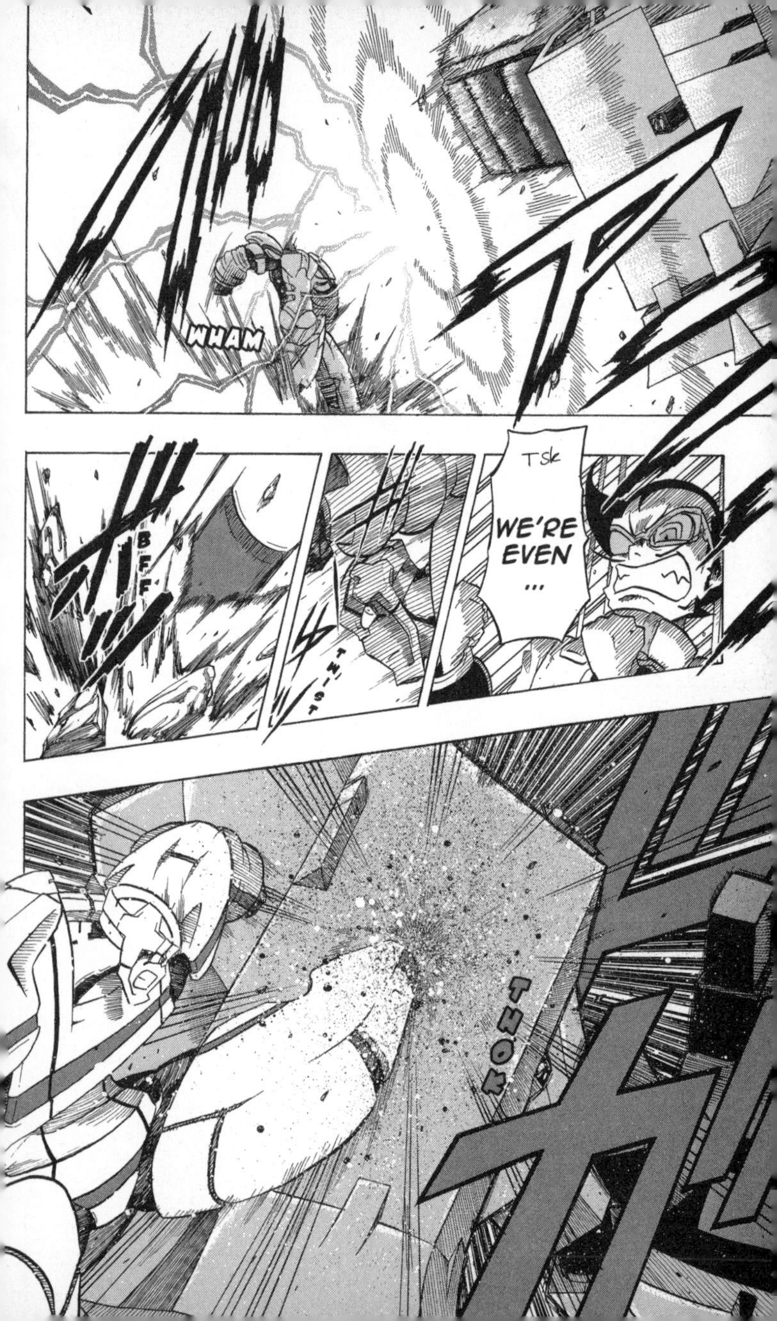
WHAM
TSK
WE'RE EVEN ...
TWIST
BFF
THOK

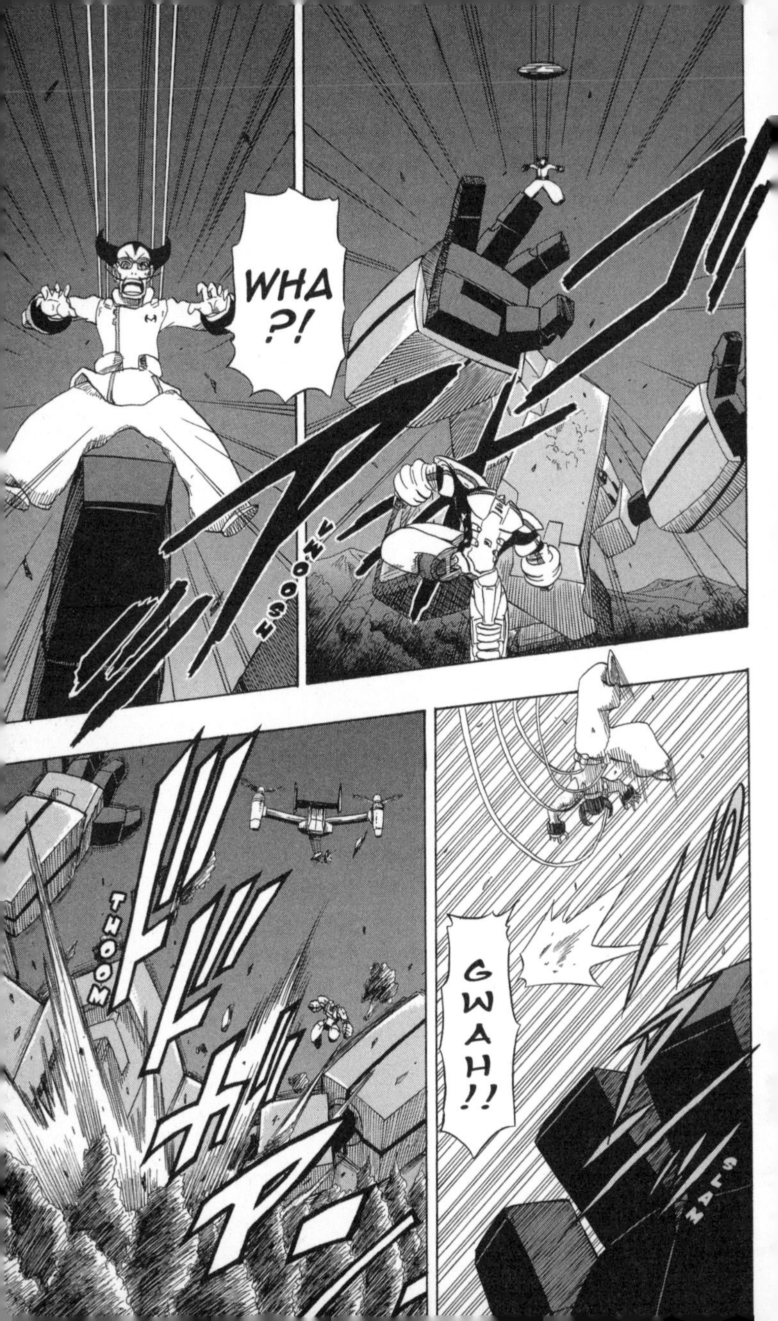
VWOOSH
WHA?!
GWAH!!
SLAM
THOOM

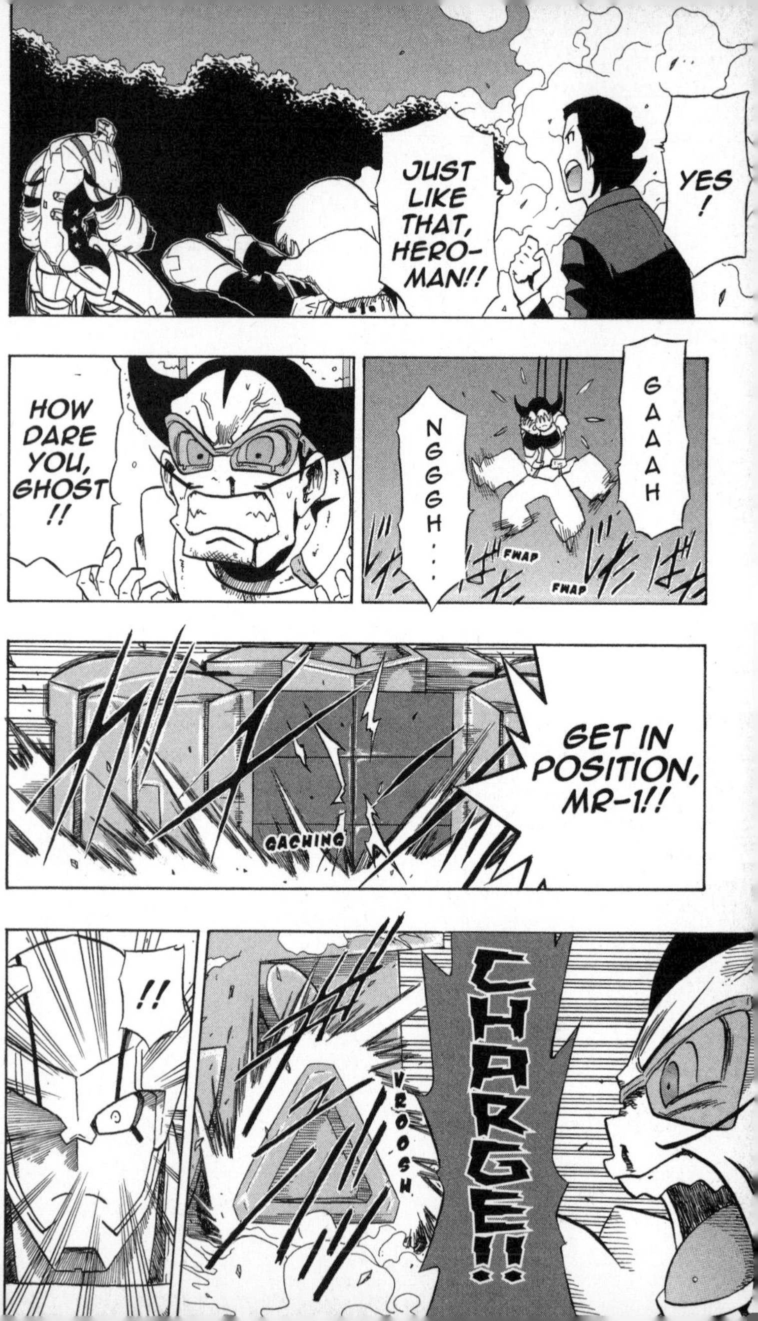
YES!
JUST LIKE THAT, HERO-MAN!!
GAAAH
NGGGH...
FWAP
FWAP
HOW DARE YOU, GHOST!!
GET IN POSITION, MR-1!!
GACHING
CHARGE!!
VROOSH
!!

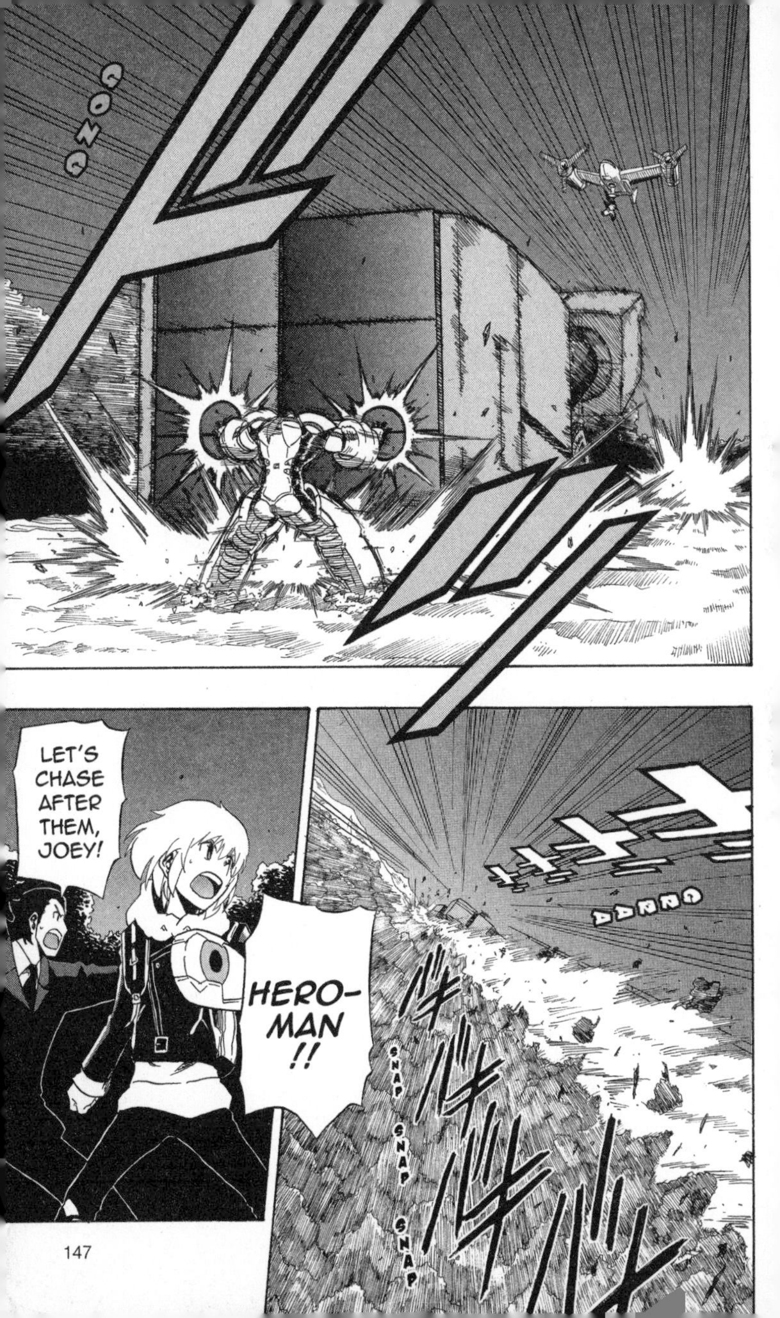
GONG
GNNAA
SNAP SNAP SNAP SNAP
LET'S CHASE AFTER THEM, JOEY!
HERO-MAN!!

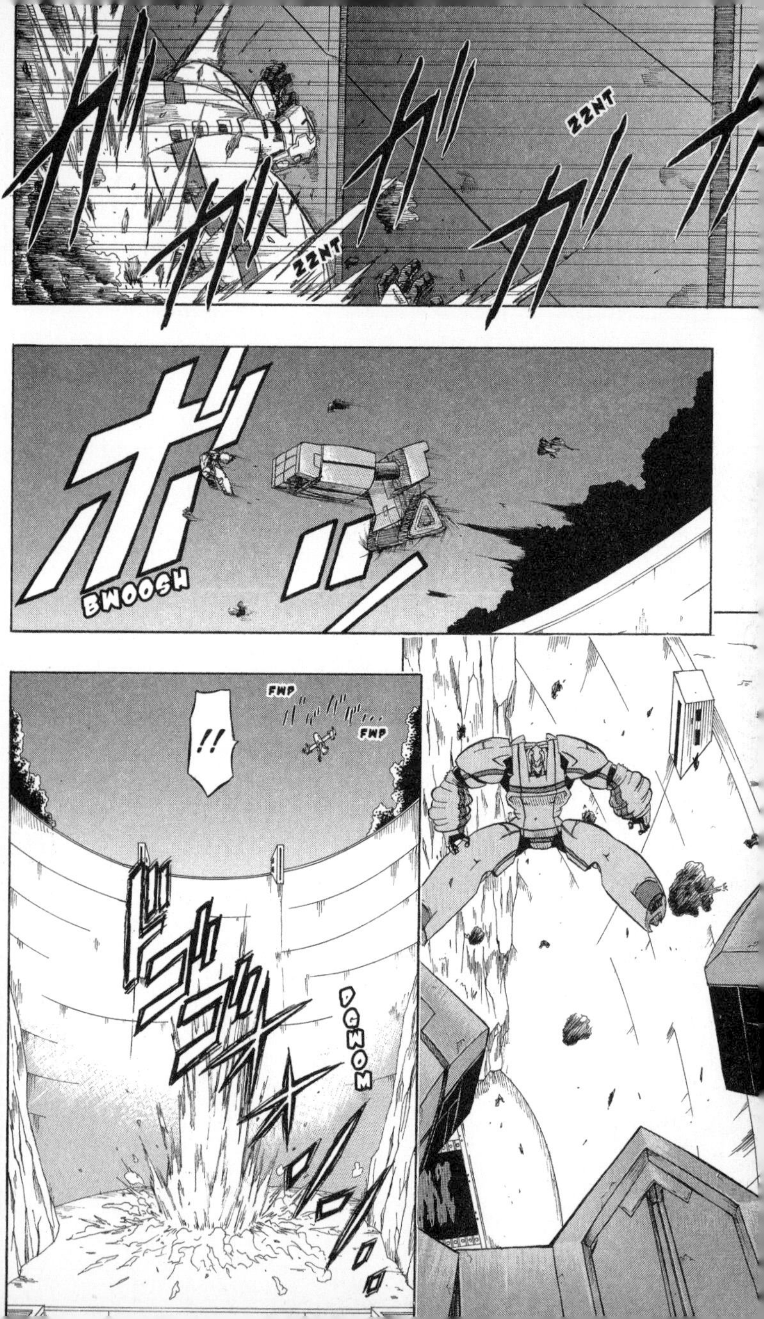
ZZNT
ZZNT
BWOOSH
FWP
FWP
!!
DGWOM

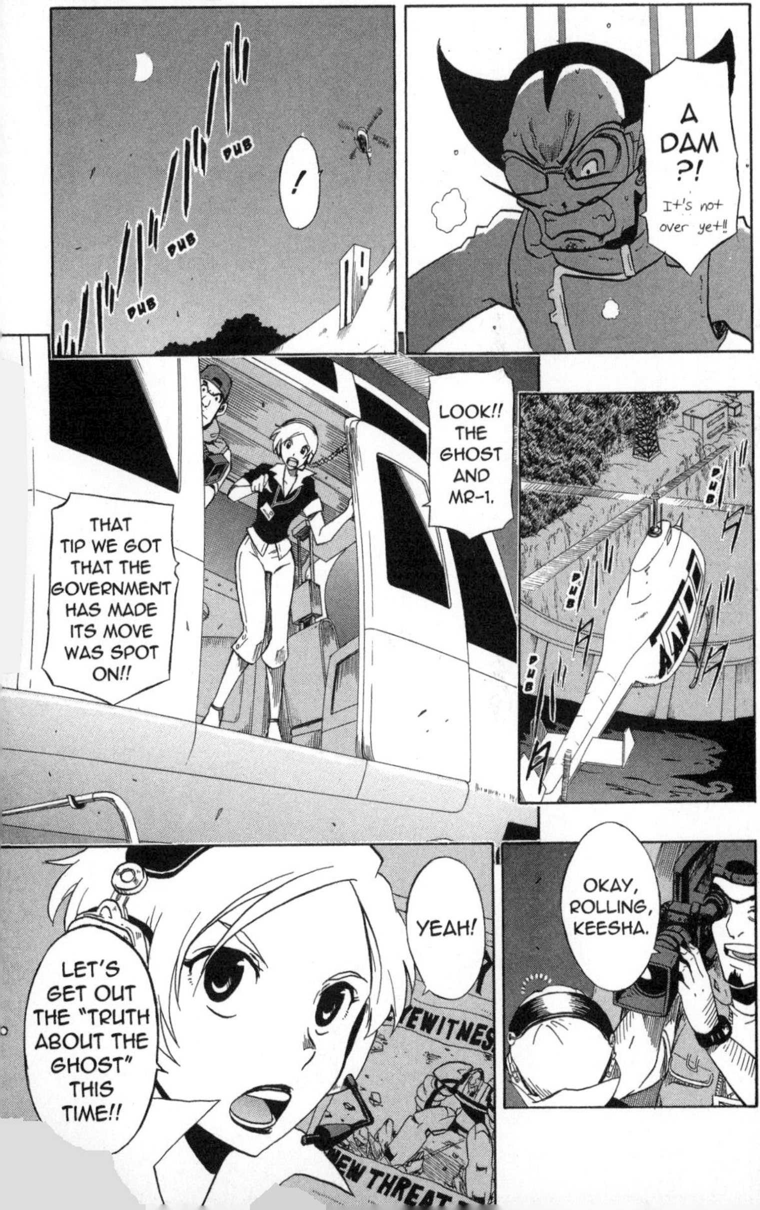
A DAM ?!
It's not over yet!!
!
DUB
DUB
DUB
DUB
DUB
DUB
LOOK!! THE GHOST AND MR-1.
THAT TIP WE GOT THAT THE GOVERNMENT HAS MADE ITS MOVE WAS SPOT ON!!
OKAY, ROLLING, KEESHA.
YEAH!
LET'S GET OUT THE "TRUTH ABOUT THE GHOST" THIS TIME!!
EWITNES
NEW THREAT

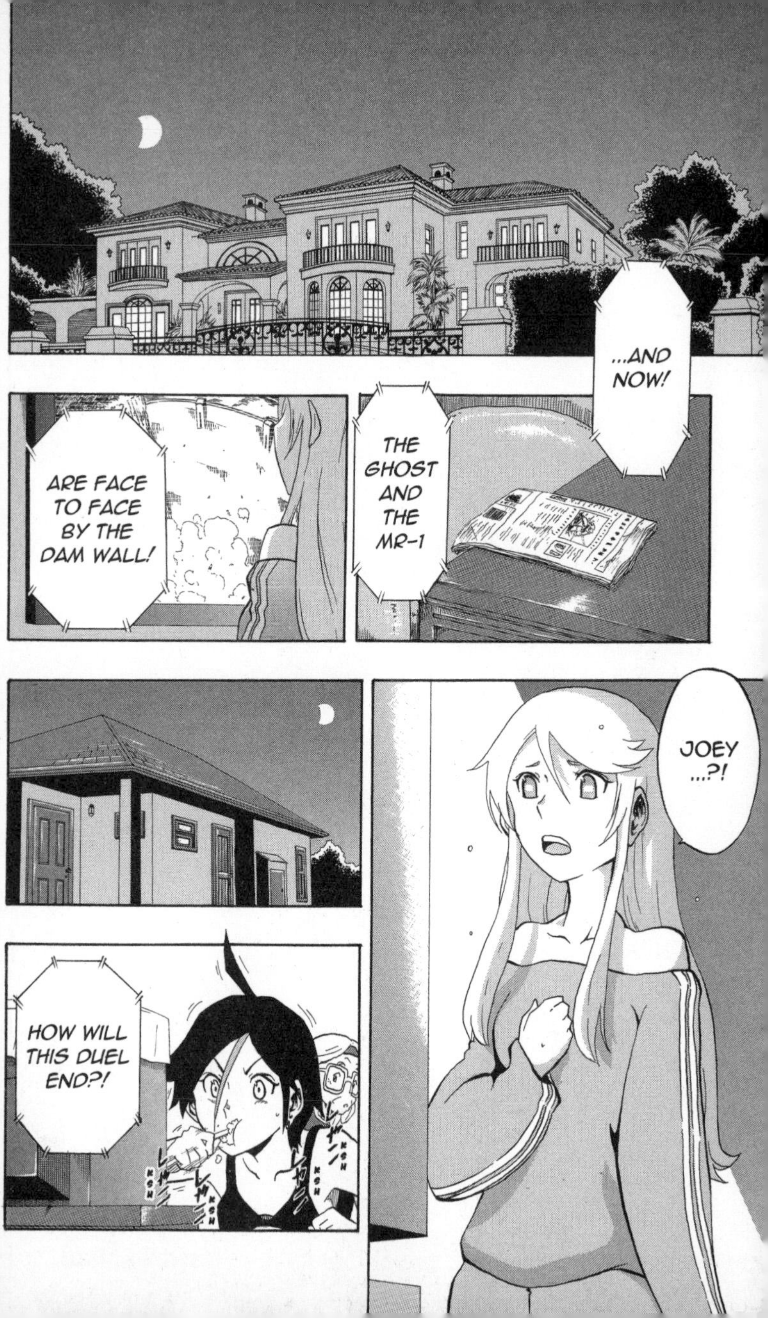
...AND NOW!
THE GHOST AND THE MR-1
ARE FACE TO FACE BY THE DAM WALL!
JOEY ...?!
HOW WILL THIS DUEL END?!
KSH
KSH
KSH
KSH

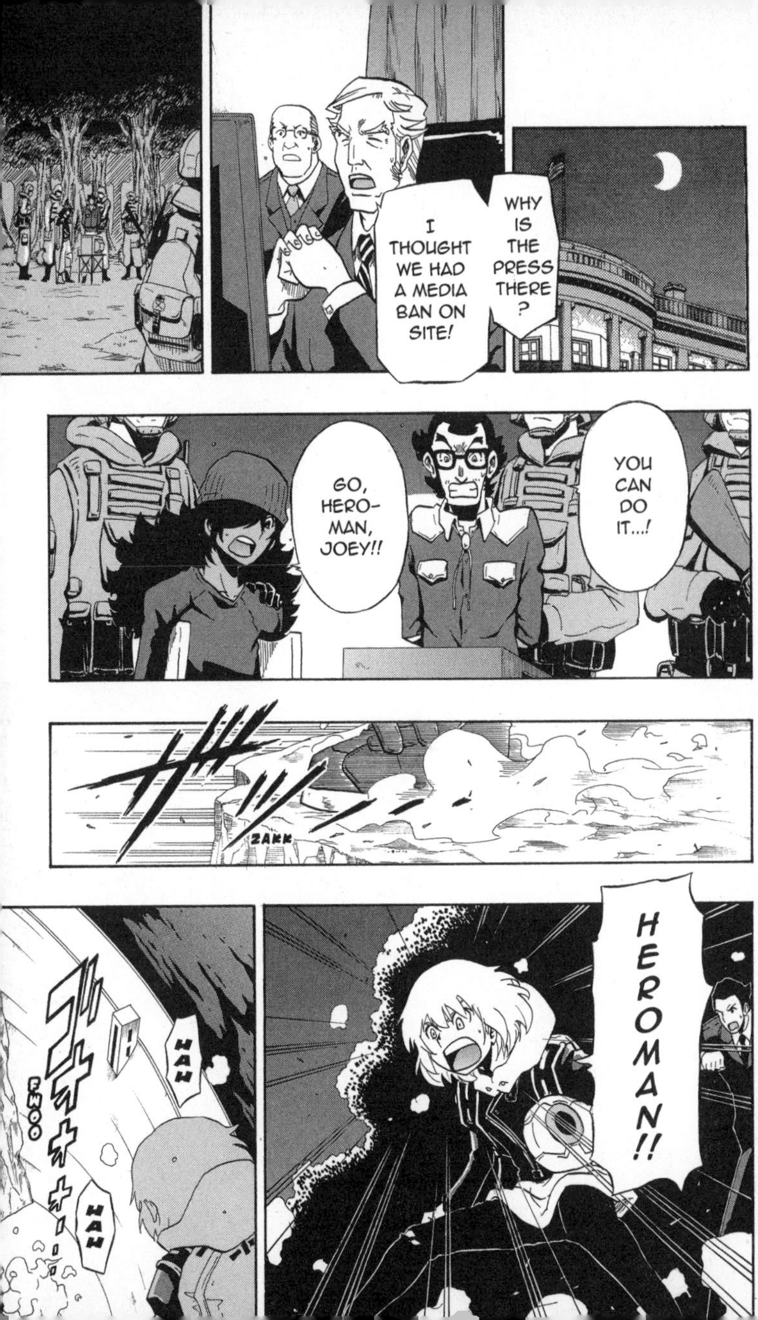
WHY IS THE PRESS THERE?
I THOUGHT WE HAD A MEDIA BAN ON SITE!
YOU CAN DO IT...!
GO, HERO-MAN, JOEY!!
ZAKK
HEROMAN!!
HAH
FWOO
HAH

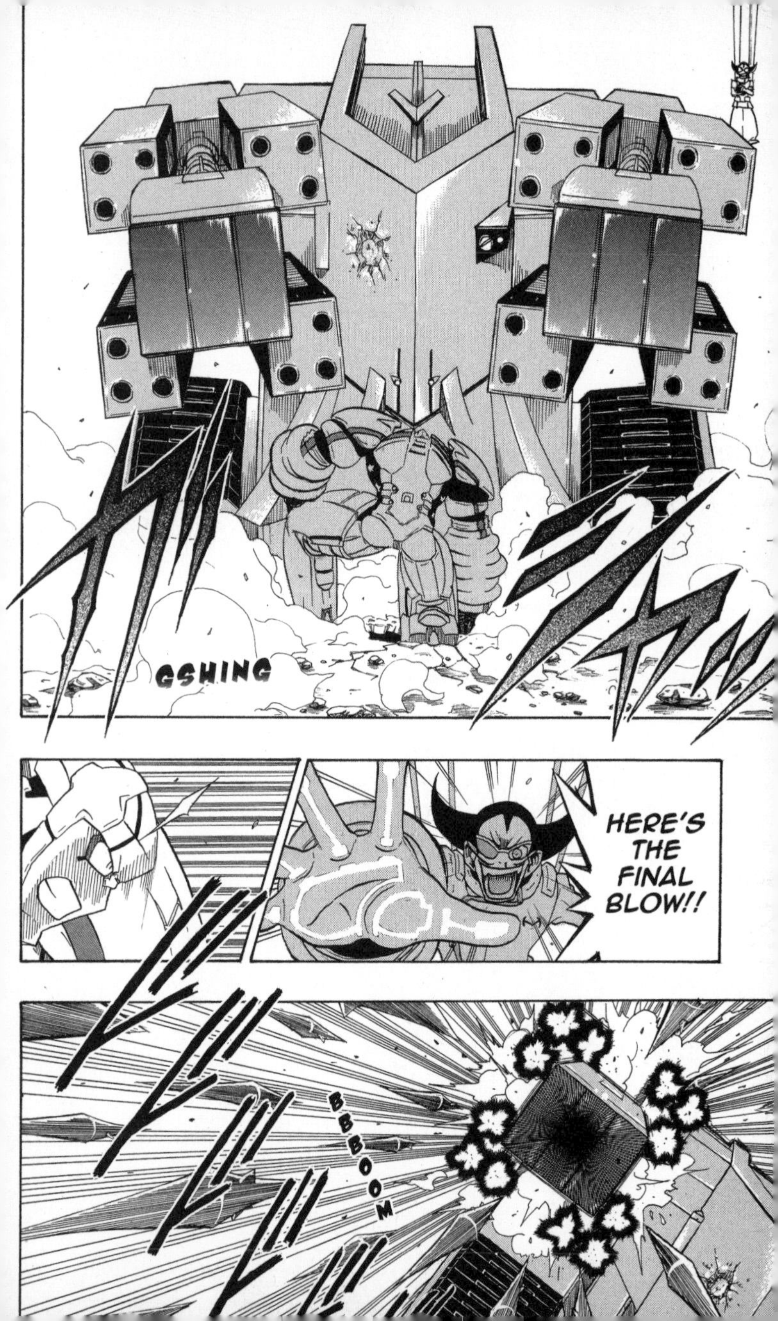
GSHING
HERE'S THE FINAL BLOW!!
BBBOOM

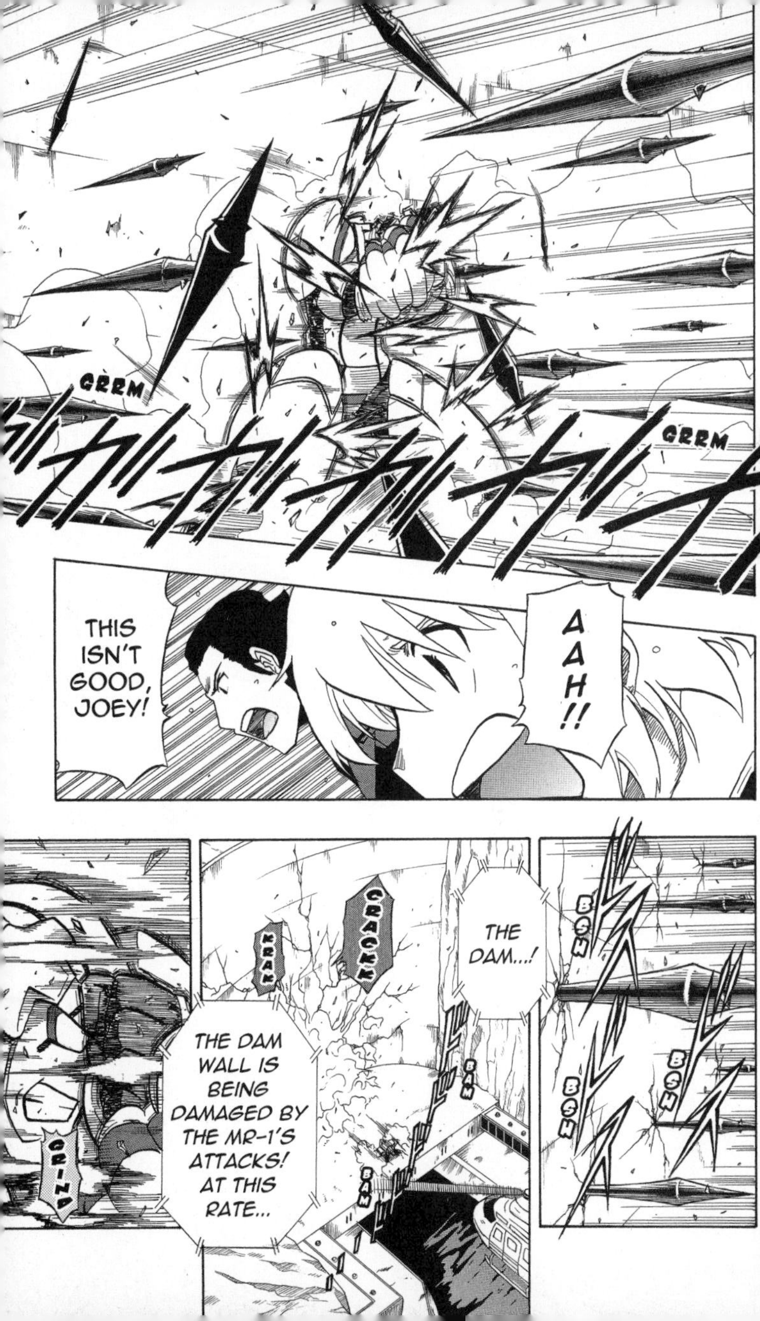
GRRM
GRRM
AAH!!
THIS ISN'T GOOD, JOEY!
BSH
BSH
BSH
THE DAM...!
CRACKK
KRAK
THE DAM WALL IS BEING DAMAGED BY THE MR-1'S ATTACKS! AT THIS RATE...
BAM
BAM
GRIND

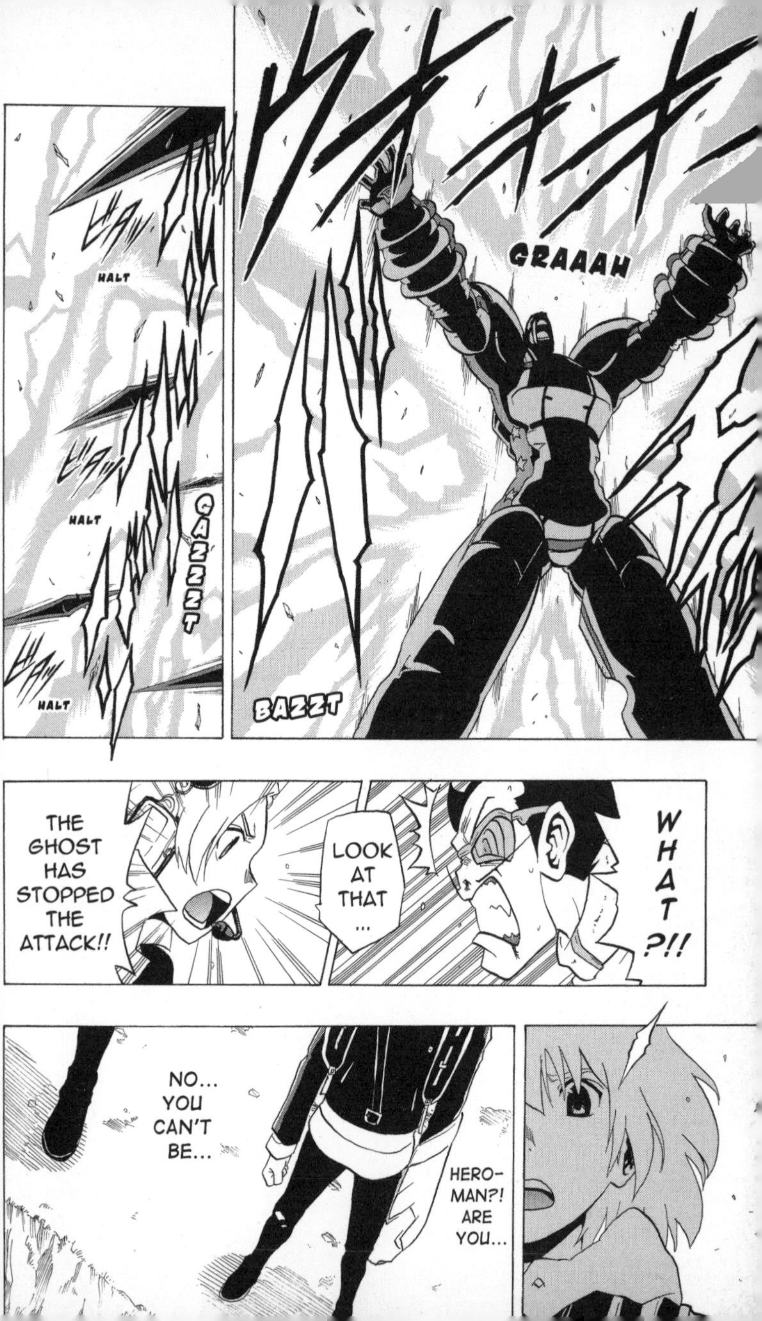
GRAAAH
BAZZT
HALT
HALT
GAZZZZT
HALT
WHAT?!!
LOOK AT THAT ...
THE GHOST HAS STOPPED THE ATTACK!!
HERO-MAN?! ARE YOU...
NO... YOU CAN'T BE...

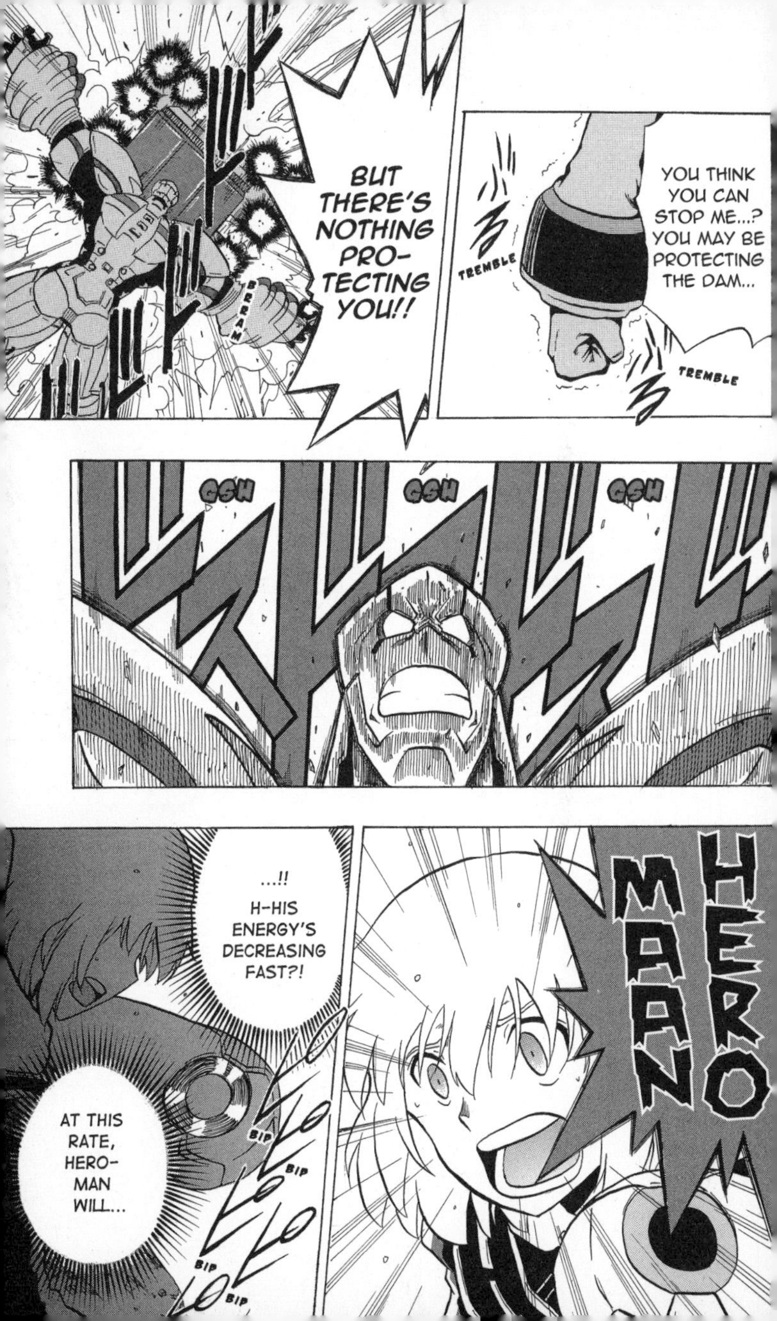

TREMBLE
YOU THINK YOU CAN STOP ME...? YOU MAY BE PROTECTING THE DAM...
TREMBLE
BUT THERE'S NOTHING PRO-TECTING YOU!!
BRRAM
GSH
GSH
GSH
HERO MAN
...!! H-HIS ENERGY'S DECREASING FAST?!
AT THIS RATE, HERO-MAN WILL...
BIP
BIP
BIP
BIP

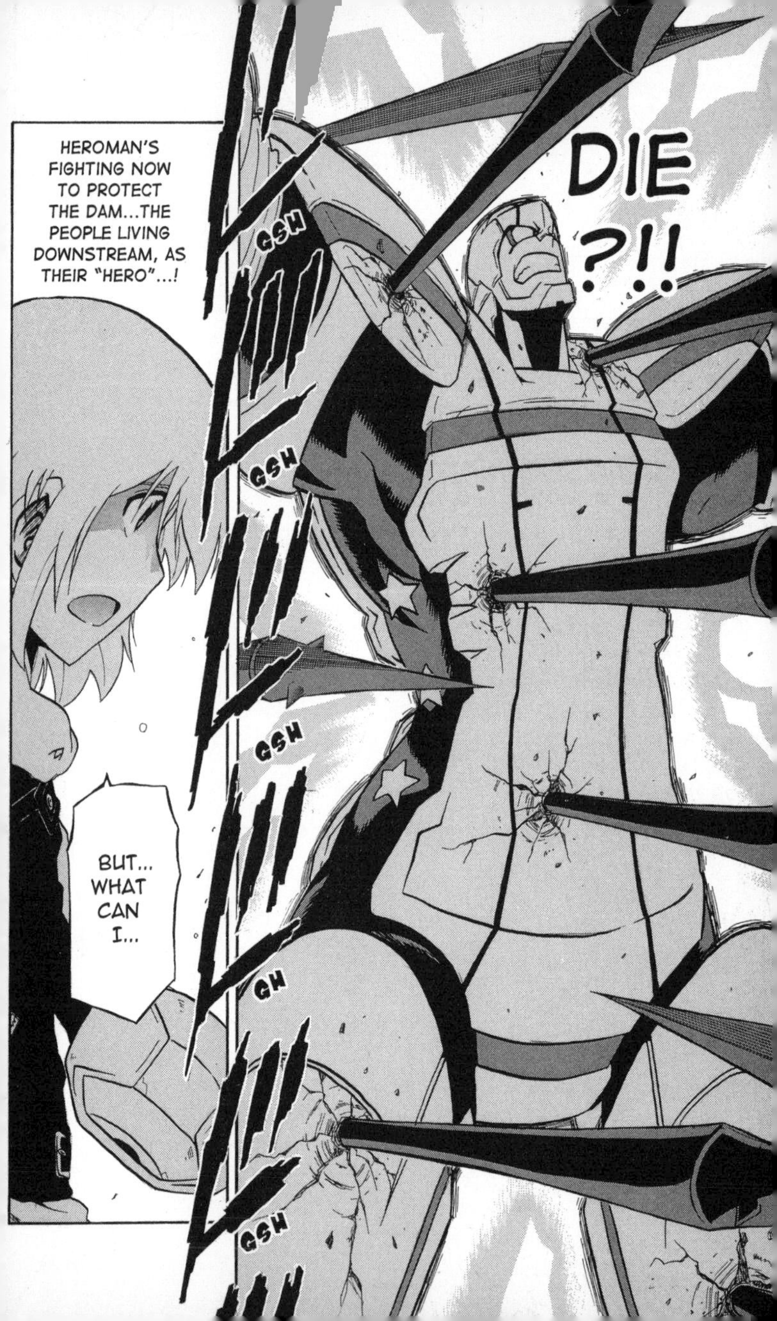
DIE ?!!
GSH
GSH
GSH
GH
GSH
HEROMAN'S FIGHTING NOW TO PROTECT THE DAM...THE PEOPLE LIVING DOWNSTREAM, AS THEIR "HERO"...!
BUT... WHAT CAN I...

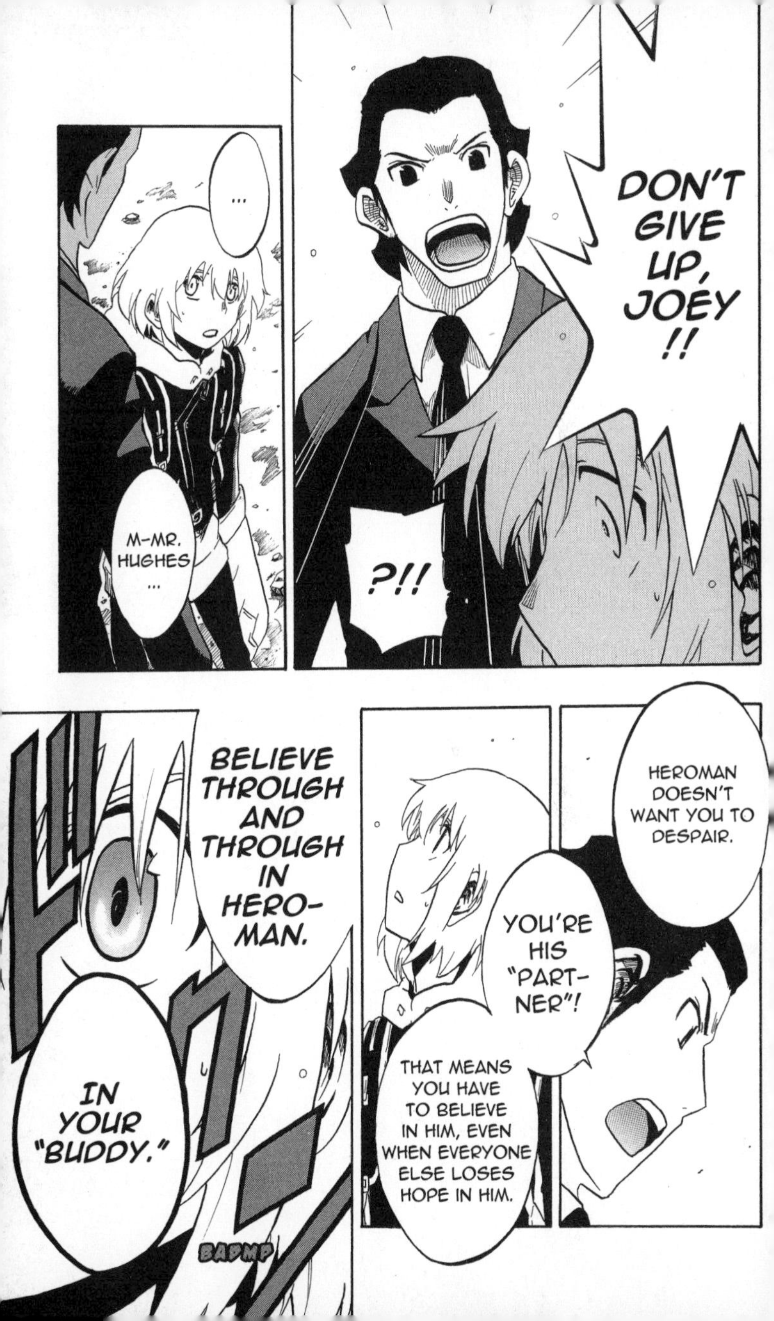
DON'T GIVE UP, JOEY !!
?!!
...
M-MR. HUGHES ...
HEROMAN DOESN'T WANT YOU TO DESPAIR.
YOU'RE HIS "PART-NER"!
THAT MEANS YOU HAVE TO BELIEVE IN HIM, EVEN WHEN EVERYONE ELSE LOSES HOPE IN HIM.
BELIEVE THROUGH AND THROUGH IN HERO-MAN.
IN YOUR "BUDDY."
BADMP

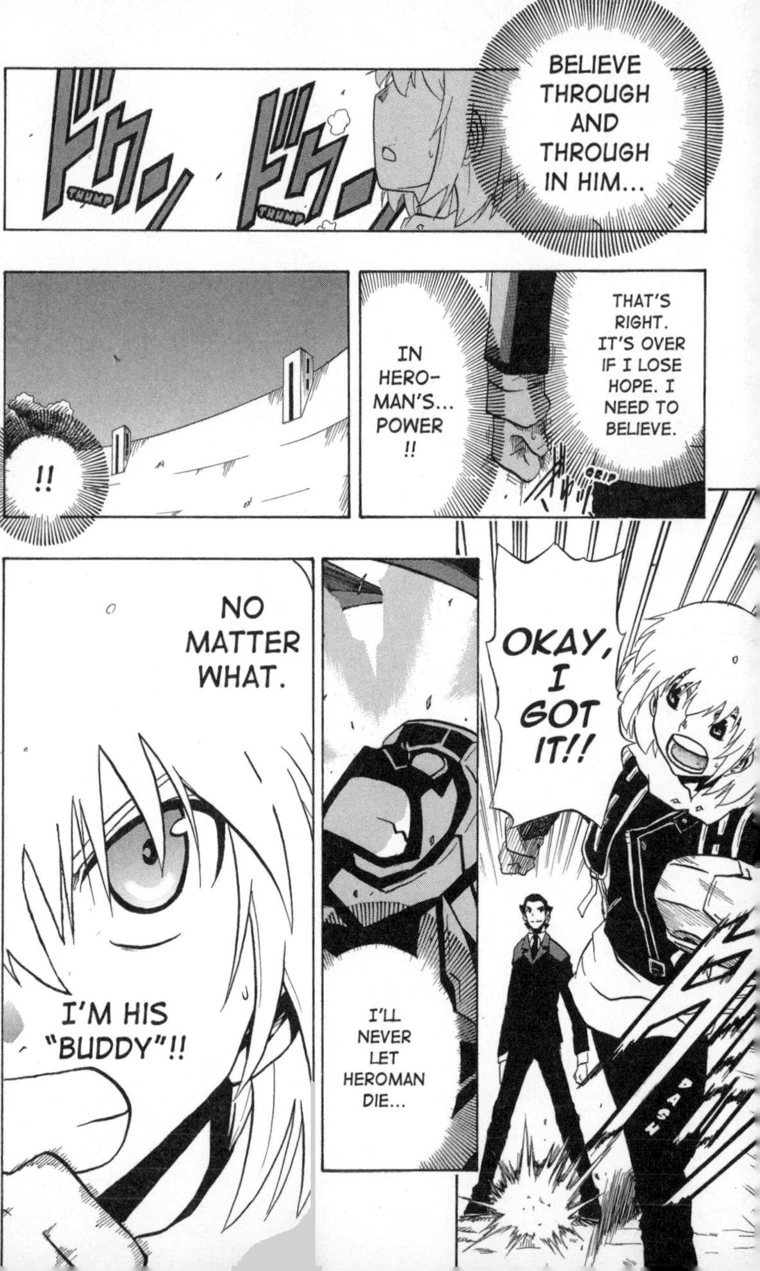
BELIEVE THROUGH AND THROUGH IN HIM...
THUMP
THUMP
THAT'S RIGHT. IT'S OVER IF I LOSE HOPE. I NEED TO BELIEVE.
IN HERO-MAN'S... POWER !!
GRIP
!!
OKAY, I GOT IT!!
DASH
I'LL NEVER LET HEROMAN DIE...
NO MATTER WHAT.
I'M HIS "BUDDY"!!

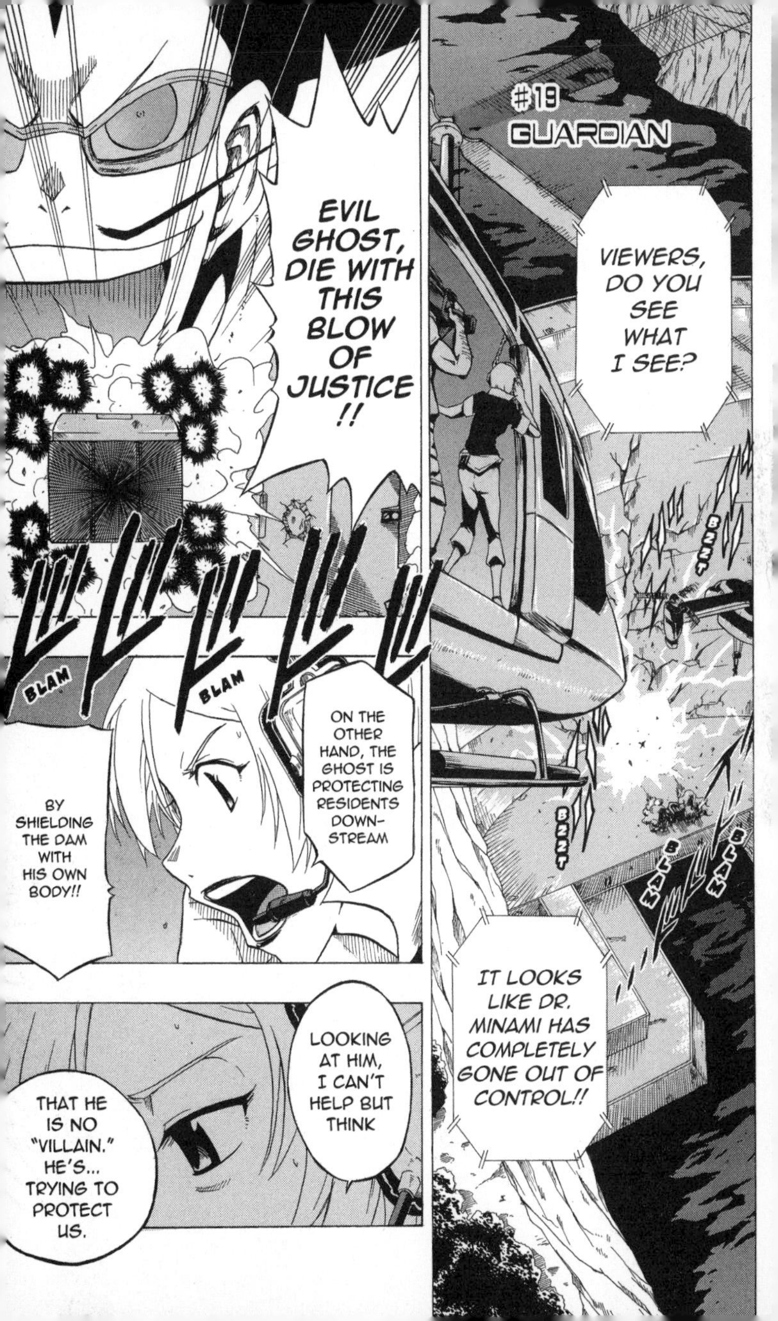
#19
GUARDIAN
VIEWERS, DO YOU SEE WHAT I SEE?
BZZT
BZZT
BLAM
BLAM
IT LOOKS LIKE DR. MINAMI HAS COMPLETELY GONE OUT OF CONTROL!!
EVIL GHOST, DIE WITH THIS BLOW OF JUSTICE!!
BLAM
BLAM
ON THE OTHER HAND, THE GHOST IS PROTECTING RESIDENTS DOWN-STREAM
BY SHIELDING THE DAM WITH HIS OWN BODY!!
LOOKING AT HIM, I CAN'T HELP BUT THINK
THAT HE IS NO "VILLAIN." HE'S... TRYING TO PROTECT US.

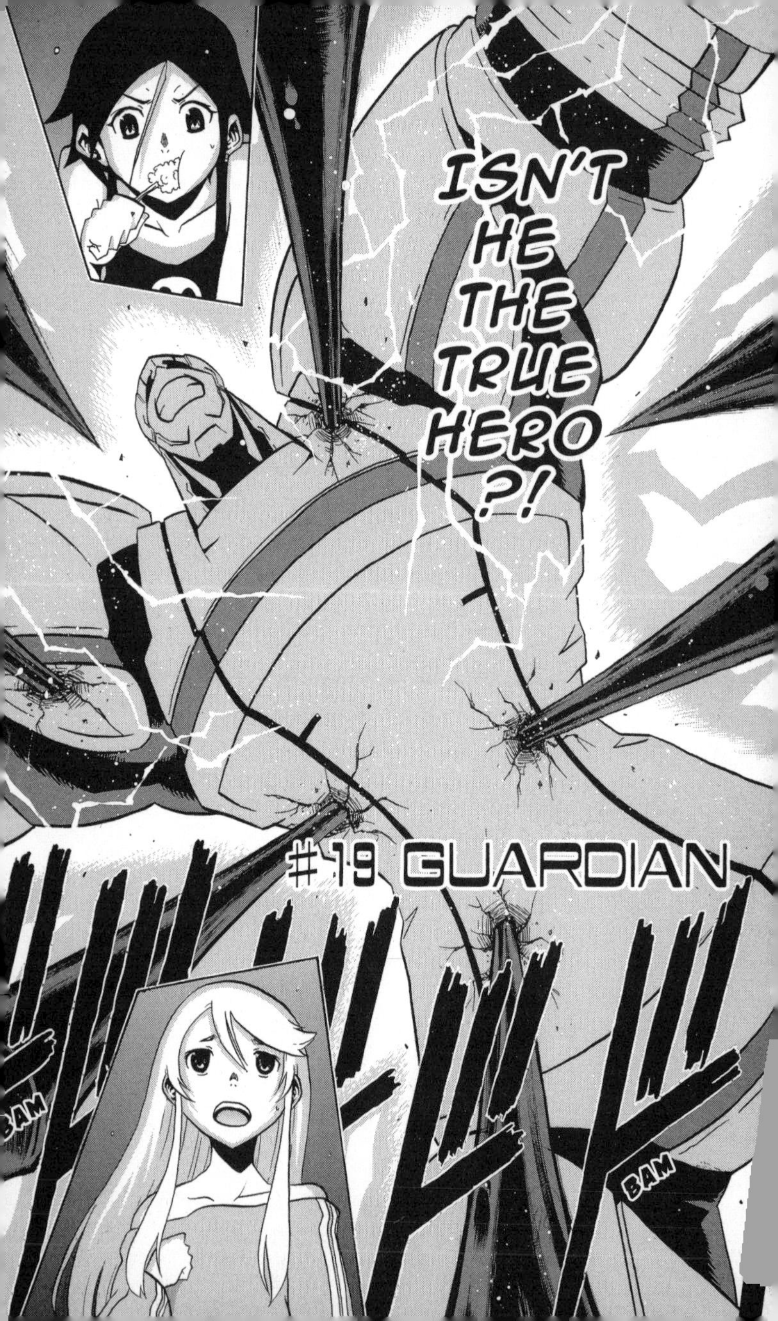
ISN'T HE THE TRUE HERO ?!
#19 GUARDIAN
BAM
BAM

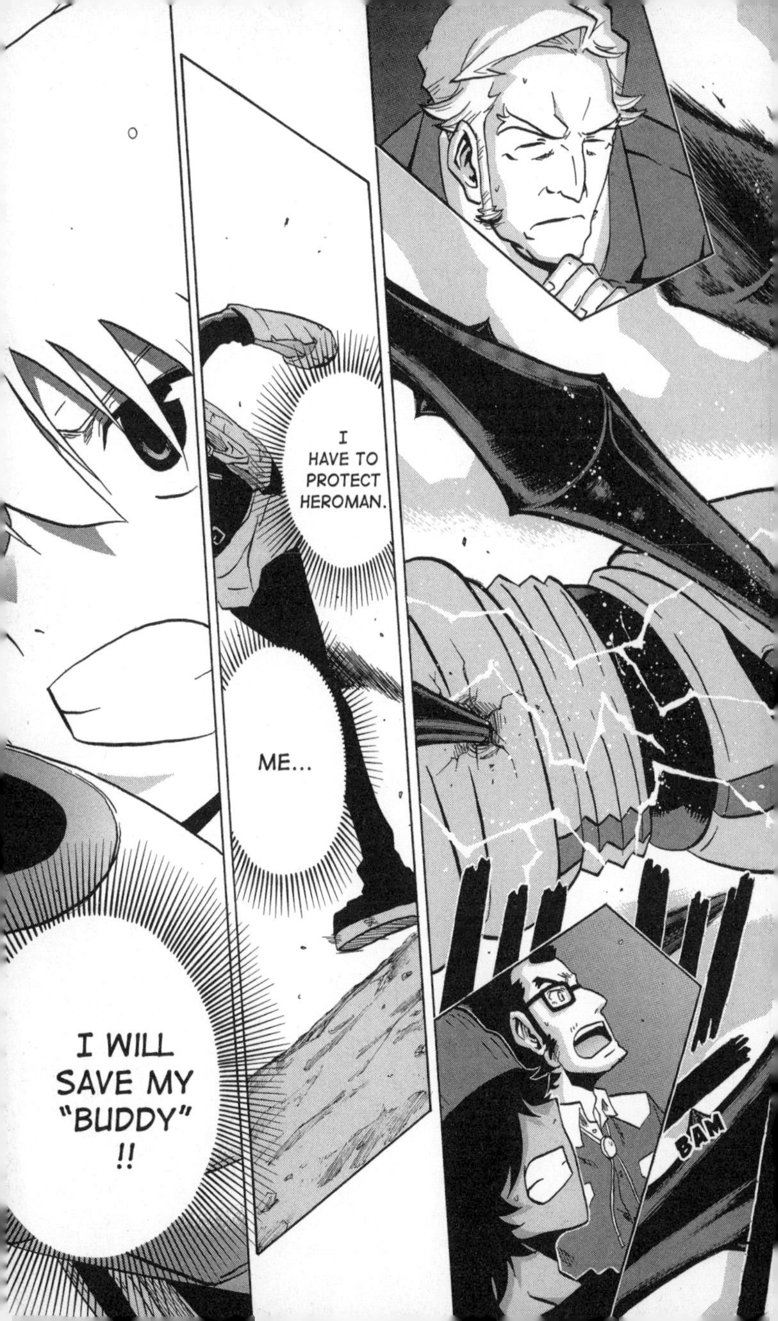
BAM
I HAVE TO PROTECT HEROMAN.
ME...
I WILL SAVE MY "BUDDY" !!

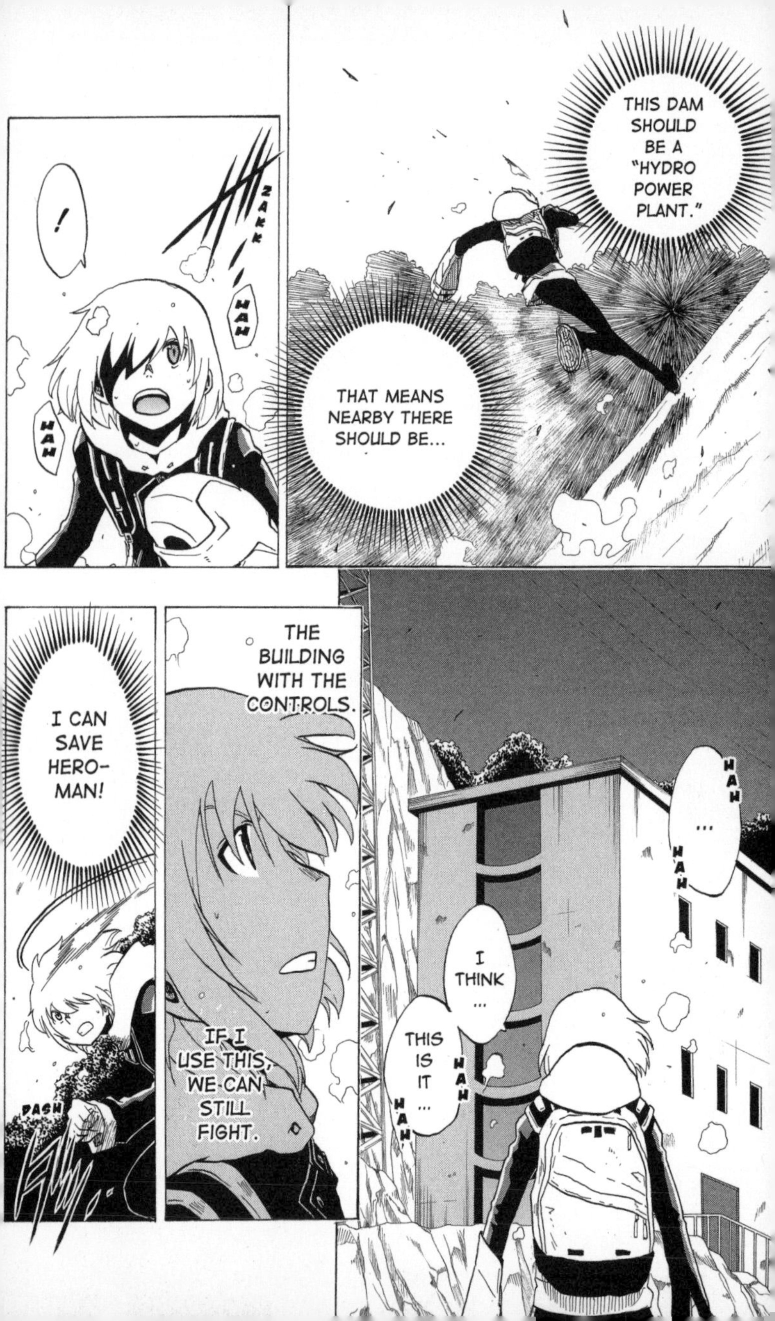
THIS DAM SHOULD BE A "HYDRO POWER PLANT."
THAT MEANS NEARBY THERE SHOULD BE...
ZAKK
!
HAH
HAH
HAH
...
HAH
I THINK ...
THIS IS IT ...
HAH
HAH
THE BUILDING WITH THE CONTROLS.
IF I USE THIS, WE CAN STILL FIGHT.
I CAN SAVE HERO-MAN!
DASH

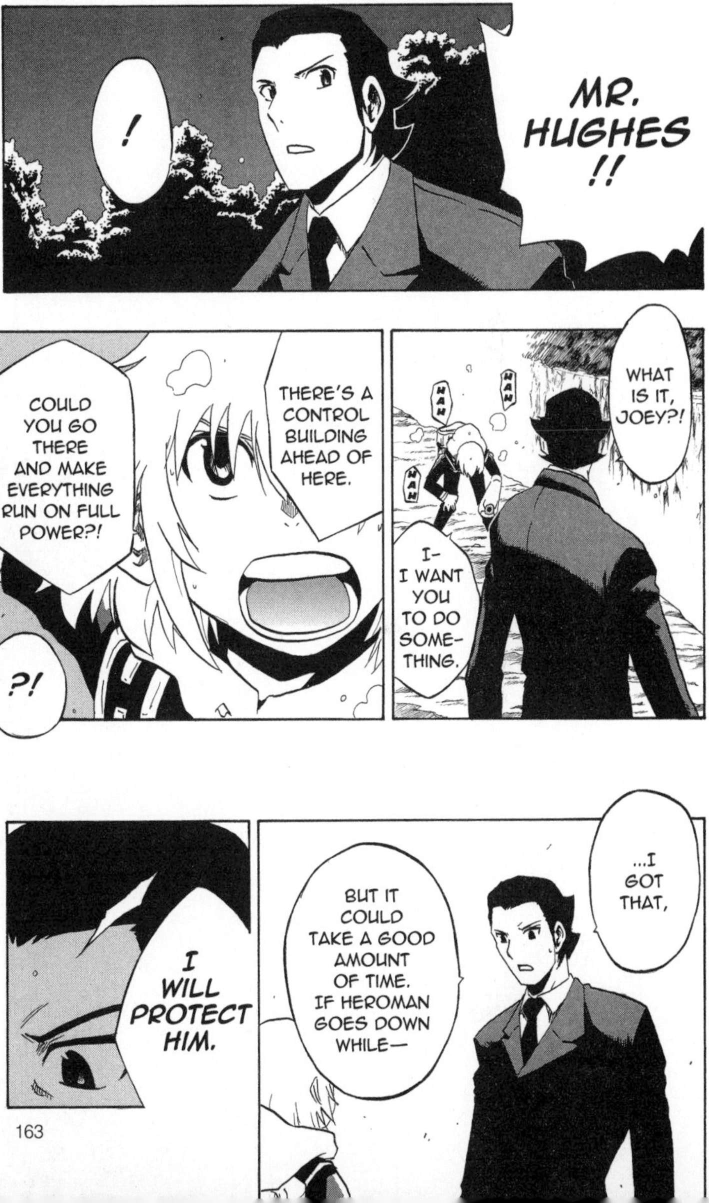
MR. HUGHES!!
!
WHAT IS IT, JOEY?!
HAH
HAH
HAH
I- I WANT YOU TO DO SOME-THING.
THERE'S A CONTROL BUILDING AHEAD OF HERE.
COULD YOU GO THERE AND MAKE EVERYTHING RUN ON FULL POWER?!
?!
...I GOT THAT,
BUT IT COULD TAKE A GOOD AMOUNT OF TIME. IF HEROMAN GOES DOWN WHILE—
I WILL PROTECT HIM.

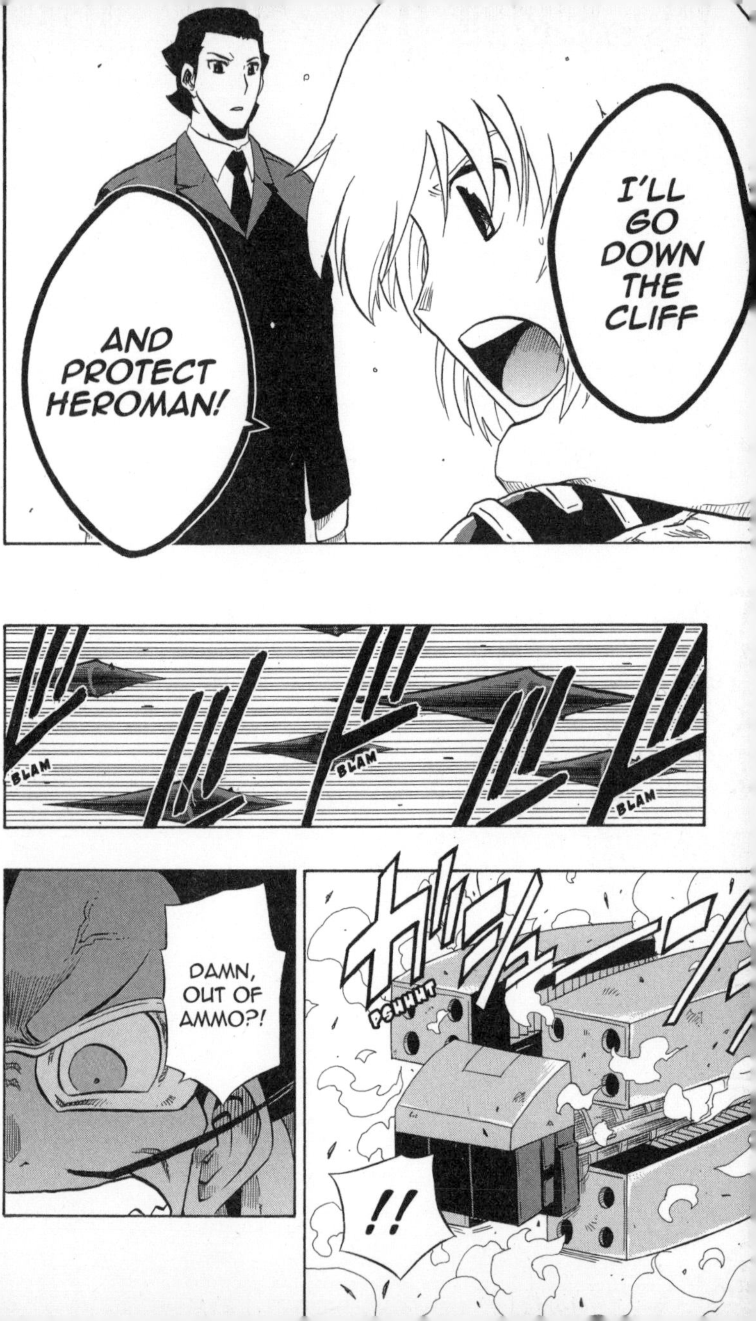
I'LL GO DOWN THE CLIFF
AND PROTECT HEROMAN!
BLAM
BLAM
BLAM
PSHHHT
!!
DAMN, OUT OF AMMO?!

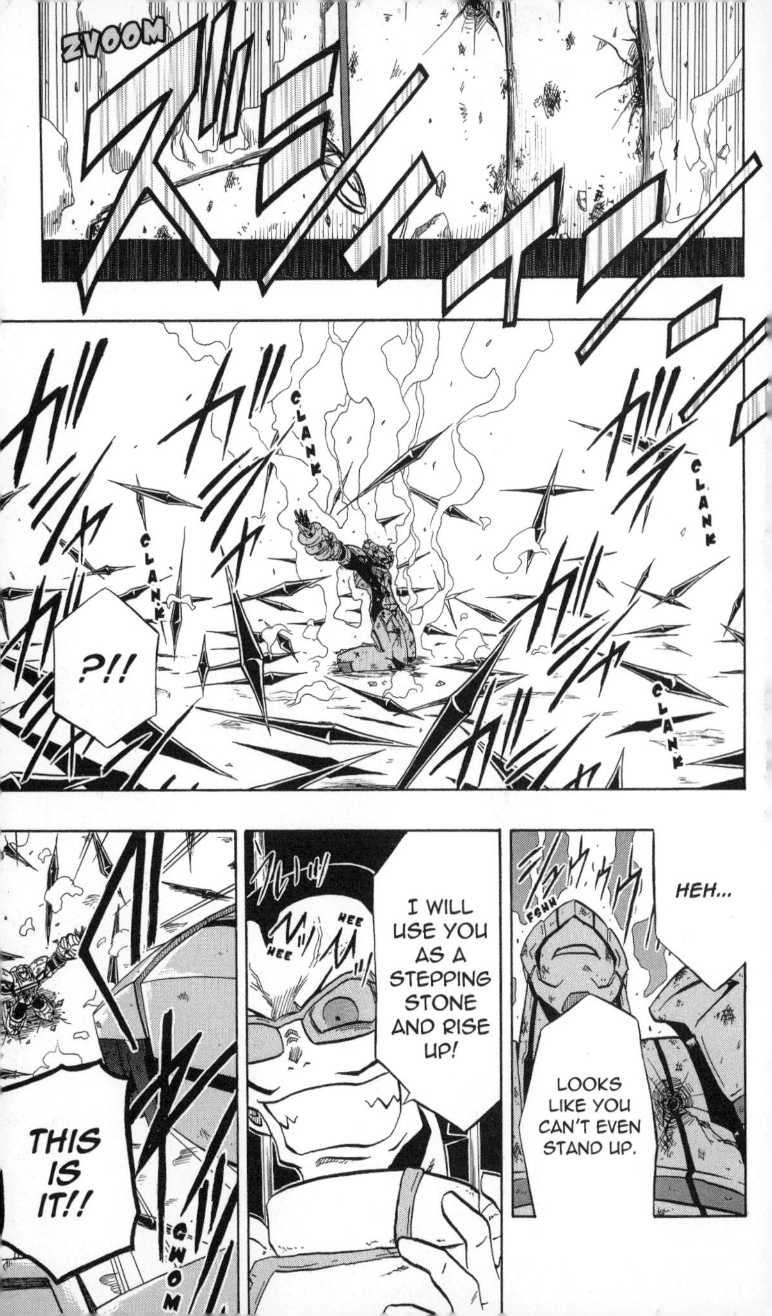
ZVOOM
CLANK
CLANK
CLANK
CLANK
?!!
HEH...
FSHH
LOOKS LIKE YOU CAN'T EVEN STAND UP.
I WILL USE YOU AS A STEPPING STONE AND RISE UP!
HEE
HEE
THIS IS IT!!
GWOM

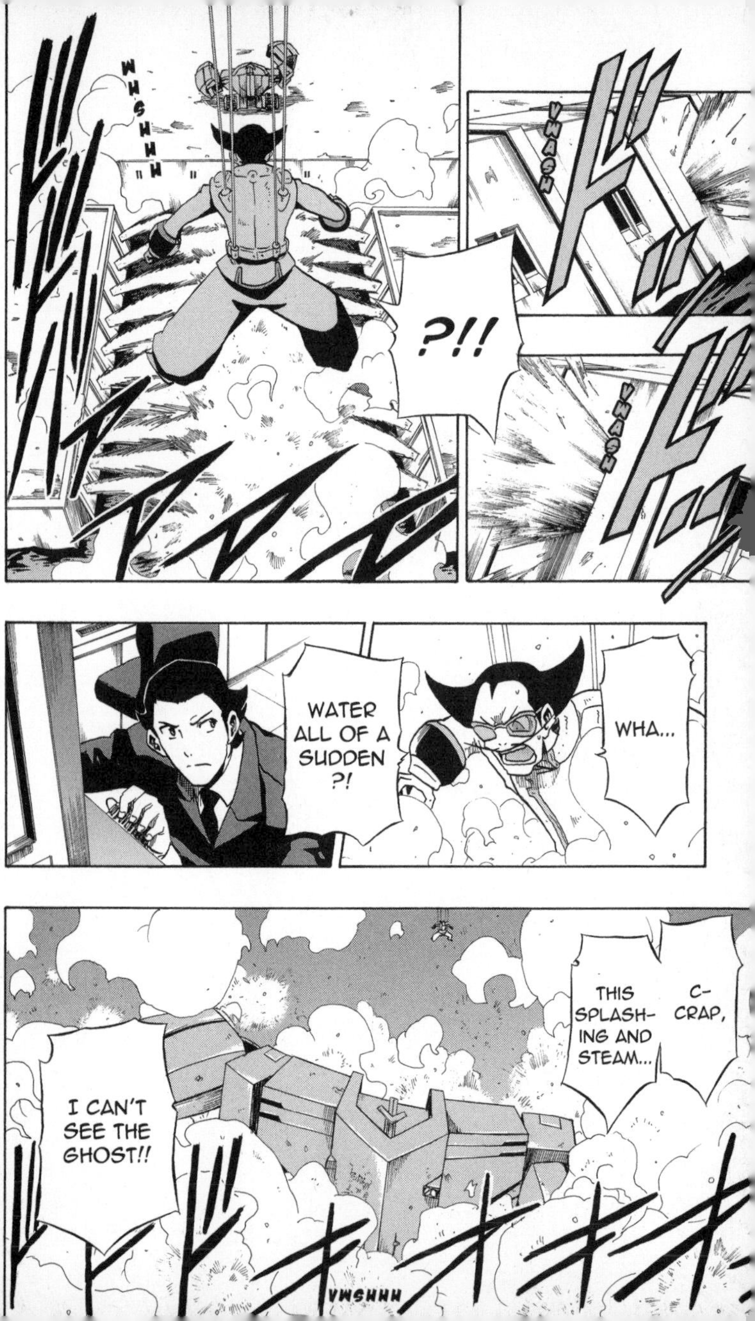
VWASH
VWASH
?!!
WHSHHH
WHA...
WATER ALL OF A SUDDEN?!
C-CRAP,
THIS SPLASHING AND STEAM...
I CAN'T SEE THE GHOST!!
VWSHHH

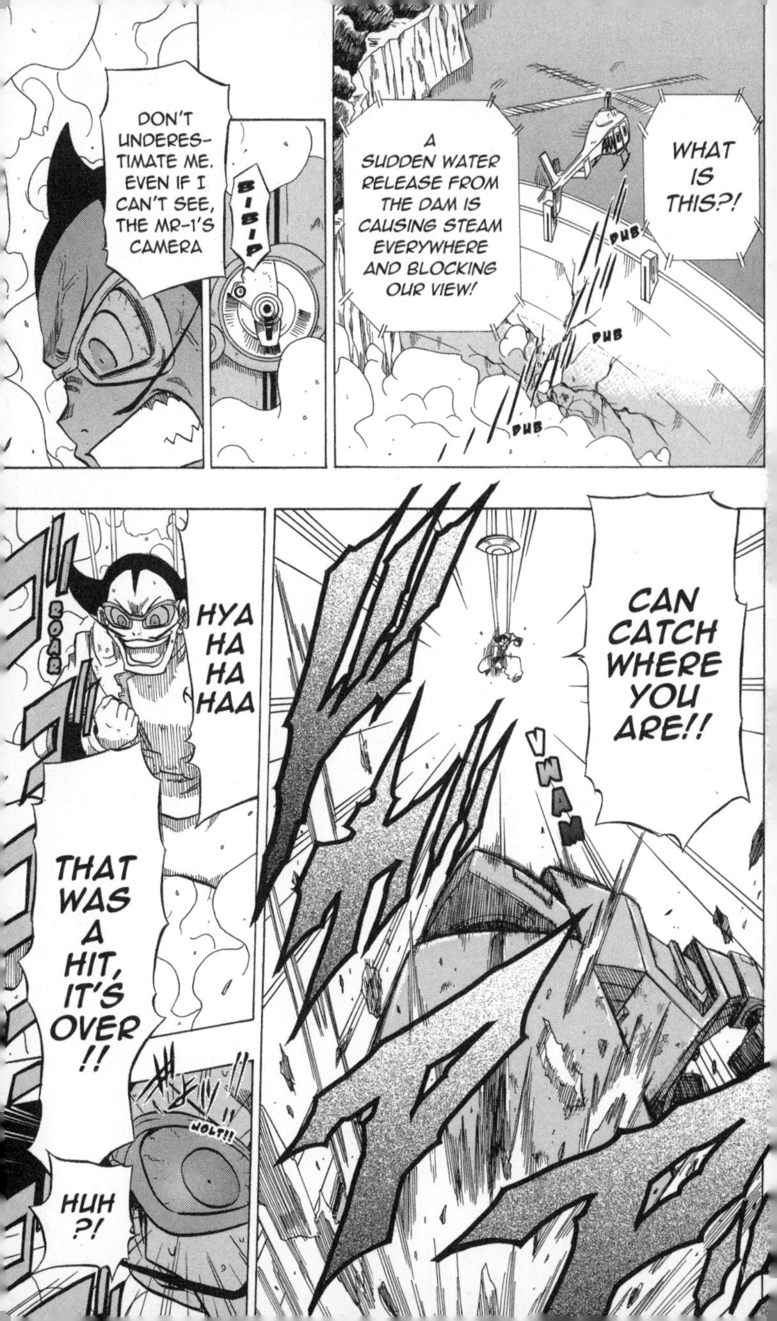
WHAT IS THIS?!
A SUDDEN WATER RELEASE FROM THE DAM IS CAUSING STEAM EVERYWHERE AND BLOCKING OUR VIEW!
DUB
DUB
DUB
BIBIP
DON'T UNDERES-TIMATE ME. EVEN IF I CAN'T SEE, THE MR-1'S CAMERA
CAN CATCH WHERE YOU ARE!!
VWAM
HYA HA HA HAA
ROAR
THAT WAS A HIT, IT'S OVER!!
JOLT!!
HUH ?!

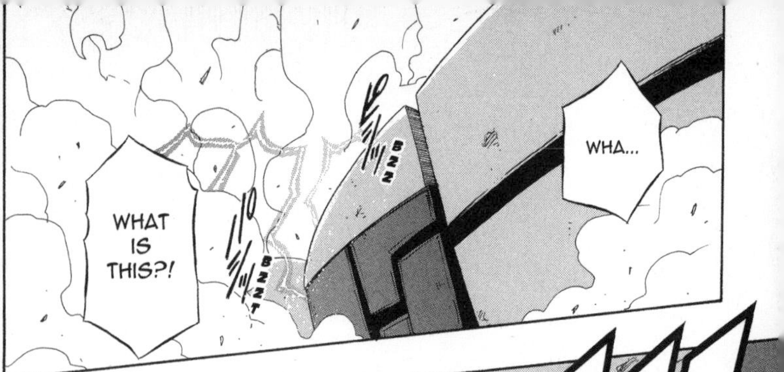
WHA...
BZZ
BZZT
WHAT IS THIS?!
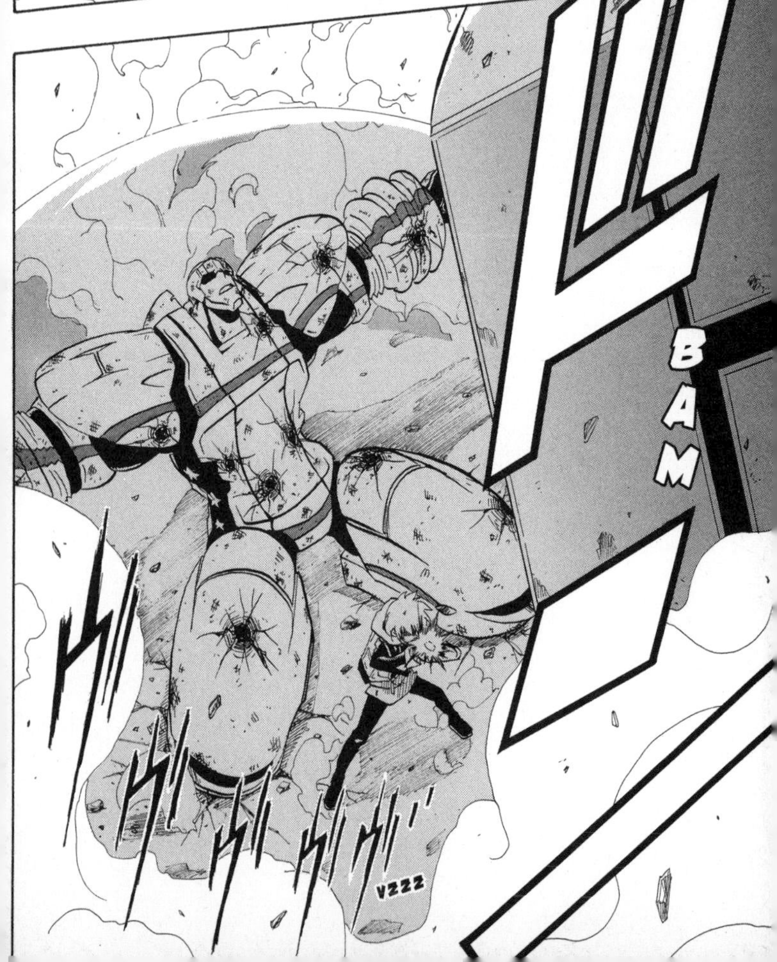
BAM
VZZZ

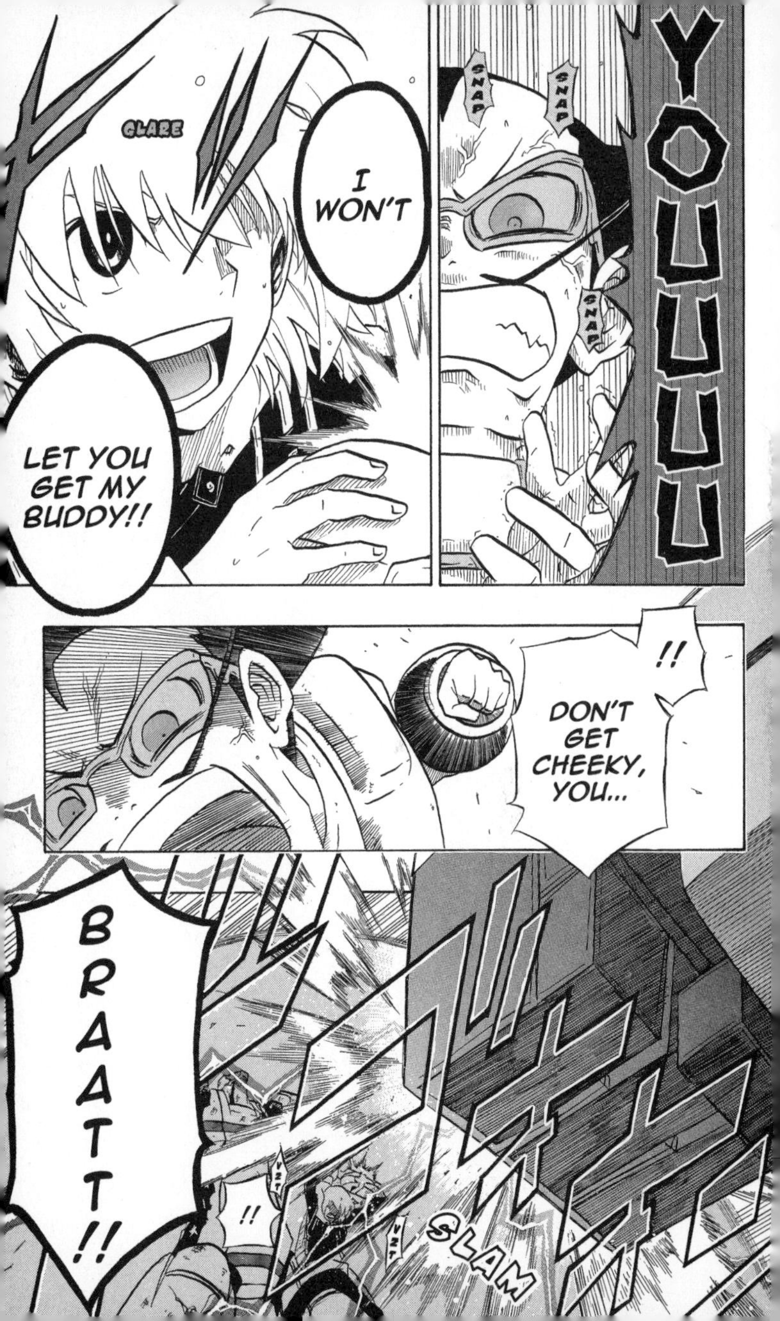
YOUUUUU
SNAP
SNAP
SNAP
GLARE
I WON'T
LET YOU GET MY BUDDY!!
!!
DON'T GET CHEEKY, YOU...
SLAM
VZT
VZT
!!
BRAATT!!

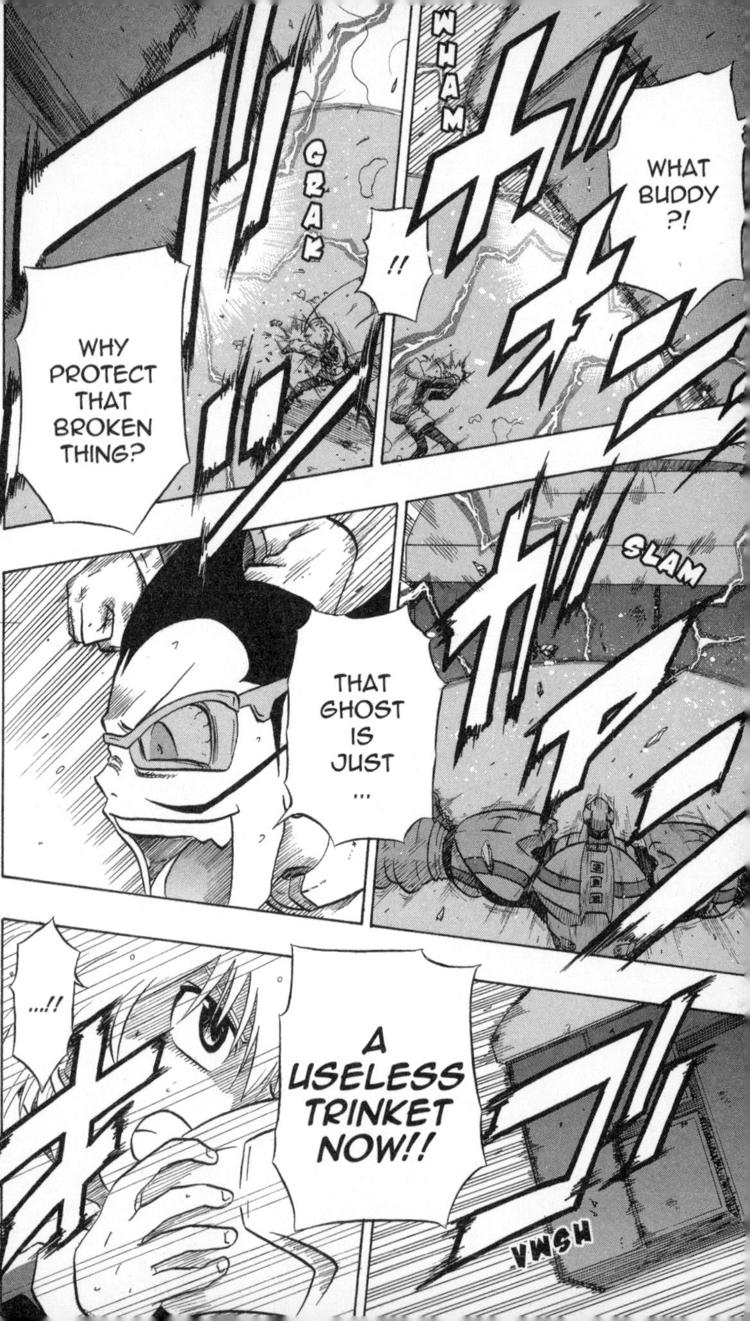
WHAM
WHAT BUDDY ?!
!!
GRAK
WHY PROTECT THAT BROKEN THING?
SLAM
THAT GHOST IS JUST ...
A USELESS TRINKET NOW!!
...!!
VWSH

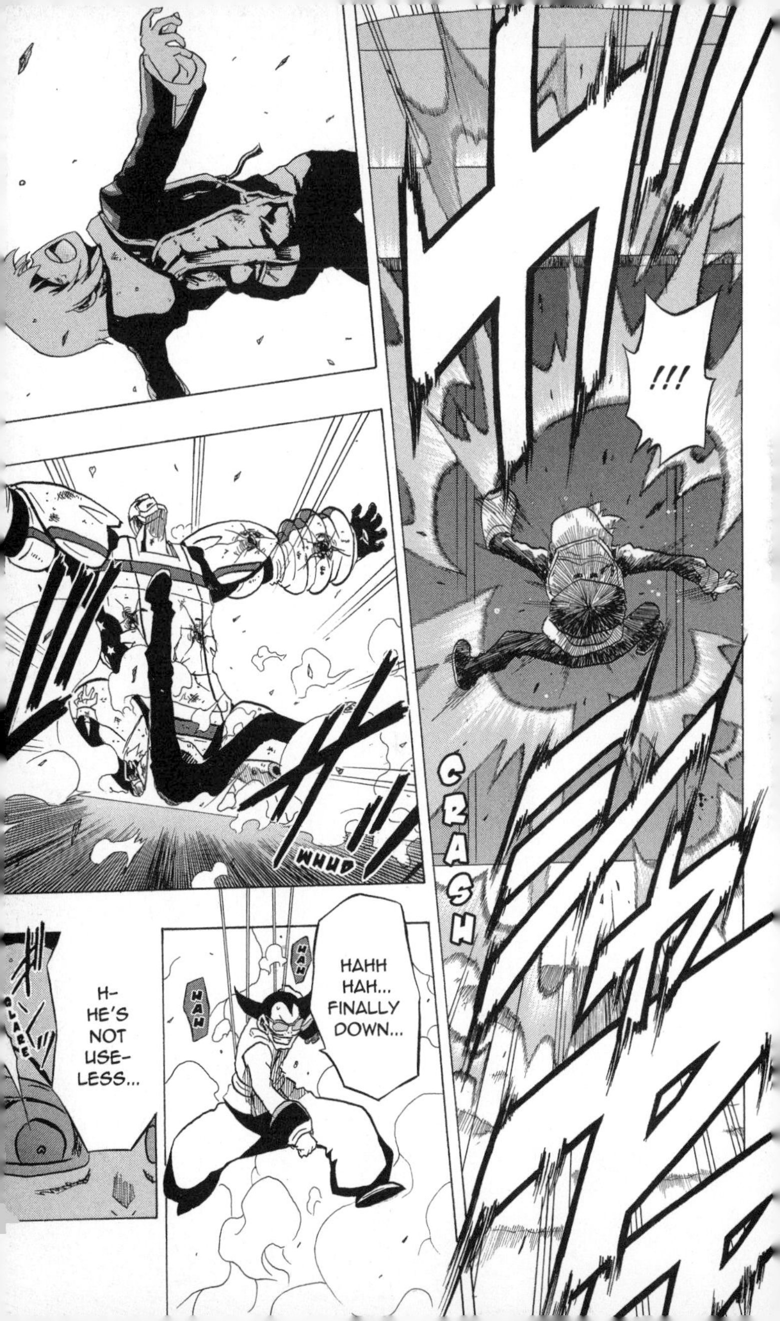
!!!
CRASH
WHUD
HAH
HAH
HAHH HAH... FINALLY DOWN...
GLARE
H- HE'S NOT USELESS...

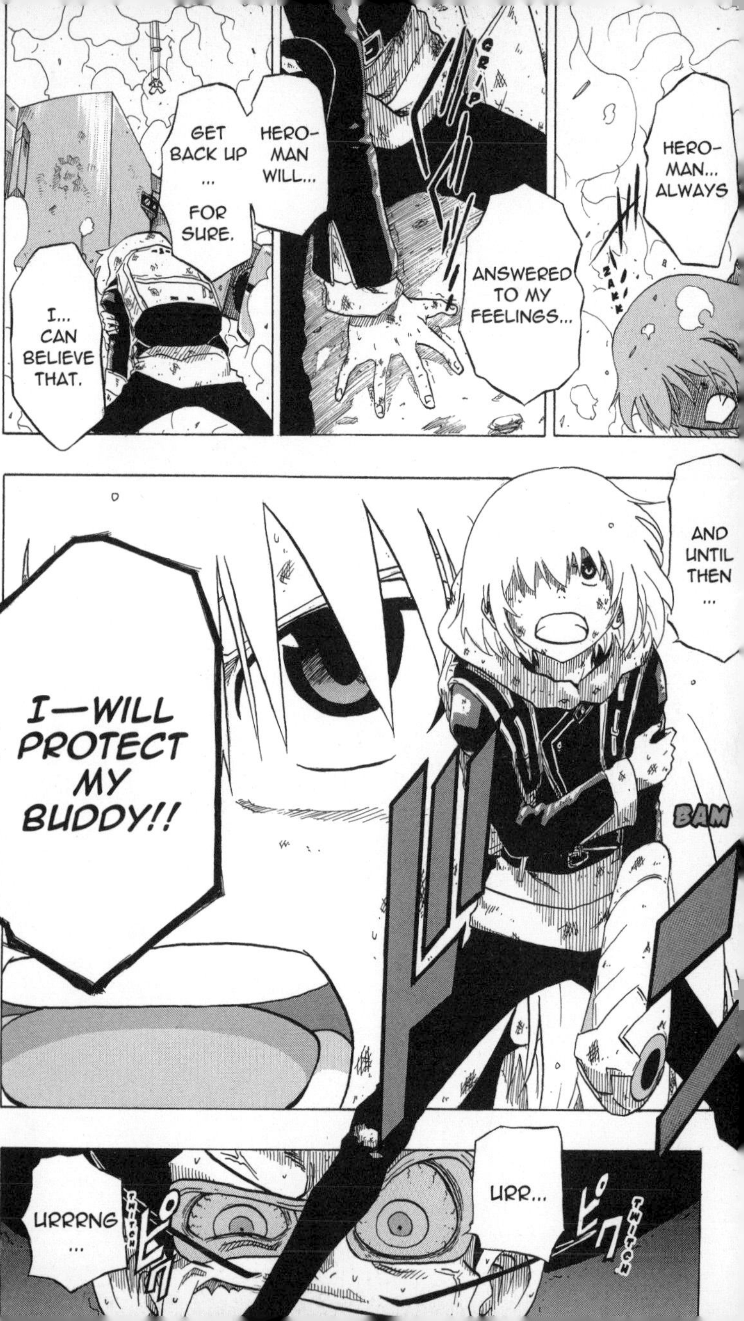
HERO-MAN... ALWAYS
ANSWERED TO MY FEELINGS...
ZAKK
GRIP
HERO-MAN WILL...
GET BACK UP ...
FOR SURE.
I... CAN BELIEVE THAT.
AND UNTIL THEN ...
BAM
I—WILL PROTECT MY BUDDY!!
URR...
TWITCH
URRRNG ...
TWITCH

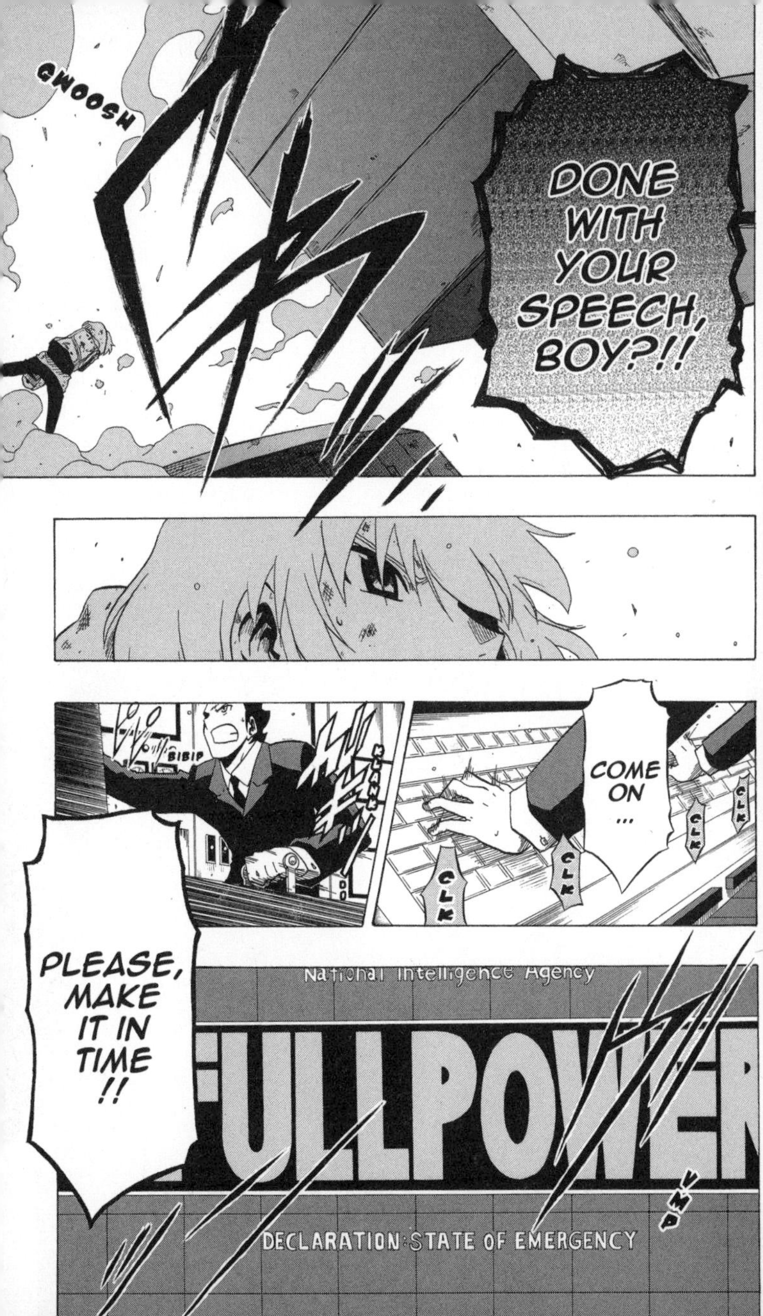
DONE WITH YOUR SPEECH, BOY?!!
GWOOSH
COME ON ...
CLK
CLK
CLK
CLK
KLANK
BIBIP
National Intelligence Agency
FULLPOWER
DECLARATION: STATE OF EMERGENCY
VMP
PLEASE, MAKE IT IN TIME!!

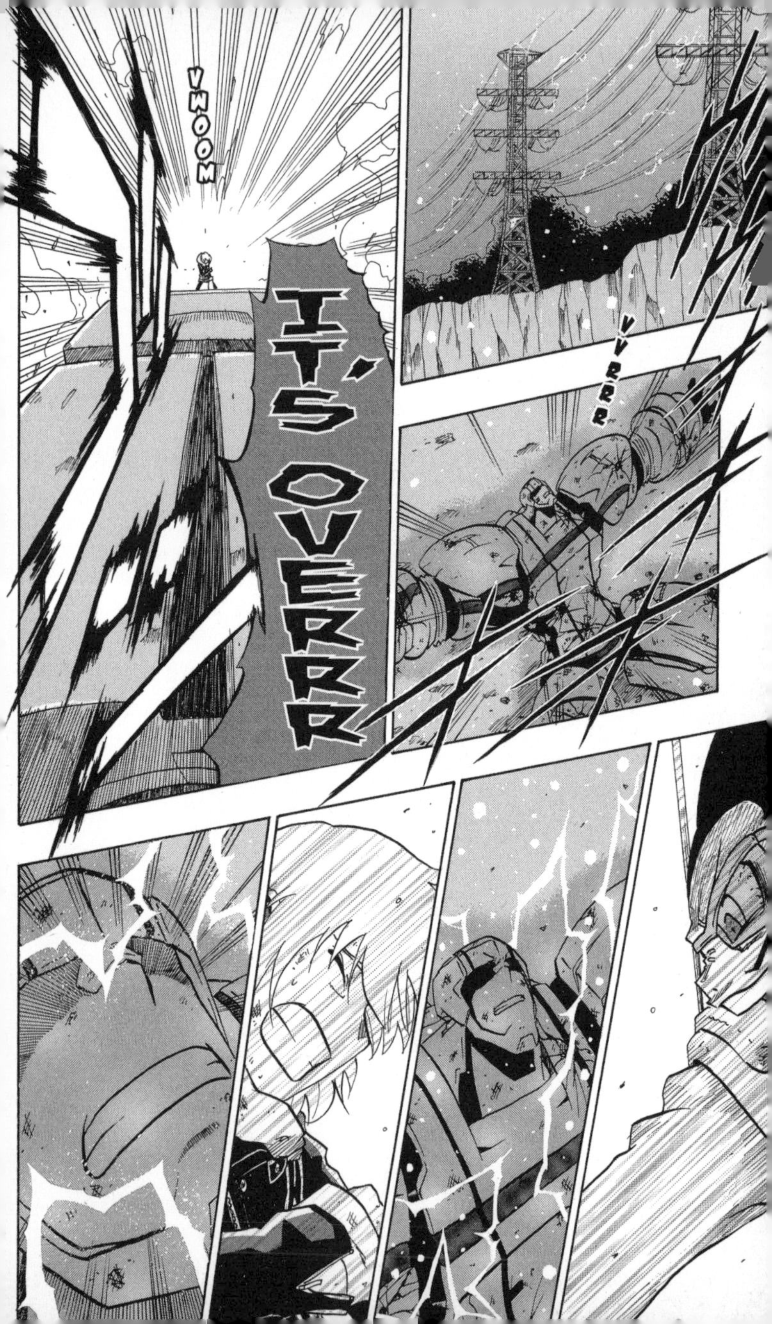
VVRRR
VWOOM
IT'S OVERRR

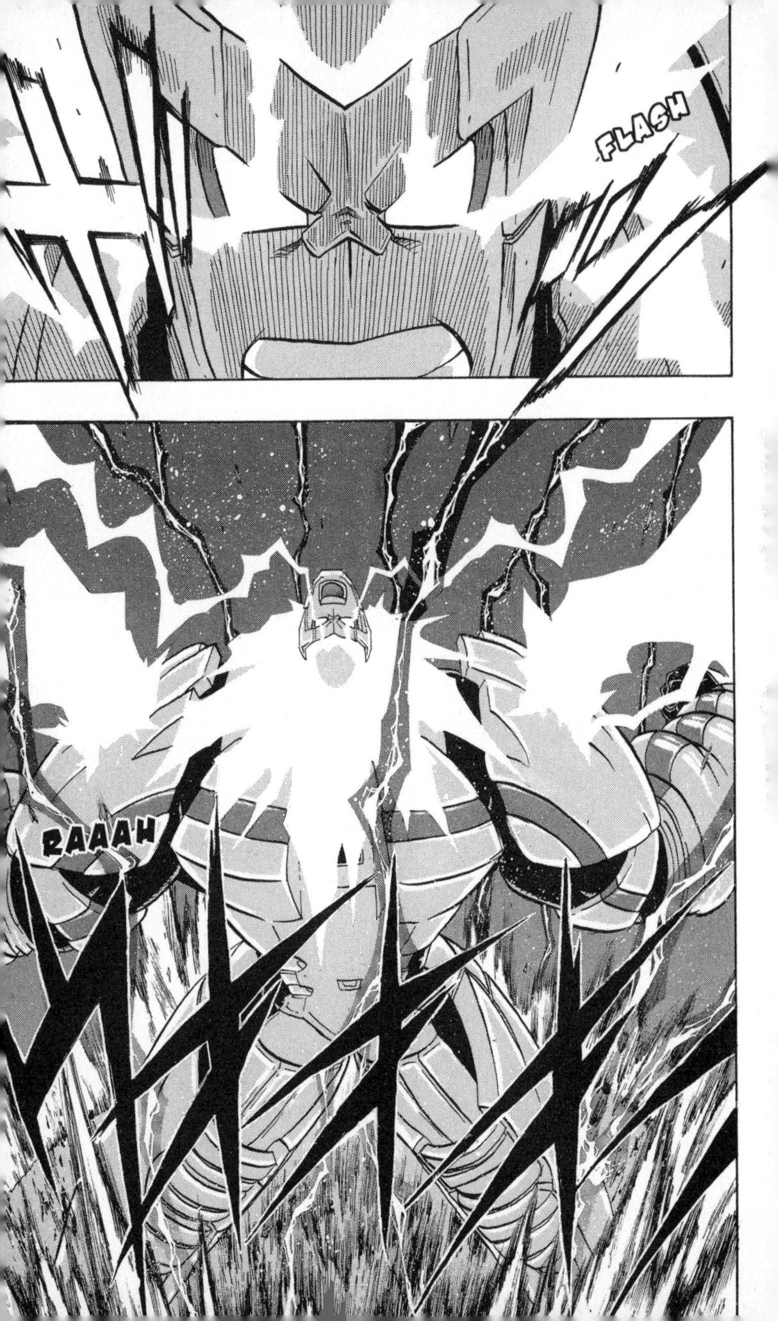
FLASH
RAAAH

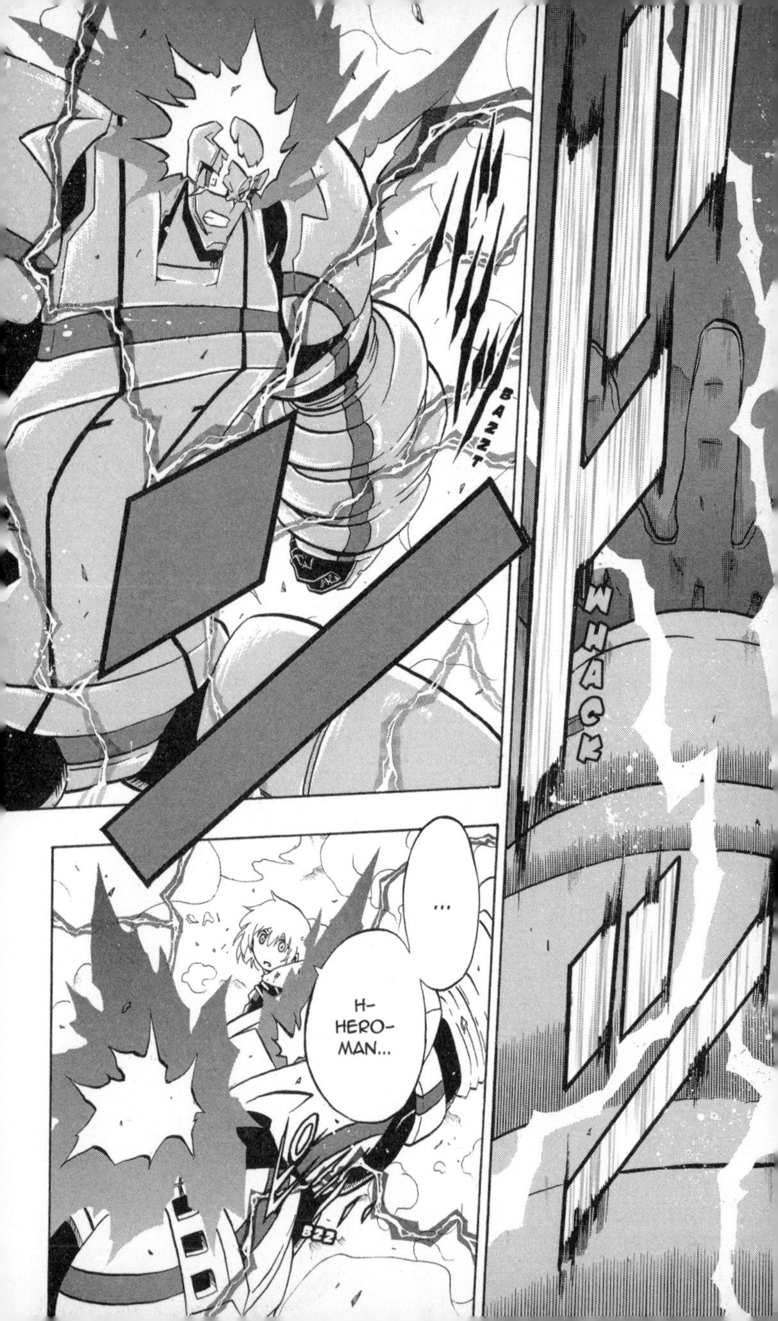
WHACK
BAZZT
...
H-HERO-MAN...
BZZ

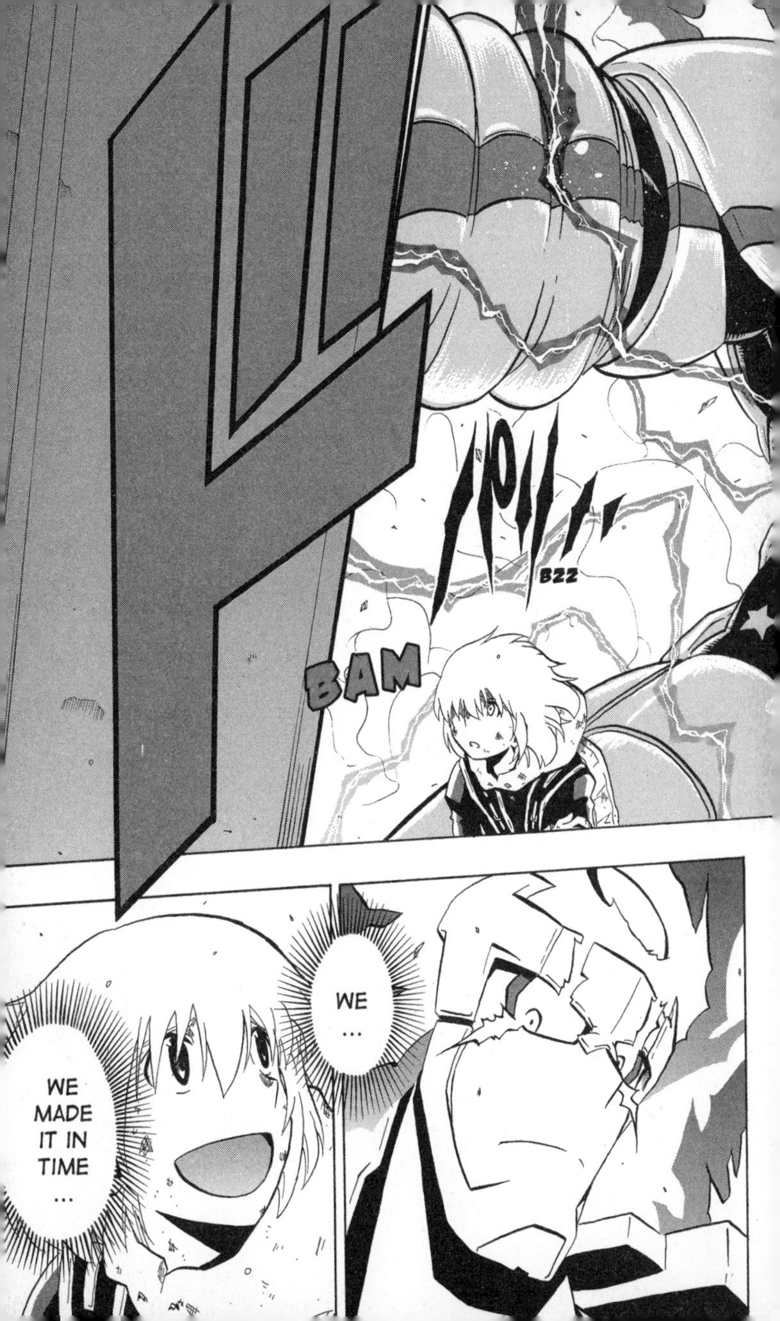
BZZ
BAM
WE ...
WE MADE IT IN TIME ...

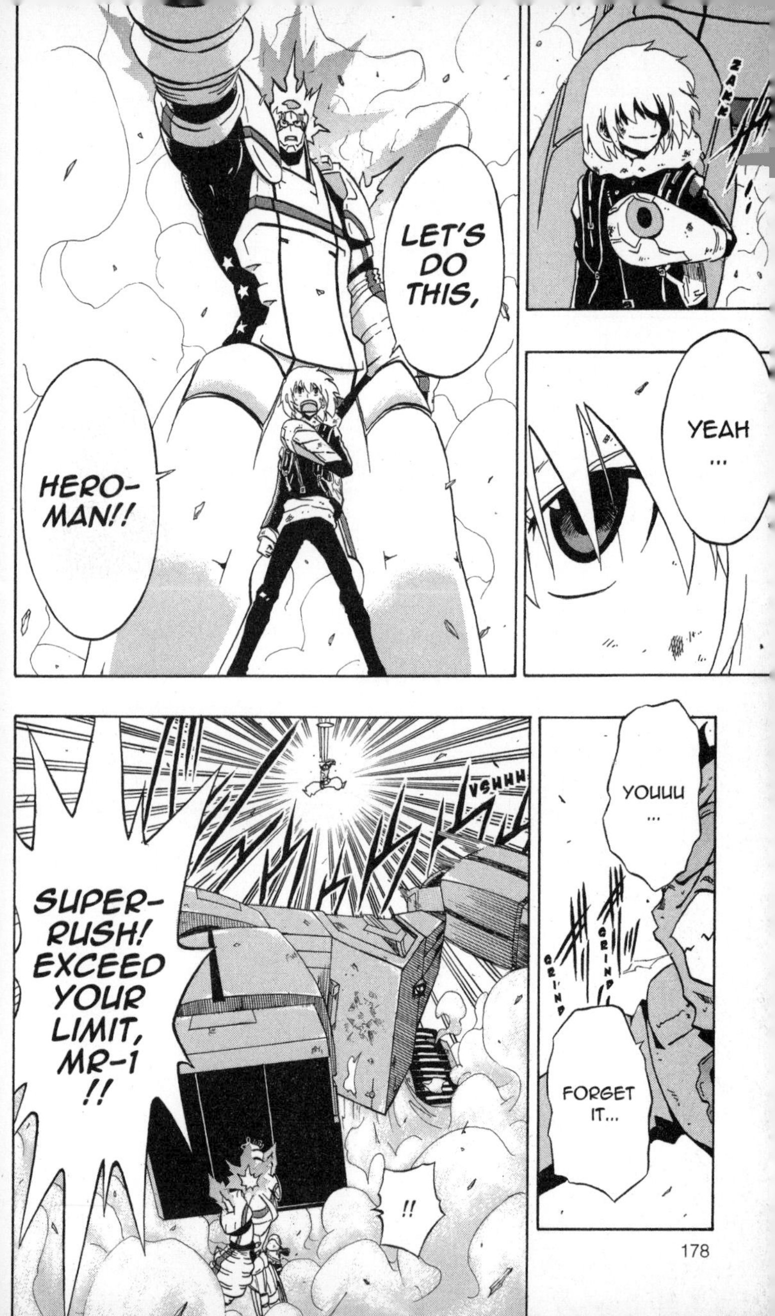
ZAKK
YEAH ...
LET'S DO THIS,
HERO-MAN!!
YOUUU ...
GRIND
GRIND
FORGET IT...
VSHHH
SUPER-RUSH! EXCEED YOUR LIMIT, MR-1 !!
!!

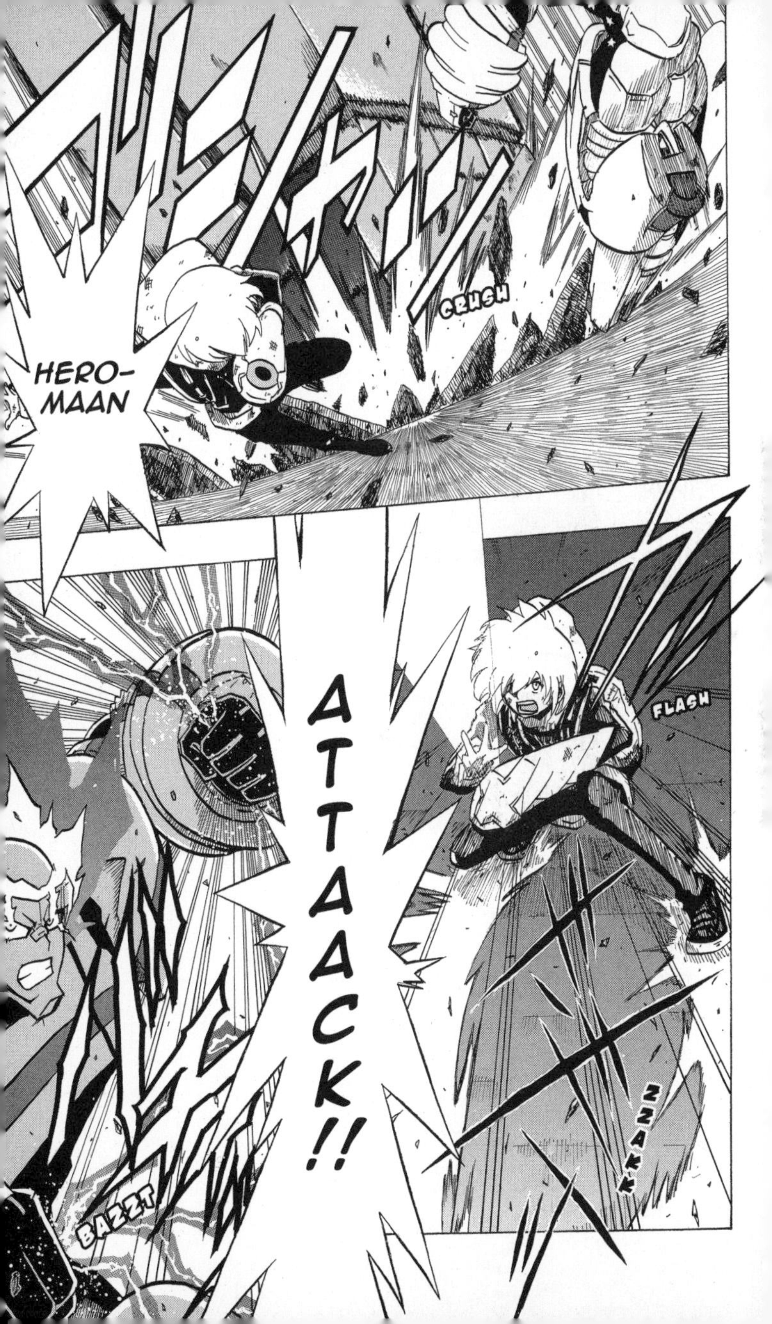

CRUSH
HERO-
MAAN
FLASH
ZZAKK
ATTAAACK!!
BAZZT

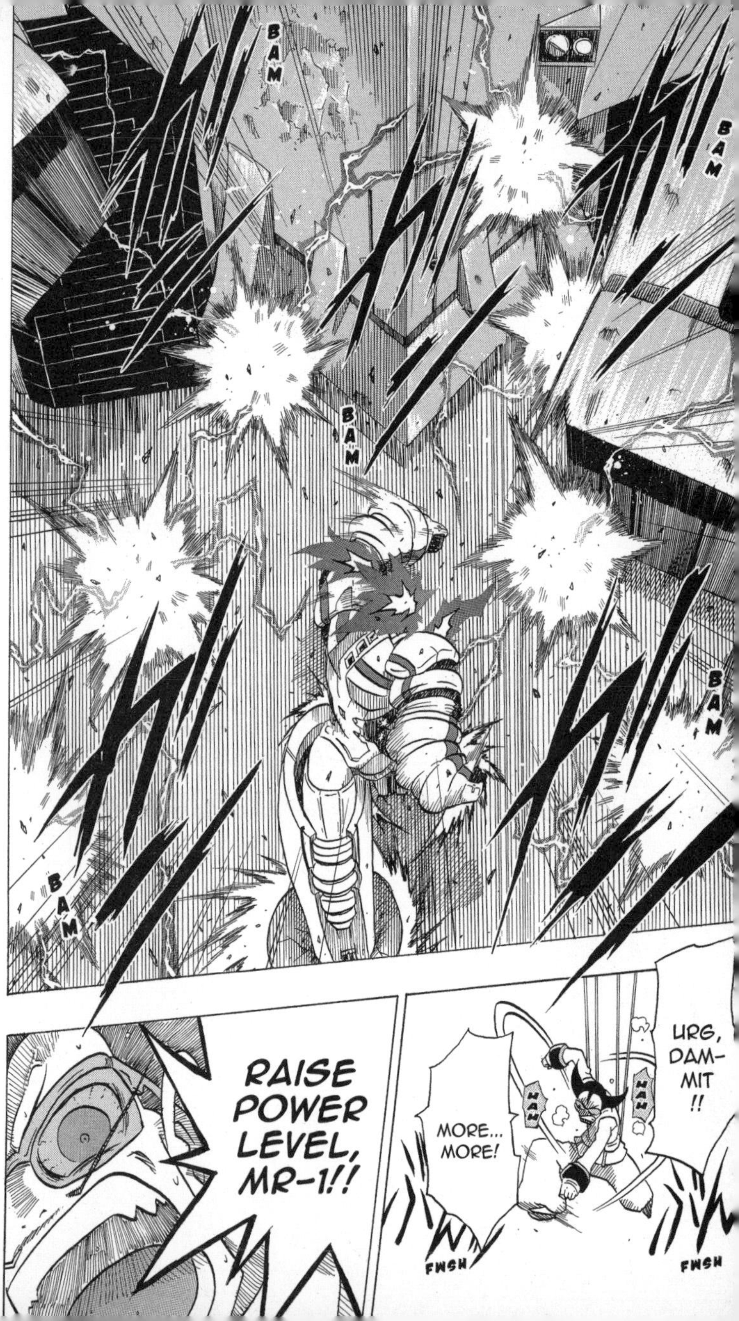
BAM
BAM
BAM
BAM
BAM
URG, DAM-MIT!!
HAH
HAH
MORE... MORE!
FWSH
FWSH
RAISE POWER LEVEL, MR-1!!

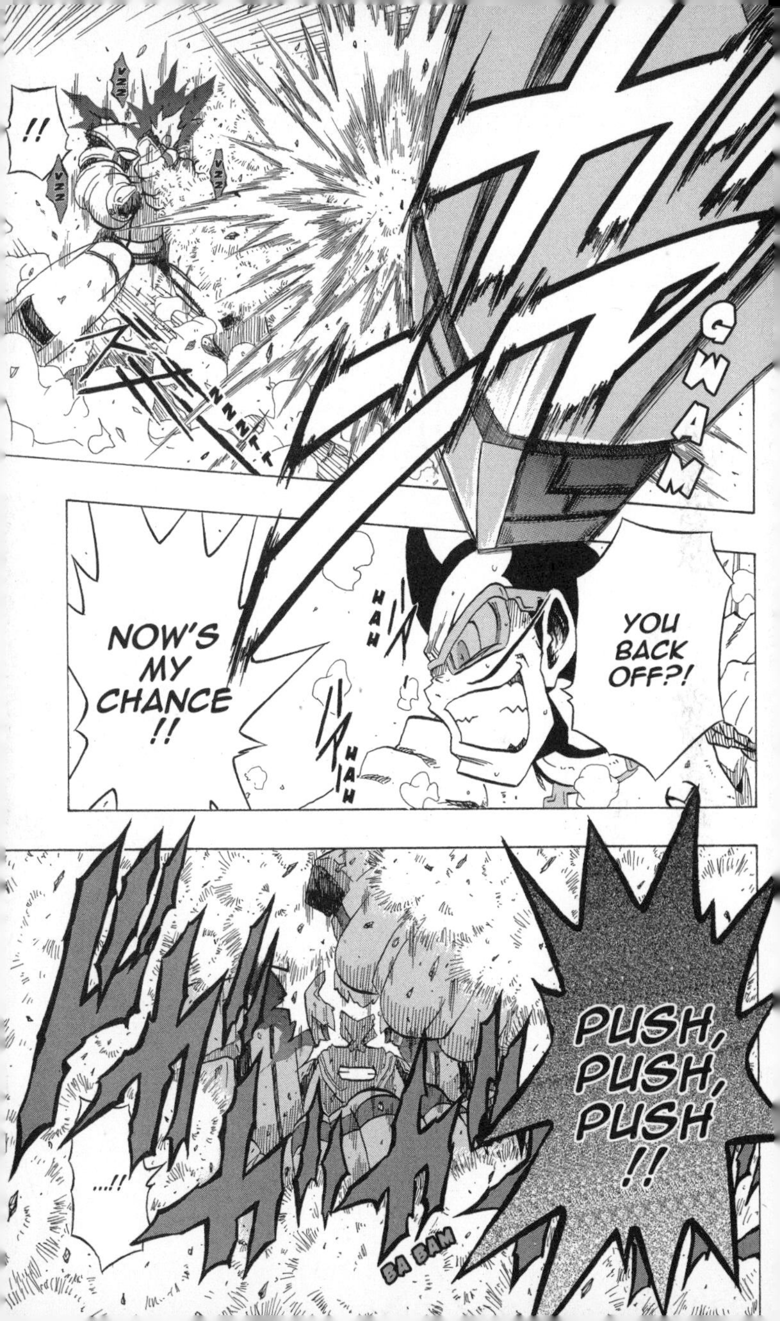

VZN
!!
VZN
VZN
NNNNT-T
GWAM
YOU BACK OFF?!
HAH
HAH
NOW'S MY CHANCE!!
PUSH, PUSH, PUSH!!
...!!
BA BAM

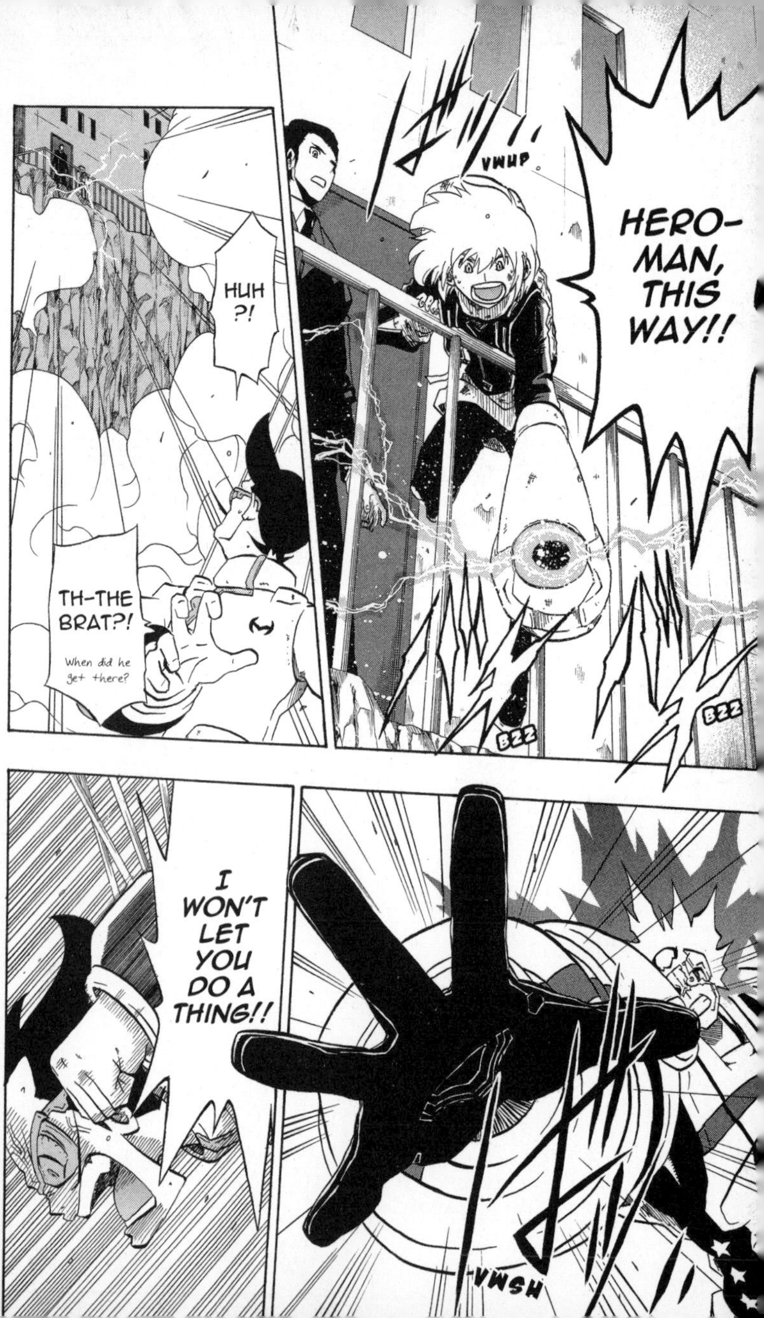
VWUP
HERO-MAN, THIS WAY!!
BZZ
BZZ
HUH?!
TH-THE BRAT?!
When did he get there?
VWSH
I WON'T LET YOU DO A THING!!

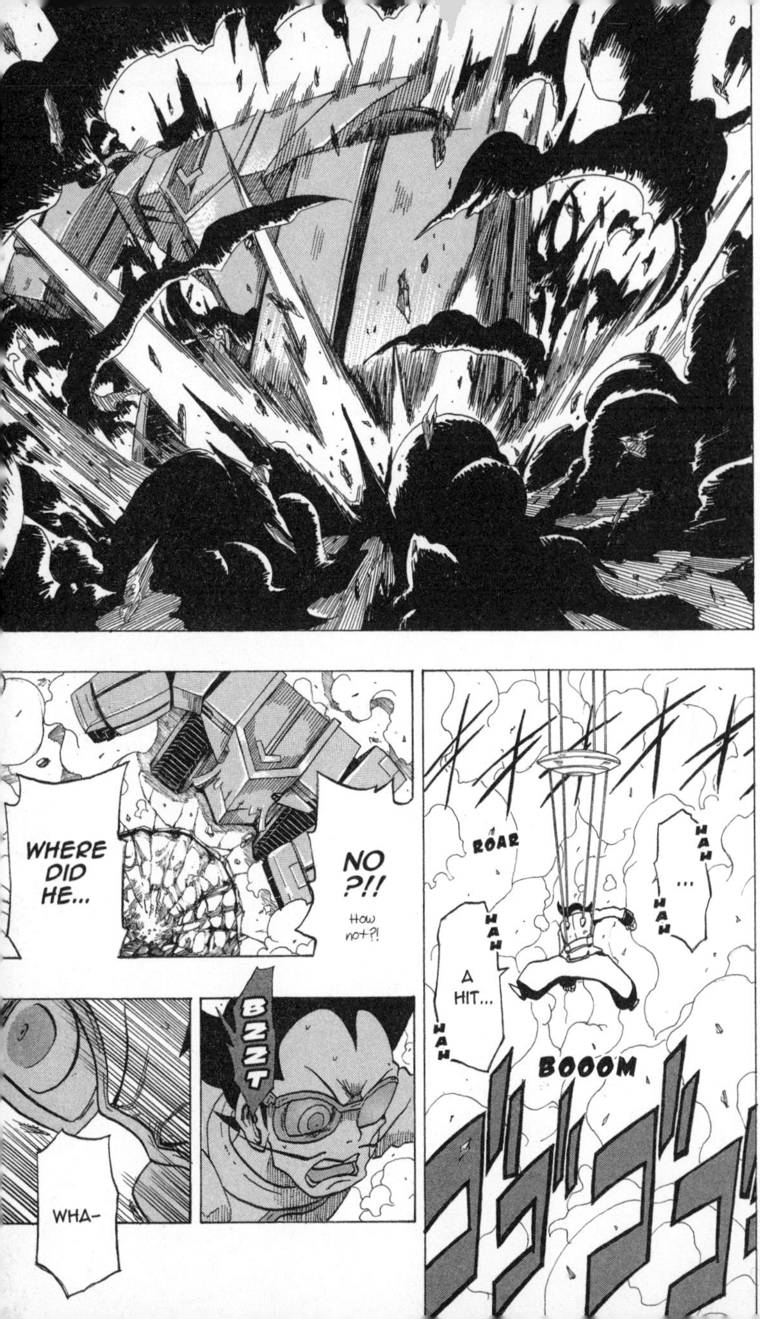
HAH ... HAH
ROAR
HAH A HIT... HAH
BOOOM
NO ?!!
How not?!
WHERE DID HE...
BZZT
WHA-

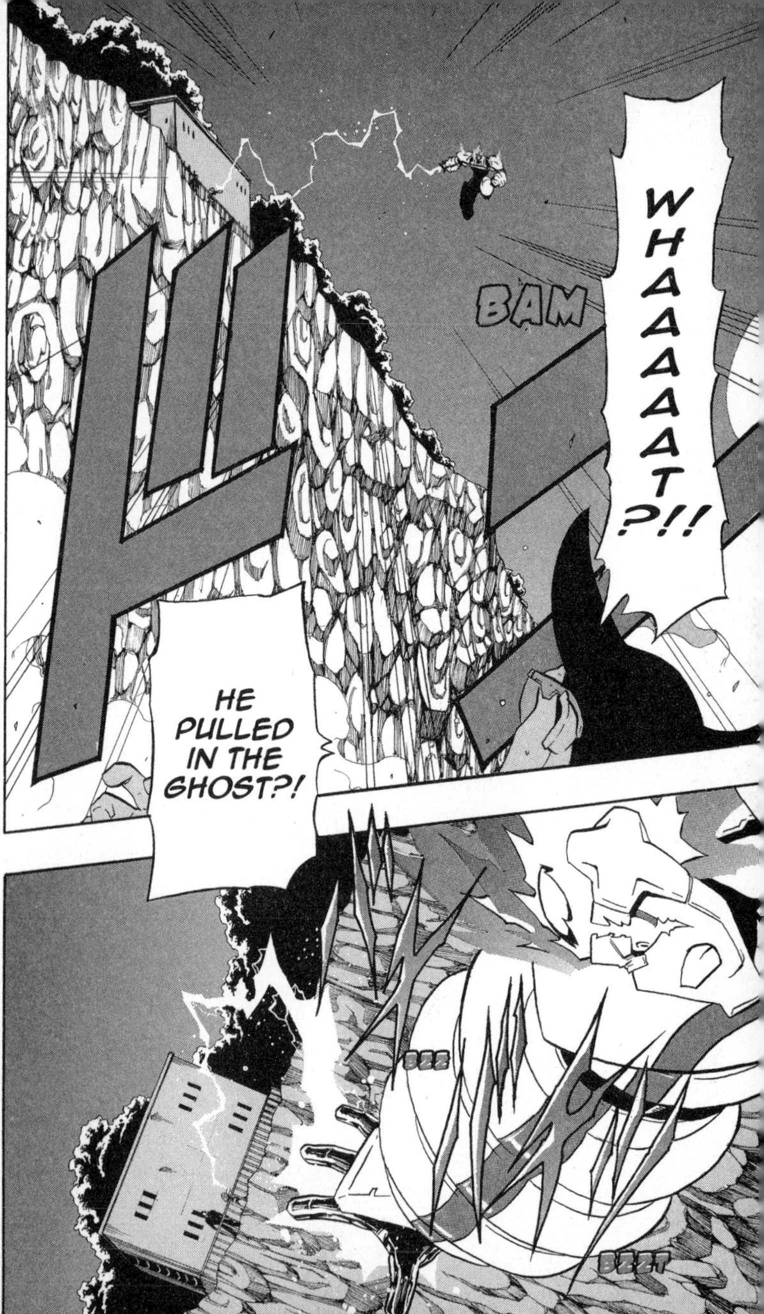
WHAAAAAT?!!
BAM
HE PULLED IN THE GHOST?!
BZZT
BZZ

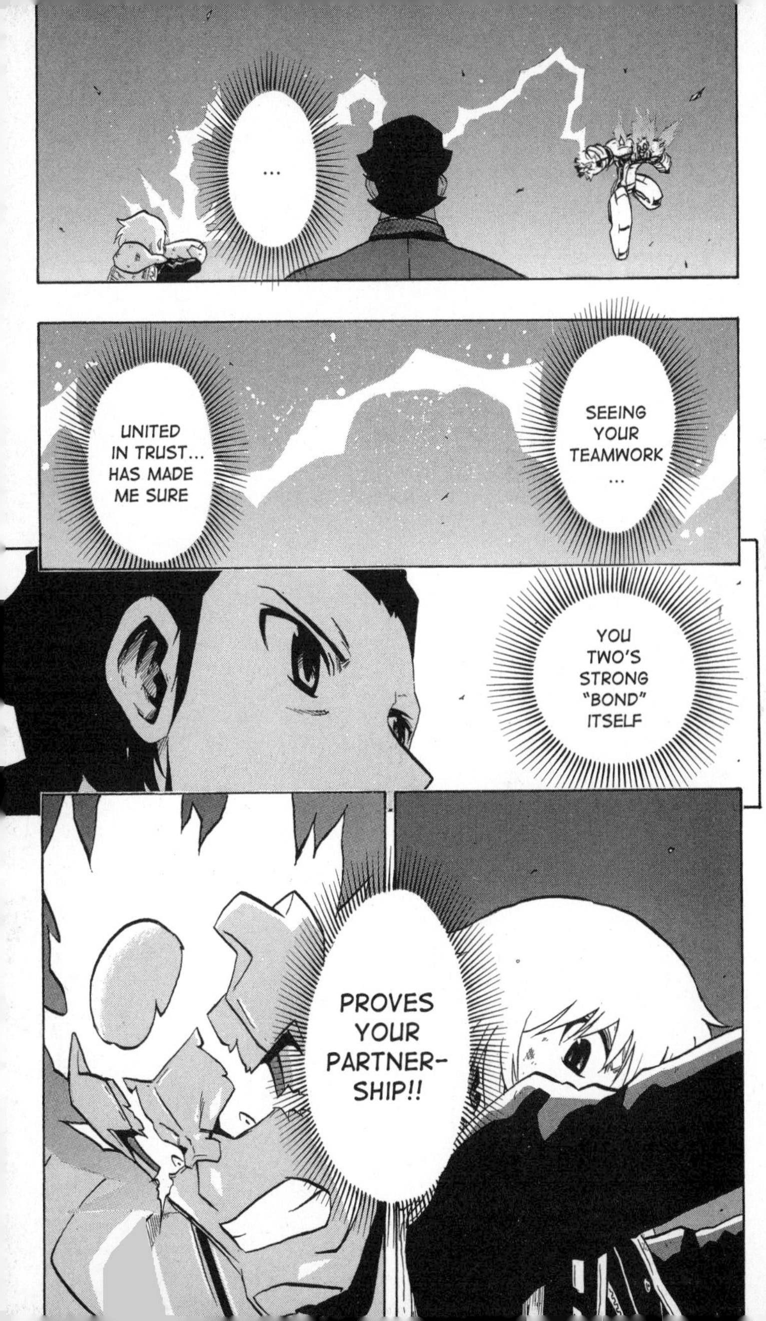
...
SEEING YOUR TEAMWORK ...
UNITED IN TRUST... HAS MADE ME SURE
YOU TWO'S STRONG "BOND" ITSELF
PROVES YOUR PARTNER-SHIP!!

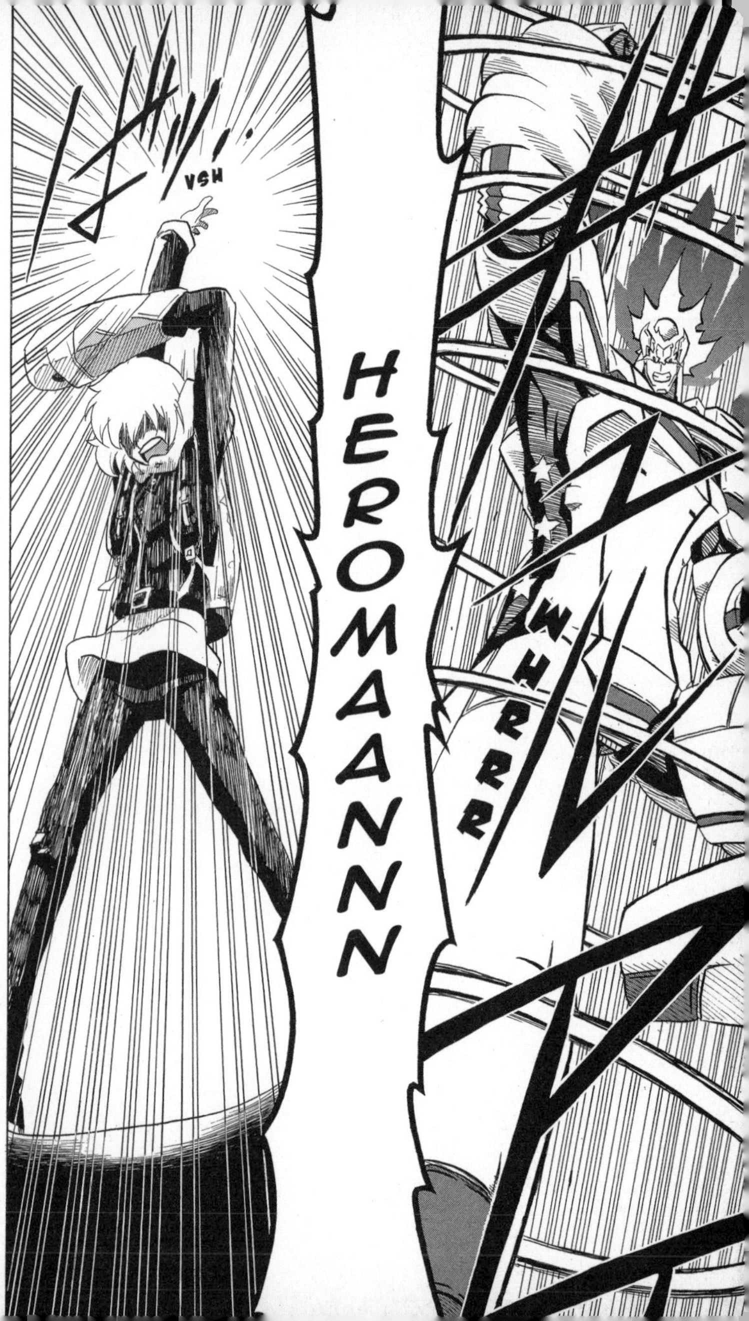
WHRRR
HEROMANNN
VSH

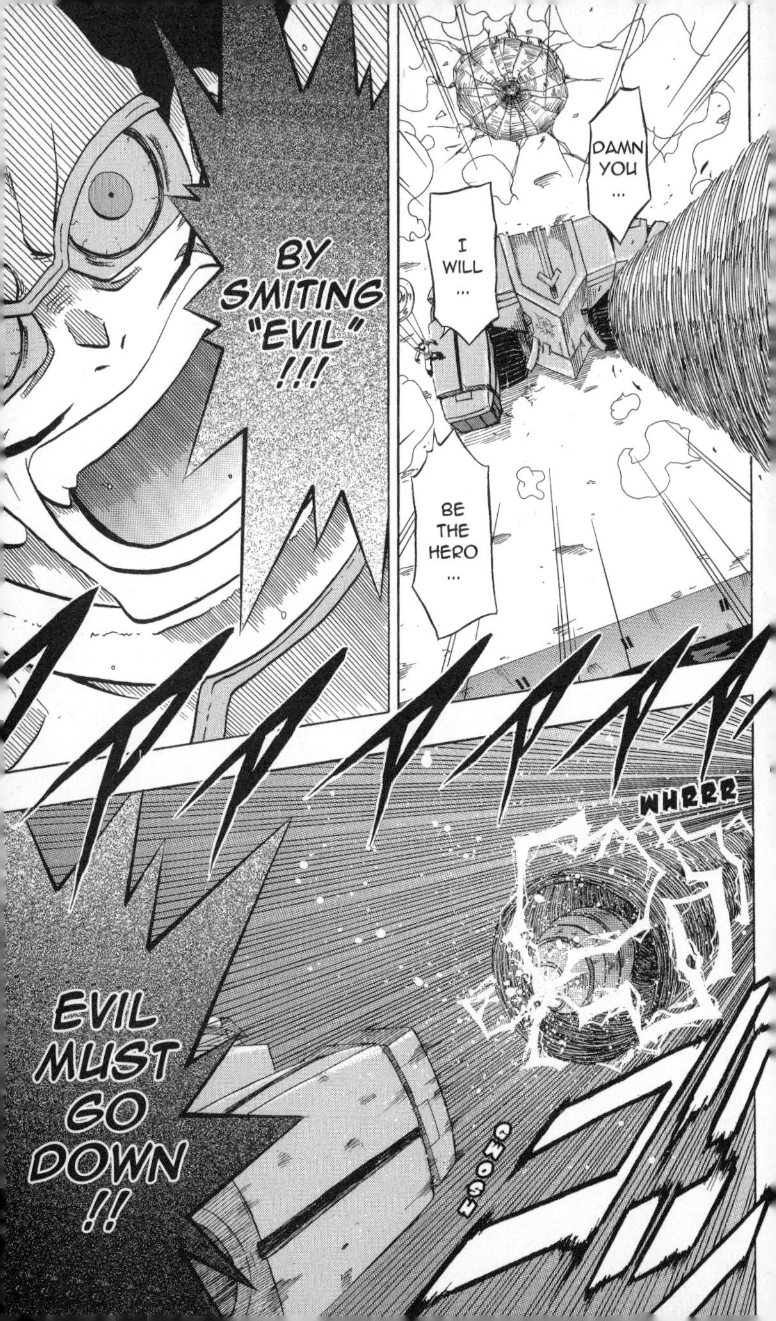

DAMN YOU ...
I WILL ...
BE THE HERO ...
BY SMITING "EVIL" !!!
WHRRR
WHOOSH
EVIL MUST GO DOWN !!

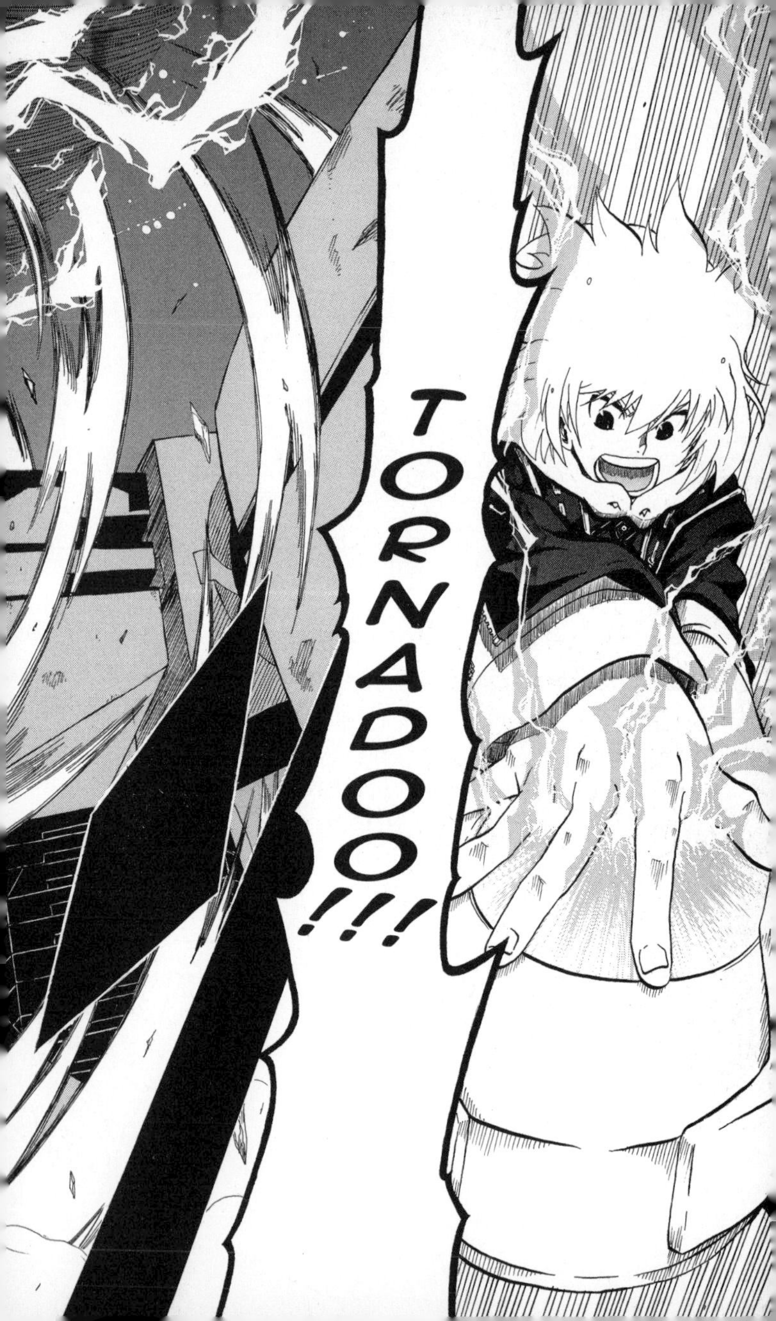
TORNADOOO!!!

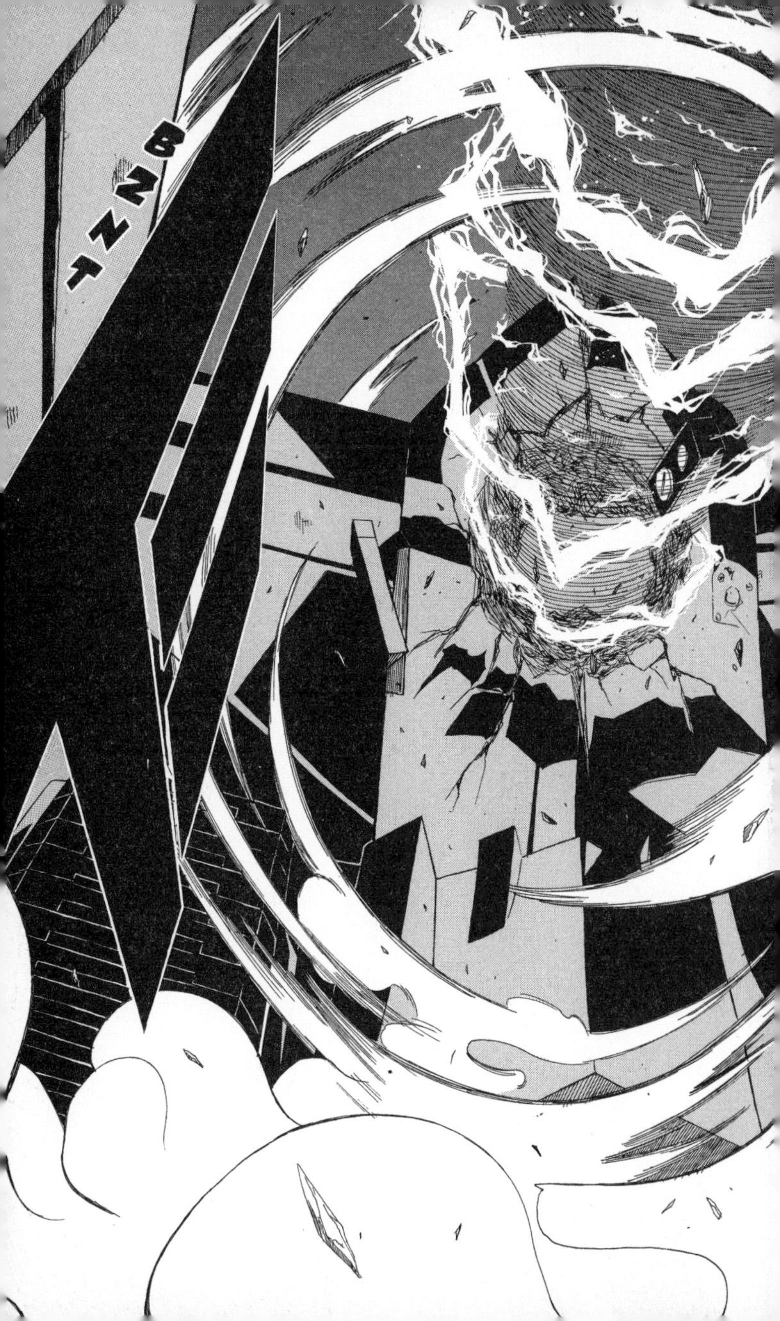
BZZT

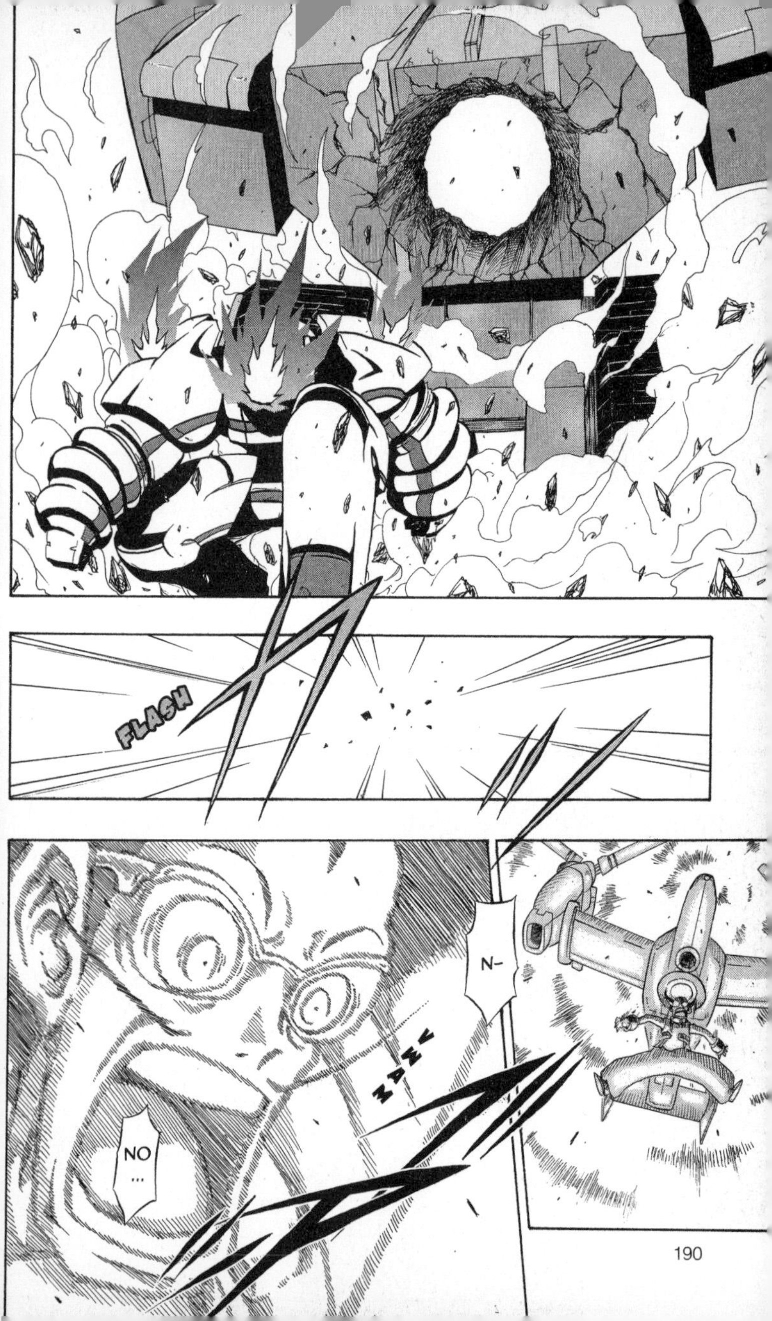
FLASH
N-
NO ...

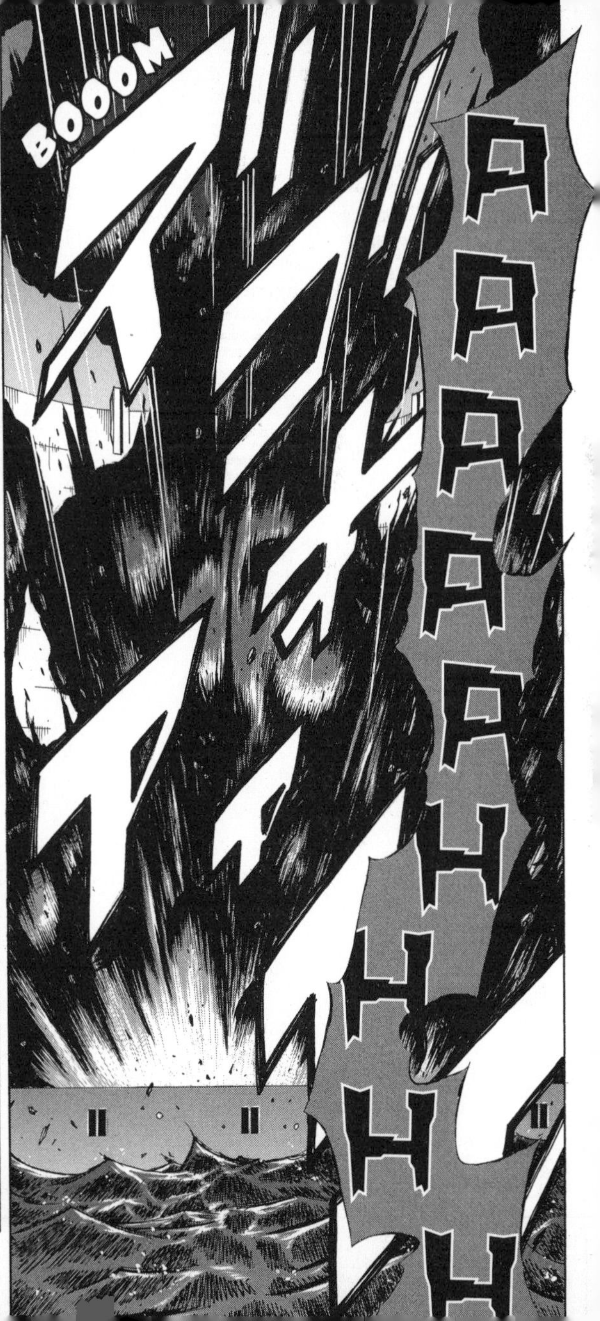
BOOOM
AAAAAHHHH
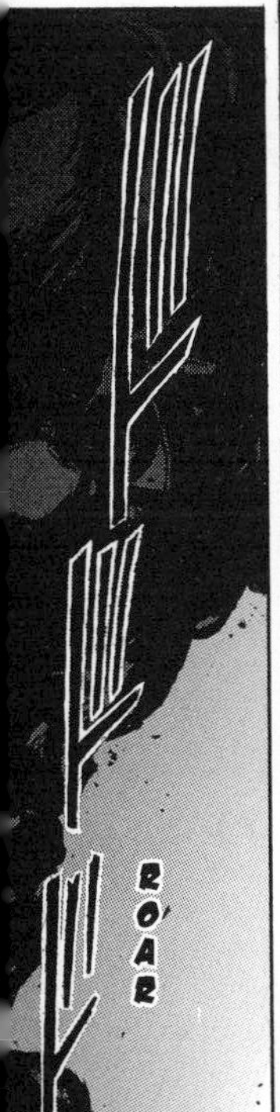
ROAR

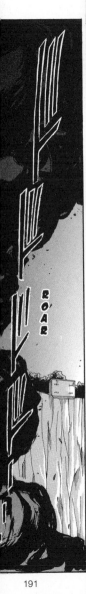

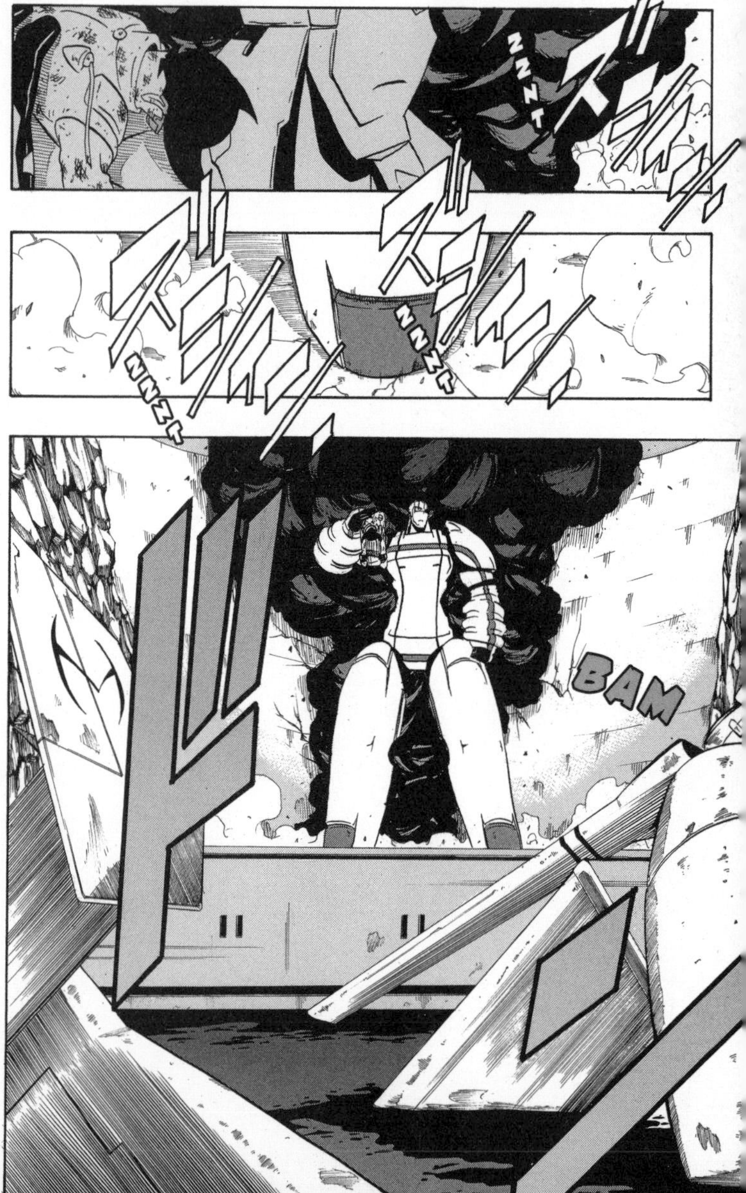
ZNNT
ZNNT
ZNNT
BAM

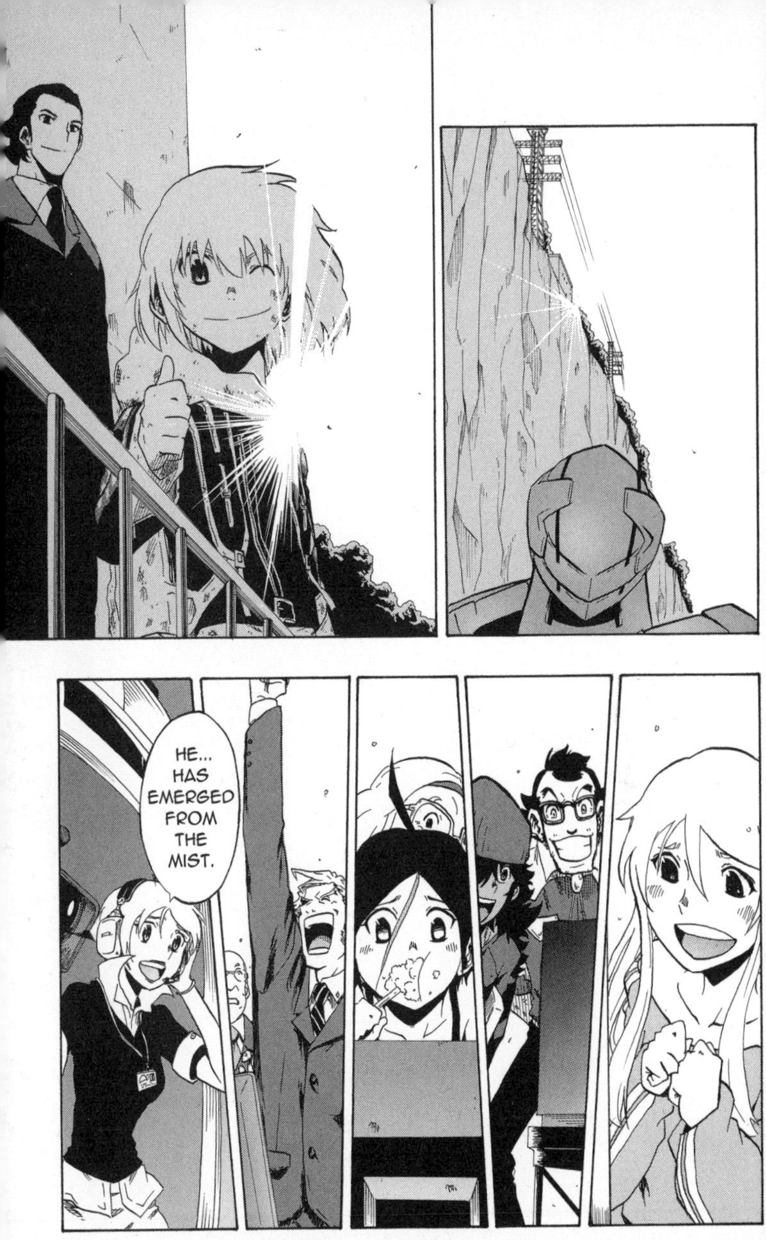
HE... HAS EMERGED FROM THE MIST.

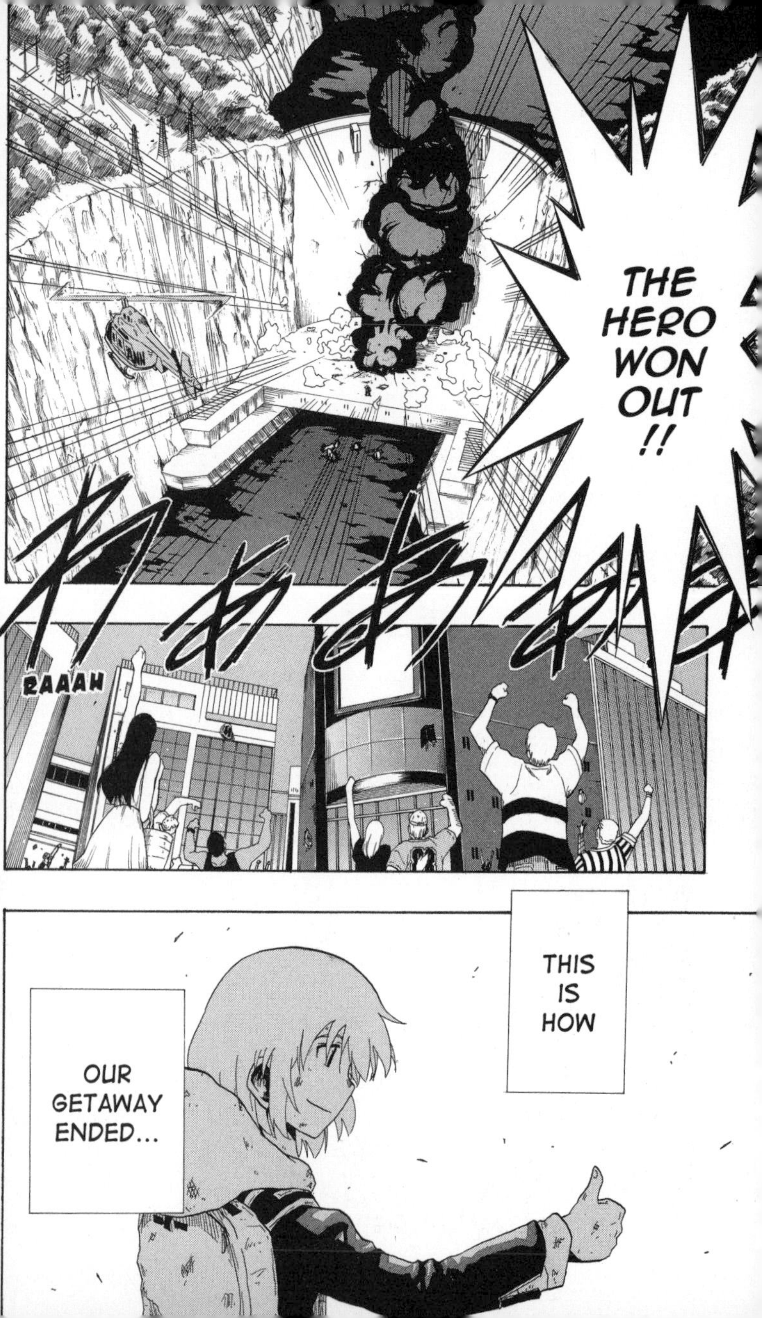
THE HERO WON OUT !!
RAAAH
THIS IS HOW
OUR GETAWAY ENDED...

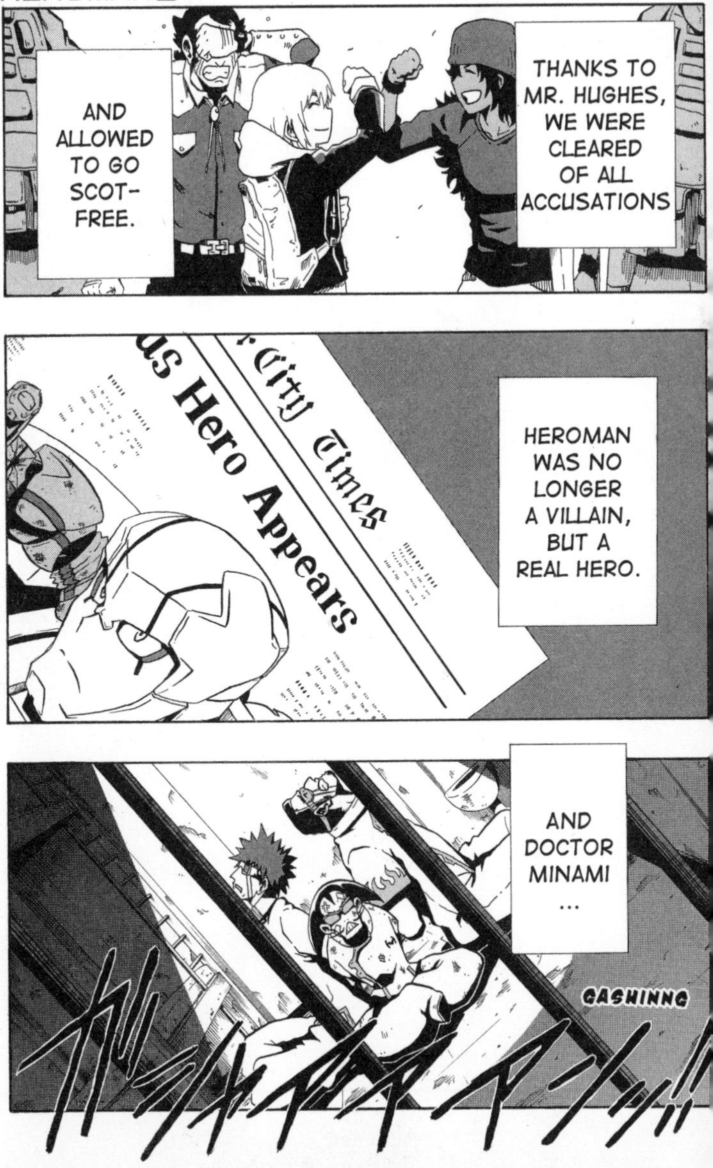
THANKS TO MR. HUGHES, WE WERE CLEARED OF ALL ACCUSATIONS
AND ALLOWED TO GO SCOT-FREE.
City Times
Hero Appears
HEROMAN WAS NO LONGER A VILLAIN, BUT A REAL HERO.
AND DOCTOR MINAMI ...
GASHINNG

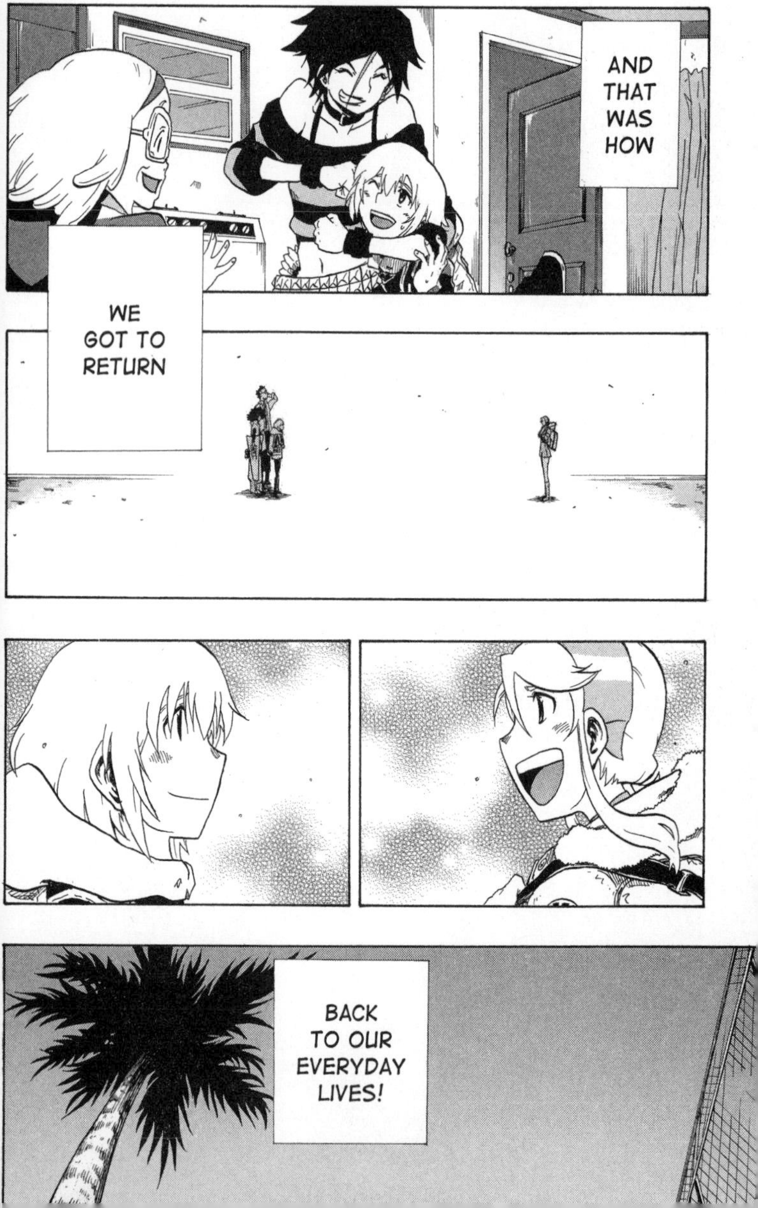
AND THAT WAS HOW
WE GOT TO RETURN
BACK TO OUR EVERYDAY LIVES!

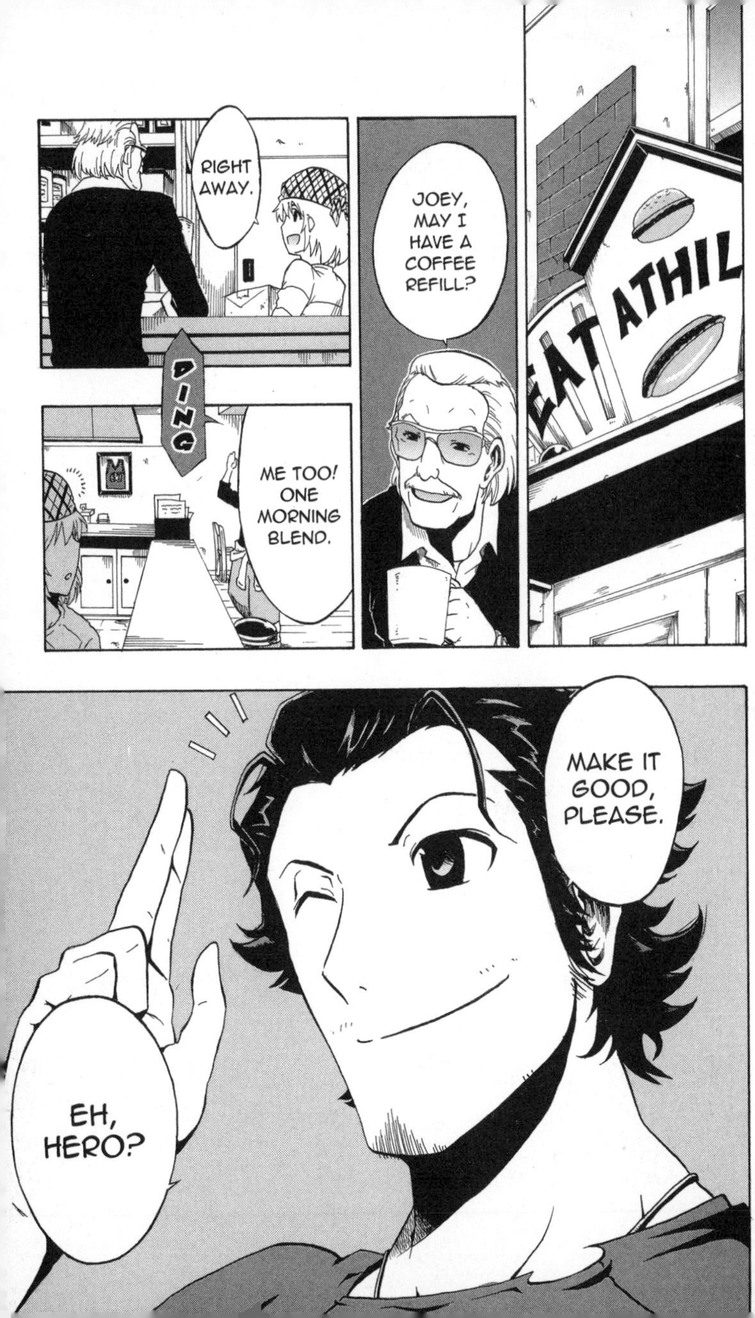
EAT ATHIL
JOEY, MAY I HAVE A COFFEE REFILL?
RIGHT AWAY.
DING
ME TOO! ONE MORNING BLEND.
MAKE IT GOOD, PLEASE.
EH, HERO?

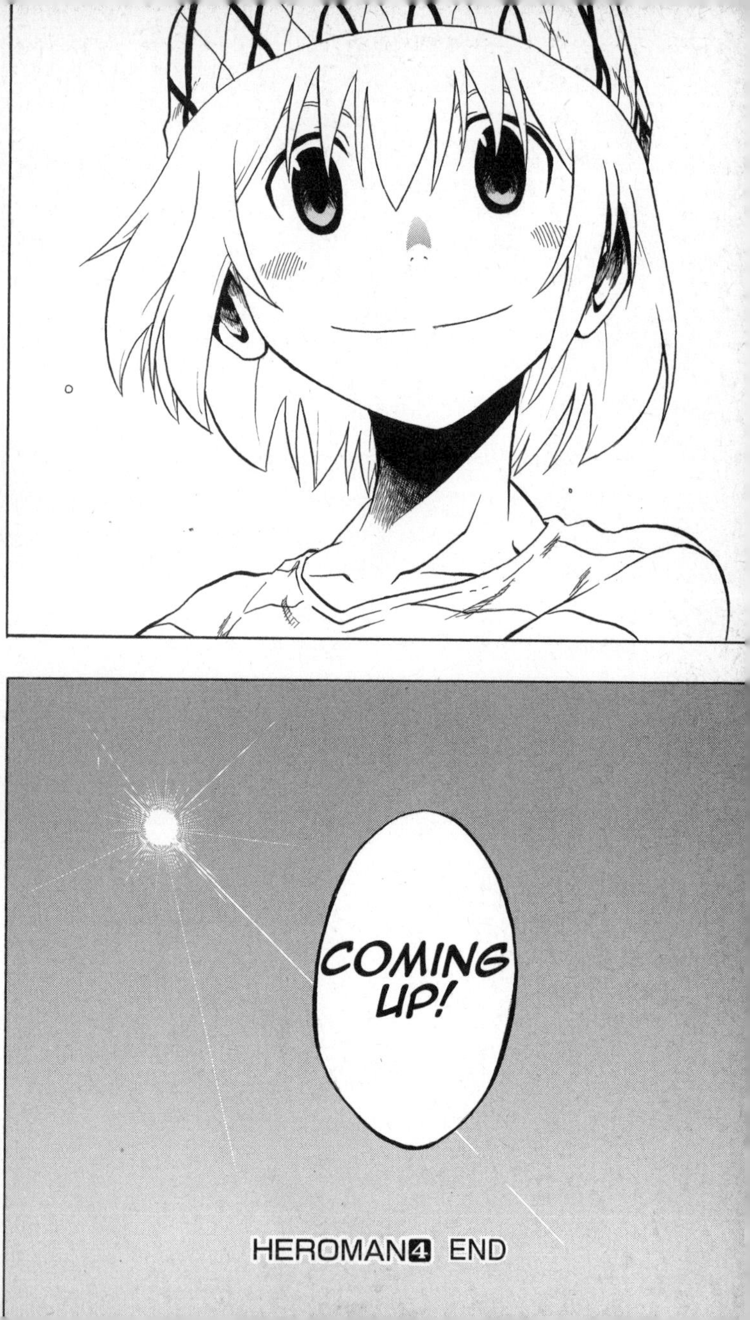
COMING UP!
HEROMAN 4 END

A monstrous evil emerges from below,
their presence threatening the entire planet.
Joey and Heroman stand up,
but will that be enough?

Carrying the hopes of mankind
on their shoulders,
the final showdown begins.

The final volume,
coming this summer!

Heroman, volume 4

Translation: Yoshito Hinton
Production: Risa Cho
            Tomoe Tsutsumi
            Daniela Yamada
            Jeremy Kahn

First published in Japan in 2011 by SQUARE ENIX CO., LTD.
English translation rights arranged with SQUARE ENIX CO., LTD. and Vertical, Inc.
through Tuttle-Mori Agency, Inc.

Translation provided by Vertical, Inc., 2013
Published by Vertical, Inc., New York

Originally published in Japanese as *HEROMAN 4* by Square Enix Co., Ltd.
First serialized in *Gekkan Shounen GanGan*, 2009-2011

This is a work of fiction.

ISBN: 978-1-935654-67-4

Manufactured in Canada

First Edition

Vertical, Inc.
451 Park Avenue South
7th Floor
New York, NY 10016
www.vertical-inc.com